D0484797

English as a
Second Language

Phase Three: Let's Write

English as a Second Language

Second Language

Phase Three:
Let's Write

William Samelson

San Antonio College

RESTON PUBLISHING COMPANY, INC., Reston, Virginia
A Prentice-Hall Company

Library of Congress Cataloging in Publication Data

Samelson, William
 English as a second language, phase III.

 Includes index.
 1. English language—Text-books for foreigners.
2. English language—Composition and exercises.
I. Title.
PE1128.S2174   428'.2'4   75-35712
ISBN 0-87909-263-7
ISBN 0-87909-262-9 pbk.

© 1976 by

RESTON PUBLISHING COMPANY, INC.
A Prentice-Hall Company
Reston, Virginia

All rights reserved. No part of this book may
be reproduced in any way, or by any means,
without permission in writing from the
publisher.

10 9 8 7 6 5 4 3

Printed in the United States of America

For *Rosi*

Preface

ENGLISH AS A SECOND LANGUAGE, PHASE THREE: LET'S WRITE, is to be used as a text for a basic course in writing and composition for students of English as a second language. It is a pre-college text of English composition. The book is intended for a one-semester course though it can be used for intensive study courses also. This book aims at developing the student's vacabulary for better comprehension. It has been designed to offer the maximum limits of writing for the basic course.

It is a well-known fact that one does not write as one speaks, though both reading and writing are communication. Thus far, the student may have learned two types of vocabulary: 1. a *speaking* vocabulary (the most limited of the vocabularies), consisting of words used in conversation; 2. a *reading* vocabulary (larger than either the *speaking* or *writing* vocabularies), containing words that can be understood on sight even though one may not be able to use them in speech or writing. LET'S WRITE offers the student a third type of vocabulary: the *writing* vocabulary. This vocabulary is more extensive than that used in conversation. The present text reinforces structures learned through oral and reading comprehension while it introduces the student to the skill of writing.

Writing will be defined here as "the ability to use the language and its graphic representations in ordinary writing situations. More specifically, . . . writing a foreign language (is) the ability to use the structures, the lexical items, and their conventional representations, in ordinary matter-of-fact writing."*

Our aim is to provide the student with the ability to write independently and competently. To achieve the above objectives we undertake the following:

I. To provide models of various types of composition (from simple one-paragraph types to the more complicated term paper), which the student will copy and ultimately learn to write independently.

II. To comment briefly on each MODEL COMPOSITION discussing distinguishing characteristics of style and organization. This will aid the students in their own writing and increase their comprehension of written material.

III. To suggest writing topics of broad and varying difficulty. This will allow the individual student to develop a writing skill reflecting his/her unique personality, background and attitude.

IV. To further enlarge the student's active vocabulary by providing alternate meanings for selected phrases and words. These are defined in the sense of the context of the MODEL COMPOSITION. Such contextual presentation reinforces the learning process, increasing the rate of retention and motivation.

To achieve the above objectives, each chapter (except CHAPTER ONE, THE WORD) comprises ten sections. Each section fulfills a unique function within the overall aim of this text.

I. MODEL COMPOSITION

The initial part of the chapter serves as an example of correct writing. Students will be expected to read the MODEL COMPOSITION with total comprehension if they are to write with reasonable skill at some future time. To achieve this goal, students will move forward cautiously through many "steps" under the guidance of their teacher. The suggested learning activities for this section are: 1. copying words or phrases; 2. copying sentences or paragraphs; and 3. writing from dictation. Exercises 2., and 3., are to be partially conducted in class under teacher's supervision.

II. WORDS IN CONTEXT

The vocabulary section comprises exercises in which the student must make considered lexical choices. Words are listed that are to be used to fill blanks in sentences. Where possible, an alternate word (*synonym*), or a phrase

---

*Robert Lado, *Language Testing*, McGraw-Hill, 1964, pp. 248-9.

that explains the meaning, may be used to fill a particular slot. The finished sentences are further altered by *substitution, replacement* or *transformation.*

III. STRUCTURES

Key words and phrases are expanded into complete sentences. This section also deals with groups of adjective-plus-preposition, verb-plus-preposition and noun-plus-preposition pairings that allow the student to generate new sentences.

IV. GRAMMAR and SYNTAX

Brief comments on the writing patterns and grammatical items contained in the MODEL COMPOSITION are made here. Further samples of writing are presented. These can be transformed by the student to express varying ideas, thus forcing production and encouraging the use of alternate vocabulary without altering syntactic structure. The student may supply all of the words on his vocabulary list that do not result in semantic absurdity.

V. IDEA RECOGNITION

Consideration is given here to the observation of logical syntactic and semantic relations within grammatically patterned sentences. The student is encouraged to develop new PATTERNS OF THOUGHT following the "kernal idea" extracted from the MODEL COMPOSITION. This practice will extend the student's sense of productivity, or creativity.

VI. VOCABULARY ENRICHMENT

To write effectively, the student learns new words. To retain these words, the student uses them repeatedly. In addition to providing the student with the useful vocabulary, all exercises within this text are organized in a manner to stimulate the student to review and reuse the expressions already learned.

This section includes some helpful techniques for vocabulary expansion. One of the exercises used is *paraphrasing* the MODEL COMPOSITION. The student completes sentences by furnishing synonyms or equivalents of a given term, thereby becoming aware that there are frequently alternate ways of expressing roughly the same idea in English.

Another helpful practice is the presentation of *lexical units*, i.e. words that may express related meanings through different structure.

> *Example:*   His *name* is Mark Anthony.
> They *call* him Mark Anthony.

Recognition of *related* words in context or in isolation may prove useful in building an active writing vocabulary. Related forms of *NOUNS, ADJEC-TIVES* and *VERBS* are requested here.

Example request for related *noun*:	Cue:	*beautiful*
	Response:	*beauty*
Example request for related *adjective*:	Cue:	*study*
	Response:	*studious*
Example request for related *verb*;	Cue:	*runner*
	Response:	*run*

VII. STEPS TO WRITING

At this point, the student will learn to rephrase excerpted model sentences by the *addition* or *deletion* of words and the revision of sentences. Small grammatical changes may also be necessitated in the process. Thus, if a model sentence reads, "He studies at the university" the assignment may call for changing "he" to "we." This change will require a substitution of "study" for "studies."

A variety of assignments related to those described above are used to force semi-independent production. This should ultimately lead to free writing.

VIII. COMPREHENSION

The comprehension exercises comprise a sequence of procedural steps. Some call for the completion of a statement by choosing phrases from the MODEL COMPOSITION. The student then adds sentences related in context. Further, the student answers questions requiring a clear understanding of *ideas* contained in the MODEL COMPOSITION. These are exercises that do not require either the production of sentences or the composition of statements.

IX. COMMENTARY ON MODEL

The student is given key words or sentences from the MODEL COMPOSITION. He is to use them in his own composition on a topic related to that of the MODEL. Although the student may express agreement with the MODEL, he is encouraged to digress or disagree with the views of the model topic. This section constitutes partially guided writing; students are free to introduce an element of originality although they use known vocabulary and structures. As the students approach the final stages of the chapter, they should have enough "control of" the language to be able to manipulate what they have learned to express their own ideas and opinions.

X. COMPOSITION

At this point, the students are ready to be assigned a topic on which they will write a short composition. The extent of FREE COMPOSITION is determined by the students' qualifications. The students may title the resulting composition with an appropriate heading.

*   *   *

The "Let's" books have been prepared as a series; *Phase One: Let's Converse*; *Phase Two: Let's Read*; *Phase Three: Let's Write*. It is not necessary, however, to establish any one book as a prerequisite for the other. Each of the three books is independent of the others, and each may be used, according to the interests and needs of the students without reference to the other two books.

The "Let's" books are essentially student-oriented. However, the instructor must determine the most suitable way of utilizing the material provided here to the particular needs of the students. It is to be understood that the exercises presented in each chapter are to serve as points of departure for whatever needs arise. This can lead to a discussion of grammatical or morphological principles. It may also necessitate differentiation between formal and idiomatic terminology.

How much time is assigned to each exercise or chapter will depend on student needs and the nature of programs for which the text will be used. It is important, however, to complete each exercise as it is undertaken for the sake of total comprehension on the part of the student. The flexibility of the present material is one of the advantages of this text. It is easily adaptable to a variety of needs. But it should be understood that it is more advantageous to deal with a portion of the text exhaustively rather than with the entire text cursorily.

The handiest books to consult when writing are a good dictionary, a thesaurus and a reference grammar. Finally, we should remember that there is ONLY ONE WAY TO LEARN TO WRITE: THAT IS TO WRITE.

Acknowledgements

With this, the last of the "LET'S" ESL series, we have come to the completion of the trilogy (LET'S CONVERSE, LET'S READ, LET'S WRITE). While in the making, the project has taken us through three years of experimentation, writing, and revision. As promising as it is to begin work on a project that aspires to lighten the burdens of those in need of it, the more so gratifying it is to see it completed.

The most profound acknowledgements seem quite inadequate when one wishes to express gratitude for aid received. My appreciations go to Isabel Y. Vera Cruz for her helpful suggestions; to all my colleagues who tried the typescript experimentally in their classes during the 1974-75 school year and offered valuable suggestions and criticism; to my secretarial staff under the direction of Lucinda Cabasos for their help in typing the manuscript. Due recognition must be given Jaime Sustaita and Adan Reyna for their fine drawings; to my twelve year old son Henry for his drawing of the poem "Live for Death."

I wish to express my thanks to the executive branch of the Reston Publishing Co., Inc. for their trust in my ability as teacher and writer and to the production staff for their patient and able guidance through a labirynth of production pitfalls. The success of the "Let's" ESL series will be largely due to their combined efforts. I accept full responsibility for any shortcomings.

Finally, no acknowledgements would be complete without recognizing the efforts of my wife Rosita who so ably "filled in" with our four children, allowing me the freedom to pursue my work.

Contents

Chapter One

The Word

Words to Remember:

recognition – discrimination –

spelling – area of meaning –

root – stem – base – prefix –

suffix – word in context –

structure – composition – word

formation – change the meaning –

change part of speech

I. *Recognition and Discrimination*

In the beginning was the Word.
                    John 1:1

A.   Composition

1. The desire to write goes one step beyond that of merely wishing to communicate: it allows us to share our knowledge, ideas, and feelings with the rest of the world. Writing also gives us the opportunity of becoming what we are, or may be.

2. In learning to write we must develop good habits as in learning to speak and to read. These habits can be formed only through practice. Observing the writings of others is only half the work; creating our own compositions is an essential activity in learning to write.

3. Let's not think that mastering a language simply means learning its vocabulary. Initially we learn to *recognize* certain basic often-used words. After that comes the time to expand our vocabulary. Words should never be studied in isolation. They are learned in relation to other words. Only then can we give full significance to a word.

4. The cosmopolitan nature of the English language is both an advantage and a disadvantage. Its advantage is that it has taken words from many sources, each with a precise definition. Its disadvantage lies in the fact that these words are often very nearly alike in definition. A writer not intimately familiar with their exact meanings will use them contrary to their correct usage.

5. It is important to use the right word in a given place. The correct definition of a term must be learned. Poor spelling is frequently the cause for misuse of words. Oftentimes, unable to spell the needed word correctly, we will use a poor compromise or an altogether wrong expression.

Examples of some commonly misspelled words are as follows:

Altogether means "thoroughly or completely."
All together means "everything or everybody collected."
>   I'm not **altogether** sure I remember.
>   They are **all together** at my home.

Already means "by the time" or "previously."
All ready means "completely ready" or "everything or everybody is ready."
>   The sightseeing tour had **already** begun.
>   The tourists were not **all ready** to travel.

Past refers to previous time or "farther than" or "beyond."
Passed is a form of the verb "pass," "successfully completed."
>   It was **past** midnight when they called.
>   They told me I **passed** my chemistry exam.

To indicates direction or is a marker of the infinitive verb.
Two is the number 2.
Too means that there is "more than enough" or "also."

> It took us **two** hours **to** drive from here **to** Jane's house.

> Her sister was there **too**. She told us that we stayed away **too** long.

Quite means "very" or "very much."
Quiet means "peaceful" or "not noisy."

> Misspelled words are **quite** frequently used.

> We can think much better when it's **quiet**.

Stationary means that something is "unchanging" or "fixed."
Stationery refers to "paper and envelopes used for letter writing."

> An acrobat seldom remains **stationary**.

> Each month I buy a box of **stationery**.

B.   **Composition by Degrees**

1. a. Copy the title of the Composition I.A.

   _____

   b. Copy the sentence that tells what was "in the beginning."

   _____

2. a. Copy the sentence that tells us what we must "develop."

   _____

   b. Copy the sentence that tells how "habits can be formed."

   _____

   c. Copy the sentence that tells us what is an "essential activity."

   _____

3. a. Copy the sentence that tells us what we "initially" learn.

   _____

   b. Copy the sentence that tells how "words should not be studied."

   _____

4. a. Copy the phrase that tells of the "nature" of the English language.

   _____

   b. Copy the sentence that tells what *kind* of words English has borrowed.

   _____

   c. Copy the phrase that tells of the "disadvantage" of the English language.

   _____

5.   Copy the sentence that tells what is "important."

   _____

C. Vocabulary Enrichment

Identify the following words in the composition and copy them below as instructed in the first paragraph.

1. Copy all nouns.

_____

2. Copy all verbs.

_____

3. Copy words ending with *-ing*.

_____

4. Copy words ending with *-ed*.

_____

5. Copy words composed of more than one syllable.

_____

D. Lexical Units

Select the word or phrase from the following list that best completes each of the sentences below.

Example: He's not *completely* sure of it.
          He's not *altogether* sure of it.

past	already	to
two	too	all together
quiet	quite	stationary
all ready	stationery	passed
altogether		

1. All the words are **collected** on this page. The words are _____ _____ on this page.
2. We have learned many words **previously**. We know many words ____ .
3. This composition is **completely** ready. It is ____ _____ .
4. He was there **after** midnight. It was _____ midnight.
5. She **successfully completed** her course. She _____ the final exam.
6. I've had **more than enough** to drink. I've drunk ____ much.
7. My friend **also** has a headache. He feels sick _____ .
8. It was a very **nice** party. It was _____ a party.

9. The neighbors asked us **not** to be **noisy**. They told us to be _____ .

10. We moved around a lot. Nobody stayed **fixed**. It is difficult to be _____ at a party.

11. Mother sent me some **letter writing** materials. I like my _____ very much.

E. Related Words

Use the **related** words to rewrite the following sentences without changing their meaning. Change the underlined word(s). Make further changes if necessary.

    Example: Paul **uses** a poor compromise.
               Paul **is using** a poor compromise.

to communicate (v.)	to learn (v.)	to wish (v.)
communicating (n.)	learning (n.)	a wish (n.)
communication (n.)		wishing (n.)
to create (v.)	to expand (v.)	to develop (v.)
creating (n.)	expanding (n.)	developing (n.)
creation (n.)	expansion (n.)	development [of] (n.)
intimate (adj.)		
intimately (adv.)		

1. **Communication** is great fun.

2. **To develop** good habits is important.

3. It is one step beyond that of **wishing** to communicate.

4. **To create** compositions is essential.

5. **Learning** a language is not simple.

6. **The expansion** of our vocabulary comes later.

7. A writer must be **intimately familiar** with words.

F. Answer these questions in writing. You may consult Composition A.

1. a. What do we share in writing?
  b. With whom do we share?
  c. What does writing do for us?

2. a. What must we develop in learning to write?
  b. How can good habits be formed?
  c. What is an essential activity in learning to write?

3. a. What do we learn initially?
   b. How can we give full significance to a word?

4. a. What is the advantage of a cosmopolitan language?
   b. What is the disadvantage of a cosmopolitan language?

5. a. What is important to use?
   b. What must be learned?
   c. What is the cause for the misused words?
   d. Why do we use a poor compromise?

G.   Write sentences using the words below.

1. desire ——————————————————————————

2. communicate ——————————————————————

3. develop ———————————————————————————

4. initially ————————————————————————————

5. definition ———————————————————————————

6. compromise ————————————————————————

II. Spelling

Polonius: *". . . What do you read, my Lord?"*
 Hamlet: *"Words, words, words."*
                              Hamlet, Act II, Scene 2

A.   Composition

In LET'S WRITE we face the task of transferring our *speaking* and *reading* vocabularies into a *writing* vocabulary. This transfer involves hard work. Our task is important, because we know that we may be judged by the manner in which we use our language. It tells about our character and the ability of our minds. If we are careless in expressing our thoughts, it may be assumed that we are likewise careless in our thinking. At this point, examples of a few commonly misused words (because of ignorance of their correct spelling) are in order.

Accept* means "to take what is offered."
Except (verb) means "to exclude."

---

*All vocabulary definitions are based on the authority of WEBSTER'S NEW WORLD DIC-TIONARY of the American Language; Second College Edition; World Publishing Co., and Prentice-Hall, Inc., 1970.

We **accept** your invitation for dinner.

People can't get along, present company **excepted**.

Adapt means "to adjust, or to make fit."

Adopt means "to select, take up or assume as one's own."

To survive, one must constantly **adapt**.

We have **adopted** a new book for the English course.

Affect (verb) means "to influence, have an effect, or produce a change."

Effect (verb) means "to produce by an action, process or agent."

The cold **affected** all of us adversely.

The cold **effected** a change on all of us.

Beside means "by or at the side of, alongside."

Besides means "in addition; as well."

The boy walked silently **beside** his uncle.

No one walked with the man **besides** the boy.

Emigrate means "to leave a country."

Immigrate means "to come into a country."

Many people **emigrated** from Europe.

They **immigrated** to the United States of America.

Some words are misused and interchanged incorrectly because they share something in common.

Legible is something "that can be read or deciphered."

Readable is something "interesting and easy to read."

His new theme is **legible**. It is **not readable**, and I find it very **dull**.

Notorious means "widely but unfavorably known."

Famous means "much talked about; being favorably known, or being a celebrity."

Capone was a **notorious** gang leader of the thirties.

Jonas Salk is a **famous** scientist and developer of an antipolio vaccine.

Well as an adverb means "in a pleasing or desirable manner."

Well as an adjective means "in good health."

Mrs. Yancey hasn't been **well** lately, but she always treats people **well**.

Students of English as a second language may find spelling in English difficult because it is not quite phonetic. *Phonetic* means that there is a close correspondence between sound and symbol. There are some very simple rules for spelling, however, samples of which are introduced below. (For a more thorough discussion of spelling rules consult a good reference grammar.)

1. **One-syllable words** ending in a consonant double that consonant when

adding a suffix beginning with a vowel, if the consonant is preceded by a **single** vowel.

plan—	She pla**nned** to go to the movies. She's a good pla**nner**.
drop—	He dro**pped** the money into the tray. They're dro**pping** him from the team.
quit—	I'm qui**tting** work early tonight. I'm not a qui**tter**.
fat—	The more you eat, the fa**tter** you get.
bat—	He is the best ba**tter** of the year. What's your ba**tting** average?
hit—	The pitcher pitched a no-hi**tter**. His hi**tting** isn't as good as it used to be.
ship—	He made a fortune in shi**pping**. They shi**pped** him overseas.
big—	The trees grow bi**gger** every day.

2. Words ending in a final **e** that is not pronounced (i.e., take, give, love, sincere, nature), drop the -e when adding a **suffix beginning** with a **vowel**.

Sincer**ity** in lov**ing** is as natur**al** as tak**ing** and giv**ing**.

3. Words ending in **-ce** and **-ge** generally **keep** the unpronounced **-e before** suffixes beginning with the vowels **a, o, u.**

notice—	It was notic**eable** from the beginning.
courage—	He was courag**eous**.

[Words ending in a final unpronounced -e generally keep that letter when the added **suffix begins** with a consonant; i.e., **pale**—The pale**ness** was evidence of her long illness.]

4. Probably the most familiar of all spelling rules is "put **i** before **e**, except after **c**."

achievement—	It was a great achi**e**vement
niece—	when my ni**e**ce received her
receive—	college diploma.

[Note: There are many exceptions to the above "**c**" rule; i.e., neither, leisure, seize, etc.]

5. Words ending in **-y** preceded by a consonant, change final **-y** to **i** before adding a suffix **beginning** with a **vowel (except i)** or a **consonant**.

happy—	The secretary was happ**ier**
marry—	when she marr**ied**
library—	the librar**ian**.

6. The general rule for **nouns** ending in -y preceded by a consonant, to which the plural -s is added is to change the -y to i and add -es.

city + -s—	He lived in many **cities.**
industry + -s—	The U.S. has varied indust**ries.**
theory + -s—	There are different scientific **theories.**

(Exceptions are one-syllable words; i.e., bay + -s—**bays** and day + -s—**days**)

7. Words ending in -c take on -k when adding a **suffix** that **begins** with a **vowel**.

picnic—	When we were picnic**king**, it rained and thundered,
panic—	and everybody panic**ked**.

B.   Composition by Degrees

1. Copy the title of Composition II.A.

_____

2. Copy the sentence that tells about the task we face here.

_____

3. Copy the sentence that tells about the transfer of vocabularies.

_____

4. Copy the sentence that contains references to our "character."

_____

5. Copy the sentence that tells about being "careless."

_____

C.   Vocabulary Enrichment

Identify the following words in the composition and copy them below as instructed.

1. Copy all words ending with **-ing.**

_____

2. Copy all words ending with **-ed.**

_____

3. Copy all **adjectives** and the nouns they modify.

_____

4. Copy all **adverbs**.

_____

5. Copy all **nouns**.

_____

D.   Lexical Units

Select the word from the following list that best completes each of the sentences below.

Example: He did not **take what was offered**.
He did not **accept** it.

legible	accept	excepted
emigrated	readable	famous
beside	immigrate	well (adv.)
affects	besides	well (adj.)
adapt	adopts	

1. Everyone gets along well, **excluding** those present. They get along, those present _____ .

2. They make things **fit** the situation. They _____ to the situation.

3. The teacher **selects** a new book. He _____ the book.

4. Learning has an **effect** on people. It _____ them.

5. The boy walks **alongside** his father. He walks_____ him.

6. There was no one there **with** the man. No one _____him was there.

7. They **left the country** to go to the U.S. They_____for the U.S.

8. **Coming into a country** is not easy. It is difficult to _____ .

9. We were soon **in good health**. We became _____ .

10. They were treated **in a pleasing manner**. They were treated _____ .

11. I was **not able to read** his handwriting. It was not _____ .

12. Before going to sleep, I read something **interesting**. The book I read was _____ .

13. Washington was a **celebrity**. He was _____ .

E.   Spelling Exercises

1. a. Practice your spelling by completing the following words:

Example: sad + -**er** = **sadder**

plan + -**ed** _____

drop + -**ed** _____

quit + -**ing** _____

fat + -**er** _____

bat + -**er** _____

hit + -**er** _____

ship + -**ing** _____

big + -**er** _____

mad + -**er** _____

care + -**ing** _____

put + -**ing** _____

red + -**est** _____

sin + -**ing** _____

2. a. Practice your spelling by completing the following words:
Example: complete + -**ing** = **completing**

sincere + -**ity** _____

love + -**ing** _____

take + -**ing** _____

give + -**ing** _____

desire + -**able** _____

measure + -**able** _____

manage + -**ing** _____

notice + -**ing** _____

b. Practice your spelling by completing the following words:
Example: notice + -**able** = **noticeable**

courage + -**ous** _____

manage + -**able** _____

place + -**able** _____

advantage + -**ous** _____

trace + -**able** _____

pleasure + -**able** _____

outrage + -**ous**   _____

3. In each of the following words, circle the letter(s) relating to the spelling rule "put **i** before **e**, except after **c**." Recopy the word. Use a dictionary to find the meaning of any new words.

achievement   _____   receipt   _____

niece   _____   ceiling   _____

receive   _____   piece   _____

deceive   _____   believe   _____

conceive   _____   brief   _____

4. a. Practice your spelling by completing the following words:
   Example: happy + -**est** = **happiest**

deny + -**ing**   _____   happy + -**er**   _____

deny + -**ed**   _____   library + -**an**   _____

marry + -**ing**   _____   study + -**ed**   _____

carry + -**ing**   _____   cry + -**ed**   _____

marry + -**ed**   _____   beauty + -**ful**   _____

carry + -**ed**   _____   supply + -**er**   _____

b. Practice your spelling by completing the following words:
   Example: ferry + -s = **ferries**

city + -s   _____   salary + -s   _____

industry + -s   _____   lady + -s   _____

theory + -s   _____   story + -s   _____

supply + -s   _____   depository + -s   _____

mystery + -s   _____   berry + -s   _____

fantasy + -s   _____   cherry + -s   _____

III. Word Formation

A. Composition

1. Many people use the word **chauvinist** nowadays but not everyone knows that it comes to us from the French language. Words such as **cliché**, **felony**, **bagatelle** and **intrigue** come from France too. These are only a few of the many important English words borrowed from other languages.

2. From Italy we have acquired such often-used words as **balcony**, **ditto**, **bandit**, **gusto** and **contraband**. The word **mosquito** originated in Spain, as did **corral** and **tornado**. Germany gave us such words as **kindergarten**, **waltz** and **blitzkrieg**. The word **blitz** is frequently used to designate a quick play in football.

3. From the Hebrew we have acquired such commonly used words as **amen**, **Sabbath** and **jubilee**. And from Arabia we received words such as **alcohol**, **algebra**, **coffee**, **ginger** and **zenith**. The American Indian also gave us many words. Among others, we have the expressions **tomahawk**, **tobacco** and **skunk**. Even from faraway China words came to us for some of our common household products; **tea**, **chop suey** and **soy** among many others.

4. The English language builds its own vocabulary with roots from Latin and Greek. A root (**origin** or **base**) of a word is that part of the word that contains the **core** of its meaning. We can understand the full meaning of a word more clearly when we observe how it was formed.

5. Learning the most common roots increases our ability to analyze the meaning of many words. For instance, knowing that the word **annus** means "year" in Latin, we will recognize the meaning in such English words as **annual**, **anniversary**, **biennial** (happening every two years or lasting two years), and **perennial** (lasting or active throughout the whole year, or continuing for a long time).

A few common roots from Latin that we can readily recognize in English words are:

Root	*Area of Meaning*	*English Derivatives*
amare	love	enamor, amateur
aptare	fit	adapt, inept
capere	take, accept	capture, capacity
civis	citizen	civilian, civilization
fortis	strong, brave	fortify, fortitude
judicium	judgment	judicious, judiciary

magnus	great	magnify, magnificent
mors	death	mortal, immortal
nomen	name	nominee, misnomer
pax	peace	pacify, pacific
populus	people	population, popular
sentire	feel	sentiment, sensation
sequi	follow	sequence, consecutive
similis	like	similar, assimilate
venire	come	convene, circumvent
videre	see	visible, audiovisual
vivere	live	vivid, survive, revive

6. Many common English words come from the Greek language. Knowing, for example, that the root **aster** means "star" and that the root **nomos** means "law," "order" or "knowledge," we can put together the word **astronomy** (literally meaning **the law of the stars**). If we know that the word **logos** means "study of" or "science of," the word **astrology** will make logical sense as the "study of the stars." Some frequently occuring Greek roots are:

Root	*Area of Meaning*	*English Derivatives*
anthropos	man	anthropology, misanthropy
aster, **astron**	star	astronomy, astronaut
bios	life	biology, biography
chroma	color	monochrome, chromosome
demos	people	democracy, epidemic
geo	earth	geography, geology
ramma	letter, written	telegram, monogram
heteros	other, different	heterosexual, heterogeneous
homos	same	homosexual, homogenized
kosmos	order, the world	cosmic, cosmos, cosmonaut
logos	study of, science of	psychology, biology
mania	madness	mania, maniac
micros	small	microscope, microfilm
nomos	law, order	economy, astronomy
onoma	name	synonym, antonym
philos	loving	philosopher, philanthropy
pseudes	false	pseudointellectual, pseudonym
psyche	mind, life, soul	psychic, psychology
tele	distant	telephone, telepathy
theos	god	theology, atheist

7. Significant also in the formation of words is the use of many **prefixes**

and **suffixes**. A **prefix** is a syllable, a group of syllables or a word united with or fixed to the beginning of another word to **change its meaning** or create a **new word.***

For example: stem—normal
                with prefix—**ab**normal

8. A **suffix** performs a function somewhat similar to the prefix, but is attached to the end of the word. Some of the roots we have listed here also serve as prefixes and suffixes of English words. The most frequently used prefixes and suffixes come to us from Latin, Greek and Anglo-Saxon. A few examples of some commonly used **prefixes** and **suffixes** are listed below:

Latin Origin

Prefix	*Area of Meaning*	*Current Word*
ab-	away from	abnormal, absent
ante-	before, in front of	antecedent, anterior
anti-	against, opposite	antisocial, antiseptic
bene-	well	benefit, benevolent
con-	with	conversation, coeducation
com-	before m, p, b	
col-	before l	
cor-	before r	
co-	means joint(ly) with	
contra-	against, opposite	contradict, contrary
de-	from, down (negative)	devalue, degrade, de-emphasize
dis-	apart, away, not (negative)	dismiss, disorder
ex-, e-	out from, former	exit, ex-president
in-	into, not	innocent
im-	before m, p, b	impossible
il-	before l	illiterate
ir-	before r	irregular
mal-	ill, bad, badly, wrong	malevolent, malformed
mis-	wrong, wrongly, not	misunderstand, mistrust
post-	behind, after	postpone, posterity
pre-	before, earlier, in front of	precede, predict
re-	back, again	repeat, return
super-	over, above, extra	supersonic, superficial
syn-, sym-	together with	synchronize, sympathy

---

*WEBSTER'S NEW WORLD DICTIONARY

| trans- | across, over, through, beyond | transatlantic, transport |
| uni- | one | uniform, unilateral, university |

Greek Origin

Prefix	*Area of Meaning*	*Current Word*
ana-	again, up, against	anarchy, anachronism
arch-	chief, primitive, the earlier	architect, archaic
cat-	down, downward	catastrophe, catapult
dia-	through, between	dialogue, diagonal
eu-	good, happy, well	eulogy, euphony
hyper-	extreme, over, above	hypertense, hyperbole
hypo-	under, below	hypodermic, hypothesis
meta-	after, beyond	metabolism, metathesis
neo-	new	neologism, neophyte
para-	beside	parapsychology, paradox
peri-	around, about	perimeter, periscope
poly-	many	polygamy, polysyllabic
syn-	with, together	synchronize, synonym

Anglo-Saxon Origin

Prefix	*Area of Meaning*	*Current Word*
be-	throughout, over	besiege, besmudge
for-	against, not	forget, forbid
mis-	error, defeat, wrong	misbehave, misconduct
out-	beyond, completely	outdo, outside, outbreak
un-	not	undo, unimaginative
under-	beneath, less than	underrate, undermine, undernourish
with-	from, against	withdraw, withhold, withstand

9. Usually a suffix **changes** the word into another **part of speech**. For example:

stem—normal (adj.)
with suffix—normal**ly** (adv.)

Photo Credits

Alamy: Jeff Greenberg 5 of 6, 45; Capstone: 138–
139; Corbis: K.J. Historical, 107; Courtesy of
Mik Mart Ice Cream: 34–35; Courtesy of Therese
R. Nicklas: 77; Faye Rusk/Junior Achievement
of Southeast Texas: 36; Flickr: Joseph, 81; Getty
Images: Tim Boyles, 160–161; Glow Images:
Corbis/Tom Stewart, 124–125; Newscom: Dan
Harr/AdMedia, 9, EPA/Felix Kaestle, 132–133;
Public Domain: 49; Shutterstock: Aaron Amat,
143, Andresr, 84, Ariwasabi, 78, Artisticco,
68–69, asife, 190, auremar, 149, baranq, 24–25,
bikeriderlondon, 4–5, 170–171, Blazej Lyjak,
192–193, blue67design, 200, Brian A Jackson,
18–19, brinkstock, 83, Carla Donofrio, 14–15,
Carlos Amarillo, 175, Creativa, 130, 150, cvalle,
148, Diego Cervo, 1, Edyta Pawlowska, 29, Eric
Isselee, 186–187, Georgios Kollidas, 80, Golden
Pixels LLC, 39, 103, Goodluz, 17, 111, hxdbzxy,
10, Horiyan, 71 (top), Iaroslav Neliubov, 63,
IhorZigor, 183, iQoncept, 22, 118, 142, iris
42, 86, isak55, 42–43, Jag_cz, 140–141, Karen
Roach, 152–153, Kheng Guan Toh, 40–41,
kovacsf, 178, kurhan, 56–57, Little Whale,
198–199, Luis Viegas, 71 (bottom), lukeruk, 73,
Mackey Creations, 67, mangostock, 114–115,
Marie C Fields, 126–127, Masson, 184–185,
michaeljung, 27, 113, 135, 154, 166, 180–181,
Michal Durinik, 94, Mmaxer, 89, Monkey
Business Images, 144–145, 162, monticello,
116, My Good Images, 159, mypokcik, 96–97,
NicoElNino, 50, ollyy, 52–53, Pavel L Photo and
Video, 156–157, Peshkova, 30–31, photastic,
74–75, ponsulak, 196–197, Pressmaster, 117,
Quka, 54, Renewer, 104, Rido, 165, Room27,
177, Samuel Borges Photography, 173, Sergey
Furtaev, 123, sheelamohanachandran2010, 91,
Stephen VanHorn, 195, Steve Cukrov, 92–93,
Stuart Jenner, 58–59, 147, Syda Productions, 61,
137, szefei, 101, Valua Vitaly, 129, Vladru, 64–65,
wavebreakmedia, 32–33, zentilia, 71 (middle),
zimmytws, 188, Zorandim, 168; SuperStock:
Cusp, 108–109; Design Elements: Shutterstock

ADDITIONAL RESOURCES

FURTHER READING

Bateman, Katherine Roberta. *The Young Investor: Projects and Activities for Making Your Money Grow.* Chicago: Chicago Review Press, 2010.

Blumenthal, Karen. *The Wall Street Journal Guide to Starting Your Financial Life.* New York: Three Rivers Press, 2009.

Chatzky, Jean Sherman. *Not Your Parents' Money Book: Making, Saving, and Spending Your Own Money.* New York: Simon & Schuster Books for Young Readers, 2010.

Gagne, Tammy. *A Teen Guide to Protecting and Insuring Assets.* Hockessin, Del.: Mitchell Lane Publishers, 2014.

Hansen, Mark. *Success 101 for Teens: Dollars and Sense for a Winning Financial Life.* St. Paul, Minn.: Paragon House, 2012.

Karchut, Wes, and Darby Karchut. *Money and Teens: Savvy Money Skills.* Colorado Springs, Colo.: Copper Square Studios, 2012.

INTERNET SITES TO EXPLORE

The College Board
https://www.collegeboard.org

The Internet Guide to Funding College and Section 529 Savings Plans
http://www.savingforcollege.com/

Junior Achievement
https://www.juniorachievement.org/web/ja-usa/home

The Mint
http://www.themint.org

MyMoney.gov—Protect
http://www.mymoney.gov/protect/Pages/Protect.aspx

Practical Money Skills
http://www.practicalmoneyskills.com

Teen Business Link
http://archive.sba.gov/teens/

Editorial Credits

Angie Kaelberer and Catherine Neitge, editors;
Ted Williams, designer; Eric Gohl, media researcher;
Charmaine Whitman, production specialist

Capstone Young Readers are published by Capstone,
1710 Roe Crest Drive, North Mankato, MN 56003
www.capstoneyoungreaders.com

Library of Congress Cataloging-in-Publication Data
McGuire, Kara.
 The teen money manual:a guide to cash, credit, spending, saving,
work, wealth, and more / by Kara McGuire.
 pages cm.
 Includes bibliographical references and index.
 ISBN 978-1-62370-135-2 (paperback)
1. Finance, Personal—Juvenile literature. 2. Teenagers—Finance,
Personal—Juvenile literature. I. Title.
 HG179.M38328 2015
 332.02400835—dc23   2014003725

Copyright © 2015 by Capstone. All rights reserved. No part of
this publication may be reproduced in whole or in part, or stored
in a retrieval system, or transmitted in any form or by any means,
electronic, mechanical, photocopying, recording, or otherwise, without
written permission of the publisher.

About the author

Kara McGuire is an award-winning personal finance writer, consumer researcher, and speaker. She writes a personal finance column for the Minneapolis *Star Tribune* and formerly worked for the public radio program *Marketplace Money*. She enjoys teaching young people and parents about money. Kara lives in St. Paul, Minnesota, with her husband, Matt, and children Charlotte, Teddy, and August.

Printed in Canada.
032014   008248FRF14

or

stem—terror (n.)
with suffix—terror**ize** (v.)

a. **Nouns** are derived from **verbs** through the addition of suffixes
-tion, **-ion**, **-sion** and **-ation**:

compile	—	compilation
examine	—	examination
denounce	—	denunciation, etc.

and the suffixes **-al**, **-se**, **-ment**, **-iture** and **-ance**:

govern	—	government
refuse	—	refusal
expend	—	expense
judge	—	judgment
furnish	—	furniture
sever	—	severance, etc.

b. **Nouns** are derived from **adjectives** through the suffixes **-ness**,
-ity, **-ce** and **-cy**:

happy	—	happiness
romance	—	romantic
fragrant	—	fragrance

c. **Adjectives** are derived from **nouns** by adding the suffixes **-ful**, **-less**,
-ious, **-ous**, **-al**, **-ic**, **-ish**, **-an**, **-ary** and **-ed**:

hope	—	hopeful
sorrow	—	sorrowful
pay	—	payless
end	—	endless
joy	—	joyous
Poland	—	Polish
America	—	American
imagination	—	imaginary
fever	—	feverish

d. **Adjectives** are derived from **verbs** by adding the suffixes
-able, **-ible** and **-ive**:

manage	—	manageable
reverse	—	reversible
evade	—	evasive
repair	—	reparable

e. **Verbs** are derived from **adjectives** by adding the suffixes -**ize**, -**en** and -**fy**:

thick	—	thicken
solid	—	solidify

f. Finally, **adverbs** are derived from **adjectives** by adding the suffix -**ly**:

handy	—	handily
suitable	—	suitably
angry	—	angrily
false	—	falsely
able	—	ably
memorable	—	memorably

10. There are many suffixes, as well as roots and prefixes, in the English language. We have only enough space here to mention a few of those commonly used. As we progress, we will learn new formations of words. For now, however, let's remember to examine old and new words in the following manner:

a. What is the **area of meaning** of the **root**?

b. What is the **area of meaning** of the **prefix**?

c. What is the **area of meaning** of the **suffix**?

d. What is the **meaning** of the **word in context**?

e. Answer the above four questions correctly and you'll never have to look up the word again.

B.   Composition by Degrees

1. a. Copy the title of Composition III.A.

————————————————————————————

b. Copy the foreign words.

————————————————————————————

c. Copy the name of the country from which these words come.

_____

2. a. Copy the words that came from Italy.

_____

b. Copy the words that originated in Spain.

_____

c. Copy the words that came from Germany.

_____

d. Copy the word that is used to describe a quick play in football.

_____

3. Copy the countries mentioned in this paragraph.

_____

4. a. Copy the sentence that tells about **roots**.

_____

b. Copy the phrase that tells why we can understand the "meaning of a word."

_____

5. a. Copy the phrase that tells what happens when you "learn the most common roots."

_____

b. Copy the words that originate from the Latin words **annus**.

_____

c. Copy the phrase that means **biennial**.

_____

d. Copy the phrase that means **perennial**.

_____

C.   Word Root

1. In the chart below, some of the most common **roots** are listed alphabetically. The area of meaning of the root is given. In the space provided on the right, write examples of words that are formed from the root. Try to find new words in the dictionary that have also been formed from the root words.

a. **Latin origin**

Example: **aptare**—fit—adapt, inept

Word Root	*Area of Meaning*	*Examples*
amare	love	_____

capere	take, accept	_____
fortis	strong, brave	_____
mors	death	_____
pax	peace	_____
sequi	follow	_____
similis	like	_____
venire	come	_____
videre	see	_____
vivere	live	_____

b. **Greek origin**

Example: **logos**—study of—logical, astrology

Word Root	*Area of Meaning*	*Examples*
anthropos	man	_____
aster	star	_____
bios	life	_____
demos	people	_____
heteros	other, different	_____
kosmos	order, world	_____
nomos	law, order	_____
onoma	name	_____
philos	loving	_____
pseudes	false	_____
psyche	mind, soul	_____
theos	god	_____

2. In the chart below, some of the most common **prefixes** are listed alphabetically. The area of meaning of the prefix is given. In the space provided on the right, write examples of words that use the prefix. Try to find new words in the dictionary that also use the prefix.

a. **Latin origin**

Example: **ante**—before, in front—antecede, antecedent, antedate

Prefix	*Area of Meaning*	*Examples*
ab-	away from	_____
anti-	against, opposite	_____
bene-	well	_____
con-	with	_____
contra-	against, opposite	_____
de-	from, down (negative)	_____

dis-	apart, away, not (negative)	_____
in-	into, not	_____
mal-	ill, bad, badly	_____
post-	behind, after	_____
pre-	before, earlier, in front of	_____
re-	back, again	_____
super-	over, above, extra	_____
syn-, sym-	together with	_____
trans-	across, over, beyond	_____
uni-	one	_____

b. Greek origin

Example: **arch-** —chief, primitive, the earlier—archaic

Prefix	*Area of Meaning*	*Examples*
ana-	again, up against	_____
cat-	down, downward	_____
dia-	through, between	_____
eu-	good, happy, well	_____
hyper-	extreme, over, above	_____
hypo-	under, below	_____
meta-	after, beyond	_____
neo-	new	_____
para-	beside	_____
peri-	around, about	_____
poly-	many	_____
syn-	with, together	_____

c. Anglo-Saxon origin

Example: **a-** —at, in, on, to—ahead, afoot, asleep

Prefix	*Area of Meaning*	*Examples*
be-	throughout, over	_____
for-	against, not	_____
mis-	error, defeat, wrong	_____
out-	beyond, completely	_____
un-	not	_____
under-	beneath, less than	_____
with-	from, against	_____

3. In the chart below, some of the most common **suffixes** are listed alphabetically in groups of varied significance. The area of meaning of the suffix is given. In the space provided on the right, write examples of words that use the suffix. Try to find similar new words in the dictionary.

a. **Abstract Nouns**

Example: -**ment**—government

Suffix	*Area of Meaning*	*Examples*
-acy	All these suffixes	_____
-age	signify **state of**, **act**	_____
-ance, -ancy	**of**, **quality of.**	_____
-ence, -ency		_____
-ation, -tion		_____
-ion, -sion		_____
-dom		_____
-hood		_____
-ice		_____
-ism		_____
-ment		_____
-ness		_____
-ship		_____
-ty, -ity		_____

b. **Concrete Nouns**

Example: -**art**—braggart

Suffix	*Area of Meaning*	*Examples*
-an, -ant	All these suffixes	_____
-ent	signify **one who does.**	_____
-ard, -art		_____
-ary		_____
-ee, -eer, -ess		_____
-er, -ar,		_____
-ier, -or		_____
-ic, -ist		_____
-ite, -yte		_____

c. **Adjectives**

Example: -**al**—cerebral

Suffix	*Area of Meaning*	*Examples*
-ac, -al, -an	All these suffixes	_____

-ar, -ary -ful -ic -ish -ive -ory	signify **resembling, full, of, belonging to.**	_____ _____ _____ _____ _____ _____
-able -ible -ile	All these suffixes signify **capable, able to.**	_____ _____ _____

d. **Verbs**

Example: **-ate**—facilitate

Suffix	*Area of Meaning*	*Examples*
-ate -en -fy -ize -ise	All these suffixes signify **to make.**	_____ _____ _____ _____ _____

D. Parts of Speech

1. a. Change **verbs** into **nouns**. Follow the examples. Consult your dictionary for new words.

Suffix			*Examples*		
-al	refuse	→ refusal	survive	→	survival
	arrive	→ arrival	approve	→	approval
	propose	→ proposal	dismiss	→	dismissal
-ance	annoy	→ annoyance	signify	→	significance
-ence	refer	→ reference	exist	→	existence
	transfer	→ transference	sever	→	severance
	defer	→ deference	accept	→	acceptance
	attend	→ attendance	disturb	→	disturbance
-ation	compile	→ compilation	relate	→	relation
-tion	examine	→ examination	nominate	→	nomination
	isolate	→ isolation	except	→	exception
	compose	→ composition	consult	→	consultation
	recognize	→ recognization	emigrate	→	emigration
	Sp. denounce	→ denuntiation	define	→	definition
	realize	→ realization	resign	→	resignation
-er	manage	→ manager	teach	→	teacher
-or	learn	→ learner	speak	→	speaker

	write	→ *writer*	read	→	*reader*
	initiate	→ *initiat*	govern	→	*governor*
	direct	→ *director*	create	→	
	develop	→ *developer*	employ	→	*employer*
-ment	develop	→ development	judge	→	*judgment*
	govern	→ government	invest	→	*investment*
	pay	→ *payment*	agree	→	*agreement*
	argue	→ *argument*	punish	→	*punishment*
-sion	decide	→ decision	expand	→	*expansion*
	impress	→ impression	divide	→	*division*
	express	→ *expression*	profess	→	*profession*
	progress	→ *progression*	collide	→	*collision*
-y	deliver	→ delivery	discover	→	*discovery*
	inquire	→ inquiry	recover	→	*recovery*
	arm	→ *army*	flatter	→	*flattery*

b. Change **nouns** into **verbs**. Follow the examples. Consult your dictionary for new words.

-ize	economy	→ economize	drama	→	*dramatize*
	terror	→ terrorize	author	→	*authorize*
	critic	→ *criticize*	familiar	→	*familiarize*
	organ	→ *organize*	final	→	*finalize*

2. Change **adjectives** into **nouns**. Follow the examples. Consult your dictionary for new words.

-ce	romantic	→ romance	fragrant	→	*fragrance*
-cy	supreme	→ supremacy	constant	→	*constancy*
	brilliant	→ *brilliancy*	coherent	→	*coherence*
-ity	agile	→ agility	artificial	→	
	able	→ *ability*	gullible	→	*gullibility*
	fragile	→ *fragility*	charitable	→	*charity*
	fatal	→ *fatality*	curious	→	*curiosity*
-ness	bashful	→ bashfulness	sleepy	→	*sleepiness*
	happy	→ happiness	pleasant	→	*pleasantness*
	kind	→ *kindness*	useful	→	*usefulness*
	childish	→ *childishness*	cheerful	→	*cheerfulness*

3. Change **nouns** into **adjectives**. Follow the examples. Consult your dictionary for new words.

-ful	hope	→ hopeful	taste	→	*tast*
	sorrow	→ *sorrowful*	waste	→	*wasteful*

	fancy	→ _____	fate	→ *joyful*
	pain	→ *painful*	tact	→ *tactful*
-less	pay	→ payless	tact	→ *tactless*
	end	→ endless	pain	→ *painless*
	power	→ *powerless*	hope	→ *hopeless*
	regard	→ *regardless*	sense	→ *senseless*
-ous	joy	→ joyous	danger	→ *dangerous*
	beauty	→ beauteous	glutton	→ *gluttonous*
	generosity	→ *generous*	fame	→ *famous*
	advantage	→ *advantageous*	outrage	→ *outrageous*
-ious	ambition	→ ambitious	atrocity	→ *atrocious*
	victory	→ *victorious*	curiosity	→ *curious*
	courtesy	→ *courteous*	labor	→ *laborious*
	luxury	→ *luxurious*	mystery	→ *mysterious*
-y	nerve	→ nervy	shadow	→ *shady*
	dirt	→ dirty	wealth	→ *wealthy*
	cloud	→ *cloudy*	guilt	→ *guilty*
-al	nature	→ natural	mechanic	→ *mechanical*
	economy	→ *economical*	music	→ *musical*
	exception	→ *exceptional*	origin	→ *original*
-ish	fever	→ feverish	fiend	→ *fiendish*
	Poland	→ Polish	self	→ *selfish*
	child	→ *childish*	fool	→ *foolish*

4. Change **verbs** into **adjectives**. Follow the examples. Consult your dictionary for new words.

-able	repair	→ reparable	notice	→ *notifiable*
	manage	→ manageable	pleasure	→ *pleasurable*
	place	→ _____	support	→ *supportable*
	trace	→ *traceable*	achievement	→ *achieveable*
-ible	reverse	→ reversible	divide	→ *divisible*
	convert	→ *convertible*	impress	→ _____
	force	→ *forcible*	attract	→ _____
-ive	evade	→ evasive	imagine	→ *imaginative*
	persuade	→ *persuasive*	impress	→ *impressive*
	destruct	→ *destructive*	select	→ *selective*

5. Change **adjectives** into **adverbs**. Follow the examples. Consult your dictionary for new words.

-ly	handy	→ handily	angry	→ angrily
	suitable	→ *suitably*	false	→ *falsely*
	able	→ *ably*	memorable	→ _____

common → *Commonly*   new → *newly*

6. **Summary** of **parts of speech**. Fill in the missing form of the word. Follow the example on top of the table. Consult your dictionary only if you are not sure of the correct form of the word.

Noun	Verb	Adjective	Adverb
economy	economize	economical	economically
_____	dramatize	_____	_____
_____	_____	hopeful	_____
_____	_____	_____	memorably
reversal	_____	_____	_____
_____	evade	_____	_____
_____	_____	memorable	_____
_____	succeed	_____	_____
_____	_____	_____	satisfactorily
consideration	_____	_____	_____
_____	_____	separate	_____

7. **Analyzing Words.** If necessary, use your dictionary to analyze the words in bold print. Write your analysis on the lines provided.

a. **amare**

(1) What is an **amorous** person?

_____

_____

(2) What is meant by the word **enamor**?

_____

_____

(3) How is the word **amateur** related to **amare**?

_____

_____

(4) Is the word **amiable** related to **amare**?

_____

_____

b. **logos—bios**

(1) What do we mean by saying "He is logical?"

_____

_____

(2) What does **biology** literally mean?

_____

_____

(3) Combine another root with **logos** and explain the meaning.

_____

_____

(4) Combine another root with **bios** and explain the meaning.

_____

_____

c. **anthropos—logos**

(1) What is the literal meaning of **anthropology**?

_____

_____

(2) How is **misanthropy** related to the root anthropos?

_____

(3) What is a "**logical**" person?

_____

_____

(4) What is another word for **misanthropy**?

_____

d. **con-, co-**

(1) What is **coeducation**?

_____

_____

(2) What is the literal meaning of **conversation**?

_____

_____

(3) What does **coexist** mean?

_____

(4) What does **contradict** mean?

_____

_____

e. **mal-**

(1) What is the meaning of the word "**malfunction?**"

_____

_____

(2) How is malevolent related to the prefix **mal-**?

_____

_____

(3) Which other word(s) will express **maltreat**?

_____

_____

(4) What is the relation of **mal-** to **mis-**?

_____

_____

    f. **fortis**

        (1) What does **fortify** mean?   (3) Is **comfort** related to **fortis**?

        _____

        _____

        (2) What does **fortitude** mean?   (4) What is a **fort**?

        _____

        _____

PART ONE

Writing the Sentence

Chapter Two

The Simple Sentence

Words to Remember:

Use: **declarative** – *makes a statement*

interrogative – *asks a question*

affirmative
  vs. negative
assertive

imperative – *command or entreaty*

exclamatory – *expresses strong feelings*

Structure: Simple sentence–one subject/one predicate

period (.)–capitalization–

question mark (?)–exclamation mark (!)

I. Model Composition

A.   Advertising

1. Advertising is an American way of life. Americans like advertising. People depend on advertising in their daily lives. People are consumers. The advertisers are manufacturers. Some advertisers are salesmen. Their merchandise needs advertising. Every product is advertised. Merchants buy ads for their products. Good advertising means success. Bad advertising can mean failure.

2. There are many ways to advertise. "Ads" come in different forms. Newspapers carry advertisements. Products are announced on TV and radio. Such announcements are called "commercials." Commercial radio stations are popular. They have a wide audience. Billboards carry much advertising. Merchants buy advertising space. It's a big industry. Many agencies furnish a variety of services. The first American advertising agency was established in Philadelphia, Pa., in 1840. Many advertising agencies are active in the U.S. today. Other advertising media include magazines and journals. Short films are produced for advertising.

3. The language of advertising is simple. Most ads have a basic appeal to children. Advertising can be funny. It tells you to eat well. It also shows you how to diet. It is contradictory. Some examples of advertising are:

a.

b.

c.

GOOD COFFEE IS IMPORTANT!

d.

HAVE YOU TRIED VIGOR CRACKERS?

4. Sometimes advertising is in the form of a dialogue. The following is an example: (Q. = question; A. = answer)

Q. Does your cereal taste good?

A. No, it doesn't.

Q. Have you tried another cereal?

A. No, I haven't.

Q. Haven't you heard of MATADOR CEREAL?

A. I've heard of it now and then.

Q. Why don't you try MATADOR CEREAL?

5. Advertising is not always truthful. A product is often misrepresented. The advertiser exaggerates the benefits of the merchandise he wants to sell. He misrepresents the truth. The consumer falls victim to advertising. Millions of people have bought advertised products. The people haven't always been satisfied. Most manufacturers guarantee their products. This is the way of free enterprise. Our business system is called the free enterprise.

B.   Composition by Degrees

1. a. Copy the title of the Model Composition.

   _____

   b. Copy the sentence that tells what "an American way of life" is.

   _____

   c. Copy the word that tells what Americans like.

   _____

   d. Copy the expression that tells what people "depend on."

   _____

   e. Copy the words that tell who the consumers are and who the advertisers are.

   _____

   f. Copy the sentence that tells what is advertised.

   _____

   g. Copy the sentence that tells what can "mean failure."

   _____

2. a. Copy the sentence that tells what the newspapers carry.

   _____

   b. Copy the sentence that contains the word "commercial."

   _____

   c. Copy the sentence that tells what the billboards carry.

   _____

   d. Copy the sentence that tells what the merchants buy.

   _____

   e. Copy the date that tells when the first advertising agency was established in America.

   _____

f. Copy the name of the city where the first agency was established in America.

_____

g. Copy the sentence that tells what radio stations are popular.

_____

3. a. Copy the word in sentence 1 that tells about the language of advertising.

_____

   b. Copy the word in sentence 2 that is short for advertising.

_____

   c. Copy the phrase that tells to whom ads appeal.

_____

   d. Copy the name of the product advertised in ad "a."

_____

   e. Copy the name of the product advertised in ad "b."

_____

   f. Copy the name of the product advertised in ad "c."

_____

   g. Copy the name of the product advertised in ad "d."

_____

   h. Copy the sentences that make advertising funny.

_____

4. a. Copy the word that describes the advertising method in paragraph 4.

_____

   b. Copy the name of the product advertised in paragraph 4.

_____

5. a. Copy the phrase that tells that advertising does not always "tell the truth."

_____

   b. Copy the phrase(s) that tell(s) that a product is "shown to be different" from what it is.

_____

   c. Copy the phrase that tells who buys advertised products.

_____

   d. Copy the sentence that tells about free enterprise.

_____

II. *Words in Context*

A. From the list of words preceding each section, fill in each blank space provided in the text. You may use a selection more than once. Also, you may use more than one word in one blank space.

1. advertise(ment)   need   depend(ent)   failure
   advertising   consumers   consume   success

In America there is a _____ to _____ . People _____
on _____ . Those who _____ are manufacturers.
Those who buy are _____ . People _____
many products. Good_____ can mean _____ .

2. different   advertise   advertisements   products
   "commercial"   advertising   industry   variety
   services   agencies   produced   commercial
   media   many

There are _____ ways to_____ . Ads come in _____
forms. Newspapers carry_____ . Radio and TV announce_____ .
Advertising on radio and TV is called _____ . Merchants buy _____
space. Advertising is a big _____ . Many _____ furnish
a _____ of_____ . Other _____ for _____
are magazines and journals. Short films are _____ for _____ .
_____ radio stations are popular.

3. language   appeal   advertising   simple
   examples

The _____ of advertising is_____ . Most ads _____
to children. There are many _____ of_____ .

4. tried   taste   dialogue   try
   advertising   another   cereal

A _____ is sometimes_____ . Does your _____
_____ good? Have you _____ _____ ? Why
don't you _____ Matador _____ ?

5. enterprise   misrepresented   truthful   exaggerates
   always   advertiser   victim   conceals
   product(s)   advertised   manufacturers   consumer
   satisfied

Advertising is not _____   _____ . A _____ is often _____ . The _____   _____ about the merchandise. The _____   _____ the truth. The___ falls _____ of advertising. Millions of people buy _____ products. The people are not always _____ . Most _____ stand behind their _____ . This is the way of free _____ .

B.   Make the necessary change(s) when you substitute the new element into your sentence.

> Example: Advertising is **an American** way of life. (a good way)
> Advertising is **a good way** of life.

1. a. **Americans like** advertising. (Mary)
   b. People depend on **advertising**. (it)
   c. **People** are consumers. (they)
   d. **The advertisers** are manufacturers. (we)
   e. Their **merchandise** needs advertising. (products)
   f. **Every product** is advertised. (the merchandise)
   g. **Merchants** buy ads for their products. (advertisers)
   h. Advertising **means success**. (sells)

2. a. There are **many** ways to advertise. (few)
   b. Ads come in **different** forms. (varied)
   c. Products are **announced** on TV and radio. (advertised)
   d. Merchants **buy** advertising space. (need)
   e. Short films are **produced** for advertising. (made)
   f. **Commercial** radio stations are popular. (which advertise)

3. a. The language of advertising is **simple**. (easy to understand)
   b. Most ads **appeal** to children. (are appealing)
   c. Advertising can be **funny**. (comical)
   d. It tells you **how to eat well**. (about the good food)
   e. It also shows you how **to diet**. (not to overeat)
   f. The first agency was **established** in 1840. (founded)

4. a. Sometimes advertising takes the form of a **dialogue**. (conversation)
   b. Have you **tried** another cereal? (eaten)
   c. I've heard it **now and then**. (from time to time)

5. a. Advertising is **not always truthful**. (sometimes a lie)
   b. **A product is** often misrepresented. (products are)
   c. The advertiser exaggerates the benefits of the **merchandise** he wants to sell. (product)
   d. He **conceals** the truth. (hides)
   e. The **consumer falls** victim to advertising. (consumers)
   f. Millions of people **buy** advertised products. (purchase)

g. The people are not always **satisfied**. (pleased)

h. Most manufacturers stand behind their **products**. (merchandise)

i. This is the way free **enterprise** works. (commerce)

III. *Structures (Key words [phrases] for composition)*

A. Use the following key words [phrases] to form complete sentences. You may consult the MODEL COMPOSITION.

Example: advertising / is / way of life

Advertising is an American way of life.

1. a. America / likes_____

   b. people / depend / advertising _____

   c. people / consumers _____

   d. advertisers / manufacturers _____

   e. Some / advertisers / salesmen _____

   f. merchandise / needs / advertising _____

   g. product / is / advertised _____

   h. advertising / means / success _____

   i. bad / can / mean / failure _____

2. a. many / ways / advertise _____

   b. ads / come / different / forms _____

   c. newspapers / carry _____

   d. products / announced / TV and Radio _____

   e. are / called / commercials _____

   f. billboards / carry / advertising _____

   g. merchants / buy / space_____

   h. advertising / media / include / magazines / journals_____

   i. short films / are / produced / advertising _____

   j. commercial / stations / are _____

3. a. language / is / simple_____

   b. ads / appeal / children _____

   c. advertising / can be / funny _____

   d. it / tells / to eat / well _____

   e. shows / to / diet _____

    f. first / agency / established _____

4. a. does / cereal / taste _____

    b. have / tried / another _____

    c. haven't / heard / **MATADOR** _____

    d. why / don't / try / **MATADOR** _____

5. a. advertising / is not / truthful _____

    b. product / is / misrepresented _____

    c. advertiser / exaggerates / merchandise _____

    d. conceals / truth _____

    e. consumer / falls / victim / advertising _____

    f. people / buy / products _____

    g. are / not / satisfied _____

    h. manufacturers / stand / behind / products _____

    i. is / way / free / enterprise _____ _____

B. Supply the missing **prepositions** for each blank space. You may consult the MODEL COMPOSITION.

    Example: Advertising is an American way ____(of)____ life.

1. a. People depend _____ advertising _____ their daily lives.

    b. Merchants buy ads _____ their products.

2. a. Ads come _____ different forms.

    b. Products are announced _____ TV and radio.

    c. Many agencies furnish a variety _____ services.

    d. Short films are produced _____ advertising.

3. a. The language _____ advertising is simple.

    b. Most ads appeal _____ to children.

    c. These are examples _____ advertising.

    d. It tells you _____ eat well.

4. a. Haven't you heard _____ MATADOR cereal?

    b. I've heard _____ it now and then.

5. a. The advertiser exaggerates _____ the merchandise.

    b. The consumer falls victim _____ advertising.

    c. Millions _____ people buy advertised products.

d. Most manufacturers stand ——————— their products.

e. This is the way ——————— free enterprise.

IV.   *Grammar and Syntax [Points of Interest]*

A.   Correctness

1. *Agreement*—Roots, prefixes and suffixes serve to form words. Sentences are formed from words. The **phrase** is the smallest unit from which a sentence is constructed. The smallest unit is called the **kernel**.

Example: **The boy sings.**

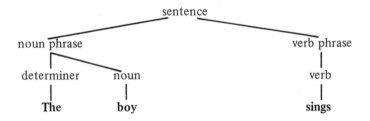

The smallest *complete* sentence is called **simple**, or **declarative**.
Example: **The man chased the dog.**

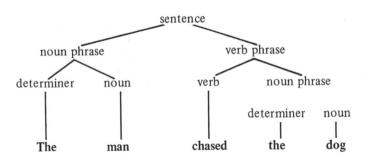

A **simple** sentence has **one independent clause**. There are no dependent clauses attached. There may be modifying phrases. There is **one subject** and **one main verb**. The subject and the verb are in agreement.

Examples:

America	needs	advertising.
subject	verb	

The advertisers	are	manufacturers.
subject	verb	

There are four basic types of simple sentences in English. Their patterns are as follows:

SUBJECT → TENSE and BE → COMPLEMENT or → ADVERBIAL
(Noun → or VERBAL → DIRECT OBJECT → (optional)
Phrase) (Noun Phrase)

Examples of the four basic types of simple sentences are:

a. Type **be**	People	**are**	consumers	(usually).
	Merchants	**are**	advertisers	(always).
b. Type **verb** **intransitive**	Manufacturers	**stand**	behind their products	(often).
c. Type **verb** **transitive**	Americans	**like**	advertising	(every day).
	Merchants	**buy**	ads	(yearly).
d. Type **verb** **linking**	Advertisers	**seem**	honest	(usually).
	Merchants	**become**	advertisers	(usually).

2. *Transformations*—The above examples show simple sentence structure in English. These simple sentences can undergo transformations. Transformations change the structure of sentences. They delete, rearrange, add or substitute some of the items within the simple sentence.

    a. *Declarative*—A declarative sentence makes or denies a statement. Examples:

> *Everyone likes advertising.*
> *The advertisers are manufacturers.*
> *Merchants buy ads for their products.*

    b. *Interrogative*—The interrogative is the ordinary pattern for asking questions. Examples:

> *Does everyone like advertising?*
> *Are the advertisers manufacturers?*
> *Do merchants buy ads for their products?*
> *Going on a diet?*
> *Have you tried VIGOR crackers?*

c. *Affirmative (assertive)*—The affirmative is like the declarative. Its purpose is to express fact and opinion. The affirmative can be expressed in several ways. Examples:

> *What* an advertisement!
> *What* a good buy!
> *How* many ways to advertise!
> *How* I love it!

The **what** and **how** affirmatives express emotion. Both the **what** and the **how** of the affirmative are close to the meaning of the word **extraordinary**. Some examples of the above can be expressed in the following way:

> It is an **extraordinary** advertisement.
> It is an **extraordinary** buy.

d. *Negative*—The word *not* is the basic clause negator.

> Did you see the advertising?
> No, I *didn't* (did *not*) see it.
> I *don't* (do *not*) like cereal.
> Pastry *isn't* (is *not*) good.

The word *not* is not the only negator. A subject can also be a negator.

(1) *Not everybody* likes commercials.

(2) *Nobody* likes commercials.

The two sentences are different in meaning. The first one can mean almost everybody. The *no* in the second sentence expresses the meaning of *zero*. Some more examples are:

(1) Advertising *won't* (will *not*) get you anywhere.

(2) Advertising will get you *nowhere*.

(1) We *don't* (do *not*) have any money.

(2) We have *no* money.

(1) I *didn't* (did *not*) see anything.

(2) I saw *nothing*.

3. *The Tenses**—Differences in *time* are called *tenses*. Time is commonly referred to as *past*, *present* and *future*. The tenses are:

a. Present	→	I (do) need advertising.
		He (does need) needs advertising.
b. Past (simple)	→	I needed (I did need) advertising.
c. Future	→	I will (I'll) need advertising.
d. Present Perfect	→	I have (I've) needed advertising.
		He has needed advertising.
e. Past Perfect	→	I had needed advertising.
f. Future Perfect	→	I will (I'll) have needed advertising.

All of the transformations can be applied to the six tenses. Example:

(Present)
I need advertising. → Do I need advertising? (Interrogative)
I don't need advertising. (Negative)

(Present Perfect)
I have needed advertising. → Have I needed advertising? (Interrogative)
I haven't needed advertising. (Negative)

[For other tenses follow the examples you've learned.]

B. Completeness

The sentence must satisfy the following requirements:

1. It gives a sense of completeness.

2. It makes sense when you read it.

3. It has a subject (someone or something).

4. It has a verb (does something).

---

*Verb Tense is extensively discussed in Chapter Five. Here we will only discuss the basic concepts of six primary tenses in the *indicative*.

5. It begins with a capital letter.

6. It ends with a period or other terminal (end) punctuation mark.

Examples:

1. Merchants buy ads for their products.

2. Bad advertising can mean failure.

3. There are many ways to advertise.

4. Products are announced on TV and radio.

5. Swoosh is strong medicine!

6. Have you tried VIGOR crackers?

7. I haven't heard of it.

8. Does your cereal taste good?

C. Punctuation

1. *The period* (.)—The period is an important mark of punctuation. It is used to end sentences or statements. Examples:

> The language of advertising is simple.
> Ads come in different forms.
> Most ads appeal to children.

Periods are used after independent clauses and dependent clauses. Examples:

> "Going on a diet?" "As soon as possible." (dependent)
> Everyone likes advertising. (independent) The sooner, the better. (dependent)

Periods are used with abbreviations. The period shows that a word has been shortened. Some examples are:

Rev.	=	Reverend
Dr.	=	doctor
Mr.	=	Mister
Ms.	=	married or unmarried woman
etc.	=	*et cetera* and so forth
e.g.	=	*exempli gratia*, for example
et al.	=	*et alii* and others
i.e.	=	that is

vs.	=	versus
Ph.D.	=	Doctor of Philosophy
Tex.	=	Texas
M.D.	=	Doctor of Medicine
a.m.	=	morning
p.m.	=	afternoon, evening
jr.	=	junior
sr.	=	senior
Inc.	=	Incorporated
Pa.	=	Pennsylvania

[NOTE: Never use the period to mark abbreviations when the period is not part of the official name. Some abbreviations have been discontinued.]

2. *Question mark* (?)—A question mark is used after a direct question. Examples:

> Have you tried VIGOR crackers?
> Does your cereal taste good?
> Haven't you heard of MATADOR cereal?

The most common direct question in English is the WH question. Examples:

> **Where** are you going?
> **How** are you?
> **What** have we here?
> **Why** aren't you ready?
> **When** will you come?

3. *Exclamation mark* (!)—In section A2(c) we used the exclamation mark as the end punctuation for the **what** and **how** affirmative sentence. The exclamation is used only after statements expressing **unusual emphasis**. Examples:

> Natural taste pastry is good!
> Good coffee is important!
> Swoosh is strong medicine!
> Do not conceal the truth!
> Think! Do it!
> You must not kill!

D.   Capitalization

1. We capitalize the first letter of a word at the beginning of a sentence.

The advertisers are manufacturers.
There are many ways to advertise.

2. **A proper noun** (name of person, place, thing or animal) is capitalized.
An **adjective** derived from that noun is also capitalized.

There are many advertising firms in America (n.).
The first American (adj.) advertising agency was established in 1840.
Winter is very long in Alaska (n.).
Alaskan (adj.) winter is long.
Sam Houston was born in Texas (n.).
Sam Houston was a Texan (adj.).

[NOTE: Proper nouns are days of the week, months, political parties, nationalities, societies, organizations, institutions, countries, cities, religions, corporations, geographic areas, states, etc.]

Examples:

On Saturday he addressed the Democratic Party.
Their first advertising appeared in May.
The West is more populated than the East.
Last July we climbed the Rocky Mountains.

E.   Exercises

1. *Subject-verb agreement*—Underline the correct verb form.

   a. Advertising (is/are) an American way of life.

   b. America (need/needs) advertising.

   c. People (is/are) consumers.

   d. The advertisers (is/are) manufacturers.

   e. Merchants (buy/buys) ads for their products.

   f. Advertising (mean/means) success.

   g. Ads (come/comes) in different ways.

   h. Newspapers (carries/carry) advertisements.

   i. Many agencies (furnishes/furnish) a variety of services.

2. *Transformations*—Transform the following sentences.

   a. Declarative to interrogative:

(1) Advertising is a way of life.

---

(2) America likes advertising.

---

(3) The advertisers are manufacturers.

---

(4) Merchants buy ads for their products.

---

(5) Their merchandise needs advertising.

---

b. Affirmative to negative:

(1) That's a good buy!

---

(2) This is the way to advertise!

---

(3) I love it!

---

(4) This is an extraordinary advertisement!

---

(5) That's delicious coffee!

---

3. *The Tenses*—Rewrite the following sentences using the tense given in parentheses.

a. There are many ways to advertise. (were)

---

b. Ads come in different forms. (came)

---

c. Products are announced on TV and radio. (have been)

---

d. Commercial radio stations are popular. (will be)

---

e. The language of advertising is simple. (has been)

---

f. It tells you to eat well. (told)

---

g. It also shows you how to diet. (showed)

_____

h. The first agency was established in 1840. (had been)

_____

i. Good coffee is important. (will be)

_____

j. Advertising hasn't always been truthful. (isn't)

_____

k. A product is often misinterpreted. (was)

_____

l. The advertiser conceals the truth. (had concealed)

_____

m. The consumer falls victim to advertising. (has fallen)

_____

n. The people haven't always been satisfied. (aren't)

_____

o. This is the way of free enterprise. (will be)

_____

4. *Completeness*—Write a complete sentence for each of the following fragments. Refer to the MODEL COMPOSITION if necessary. All of the fragments can be found in paragraphs 1 and 2.

a. is an American way of life

_____

b. depend on advertisement in their daily life

_____

c. are manufacturers

_____

d. product is advertised

_____

e. buy ads for their products

_____

f. bad advertising means failure

_____

g. are many ways to advertise

_____

h. carry advertisements

_____

i. buy advertising space

_____

j. other advertising mediums magazines and journals

_____

5. *Punctuation*—Punctuate the following passage. Use only **periods** (.), **question marks** (?) and **exclamation marks** (!). Capitalize where you think it necessary. The number on the right indicates how many corrections are needed.

mr. Jones needed some advertising He was a manufacturer.	2
Mrs Jones worked at the methodist Hospital She was a nurse.	3
the M D 's name was hendricks He was a specialist Mr. jones	7
bought two ads. he manufactured nuts, bolts, etc Business	2
wasn't good. mr and mrs. Jones hoped the advertising would	3
help their business	1
"what do you like " the man asked	3
"I like to buy an ad " Mr Jones replied	3
"What size ad would you like "	1
"I prefer a small one " said mr. jones.	3
it was a hard day. Mr and Mrs. Jones were glad it was over	3
They had worked from 7 a m to 6 p m. They were tired	4

V. *Idea Recognition*

Copy from the **MODEL COMPOSITION** the sentences expressing:

A. an American way of life . . .

_____

B. why America likes advertising . . .

_____

C. who the manufacturers are . . .

_____

D. what good advertising means . . .

_____

E. what bad advertising means . . .

_____

F. in what forms ads come . . .

_____

G. what the radio and TV announcements are . . .

_____

H.   what kind of films for advertising are produced . . .

_____

I.   about the advertising language . . .

_____

J.   to whom advertising language appeals . . .

_____

K.   how advertising can be . . .

_____

L.   how advertising hasn't always been . . .

_____

M.   what the advertiser exaggerates about . . .

_____

N.   what the advertiser conceals . . .

_____

O.   the satisfaction of the people . . .

_____

VI.   *Vocabulary Enrichment*

A.   Paraphrasing

Paraphrasing involves rephrasing specific expressions or words without changing their meaning. Write the expressions found in the MODEL COMPOSITION that correspond to the paraphrases below.

Example: a way of life   **It is the way people live.**

1. people who buy things _____

2. people who tell about things _____

3. people who sell things _____

4. good advertising _____

5. bad advertising _____

6. announcements on radio _____

7. people who sell advertising_____

8. doing the advertising _____

9. can be easily understood _____

10. don't tell the right thing _____

B. Lexical Units

Select the word (phrase) from the following list that best completes each of the sentences below. You may use a selection more than once.

Example:

They **exaggerate** about their product.
They **misrepresent** the truth about it.

tell	way of life	dependent	sell
advertising	commercial	widely	contradictory
basic	conversation		

1. America **likes** advertising. It is an American _____ .
2. People **depend** on advertising. They are _____ .
3. The manufacturers **advertise**. They _____ about their product.
4. The salesmen **advertise**. They want to _____ merchandise.
5. Products are **announced** on radio and TV. This is called a _____ .
6. Magazines carry **announcements**. They are a medium for _____ .
7. Commercial radio stations are **popular**. They are _____ listened to.
8. The language of advertising is **simple**. Its structure is _____ .
9. Advertising is sometimes **funny**. This happens when advertising becomes _____ .
10. Some ads are presented as **dialogues**. People understand _____ better than pictures.

C. Related Words

Use the **related words** to rewrite the following sentences without changing their meanings. Change the underlined word. Make further changes if necessary.

Example: to buy (v.) buyer (n.)
Merchants **buy** much advertising.
Merchants are **buyers** of much advertising.

to advertise (v.)	to produce (v.)	to establish (v.)
advertising (n.)	products (n.)	establishment (n.)
advertisement (n.)	production (n.)	
to succeed (v.)	to consume (v.)	to fail (v.)
success (n.)	consumer (n.)	failure (n.)

to depend (v.)   to announce (v.)
   dependence (n.)   announcements (n.)
   dependent (adj.)

1. **Advertising** is a necessity. _____

2. Without ads they **fail**. _____

3. They **announce** products on TV. _____

4. They **depend** on advertising. _____

5. Advertising helps **succeed**. _____

6. What they **produce** is good. _____

7. The public **consumes** products. _____

8. There are old **established** firms. _____

VII. *Steps in Writing*

A.   Add new words and revise the sentence to suit the changes indicated in parentheses.

Example: **America** likes advertising. (Americans)
            Americans **like** advertising.

1. **The consumer** needs advertising. (consumers)

   _____

2. **People** depend on advertisement. (He)

   _____

3. **They** are consumers. (She)

   _____

4. **Every** product is advertised. (some)

   _____

5. Merchants **buy** ads for their products. (need)

   _____

6. Ads **come in different forms**. (are differently formed)

   _____

7. **Newspapers** carry advertisements. (our newspaper)

   _____

8. **Many agencies** furnish a variety of services. (My agency)

   _____

9. **They have** a wide audience. (their audience is)

   _____

10. **Their language is simple.** (they speak simply)

_____

11. **Ads** have a basic appeal to children. (advertising)

_____

B. Opposites

Use the **opposites** to rewrite the following sentences. Make the necessary changes to suit the new sentences.

     Example: likes—dislikes

          America likes advertising.

          America **dislikes** advertising.

sad	agreeable	complicated	few	tells the truth
limited	bad	unimportant	weak	never
satisfied				

1. The language is **simple.** _____
2. **Most** ads appeal to children. _____
3. Ads can be **funny.** _____
4. It is often **contradictory.** _____
5. They have a **wide** audience. _____
6. Natural taste pastry is **good.** _____
7. Swoosh is **strong** medicine! _____
8. Good coffee is **important!** _____
9. The advertiser **lies** about the product. _____
10. People are **always** satisfied. _____
11. Sometimes they are **dissatisfied.** _____

VIII. Comprehension

A. Complete the sentence and add as many related sentences as you can find in the MODEL COMPOSITION.

     Example: Advertising is an **American way of life.**

          America likes advertising. People depend on advertising in their daily life.

1. Merchants buy ads _____

_____

2. Products are announced on TV _____

_____

3. The first American advertising agency was established _____

_____

4. Commercial radio stations are _____

_____

5. The language of advertising is _____

_____

B.   Reply with complete sentences.
      Example: Who advertises?
                 Merchants and salesmen advertise.

1. Why do people depend on advertising? _____

_____

2. What happens with bad advertising? _____

_____

3. Are there many ways to advertise? What are they? _____

_____

4. How do we know that commercial radio stations are popular? _____

_____

5. What is the language of advertising? _____

_____

6. Why is some advertising funny? _____

_____

7. What does ad "a" say about "Swoosh?" _____

_____

8. What does ad "d" advertise? _____

_____

9. Has advertising always been truthful? _____

_____

10. What often happens to an advertised product? _____

_____

11. What happens to the consumer when truth is misrepresented? _____

_____

12. Have the people always been satisfied? _____

_____

13. Do most manufacturers stand behind their products? _____

_____

14. What is our business system called? ———————————————

———————————————————————————

IX. Commentary on Model

A. 1. Describe ad "a."

2. Describe ad "d."

3. Discuss the importance of advertising.

4. Discuss why the language of advertising is simple.

5. Give an appropriate title to your composition.

B. 1. Discuss the points in the MODEL COMPOSITION that you like.

2. Discuss the points in the MODEL COMPOSITION with which you disagree.

3. Tell briefly what you think about advertising.

4. Give an appropriate heading to your composition.

X. Composition

A. Using the key words and phrases from the MODEL COMPOSITION, write your own composition on a related topic.

way of life	depend on advertisement	consumers
manufacturers	salesmen	success
products	bad advertising	commercials
failure	TV and radio	popular
advertising space	variety of services	established
simple language	contradictory	public falls victim
misrepresent	exaggerate	

B. 1. Rewrite section 1 of the MODEL COMPOSITION in the **I** person. Make all appropriate changes.

> Example: Advertising is **my** way of life.

2. Rewrite section 4, changing singular forms to their plural forms (i.e. **product** to **products**, **advertiser** to **advertisers**, etc.). Make all appropriate changes.

C. Describe briefly what you see in the picture below.

Chapter Three

The Compound Sentence

Words to Remember:

compound = *two or more main*

(independent) clauses

Coordination—Coordinators

and, but, for, nor, or, so, yet

Parallelism—Faulty Parallelism

semicolon (;) comma (,)

hyphen (-)

I.   *Model Composition*

> *"I think; therefore I am."*
>   Descartes

A.   Creative Thought

1. What is thought? The question is as old and puzzling as man himself. The other day I heard someone say, "This is food for thought." What did that mean? It was, perhaps, a way to encourage creative thought.

2. There are many ways in which our thinking is stimulated. To be productive individuals, we must think. When we study English, we think. We speak and create new thoughts. We write and think only in English. Thinking in one language, but learning another, makes it harder to progress creatively. When we study English, we must think in English.

3. Once I walked slowly and leisurely across a large meadow. There were many flowers and trees in bloom. The landscape looked peaceful and inviting. I was in a hurry, but not seeing anyone present, I remained for a while. Thoughts came to me readily, and I felt creative. There was silence around me, but there was a very special "buzzing" in my mind. That "buzzing" I called thought. Some people call it meditation.

4. The other day there were twenty-one children on the meadow. They were very noisy. One small boy was from Indiana; the others were Texans. I guessed that, because the Texans called the small boy "Hoosier." I listened to him, and he was glad. His father was an attorney-at-law in a small town. His grandfather took part in the Spanish-American War. The boy was proud of his heritage.

5. I wondered why the small boy confided in a stranger; I was a stranger to him. Now it was quiet on the meadow. There was no one present to disturb me. People are lonely, I thought. They need someone to talk to, yet they seldom listen. We must listen to children, so that we can understand them. We are called "thoughtful" when we are considerate and listen.

6. Not all thinking is creative. A painter creates his work in his thoughts, so does a writer, or a dancer. That is creative thought. But a person can simply think before he acts; that kind of thought is called "wisdom." When people think and listen, they commit fewer mistakes. Many misunderstandings are avoided this way. In a manner of speaking, this type of thought can be called creative too. Things that are not destructive may well be considered creative.

B.   Composition by Degrees

1. a. Copy the title of the MODEL COMPOSITION. _____

   b. Copy the sentence that tells what is "puzzling." _____

   c. Copy the sentence that tells the meaning of "food for thought." ___

2. a. Copy the sentence that tells what individuals must do to be productive. _____

   b. Copy the sentence that tells what makes it harder to "progress creatively." _____

   c. Copy the sentence that tells what we must do when "we study English." _____

3. a. Copy the sentence that tells where the narrator walked. _____

   b. Copy the sentence that tells what looked "peaceful and inviting."

   c. Copy the sentence that tells in what manner the narrator's thoughts came. _____

   d. Copy the phrase that tells how the narrator felt. _____

   e. Copy the phrase that tells what was on the narrator's mind. _____

   f. Copy the phrase that tells what the narrator called the "buzzing."

4. a. Copy the phrase that tells how many children were on the meadow.

   b. Copy the phrase that describes how the children were. _____

   c. Copy the phrase that describes the boy from Indiana. _____

   d. Copy the sentence that tells the profession of the boy's father.

5. a. Copy the phrase that tells what the narrator wondered. _____
_____

b. Copy the sentence that tells how people are. _____
_____

c. Copy the sentence that tells what people need. _____
_____

d. Copy the sentence that tells what we must do with children. _____
_____

e. Copy the phrase that tells what we are called when we listen. _____
_____

6. a. Copy the sentence that tells how a painter creates his work. _____
_____

b. Copy the sentence that tells what a person can do before acting.
_____

c. Copy the sentence that tells what happens when we "think and listen." _____

d. Copy the phrase that tells what the things are called that are "not destructive." _____
_____

II. *Words in Context*

A. From the list of words and phrases preceding each section, fill in each blank space provided in the text. You may use a selection more than once. Also, you may use more than one word in one blank space.

1. puzzling other perhaps   creative
  someone thought encourage

The question about_____ is as old and _____ as man himself.
The _____ day I heard _____ say, "This is food for_____ ."
It was, _____, a way to _____ _____ _____ .

2. thinking think create productive
  learning progress

Our _____ is stimulated in many ways. To be _____ individuals,
we must _____ . When we study English, we _____ .
We write and _____ only in English. _____ in one
language, but _____ another, makes it harder to _____creatively.

3. leisurely   peaceful   hurry   remained
    seeing   thought(s) silence   "buzzing"

Slowly and _____ I walked across a large meadow. The landscape looked _____ and inviting. I was in a _____ , but not _____ anyone present, I remained for a while. _____ came to me. There was _____ , but there was a very special _____ in my mind. That _____ I called _____ .

4. twenty-one   listened   glad   noisy   boy
    attorney-at-law proud   heritage Spanish-American

There were _____ children on the meadow. They were _____ . One small _____ was from Indiana. I _____ to him, and he was _____ . His father was an _____ . His grandfather took part in the _____ War. The boy was _____ of his _____ .

5. quiet   considerate   disturb   lonely
    confided   seldom   "thoughtful" stranger
    thought   listen   wondered

I _____ why the boy _____ in me. I was a _____ to him. Now it was _____ on the meadow. There was no one_____ to _____ us. People are _____ , I _____ . They _____ listen. We must _____ to children. We are_____ called_____ when we are _____ and_____ .

6. thought(s)   think   commit   misunderstandings
    creative   listen   acts   considered
    destructive thinking creates

Not all _____ is _____ . The painter _____ his work in his _____ . A person can simply _____ before he _____ . When people _____ and_____ they _____ fewer mistakes. Many _____ are avoided this way. This type of _____ can be called_____ too. Things that are not _____ , may well be _____ _____ .

B. Make any necessary change(s) when you substitute the new element into your sentence.
    Example: I think; therefore I **am.** (exist)
               I think; therefore I **exist.**

1. a. What **is thought**? (thoughts) _____

   _____

   b. The question is as old and puzzling as **man**. (ourselves) _____

   _____

   c. What did **that** mean? (it) _____

   _____

   d. It was **a way** to encourage thought. (meant) _____

   _____

2. a. Our **thinking is** stimulated. (thoughts) _____

   _____

   b. To be **productive**, we think. (creative) _____

   _____

   c. **When we study** English, we think. (while studying) _____

   _____

   d. We speak and create new **thoughts**. (ideas) _____

   _____

3. a. I **walked** across a large meadow. (was walking) _____

   _____

   b. There **were many** flowers in bloom. (was a) _____

   _____

   c. **The landscape** looked peaceful. (it) _____

   _____

   d. **I was** in a hurry. (we) _____

   _____

   e. I remained for a while. (we) _____

   _____

   f. **There** was **silence** around me. (it, silent) _____

   _____

   g. That "buzzing" **I called** thought. (we call) _____

   _____

4. a. There **were twenty-one children**. (was one) _____

   _____

   b. **They were** very noisy. (I) _____

   _____

   c. **One** small **boy was** from Indiana. (twenty-one) _____

   _____

   d. I listened to **him**. (they, me) _____

   _____

e. His father was an **attorney-at-law**. (teacher) ———————

————————————————————————

f. **The boy was** proud of **his** heritage. (we are) ———————

————————————————————————

5. a. The small boy confided in **a stranger**. (me) ———————

————————————————————————

b. Now it was **quiet** on the meadow. (peaceful) ———————

c. People are **lonely**. (friendly) ————————————

————————————————————————

d. **They** need someone to talk to. (we)———————————

————————————————————————

e. **We** must listen to children. (you) ———————————

————————————————————————

f. We are called **thoughtful**. (considerate) ———————

————————————————————————

6. a. **A painter creates his** work in **his** thoughts. (painters) ———

————————————————————————

b. **A person** can think before **he acts**. (I) ———————————

c. **People** commit fewer mistakes when **they** listen. (we) ———

————————————————————————

d. Many misunderstandings **are** avoided. (can be) ———————

————————————————————————

III. *Structures (Key words [phrases] for composition)*

A. Use the following key words [phrases] to form complete sentences. You may consult the MODEL COMPOSITION.
> Example: I think / I am
> **I think; therefore I am.**

1. a. question / is / old and puzzling ———————————
   b. is / food / thought ————————————————
   c. is / way / to encourage ——————————————
2. a. are / many ways / thinking / stimulated ———————

   ————————————————————————

   b. are / productive / individuals ——————————

    c. study / English _____

    d. speak / create / thought _____

    e. write / think / English _____

    f. learning / one language / learning another / harder to progress _____
_____

3. a. went / slowly and leisurely / across _____
_____

    b. flowers / trees / were / in bloom _____

    c. landscape / was / inviting _____

    d. thoughts / readily / creative _____

    e. was / silence / around _____

    f. was / a special / buzzing _____

    g. buzzing / called / thought _____

4. a. were / twenty-one / on the meadow _____
_____

    b. were / very / noisy _____

    c. boy / was / from / Indiana _____

    d. I listened / was / glad _____

    e. father / was / attorney-at-law _____

    f. boy / was / proud / heritage _____

5. a. wondered / boy / confided _____

    b. was / quiet / meadow _____

    c. was / present / to disturb _____

    d. people / are / lonely _____

    e. need / someone / to talk _____

    f. must / listen / children _____

    g. called / thoughtful / listen _____

6. a. not all / thinking / is _____

    b. painter / creates / work _____

    c. person / can think _____

    d. that kind / is called _____

    e. misunderstandings / are avoided _____

    f. type of thought / called / creative _____
_____

g. are / not destructive / considered / creative _____

_____

B. Supply the missing **preposition** for each blank space. You may consult the MODEL COMPOSITION.

Example: ___(To)___ think, is___(to)___ exist.

1. a. This is food _____ thought.

   b. It was a way _____ encourage thought.

2. a. There are many ways _____ which thinking is stimulated.

   b. We write and think only _____ English.

   c. Thinking _____ one language, but learning another, makes it harder _____ progress creatively.

3. a. I walked _____ a large meadow.

   b. There were many flowers _____ bloom.

   c. I was _____ a hurry.

   d. I remained _____ a while.

   e. Thoughts came _____ me readily.

   f. There was silence _____ me.

   g. There was a very special buzzing _____ my mind.

4. a. There were twenty-one children _____ the meadow.

   b. One boy was _____ Indiana.

   c. I listened _____ him.

   d. His grandfather took part _____ the Spanish-American War.

   e. The boy was proud _____ his heritage.

5. a. The boy confided _____ a stranger.

   b. It was quiet _____ the meadow.

   c. There was no one present _____ disturb me.

   d. People need someone _____ talk to.

   e. We must listen _____ children.

6. a. He creates his work _____ his mind.

   b. That kind _____ thought is called creative.

   c. In a manner _____ speaking, this type _____ thought is creative.

IV.   Grammar and Syntax [Points of Interest]

A.   Coordination and Coordinators

1. The COMPOUND SENTENCE has two or more full PREDICATIONS in the form of **independent clauses**. Each of the ideas expressed are closely related. The clauses are really two or more simple sentences joined together by connecting words (COORDINATORS) such as **and, but, for, nor, or, so** and **yet**.

2. COORDINATORS **and, but** and **or** serve to connect several grammatical units.

Example: **Susan and I** are good students. (n.)
Susan **reads and studies** her lesson. (v.)
Susan is **pretty but shy.** (adj.)
Susan calls me up **once or twice** a week. (adv.)

3. Expressions that indicate a definite relationship between stated ideas are connected frequently by the words **however, therefore, on the other hand, nevertheless, for example, consequently** or by a **semicolon** (;).

Examples: Two **simple** sentences: The question is old.
The question is not puzzling.

Compound sentence: The question is old, but it is not puzzling.

Two **simple** sentences: Thoughts came to me readily.
I felt creative.

Compound sentence: Thoughts came to me readily, and I felt creative.

Two **simple** sentences: There was silence around me.
There was a very special "buzzing" in my mind.

Compound sentence: There was silence around me, but there was a very special "buzzing" in my mind.

Two **simple** sentences: I listened to him.
He was glad.

Compound sentence: I listened to him, and he was glad.

Three **simple** sentences: People are lonely.
They need someone to talk to.
They seldom listen.

Compound sentence:	People are lonely and they need someone to talk to, yet they seldom listen.
Three **simple** sentences:	There were twenty-one children on the meadow. They were noisy. One small boy was very quiet.
Compound sentence:	There were twenty-one children on the meadow and they were noisy, but one small boy was very quiet.

[NOTE: We must not leave out completely the punctuation mark or the coordinator. The coordinators can be used without a comma, but a comma may not be used without a coordinator.]

Wrong:　　I was in a hurry, not seeing anyone present, I remained for a while.

Correct:　　I was in a hurry, but not seeing anyone present, I remained for a while.

Wrong:　　There was silence around me, there was a very special "buzzing" in my mind.

Correct:　　There was silence around me, but there was a very special "buzzing" in my mind.

B.　Sentence Faults

1. Coordinators are used to join equal grammatical structures. This joining of grammatical structures is called PARALLELISM. It is an arrangement of **words, phrases, clauses** or **sentences** of similar or logically related ideas.

A correct parallel structure will relate a **noun** with a **noun**, an **infinitive** with another **infinitive**, an **adjective** with an **adjective**, etc.

Examples:　They learn about the **origin** and **development** of meditation.

Susan likes **to study** and **to read**.

School has taught us **to encourage** thought and **to learn** by experience.

We **speak** and **create** new thoughts.

The children were very **noisy** and **playful**.

2. **Faulty Parrallelism** develops when **unparalleled** grammatical structures are joined into sentences.

Faulty Parallelism	*Corrected Parallelism*
Susan likes to study and reading.	Susan likes to study and to read.
I'm reading about thought and how it developed.	I'm reading about thought and its development.
Thinking on the meadow and to walk on it is a great pleasure.	Thinking and walking on the meadow is a great pleasure.
The boy was small, with brown hair, and who had a happy face.	The boy was small, brown-haired, and happy-faced.

C.   Punctuation

1. The COMMA is followed by the coordinators **and, but, for, yet, or, nor** and **so** when it joins two (or more) main clauses in a COMPOUND SENTENCE.

> Examples: We study English, and we think in English.
> (2 main clauses)
>
> I listened to him, and he was glad.
> (2 main clauses)
>
> People are lonely, but they don't listen.
> (2 main clauses)
>
> They need someone to talk to, yet they seldom listen.
> (2 main clauses)

2. The SEMICOLON SEPARATES two independent clauses (COMPOUND SENTENCE) when a coordinator is not used.

> Examples: We are productive individuals; we think.
> I think; therefore I am.
>
> I wondered why the small boy confided in a stranger; I was a stranger to him.
>
> A person can simply think before he acts; that kind of thought is called "wisdom."

3. The HYPHEN is used here for the purpose of connecting.

a. **multiple numbers**: There were twenty-one children on the meadow.

b. **describing a profession**: His father was an attorney-at-law.

    c. connecting **adjectives** describing countries: His grandfather took part in the Spanish-American War.

D.   Exercises

1. The following sentences are incorrectly joined. Select one of the CO-ORDINATORS (and, but, for, nor, or, so, yet) to make the necessary correction.

        Example: We have a lot to read, we will need to hurry.
                   We have a lot to read, and we will need to hurry.

a. The question is old, it is not puzzling. _____

b. Thoughts came to me readily, I felt creative. _____

c. There was silence around me, there was a very special "buzzing" in my mind. _____

d. I listened to him, he was glad._____

e. People are lonely, they need someone to talk to, they seldom listen.

f. There were twenty-one children on the meadow, they were noisy, one small boy was very quiet._____

g. I was in a hurry, not seeing anyone present, I remained for a while.

h. There was silence around me, there were twenty-one children on the meadow. _____

i. Thinking in one language, learning another, makes it harder to progress creatively. _____

j. A painter creates his work in his thoughts, does a writer, a dancer.

2. Transform the **simple** sentences into **compound** sentences. Make up simple sentences and add them on to those given below to form the compound sentences.

Example: I was in a hurry. **I did not see anyone.**
Compound: I was in a hurry, and I did not see anyone.

a. The question is old. _____

_____

b. We see productive individuals. _____

_____

c. We write compositions. _____

_____

d. They think in one language. _____

_____

e. She studies English. _____

_____

f. I walked very slowly. _____

_____

g. The landscape looked peaceful. _____

_____

h. I was in a hurry. _____

_____

i. Thoughts came to me readily. _____

_____

j. There was silence around me. _____

_____

k. I listened to the boy. _____

_____

l. His father was an attorney-at-law. _____

_____

m. It was quiet on the meadow. _____

_____

n. People need someone to talk to. _____

_____

o. We must listen to children. _____

_____

p. We are called thoughtful. _____

_____

q. A painter creates his work in his thought. _____

_____

r. People think and listen. _____

s. Things are not destructive. _____

3. In the spaces provided below, write your own **compound** sentences. Follow the directions given before each group.

    a. Use a **comma** (,) and the coordinator "and."
      (1) _____
      (2) _____
    b. Use a **comma** (,) and the coordinator "but."
      (1) _____
      (2) _____
    c. Use a **comma** (,) and the coordinator "yet."
      (1) _____
      (2) _____

4. Correct the following sentences for FAULTY PARALLELISM. Write the corrected sentence in the space provided.

    a. Mike likes to think and to reading. _____
_____

    b. We're learning about thought and how it developed. _____
_____

    c. Thinking on the meadow and to walk on it is fun. _____
_____

    d. Speaking and to create new thoughts is hard. _____
_____

    e. He taught them to encourage thought and learning. _____
_____

    f. Susan likes studying and to read. _____
_____

    g. The boy was small, with brown hair, and who had a happy face.
_____
_____

    h. To buy ads means selling products. _____
_____

    i. He wanted to listen and playing with me. _____
_____

5. Punctuate the following passages. Use periods (.), question marks (?), exclamation marks (!), commas (,), semicolons(;) and hyphens (-) where they are necessary. The number on the right margin indicates how many corrections are needed.

What is thought What does it mean To be	2
productive individuals we must think Thinking in	2
one language but learning another makes it harder	2
to progress creatively When we study English we	2
must think in English	1
There were twenty one children on the meadow	1
One small boy was from Indiana The others were	1
Texans I wondered why the boy confided in	1
a stranger I was a stranger to him People are	2
lonely I thought They need someone yet they	3
seldom listen A person can think before he acts	2
That kind of thought is called "wisdom "	1

V. *Idea Recognition*

Copy from the MODEL COMPOSITION the sentences expressing:

A. how old the question about thought is . . .

_____

B. what explains the expression "food for thought" . . .

_____

C. what the productive individual must do . . .

_____

D. what we do when we study English . . .

_____

E. what we must do when we study English . . .

_____

F. the way thoughts came to the narrator . . .

_____

G. the way the narrator felt . . .

_____

H. what the narrator called "buzzing" . . .

_____

I. why the narrator knew that the small boy was from Indiana . . .

_____

J. what the people need . . .

_____

K. what we must do with children . . .

_____

L. what we are called when we listen . . .

_____

M. what happens when people think and listen . . .

_____

N. what things can be considered when they're not destructive . . .

_____

VI. *Vocabulary Enrichment*

A. Paraphrasing

The following are **paraphrases** (rephrasing expressions or words without changing their meaning) of expressions or words found in the narrative. Write the expressions found in the MODEL COMPOSITION that correspond to the paraphrases below.

> Example: food for thought
> **things that stimulate meditation**

1. someone who thinks _____

2. someone who creates _____

3. difficult to continue creating _____

4. relax while walking _____

5. a pleasant countryside _____

6. pleased about one's past _____

7. he told the stranger about himself _____

8. no one likes to be alone _____

9. thinking means intelligence _____

B. Lexical Units

Select the word (or phrase) from the following list that best completes each of the sentences below. You may use one selection more than once.

Example: I think; therefore I **am**.
         I think; therefore I **exist**.

stimulated	encourage	thought	progress
quiet	relax	quickly	talked readily
meditating	don't, often		

1. This is a way **to make you think**. It is a way to _____ .

2. Our **thinking grows** in many ways. Thinking is _____ in many ways.

3. Sometimes it is hard **to advance**. Learning one language, and thinking in another makes it hard to _____ .

4. He walked **slowly** and **leisurely**. He wanted to _____ .

5. The landscape looked **peaceful**. It was _____ .

6. He was in a **hurry**. He wanted to get somewhere _____ .

7. Thoughts came to him **readily**. His thinking was _____ .

8. There was a special **buzzing** in his mind. He called it _____ .

9. The small boy **confided** in a stranger. He _____ to him.

10. People are lonely. They **seldom** listen. They are lonely but they _____ _____ listen.

C.   Related Words

Use the **related words** to rewrite the following sentences without changing their meanings. Change the underlined word. Make further changes if necessary.

Example: to think (v.)   thinking (n.)
         I **think**, therefore I am.
         Thinking is being.

puzzle (n.)	to encourage (v.)	to study (v.)
puzzling (adj.)	encouraging (adj.)	study (n.)
		studying (v.)
to think (v.)	leisure (n.)	
thought (n.)	leisurely (adv.)	

1. The question is **puzzling**. _____

2. It is a way to **encourage** thought. _____

3. **To study** English requires thought. _____

4. I walked **leisurely** across the meadow. _____

5. Not all **thinking** is creative. ───────────────

VII. *Steps in Writing*

A. Add new words and revise the sentence, if necessary, to suit the changes indicated in parentheses.

> Example: **I** think; therefore I am. (he)
> He **thinks**; therefore he is.

1. To be productive **individuals**, we must think. (individual)

───────────────────────────────

2. When **we** study English, **we** think. (he)

───────────────────────────────

3. **We** speak and create new thought. (One)

───────────────────────────────

4. **We write** and think only in English. (He speaks)

───────────────────────────────

5. **I walked slowly and leisurely** across a meadow. (He ran quickly)

───────────────────────────────

6. **I** was in a hurry. (We)

───────────────────────────────

7. Thoughts came to **me** readily. (her)

───────────────────────────────

8. There were **twenty-one** children on the meadow. (32)

───────────────────────────────

9. **The boy** was proud of **his** heritage. (We)

───────────────────────────────

10. **I** was a stranger to **him**. (They, us)

───────────────────────────────

11. **People** are lonely. (We)

───────────────────────────────

12. **They** seldom listen. (She)

───────────────────────────────

13. **We** must listen to children. (You)

───────────────────────────────

14. **A painter** creates **his** work in **his** thoughts. (Painters)

───────────────────────────────

15. **This** is creative thought. (Those)

_____

B.   Opposites

Use the **opposites** to rewrite the following sentences. Make the necessary changes to suit the new sentences.

        Example: puzzling—clear
                  The question is **puzzling**.
                  The question is **clear**.

discourage	unproductive	regress	deadened	destructive
with effort	quickly	quiet	noisy	inconsiderate

1. This is a way to **encourage** thought. _____

_____

2. Our desires are **stimulated**. _____

_____

3. When we don't think, we are **productive**. _____

_____

4. Things that are unproductive are **creative**. _____

_____

5. When we are destructive, we **progress**. _____

_____

6. He walked **slowly**; he was in a hurry. _____

_____

7. He couldn't think; thoughts came **readily**. _____

_____

8. The children were peaceful. They were **loud**. _____

_____

9. It was **quiet** on the meadow. _____

_____

10. When we don't listen we are **considerate**. _____

_____

VIII.   Comprehension

A.   Complete the following sentences and add as many related sentences as you can find in the MODEL COMPOSITION.

> Example: The other day I heard someone say, **"This is food for thought." It was, perhaps, a way to encourage creative thought.**

1. There are many ways _____

2. When we study English, _____

3. Thinking in one language, but learning another, _____
_____

4. Once I walked slowly and leisurely _____
_____

5. I was in a hurry _____
_____

6. Thoughts came to me readily,_____
_____

7. I listened to the boy, _____
_____

8. Now it was quiet _____
_____

9. People are lonely, _____
_____

10. A painter creates _____
_____

11. But a person can simply think _____
_____

12. When people think and listen _____
_____

13. In a manner of speaking _____
_____

14. Things that are not destructive, _____
_____

B.   Answer each question with a complete sentence.

> Example: Why am I?
>   I am; because I think.

1. What is old and puzzling? _____

2. What was it the narrator heard someone say?_____

_____

3. Why must we think?_____

_____

4. When do we create new thoughts?_____

_____

5. When must we think in English?_____

_____

6. Where did the narrator walk?_____

_____

7. Why did the narrator remain on the meadow?_____

_____

8. How did the thoughts come to him?_____

_____

9. What was it the narrator called the "buzzing"?_____

_____

10. How many children were there on the meadow?_____

_____

11. Where did the small boy come from?_____

_____

12. Did the small boy know the narrator?_____

_____

13. What was the boy's father? Grandfather?_____

_____

14. Why was the boy glad?_____

_____

15. What do people need?_____

_____

16. Why must we listen to children?_____

_____

17. What do we call a considerate person?_____

_____

18. How does a painter create his work?_____

_____

19. When do people commit fewer mistakes?_____

_____

20. How is misunderstanding avoided?_____

_____

IX. *Commentary on Model*

A. 1. Tell what you learned about **thought** from section 2 of MODEL COMPOSITION.

2. Tell what you learned about **people** and **children** from paragraphs 4 and 5 of MODEL COMPOSITION.

3. Discuss why thinking is not always **creative**.

4. Give an appropriate title to your composition.

B. 1. Discuss the points in the MODEL COMPOSITION with which you agree.

2. Discuss the points in the MODEL COMPOSITION with which you disagree.

3. Tell in your own words what **you've** learned about creative thought.

4. Give an appropriate title to your composition.

X. *Composition*

A. Using the following key words and phrases from the MODEL COMPOSITION, write your own composition on a related topic.

old and puzzling	food for thought	encourage creative thought
thinking is stimulated	speak and create	progress
meditation	peaceful and inviting	silence
· children	people	lonely
considerate	listen	understand
wisdom	create	misunderstanding
mistake	destructive	creative

B. 1. Rewrite section 2 in the **I** person. Make all appropriate changes.

Example: There are many ways in which **my** thinking is stimulated.

2. Rewrite section 3 changing **I** to **Susan** and **Mark**. Make all appropriate changes.

Example: Once **Susan** and **Mark** walked slowly and leisurely across the meadow.

C. Describe briefly what you see in the picture below.

Chapter Four

The Complex Sentence

Words to remember:

Complex Sentence

Main = Independent Clause
Subordinate = Dependent Clause

Relationships
Subordination and Subordinators
(Clause Markers)

*Time (***after***) − Place (***where***) − Contrast*

*(***although***) − Condition (***although***)*

*Purpose (***in order that***) − Cause (***as***)*

*Manner and Comparison (***as though***)*

Comma (,) − Colon (:) − Quotation Marks (" ")

I.   Model Composition

A.   Love

1. Although much has been written about this subject, whenever we are puzzled about it, we ask the question: What is love? Love means different things to different people. Children regard love from their point of view, while they are very young. As we grow older, love grows into different dimensions with our maturing. Love changes constantly, because we change from day to day.

2. There are different kinds of love. Whereas we live in a mechanized world, we hold a special affection for nature. When you look at the lake, your heart is glad that the water is there. Unless you spend a week in the mountains, you will not know the beneficial effects of mountain air. As soon as the tidal sea wave touched your feet, you realized why you had always wanted to be at the seashore. My father used to say: "Man goes back to water, as though he had come from its depths."

3. Wherever there is a family, there is the love of a parent for the child. Warmth and support are basic needs. There is also the love of a child for its parent. Family love means being your natural self, in order that fear and deception vanish. For parents, it means caring for someone's needs more than for themselves. Before thinking of themselves, parents will help their children. Once you have found the need to be with someone, you will also feel the desire to share and to care. As long as man has existed, family love has been the cornerstone of civilized society.

4. When true love comes, you do not seek sensations, which are independent of one another and soon forgotten. You feel a lasting affection for each other, in that you long for one another. Two people unite into one. You want to give everything to the person you love. You're not afraid of death. Now that you've found love, you're only afraid that your loved one might die first.

5. The love between man and woman is strong, although at times it seems confusing. Whether it is a lasting bond, or simply the moment of the act of love, it leaves a deep feeling of joy and fulfillment. In love-making there is a complete giving of oneself to another person, since there is a unity of body and mind. This giving is truly unselfish, as it aims only at pleasing the other person.

6. Love has been called an "abstract" thing, which means that it is difficult to define. But for those who seek it, it is very real. They find comfort in the touch of a hand, or a kiss or being close to someone dear. Sick persons can become well again, as soon as love enters their hearts. Love can overcome family

feuds, it can bring together people of different ages, as well as ethnic and national backgrounds. Love brings people together, because they care.

B.   Composition by Degrees

1. a. Copy the title of the MODEL COMPOSITION.

   _____

   b. Copy the question we ask when we are puzzled.

   _____

   c. Copy the sentence that tells what love "means to different people."

   _____

   d. Copy the sentence that tells how "children regard" love.

   _____

   e. Copy the sentence that tells how "love changes."

   _____

2. a. Copy the phrase that tells what we "hold" for nature.

   _____

   b. Copy the phrase that tells why your "heart is glad."

   _____

   c. Copy the sentence that tells about the mountains.

   _____

   d. Copy the sentence that tells you why man goes "back to water."

   _____

3. a. Copy the sentence that tells about "warmth and support."

   _____

   b. Copy the sentence that tells about "parents' caring."

   _____

   c. Copy the sentence that tells about "parents helping their children."

   _____

   d. Copy the sentence that tells about the "desire to share and to care."

   _____

   e. Copy the sentence that tells about the "cornerstone of civilized society."

   _____

4. a. Copy the sentence that tells what happens "when true love comes."

   _____

   b. Copy the phrase that tells what you "feel for each other."

   _____

c. Copy the phrase that tells what "two people" do.

_____

d. Copy the phrase that tells what you "want to give to the person you love."

_____

e. Copy the sentence that tells about "death."

_____

5. a. Copy the sentence that tells about the "love between man and woman."

_____

b. Copy the phrase that tells what "love leaves."

_____

c. Copy the phrase that tells what there is in "love-making."

_____

d. Copy the phrase that tells how the giving "truly is."

_____

6. a. Copy the phrase that tells what love has "been called."

_____

b. Copy the sentence that tells for whom love is "very real."

_____

c. Copy the sentence that tells what happens when "love enters their hearts."

_____

d. Copy the phrases that tell what "love can overcome."

_____

II. Words in Context

A. From the list of words and phrases preceding each section fill in each blank space provided in the text. You may use a selection more than once. Also, you may use more than one word in one blank space.

1. subject	whenever	love	although
older	maturing	grow(s)	dimensions
while	point of view	different	

_____ much has been written about this_____ matter, _____ we are puzzled about it we ask the question: What is _____? _____ means _____ things to _____ people. Children regard _____

from their _____ _____ _____ they are very young. As we _____
older, _____ _____ into _____ with our _____ .

2. glad   as soon as   whereas   mechanized
   when   unless   as though   depths
   affection   beneficial   mountain(s)   touched

_____ we live in a _____ world, we hold a special _____
for nature. _____ you look at a lake, your heart is _____ that the
water is there. _____ you spend a week in the _____ you will not
know the _____ effects of _____ air. _____ the tidal sea wave
_____ your feet you realize why you had always wanted to be at the seashore. Man goes back to water, _____ he had come from its _____ .

3. in order that   family   before   wherever once
   child(ren)   care   parents   love   need
   share   as long as   cornerstone

_____ there is a _____ , there is the _____ of a parent
for the _____ . _____ means being your natural self, _____
fear and deception vanish. _____ thinking of themselves, _____ will
help their _____ . _____ you have found the _____ to be with
someone, you will also find the desire to _____ and to _____ .
_____ man has existed, _____ has been the _____ of civilized
society.

4. sensations   forgotten   when   love   independent
   in that   now that   afraid   affection

_____ true _____ comes, man does not seek _____ , which
are _____ of one another and soon _____ . You feel a lasting _____
for each other, _____ you search out one another. _____ you've
found love, you're only _____ that your loved one might die first.

5. confusing*   as   complete   although   strong
   since   unselfish   unity   oneself

The love between man and woman is _____ , _____ at
times it seems _____ . In love-making there is a _____ giving of
_____ to another person, _____ there is a _____ of body and
mind. This giving is truly _____ , _____ it aims only at pleasing the
other person.

6. love   which   person(s)   abstract
   as soon as   heart(s)   define
   feuds   together   backgrounds

_____ has been called an _____ thing, _____ means
that it is difficult to _____ . Sick _____ can become well again,
_____ _____ enters their _____. _____ can overcome
family_____ , it can bring_____ people of different ages, as well as
ethnic and national _____.

B.   Make any necessary changes when you substitute the new element into
your sentence.

> Example: Whenever **we are** puzzled about it, **we** ask the question. (I)
>   Whenever **I am** puzzled about it, **I** ask the question.

1. a. Love means different things to different **people**. (men)

   _____

   b. **Children** regard love from **their** point of view. (we)

   _____

   c. As **we** grow older, love changes. (they)

   _____

   d. Love changes constantly because **we** change. (you)

   _____

2. a. Whereas **we** live in a mechanized world, **we** hold a special affection
      for nature. (she)

   _____

   b. When **you** look at a lake, **you are** happy. (I)

   _____

   c. Unless **you** spend a week in the mountains, **you** will not appreciate
      the mountain air. (we)

   _____

   d. **Man goes** back to water, as though **he** had come from its depths. (we)

   _____

3. a. Family love means being **your** natural self. (my)

   _____

   b. Before thinking of **themselves, parents** will help **their** children. (my-
      self, I, my)

   _____

c. As long as **man has** existed, family love has been the cornerstone of civilized society. (we)

_____

4. a. **You feel** a lasting affection. (she)

_____

b. **You** search out one another. (we)

_____

c. **Two people** unite into one. (they)

_____

d. **You** want to give everything to **the person you love.** (I, her)

_____

e. **You're not** afraid of death. (one is)

_____

5. a. The love between **man and woman** is strong. (them)

_____

b. It leaves a deep feeling of **joy.** (fulfillment)

_____

c. **There is a** unity of mind and body. (it results in)

_____

d. **It** aims at pleasing **the other person.** (she, him)

_____

6. a. **Love** is difficult to define. (it)

_____

b. **They** find comfort in the touch of a hand. (some people)

_____

c. Sick **persons** can become well again. (people)

_____

d. Love can overcome family **feuds.** (hatreds)

_____

e. Love **brings together** people of different nationalities. (unites)

_____

III. Structures (Key words [phrases] for composition)

A. Use the following key words [phrases] to form complete sentences. You may consult the MODEL COMPOSITION.

Example: much / been / about / subject matter
Much has been written about this subject matter.

1. a. love / means / different things _____

   b. regard / love / point of view _____

   c. love / changes _____

   d. we / change _____

2. a. are / kinds / of love _____

   b. hold / special / affection _____

   c. spend / week / in the mountains _____

   d. realize / you / wanted / seashore _____

   e. goes / to water _____

3. a. wherever / family / the love / parent / child _____

   b. are / basic _____

   c. is / love / child / parent _____

   d. means / being / natural /self _____

   e. caring / someone's / needs / more _____

   f. family / has been / cornerstone _____

4. a. feel / lasting / affection _____

   b. people / unite _____

   c. want / to give / the person _____

d. not / afraid / death _____

5. a. between / man and woman _____

   b. leaves / deep feeling / joy _____

   c. is / truly / unselfish _____

   d. aims / pleasing / person _____

6. a. has been / called / abstract _____

   b. is / difficult / define _____

   c. seek / it / real _____

   d. find / comfort / in the touch _____

   e. can / become / well _____

   f. overcome / feuds / bring / people / different / backgrounds _____

B. Supply the missing **subordinators (clause markers)** for each blank space. You may consult the MODEL COMPOSITION.

Example: <u>(Although)</u>   much has been written about love, we love.

1. a. _____ we are puzzled, we ask "what is love?"

   b. Some regard love from one point of view, _____they are very young.

   c. _____ we grow older, love grows with us.

2. a. _____ we live in cities, we hold an affection for nature.

   b. _____ you see a lake, you are happy.

   c. _____ you spend vacations in the mountains, you will not appreciate mountain air.

   d. _____ the water has touched your feet, you know why you love the seashore.

e. Man goes back to water, _____ he had come from its depths.

3. a. _____ there is a family, there is love.

   b. It means being your natural self, _____ fear and deception vanish.

   c. _____ thinking of themselves, parents will help their children.

   d. _____ you have found the need to be with someone, you'll also feel the desire to share and care.

   e. _____ man lives, love is important.

4. a. _____ true love comes, you feel happy.

   b. You feel a lasting affection for each other, _____ you search out one another.

   c. _____ you've found love, you're no longer afraid.

5. a. The love between man and woman is strong, _____ it seems confusing.

   b. _____ it is a lasting bond, _____ simply the act of love, it leaves a deep feeling of joy.

   c. There is a complete giving of oneself, _____there is a unity of body and mind.

   d. Giving is truly unselfish, _____ it aims only at pleasing the other person.

6. a. Sick persons can become well again, _____ love enters their hearts.

   b. Love brings people together, _____they care.

IV.   Grammar and Syntax [Points of Interest]

A.   Subordination and Subordinators

1. The COMPLEX SENTENCE has one main (independent) clause and one or more subordinate (dependent) clauses. The **main clause** contains a completely stated thought. The **subordinate** clause lacks the sense of completeness; for that reason, it is called the **dependent clause**.

The subordinate (dependent) clause depends on a main (independent) clause. The dependent clause is introduced by means of SUBORDINATORS (subordinate conjunctions). Since the subordinator is part of the clause it introduces, there is no need to separate it from its clause by a comma or any other punctuation mark.

The SUBORDINATORS (clause markers) show different RELATION-SHIPS.

a. Time Relationship:

After we said goodbye, I went home.

As we grow older, love grows into different dimensions.

Before thinking of themselves, parents will help their children.

Now that love is here, you're happy.

Once you have found the need to be with someone, you will also feel the desire to share.

Until that day comes, there will be no happiness.

When you look at a lake, your heart is glad that the water is there.

Whenever we are puzzled about it, we ask the question.

Children regard love from their point of view, **while** they are very young.

As long as man has existed, family love has been the cornerstone of civilized society.

As soon as the tidal sea wave touched your feet, you realized why you had always wanted to be at the sea shore.

b. Place Relationship:

Where there is a will, there is a way.

Wherever there is a family, there is love of a parent for a child.

c. Manner and Comparison:

Man goes back to water, **as though** he had come from its depths.

d. Contrast of Ideas:

Although much has been written about this subject, we still ask the question: What is love?

Whereas we live in a mechanized world, we hold a special affection for nature.

e. Condition:

Unless you spend a week in the mountains, you will not know the beneficial effects of mountain air.

f. Cause:

Love changes constantly, **because** we change from day to day.

You feel a lasting affection for each other, **in that** you search out one another.

In love-making there is a complete giving of oneself, **since** there is a unity of body and mind.

g. **Purpose**:

We must grow older, **in order that** we may better understand love.

The following CLAUSE MARKERS were introduced in the MODEL COMPOSITION:

Time Relationship	— **after, before, now that, once, until, when, whenever, while, as soon as**
Place Relationship	— **where, wherever**
Manner and Comparison	— **as though**
Contrast of Ideas	— **although, whereas**
Condition	— **unless**
Cause	— **because, in that, since**

B.   Sentence Faults

1. Normally, English sentence order is SUBJECT, VERB AND COMPLE-MENT. MODIFIERS appear either before or after the word they modify. The modifier is placed as closely as possible to the word it modifies. When related parts of the sentence are unnecessarily split, the sentence is confusing and often misleading.

A modifier is called a "dangling modifier" when it has no word in a sentence to modify.

Example:
Walking into the hall, the air felt cooler.

In the above sentence, the writer took for granted that the reader would understand that somebody walked into the hall. But in the main clause, "the air felt cooler," the only noun is **air**. The air cannot walk into the hall. We could correct the sentence, by supplying the noun or the pronoun described by the **participial phrase**:

Corrected Example:
Walking into the hall, she felt the air grow cooler.

or
> **As she walked** into the hall, the air felt cooler.

2. When two **main clauses** are joined with a comma between them, the resulting sentence can be confusing. This is called **comma splice**.

> Examples of **comma splices**:
>> We are puzzled about it, we ask a question.
>>
>> We grow older, love grows into different dimensions.
>>
>> You spend a week in the mountains, you will not know the beneficial effects of mountain air.

The way to correct the **comma splice** sentence, is to **subordinate** one of the main clauses.

> Examples:

Comma splice	— We are puzzled about it, we ask a question.
Subordination	— **Whenever** we are puzzled about it, we ask a question.
Comma splice	— We grow older, love grows into different dimensions.
Subordination	— **As** we grow older, love grows into different dimensions.
Comma splice	— You spend a week in the mountains, you will not know the beneficial effects of mountain air.
Subordination	— Unless you spend a week in the mountains, you will not know the beneficial effects of mountain air.

C.   Punctuation

1. The COMMA (,) is generally considered an **interruption** to the flow of thought in a sentence. It is followed by the coordinators **and, but, for, yet, or, nor** and **so** when it joins two (or more) **main clauses** in a COMPOUND SENTENCE (Chapter Three).

The COMMA is used after a **dependent clause** beginning a sentence. When a dependent clause comes after the main clause, there is no comma.

> Examples:
>> Whereas we live in a mechanized world, we hold a special

affection for nature.

When you look at a lake, your heart is glad that the water is there.

Wherever there is a family, there is the love of a parent for the child.

Use a COMMA before the **subordinators as, because** and **for** to make the meaning clear.

Example:

Love brings people together, because they care.

2. The COLON (:) indicates that a **list of things follows**. It can also be used before direct **quotations**.

Examples:

Whenever we are puzzled about it, we ask the question: What is love? What is affection? What is feeling?

My father used to say: "Man goes back to water as though he had come from its depths."

3. The double QUOTATION MARKS (" ") are used **before** and **after** words or phrases uttered by someone else and quoted directly.

Example:

My father used to say: "Man goes to water, as though he had come from its depths."

D.   Exercises

1. The following sentences are incorrectly joined. Select one of the SUB-ORDINATORS given for each section to make the necessary correction.

Example:

The tidal wave touched my feet, I liked it. (when)
When the tidal wave touched my feet, I liked it.

a. once	now that	before	after
whenever	until	when	as
as long as	while	as soon as	

(1) We said goodbye, I went home.———————————
————————————————————————————————

(2) We grow older, love grows into different dimensions. _____

_____

(3) Thinking of themselves, parents will help their children. _____

_____

(4) We are puzzled about it, we ask the question. _____

_____

(5) Children regard love from their point of view, they are very young. _____

_____

(6) Man has existed, family love has been the cornerstone of civilized society. _____

_____

(7) The tidal sea wave touched your feet, you realize why you had always wanted to be at the sea shore._____

_____

(8) Love is here, you're happy. _____

_____

(9) You have found the need to be with someone, you will also feel the desire to share._____

_____

(10) That day comes, there is no happiness._____

_____

(11) You look at a lake, your heart is glad that the water is there. __

_____

b. as though   where   although   in that
    whereas   unless   because   wherever
    since   in order that

(1) We must grow older, we may better understand love. _____

_____

(2) In love-making there is a complete giving of oneself, there is a unity of body and mind. _____

_____

(3) There is a will, there is a way._____

_____

(4) There is a family, there is love of a parent for the child. _____

_____

(5) Man goes back to water, he had come from its depths. _____

(6) Much has been written about this subject, we still ask the question: What is love? _____

(7) We live in a mechanized world, we hold a special affection for nature. _____

(8) You spend a week in the mountains, you will not know the beneficial effects of mountain air. _____

(9) Love changes constantly, we change from day to day. _____

(10) You feel a lasting affection for each other, you search out one another. _____

2. Complete the following expressions by adding either a **dependent** clause or an **independent** clause to make **complex** sentences.

Example:
Although much has been written about this subject matter, **whenever we are puzzled, we ask the question: What is love?**

a. Children regard love from their point of view, _____

b. Love changes constantly, _____

c. Whereas we live in a mechanized world, _____

d. When you look at a lake, _____

e. Unless you spend a week in the mountains, _____

f. As soon as the tidal wave touched your feet, _____

g. Man goes back to water, _____

h. Wherever there is a family, _____

i. Family love means being your natural self, _____

j. Before thinking of themselves, _____

k. When true love comes, _____

l. You feel a lasting affection for each other, _____

m. Now that you've found love, _____

n. The love between man and woman is strong, _____

o. Whether it is a lasting bond, _____

p. In love-making there is a complete giving of oneself to another person, _____

q. This giving is truly unselfish, _____

r. Love has been called an "abstract" thing, _____

s. But for those who seek it, _____

t. They find comfort in the touch of a hand, _____

u. Sick persons can become well again, _____

v. Love can overcome family feuds, _____

w. Love brings people together, _____

3. In the spaces provided below, write your own **complex** sentences. Follow the directions given before each group.

    a. Use a comma (,) and the subordinator "after."

        (1) _____

        (2) _____

  b. Use a comma (,) and the subordinator "where."

    (1) —————————————————————————————

    (2) —————————————————————————————

  c. Use a comma (,) and the subordinator "although."

    (1) —————————————————————————————

    (2) —————————————————————————————

  d. Use a comma (,) and the subordinator "as though."

    (1) —————————————————————————————

    (2) —————————————————————————————

  e. Use a colon (:) and a direct quotation (" ").

    (1) —————————————————————————————

    (2) —————————————————————————————

4. Correct the following sentences for DANGLING MODIFIERS. Write the corrected sentence in the space provided.

    Example:
        Walking into the hall, the air felt cooler.
        Walking into the hall, she felt the air grow cooler.

  a. Singing a song, the place was much happier. ——————————
  ————————————————————————————————

  b. Reaching maturity, my mother allowed me to go out on a date. ——
  ————————————————————————————————

  c. Spending a week in the mountains, the home was more enjoyable. —
  ————————————————————————————————

  d. Realizing the need for each other, the house was filled with love. ——
  ————————————————————————————————

  e. Looking out of the window, the landscape was beautiful. ————————
  ————————————————————————————————

5. Punctuate the following passages. Use periods (.), commas (,), colons (:), dashes (-) and quotation marks (" ") where they are necessary. The number on the right margin indicates how many corrections are needed.

There are different kinds of love Whereas we live in a	1
mechanized world we hold a special affection for nature When	2
you look at a lake your heart is glad that the water is there	2

Unless you spend a week in the mountains you will not know the   1
beneficial effects of mountain air As soon as the tidal sea   1
wave touched your feet you realize why you had always wanted to   1
be at the seashore My father used to say Man goes back to   3
water as though he had come from its depths   3

The love between man and woman is strong although at times   1
it seems confusing Whether it is a lasting bond or simply the   2
moment of the act of love it leaves a deep feeling of joy and   1
fulfillment In love making there is a complete giving of   2
oneself to another person since there is a unity of body and   1
mind This giving is truly unselfish as it aims only at pleasing   2
the other person   1

V.   *Idea Recognition*

Copy from the MODEL COMPOSITION the sentences expressing:

A.   what we are puzzled about . . .

_____

B.   what love means to different people . . .

_____

C.   how children regard love . . .

_____

D.   how love changes . . .

_____

E.   what we hold for nature . . .

_____

F.   why you realize the need to be at the sea shore . . .

_____

G.   when there is a love of a parent for the child . . .

_____

H.   what family love means . . .

_____

I.   what parents will do before thinking of themselves . . .

_____

J.   how long love has been the cornerstone of civilized society . . .

_____

K.   what happens when true love comes . . .

_____

L. what you want to give to the person you love . . .

_____

M. how the love of man and woman is . . .

_____

N. what kind of giving love truly is . . .

_____

O. how love is for those who seek it . . .

_____

P. what love can overcome . . .

_____

Q. why love brings people together . . .

_____

VI. *Vocabulary Enrichment*

A. Paraphrasing

The following are **paraphrases** (rephrasing expressions or words without changing their meaning) of expressions or words found in the narrative. Write the expressions found in the MODEL COMPOSITION that correspond to the paraphrases below.

> Example: children see love differently
> **children regard love from their point of view**

1. with years, love changes _____

2. we don't dislike nature _____

3. mountain air is useful _____

4. man is attracted to water _____

5. family love has no falsehood _____

6. parents are unselfish _____

7. true love is not for the moment _____

8. two people become one _____
   _____

9. love is giving and pleasing the other _____
   _____

10. love is stronger than disagreement _____
    _____

B. Lexical Units

Select the word (phrase) from the following list that best completes each of the sentences below. You may use one word more than once.

> Example: We are **puzzled** about love.
> Love is **mysterious**.

good	origin	unselfish	assurance	become
changes	deception	lasting	strong	natural

1. Love means **different** things to **different** people. Love _____ from one person to another.
2. We hold a **special affection** for nature. It is _____ for man to love his environment.
3. Mountain air has a **beneficial** effect on man. It is _____ to breathe in mountain air.
4. Man may have **come from** the water. Water may have been man's _____ .
5. In a family you can **be yourself**. There is no need for _____ .
6. Parents **care more for their children** than for themselves. They are _____ .
7. Family love has been a **cornerstone** of society. It makes society _____ .
8. True love is not a sensation to be **soon forgotten**. It is a_____ relationship.
9. Two people **unite** into one. They _____ one.
10. Giving in love aims at **pleasing the other person**. This giving is truly _____ .
11. Those who seek love, **find comfort** in the touch of a hand. They seek _____ in touching.

C.   Related Words

Use the **related words** to rewrite the following sentences without changing their meanings. Change the underlined word. Make further changes if necessary.

Example: puzzle (n.)   puzzling (adj.)
          It's a **puzzle**.   It's **puzzling**.

to seek (v.)   to need (v.)   to love (v.)   to look (v.)
   seeking (v.)   need (n.)   love (n.)   look (n.)
                       needing (v.)   loving (v.)   looking (v.)
to grow (v.)
   growing (v.)

1. **To love** means wanting to touch. _____
_____

2. When **you look** at a lake, you're glad. _____
_____

3. While **you grow** older, you change. _____
_____

4. Not all **love** is lasting. _____
_____

5. To **seek** love, means to need it. _____
_____

VII.   *Steps in Composition*

A.   Add new words and revise the sentence, if necessary, to suit the changes indicated in parentheses.

Example: **It** is a lasting love. (mine)
          Mine is a lasting love.

1. **Love** means different things to different people. (loving)
_____

2. **Children** regard love from **their** point of view. (we)
_____

3. There are **different** kinds of love. (many)
_____

4. We hold a special affection for **nature**. (our family)
_____

5. He has always wanted to be **in the mountains.** (at the seashore)

_____

6. **Warmth** and **support** are basic needs. (love, affection)

_____

7. There is the love of **a child** for **its parents.** (parent, children)

_____

8. **They** care for someone's needs. (I)

_____

9. You feel the desire to **share.** (give)

_____

10. **You** feel a lasting affection for **each other.** (I, you)

_____

11. **Two people** unite into one. (we both)

_____

12. **You** want to give to the person **you** love. (we)

_____

13. **You're not** afraid of death. (no one is)

_____

14. The love between **man** and **woman** is strong. (parent, child)

_____

15. Love brings **people** together, because **they** care. (us, we)

_____

B. Opposites

Use the **opposites** to rewrite the following sentences. Make any necessary changes to suit the new sentence.

> Example: question—answer
> We ask a **question.**
> We give an **answer.**

appear	strong	uncivilized	same	together
sick	unselfish	sad	comfort	natural

1. Love brings on **different** feelings. _____

_____

2. We live in a **civilized** world. _____

_____

3. My heart is **glad**. _____

_____

4. Love means being your **unnatural** self. _____

_____

5. Where there is no love, fear and deception **vanish**. _____

_____

6. The love between man and woman is **weak**. _____

_____

7. The giving in love is **selfish**. _____

_____

8. **Healthy** persons can become well again. _____

_____

9. They find **discomfort** in the touch of a hand. _____

_____

10. Love can bring **apart** people of different ages. _____

_____

VIII.   Comprehension

A.   Complete the sentence and add as many related sentences as you can find in the MODEL COMPOSITION.

> Example: Although much has been written about this subject matter, **whenever we are puzzled, we ask the question: What is love?**

1. Love means different things _____

_____

2. Children regard love from their point of view, _____

_____

3. Whereas we live in a mechanized world, _____

_____

4. Wherever there is a family, _____

_____

5. Once you have found the need to be with someone, _____

_____

6. When true love comes, _____

_____

7. The love between man and woman is strong, _____

8. In love-making _____

9. Love has been called an "abstract" thing _____

10. Sick persons can become well again, _____

11. Love brings people together, _____

B. Answer each of the following questions with a complete sentence.

Example: What are we puzzled about?
We're puzzled about love.

1. How do children regard love? _____

2. Why does love change constantly? _____

3. What do we hold for nature? _____

4. Why does man go back to water? _____

5. What are the basic needs? _____

6. What does family love mean? _____

7. When will parents help their children? _____

8. How long has family love been the cornerstone of civilized society?___

9. What happens when true love comes? _____

10. What kind of affection do people in love feel for each other? _____

11. Why do you want to give everything to the person you love? _____

12. What are you not afraid of? _____

13. What are you afraid of? _____

14. How is the love between man and woman? _____

15. What happens in love-making? _____

16. Why has love been called "abstract"? _____

17. What is love for those who seek it? _____

18. Who can become well again in love?_____

19. Whom does love bring together? Why? _____

IX.   *Commentary on Model*

A.   1. Tell what you learned about the **family** from section 3 of the MODEL COMPOSITION.

2. Tell what you learned about **true love** from section 4.

3. Discuss why love is **puzzling**.

4. Give an appropriate title to your composition.

B.   1. Discuss the points in the MODEL COMPOSITION with which you agree.

2. Discuss the points in the MODEL COMPOSITION with which you disagree.

3. Tell in your own words what you've learned about love.

4. Give an appropriate title to your composition.

X.   *Composition*

A. Using the key words and phrases from the MODEL COMPOSITION, write your own composition on a related topic.

love	people grow older	changes constantly
different kinds	affection for nature	mountain air
family love	parents and children	true love
man and woman	love-making	give everything
truly unselfish	comfort	touch
together	care	kiss

B. Rewrite section 4 of the MODEL COMPOSITION changing **you** to **I**.

Example: When true love comes, **I** do not seek sensations, etc.

C. Describe briefly what you see in the picture below.

Chapter Five

Logical or Natural Sequence of Tenses

Words to Remember:	
after	*in (year)*
always	*later*
at birth, in childhood, etc.	*now*
at last	*nowadays*
at the turn of the (century, decade, etc.)	*next*
before	*previously*
during	*prior to*
earlier	*since*
every (number) (moment, year, month, day, etc.)	*soon*
finally	*then*
formerly	*when*
frequently	*while*

I. *Model Composition*

A. Remembrance

1. The street on which the Axbys now live is called Shadywood. It is called Shadywood because there are many shade trees there. Prior to moving there, the Axbys lived on Blanco Street. Mr. Axby is a school teacher and a widower. Mrs. Axby died during the past summer after a long illness. The children go to neighborhood schools. Ralph is the oldest and the tallest at the age of seventeen. He attends Meridian High School and plays tennis on the team. His brother John is a freshman at the same school. John loves to study and to read. Their sister Dorothy is in the eighth grade. She loves studying but not reading. She is in a habit of reading rapidly but is unable to learn well.

2. Dorothy was ill last week, but she is feeling better now. She stayed in bed several days, but she is doing some chores around the house today. She vacuums her room every day and prepares her clothing for the next day. Her father went to town earlier in the day and bought Dorothy a new dress. She was happy and tried it on right away.

3. Mr. Axby often waits in the car while his children come out of school. This happens only on days when it rains. Mrs. Axby used to attend to this chore in her lifetime. At times there is too much traffic, and Mr. Axby cannot find a place to park. When this happens, he drives many times around the block. The siblings are worried, but their father arrives as soon as the space is available.

4. Once every week the Axbys go to the cemetery and place flowers on Mrs. Axby's grave. While they stand at the graveside, they remember the good times. Mrs. Axby always told them to remember her and to be happy. Nowadays, they miss her cheerful personality. She was always happy and resourceful. The day always ends with a long hike after they leave for home. The Axbys remember and cherish their memories. It is important to remember our loved ones.

B. Composition by Degrees

1. a. Copy the title of the MODEL COMPOSITION. _____
   _____

   b. What does the title tell you? The title tells that the composition is about _____
   _____

   c. Copy the name of the street on which the Axbys live. _____

   d. Why is the street called by its name? Because there are many _____

   e. Copy the word in paragraph 1 that says that Mr. Axby has no wife.
   _____

   f. Copy the word in paragraph 1 that expresses "brothers and sisters."
   _____

   g. Copy the name of the high school attended by the two brothers. ___
   _____

   h. Copy the word in paragraph 1 that says that Dorothy cannot learn
   well. _____

2. a. Copy the sentence that explains why Dorothy stayed in bed several
   days. _____
   _____

   b. Copy the phrase that tells why Dorothy can do some chores around
   the house. _____

   c. Copy the sentence that tells why Dorothy was happy. _____
   _____

3. a. Copy the phrase that tells why Mr. Axby waits in the car. _____
   _____

   b. Copy the phrase that tells when Mr. Axby waits for his children.___
   _____

   c. Copy the phrase that explains why Mr. Axby drives around the
   block. _____

   d. Copy the phrase that tells how soon the father arrives. _____
   _____

4. a. Copy the phrase that tells how often the Axbys go to the cemetery.
   _____

   b. Copy the reason for which the Axbys go to the cemetery. _____
   _____

   c. Copy the phrase that tells where the Axbys stand. _____
   _____

   d. Copy the phrase that tells what the Axbys remember._____
   _____

   e. Copy the phrase that tells about Mrs. Axby's personality. _____
   _____

   f. Copy the phrase that tells when the Axbys go on a hike. _____
   _____

II. *Words in Context*

A. From the list of words and phrases preceding each section fill in each blank space provided in the text. You may use a selection more than once. Also, you may use more than one word in one blank space.

1.
live	died	does
is called	has	loves
are	go	read
is	moving	to read
reading	attends	studying
learn	to study	

The street on which the Axbys now _____ is called Shadywood. It ____ _____ Shadywood because there _____ many shade trees there. Prior to _____ there, the Axbys _____ on Blanco Street. Mr. Axby _____ a school teacher and a widower. Mrs. Axby _____ during the past summer after a long illness. Mr. Axby _____ three children who_____ still of school age. The siblings _____ to neighborhood schools. Ralph _____ the oldest and the tallest at the age of seventeen. He_____Meridian High School and _____ well in school. John_____ _____ and ____ _____. Their sister Dorothy _____ in the eighth grade. She _____ _____ but not_____. She ____ in the habit of _____ rapidly but unable _____ _____ well.

2.
several	next	last	feeling
around	new	some	today
happy	now	every	
right away	other	earlier	

Dorothy was ill_____week, but she is _____better_____. She stayed in bed_____days, but she is doing _____chores_____the house _____. She vacuums her room _____ day and prepares her clothing for the _____ day. Her father went to town_____ in the day and bought Dorothy a _____ dress. She was_____and tried it on_____ _____.

3.
siblings	car	children
school	block	space
traffic	father	place
days		

Mr. Axby waits in the _____ while his _____ come out of _____. This happens only on_____when it rains. At times there is too much _____ and Mr. Axby cannot find a _____to park. When this happens, he drives many times around the _____. The _____ are worried, but their _____ arrives as soon as the _____ is available.

4.
at	to the cemetery	miss
at the	stand	usually
remember	happy	while
cheerful	resourceful	grave
after	recall	nowadays
always	graveside	cherish
every	memories	long

_____ year the Axbys go ____ ____ ____ and place flowers on Mrs. Axby's_____. _____ they stand____ _____ graveside, they _____ the good times. Mrs. Axby always told them to_____ her and reminded them to be _____. _____ , they_____ her _____ personality. She was _____ _____and _____. The day _____ ends with a long hike _____ they leave for home. The Axbys remember and _____ their _____ .

B.   Make the necessary change(s) when you substitute the new element into your sentence.

> Example: **The Axbys** live on Shadywood street. (Ralph)
> Ralph **lives** on Shadywood street.

1. **The siblings** go to the neighborhood school. (Dorothy)

   _____

2. Mr. Axby has **three** children. (one)

   _____

3. **He attends** Meridian High. (They)

   _____

4. **He** does well in school. (We)

   _____

5. **John** loves to study and to read. (I)

   _____

6. **She** loves studying but not reading. (They)

   _____

7. **She** is in a habit of reading rapidly. (I)

   _____

8. **Dorothy** was ill all of last week. (We)

_____

9. **She** is doing some chores around the house. (Ralph and Susan)

_____

10. **She** vacuums her room. (They)

_____

11. **He** prepares his clothing. (We)

_____

C.   Replace each underlined **noun** or **phrase** with an appropriate **pronoun**. Change the sentence structure where necessary.

> Example: **Mr. Axby** has three children.
> **He** has three children.

1. **Dorothy** was ill last week. _____

_____

2. She vacuums **her room** every day. _____

_____

3. **Her father** went to town the other day. _____

_____

4. He bought **Dorothy** a new dress. _____

_____

5. She tried on the **dress** right away. _____

_____

6. Mr. Axby often waits in the car while **his children** come out of school.

_____

7. **The children** are worried. _____

_____

8. **Their father** arrives as soon as **the space** is available. _____

_____

D.   Change the subjects from singular to plural and make the necessary changes.

> Example: **He waits** in the car. (they)
> **They wait** in cars.

1. **She** places flowers on Mrs. Axby's grave. (They)

   _____

2. **He** stands at the graveside. (we)

   _____

3. **She** remembers the good times. (they)

   _____

4. Nowadays, **he** misses her cheerful personality. (we)

   _____

5. **I** was always happy and resourceful. (we)

   _____

6. The **day** always ends with a long hike. (days)

   _____

7. **I** remember and cherish **my** memories. (They, their)

   _____

III.   Structures (Key words [phrases] for composition)

A.   Use the following key words [phrases] to form complete sentences. You may consult the MODEL COMPOSITION.

> Example: street / live
> **The Axbys now live on Shadywood Street.**

1. street / live / is called _____

2. there are / shade trees _____

3. is / a teacher / a widower _____

4. died / after / illness _____

5. has / children / still of school age _____

6. the children / go _____

7. is / oldest / tallest _____

8. attends / does well _____

9. his brother / freshman / same school _____

10. loves / study / read _____

11. sister / is / eighth grade _____

12. studying / reading _____

B.   Supply the missing **prepositions** for each blank space.

Example: Use key words ___(to)___ form complete sentences.

1. The street _____which the Axbys now live is called Shadywood.
2. Prior _____ moving there, the Axbys lived _____Blanco Street.
3. Mrs. Axby died _____ a long illness.
4. Three children are _____ school age.
5. The siblings go_____neighborhood schools.
6. He is the tallest _____the age of seventeen.
7. John is a freshman _____ the same school.
8. He loves _____ study and _____read.
9. Their sister is_____the eighth grade.
10. She is _____ a habit _____ reading rapidly but is unable _____ learn well.
11. She stayed _____ bed several days.
12. She is doing some chores _____ the house now.
13. They prepare their clothing _____ the next day.
14. Her father went _____ town.
15. She tried _____ the dress right away.
16. Mr. Axby waits_____the car_____his children come _____ school.
17. This happens _____days when it rains.
18. _____ times there is too much traffic.
19. He cannot find a place _____ park.
20. The Axbys go_____the cemetery.

21. They place flowers _____ Mrs. Axby's grave.

22. He stands _____ the graveside.

23. She told them _____ remember and _____ be happy.

24. They go hiking after they leave _____ home.

C.   Complete the following sentences.

Example: The street on which Ralph lives **is called Shadywood.**

1. It is called Shadywood because there _____
   _____ .

2. Dorothy was ill during last week, but _____
   _____ .

3. Her father went to town earlier in the day and _____
   _____ .

4. She was happy and _____
   _____ .

5. Though times were often hard, she _____
   _____ .

6. Mr. Axby often waits in the car _____
   _____ .

7. The Axbys go to the cemetery _____
   _____ .

8. They remember the good times _____
   _____ .

9. They miss her cheerful personality _____
   _____ .

10. The day always ends with a long hike _____
    _____ .

IV.   *Grammar and Syntax* [Points Of Interest]

A.   Comments and Model Samples

1. VERB TENSE

Tense signifies the different verb forms which indicate the **difference of time**. There are six such tenses in English.

a. **Present** and **Present Progressive** indicate

   (1) an action going on or a condition existing **now**.

   Examples: Ralph **lives** on Shadywood Street.
   Dorothy **is learning** her lesson.

   (2) a customary or general action (with such added words as **frequently, every day, always,** etc.).

   Examples: The children **go** to school every day.
   They always **do** their homework.

b. **Simple Past** and **Past Progressive** indicate

   (1) that action took place or existed in some definite time in the past.

   Examples: She **was** happy and she **smiled.**
   They **ate** their breakfast this morning.

   (2) that action took place or continued at some particular time in the past when something else happened.

   Examples: She **was studying** when her father came in.
   While they **were driving** to school, they saw their teacher.

c. **Future** indicates an action that will take place or will exist.

   Examples: They **will visit** us next year.
   They **visit** us next year.
   They **are visiting** us next year.
   They **shall be visiting** us next year.
   They **are going to visit** us next year.

d. **Present Perfect Tense** indicates

   (1) that an action began in the past and continues to the present (connects the past to the present).

   Examples: She **has encouraged (has been encouraging)** Dorothy to study English for several years.

Dorothy **has worked (has been working)** hard since last week.

(2) that an action happened in an indefinite time in the past. The time of action is neither expressed nor implied.

Examples: They **have visited** the cemetery.
Have you ever **vacuumed** a room?
She **has vacuumed** her room already.

(3) that an action was repeated several times in an indefinite past.

Examples: We **have visited** her often.
He **has picked** them up time and again.

e. **Past Perfect Tense** expresses an action or condition completed before a certain time in the past or before another past action.

Examples: We **had left** before they **arrived**.
She **got** out of bed after the doctor **had given** her the injection.

f. **Future Perfect** tells of an action that began in the past and is to be completed at a future time **before** another future action will take place.

Examples: By Friday next week **we shall have finished** the chapter.
Dorothy **will have gotten** well before next Monday.
They'll **have learned** to study before they finish the course.

2. SEQUENCE OF TENSES

In the speaker's mind, the time an action takes place depends on how it relates to the time of speaking. For example, if the speaker says, "I bought Dorothy a new dress today," the time he **purchased** the dress is **past** in his mind. The verb **bought** is in the simple past. It expresses action **completed** in the past.

a. Coordination in a sentence means that the sentence is well **balanced**, it expresses concepts of equality, and it contains **parallel** structures (**parallelism**). Some examples of balanced sentences are:

(1) **Verb** with **verb**:
He loves **to study and to read**.

He loves **to study but** not **to read**.
He probably loves **either to study or to read**.
She loves **studying and reading**.
She loves **studying but** not **reading**.
She probably loves **either studying or reading**.

(2) **Adjective** with **adjective**:
He is the **oldest** and **tallest**.
Dorothy was **happy** and **resourceful**.
Ralph has a **younger** sister and **smaller** brother.

(3) **Adverb** with **adverb**:
She is in a habit of reading **rapidly** without learning **well**.
Although he drives **fast** he does it **well**.

b. LOGICAL or NATURAL SEQUENCE in a sentence means using tenses that naturally, or logically, follow a sequence in describing some activities. Events logically precede or succeed one another and have to be placed in their proper order in time. It is not logical, or natural, to say, "Her father **went** to town earlier in the day and **buy** Dorothy a new dress." The logical, or natural, sequence is "Her father **went** to town earlier in the day and **bought** Dorothy a new dress." Some examples of logical sequence follow:

(1) **Present** with **Present** (action takes place at the same time):
Mr. Axby **has** three children who **are** still of school age.
Mr. Axby often **waits** in the car while his children **come out** of school.
He seldom **waits** until I **come**.
At times there **is** too much traffic, and he cannot **find** a place to park.
But this **happens** only on days when it **rains**.
When this **happens**, he **drives** many times around the block.
The siblings **are** worried, but their father **comes** as soon as the space **is** available.
Every year the Axbys **go** to the cemetery and **place** flowers on Mrs. Axby's grave.
While they **stand** at the graveside, they **remember** the good times.
They **do**, but they **miss** her cheerful personality.
The Axbys **are** a closely knit family, and that **is** why they **miss** the departed Mrs. Axby.
The Axbys **remember** and **cherish** their memories.

(2) **Present Habitual** (action takes place as a consequence of another

action in the present):

The street on which Ralph **lives is called** Shadywood.

It **is called** Shadywood because **there** are many shade trees there.

I often **wait** until she comes.

Dorothy usually **waits** until we come.

They usually **recall** the past while they **are standing** at the grave-side.

The day always **ends** with a long hike as soon as they **leave** for home.

(3) **Past** with **Present** (action does not take place at the same time):

Dorothy **was** ill all of last week, but she **is feeling** better today.

She **stayed** in bed several days, but she **is doing** some chores around the house now.

She **vacuumed** her room yesterday; now she **is preparing** her clothing for the next day.

(4) **Past** with **Past** (action takes place at the same time):

She **was** happy and **tried** it on right away.

Mrs. Axby always **told** them to remember her, and **reminded** them to be happy.

Though times **were** often hard, she never **complained**.

c. Time sequence of tenses other than those discussed already follows similar logic. Below are some samples of logical or natural sequence in varied tense combinations.

(1) **Past** with **Present** and **Future**:

Dorothy **was** ill last week, she **is feeling** better today, and she **will be** in school tomorrow.

Mr. Axby **went** to town yesterday, but he **is staying** home today, and **he'll go** to town again on Tuesday.

(2) **Past Perfect** with **Past**:

The siblings **had left** before their father **came**.

Dorothy **went** to town after she **had received** some money.

(3) **Present** with **Future Perfect**:

Before she **vacuums** her room Dorothy **will have prepared** her clothing for the next day.

When their father **arrives**, the siblings **will have waited** a long time.

d. Logical sequence may also come as a result of various **clause** constructions. Examples:

(1) NOUN CLAUSE:
He **says** that he **studies** at Meridian High.
He **says** that he **studied** at Meridian High.
He **says** that he **will study** at Meridian High.
He **says** that he **has studied (has been studying)** at Meridian High.
He **said** that he **studies** at Meridian High. (never **studies**)
He **said** that he **would study** at Meridian High. (never **will study**)
He **said** that he **had studied** at Meridian High. (never **has studied**)

(2) ADVERBIAL CLAUSE: An adverbial clause modifies a verb.

(a) Main verb in the **present tense**:
A good student does not quit **as soon as his teacher leaves.**
while others are studying.
before he has finished his work.
until he has finished his work.

(b) Main verb in the **past tense**:
The children waited **until their father came.**
after they finished school.

(c) Main verb in the **future tense**:
They'll wait **until the traffic lets up.**
while Mr. Axby's getting ready.
until Ralph has finished his game.

(d) Main verb in the **past progressive tense**:
The children were waiting **when Mr. Axby got there.**
while Ralph was playing tennis.

(e) Main verb in the **present perfect tense**:
They have recalled the past **since Mrs. Axby died, because Mrs. Axby has asked them to.**
so that they will be able to cherish their memories.

(3) ADJECTIVAL CLAUSE: An adjectival clause modifies a noun and is not necessarily related to the action expressed by the verb. It involves a different concept of time in the mind of the speaker.

    (a) The Ralph **that I know** attends Meridian High.
                                  played tennis last Monday.

    (b) The dress **that he bought** yesterday is in the closet.
                                    was too long.

    (c) Last night **I waited for the man** who was remembered by my children.
                                    who will be our neighbor.
                                    who is considered a good teacher.

B.   **Exercises**

1. Write the appropriate **present tense** form of the verb in parentheses:

    a. The street on which Ralph _____ (to live) is called Shadywood.

    b. It _____ (to be called) Shadywood because there _____ (to be) many shade trees there.

    c. Mr. Axby _____ (to have) three children who _____ (to be) still of school age.

    d. Ralph _____ (to have) a brother and a sister.

    e. He _____ (to attend) Meridian high school and _____ (to play) tennis on the team.

2. Change the above to the **past tense**.

3. Write the appropriate **past tense** form of the verb in parentheses:

    a. Ralph _____ (to go) to school at 7:30 this morning.

    b. Dorothy _____ (to be) ill yesterday.

    c. She _____ (to stay) in bed several days.

    d. Her father _____ (to go) to town the other day.

    e. He _____ (to buy) Dorothy a new dress.

4. Insert the correct form of the verb in parentheses:

    a. Dorothy _____ (to be) ill during last week, she _____ (to be) feeling better now, and she _____ (to be) in school tomorrow.

    b. Mr. Axby _____ (to go) to town yesterday, but he _____ (to be, to stay) home today, and he _____ (to go) to town again on Tuesday.

c. The children _____ _____ (to have, to leave) before their father _____ (to come).

d. Dorothy _____ (to go) to town after she _____ _____ (to have, to receive) some money.

e. Before she _____ (to vacuum) her room, Dorothy _____ _____ (to have, to prepare) her clothing for the next day.

f. When their father _____ (to arrive), the siblings _____ _____ (to have, to wait) a long time.

V. *Idea Recognition*

A. Copy from the MODEL COMPOSITION the sentences expressing:

1. where the Axbys live . . .

_____

2. why Mr. Axby is a widower . . .

_____

3. why John is a good student . . .

_____

4. why his sister Dorothy is not as good a student as John . . .

_____

5. why Dorothy stayed in bed . . .

_____

6. why Dorothy was happy . . .

_____

7. what happens when it rains . . .

_____

8. what happens when there is much traffic . . .

_____

9. why the children are worried . . .

_____

10. why the Axbys remember the good times . . .

_____

11. how Mrs. Axby was . . .

_____

12. who the Axbys miss . . .

_____

13. how the day ends . . .

_____

14. about the Axbys' memories . . .

_____

B.   Describe what is **happening** in relation to the following general statements according to the MODEL COMPOSITION. Write as many new sentences as you think possible.

> Example: **The street is called Shadywood.**
> **Ralph lives on Shadywood street.**
> **There are many shady trees on Shadywood street.**

1. Mrs. Axby died. _____

_____

_____

2. There are three children. _____

_____

_____

3. Ralph is seventeen years of age. _____

_____

_____

4. John is a good student. _____

_____

_____

5. Dorothy is not as good a student as John. _____

_____

_____

6. Dorothy was ill. _____

_____

_____

7. She stayed in bed. _____

_____

_____

8. Her father bought Dorothy a dress. _____

_____

_____

9. The children come out of school. _____

_____

_____

10. It rains. _____
_____
_____

11. There is too much traffic. _____
_____
_____

12. There are flowers on the grave. _____
_____
_____

13. They remember the good times. _____
_____
_____

14. Mrs. Axby was happy. _____
_____
_____

VI.   *Vocabulary Enrichment*

A.   Paraphrasing

The following are **paraphrases** (rephrasing expressions or words without changing their meaning) of expressions or words found in the narrative. Write the expressions found in the MODEL COMPOSITION that correspond to the paraphrases below.

> Example: a street called Shadywood
> **It is a place with many shade trees.**

1. man whose wife died _____
2. brothers and sisters _____
3. a tennis player _____
4. first-year student _____
5. an habitual reader _____
6. a rainy day _____
7. a parking place _____
8. at the graveside _____
9. a happy person _____
10. a long walk _____

B.   Lexical Units

Select the word (or phrase) from the following list that best completes each of the sentences below. You may use one selection more than once.

Example: This lesson is **easy**. The words are **not difficult**.

nearby	to leave	called
quick	rainy weather	parking place
is busy	dead	illness
purchase		

1. The **name** of the street is Shadywood. It is_____ Shadywood Street.

2. Mrs. Axby **died** after a long illness. She has been _____ since the past summer.

3. The children go to **neighborhood** schools. They go to _____ schools.

4. She is in a habit of reading **rapidly**. She is a_____reader.

5. Dorothy was **ill** during last week. Her _____ lasted one week.

6. She is **doing** some **chores** around the house. She_____ around the house.

7. Her father **bought** Dorothy a new dress. He went to town to _____ a dress for Dorothy.

8. Mr. Axby waits until his children **come out** of school. He waits for his children _____ _____school.

9. This happens on **days when it rains**. It happens during_____ _____ .

10. Mr. Axby cannot find a **place to park**. He cannot find a_____ _____ .

C.   Related Words

Use the **related words** to rewrite the following sentences without changing their meaning. Change the underlined word. Make further changes if necessary.

Example: love (n.)   to love (v.)
Dorothy **loves** studying.
Dorothy has a love for studying.

to play (v.)	rapid (adj.)	to read (v.)
playing (v.)	rapidly (adv.)	reading (n.)
		reader (n.)
hike (n.)	shade (n.)	habit (n.)

hiking (v.)   shady (adj.)   habitual (adj.)
                                                              habitually (adv.)

to study (v.)   to park (v.)
studying (n.)   parking (n.)

1. Ralph **plays** tennis on the team. _____

_____

2. The trees provide a lot of **shade.** _____

_____

3. She is in a **habit** of **reading.** _____

_____

4. He loves to **study** and to **read.** _____

_____

5. He is a **rapid reader.** _____

_____

6. They all go on a **hike.** _____

_____

7. Mr. Axby can find a place to **park.** _____

_____

VII.   Steps to Writing

A.   Add new words and revise the sentence, if necessary, to suit the changes indicated in parentheses.

> Example: She reads rapidly. (we)
> **We read** rapidly.

1. **The Axbys** live on Shadywood Street. (she)

_____

2. **The children** go to neighborhood schools. (all of us)

_____

3. **Ralph** plays tennis on the team. (Dorothy and John don't)

_____

4. **John** loves to study and to read. (we don't always)

_____

5. **She** is in a habit of reading rapidly. (most people)

_____

6. **She** is doing some chores around the house. (they)

7. **Dorothy vacuums** her room and prepares her clothing. (we vacuumed)

8. **Her father** went to town and bought her a dress. (they will go)

9. **She** was happy and tried it on right away. (we)

10. This happens only on days **when it rains**. (rainy)

11. When they **stand** at the graveside, they remember the good times. (are standing)

B. Opposites

Use the **opposites** to rewrite the following sentences. Make the necessary changes to suit the new sentence.

> Example: bachelor—married man
> Mr. Rowan is a **bachelor**.
> He is a married man.

| bright | youngest | not feeling well | does not like | student |
| slowly | looks for | composed | displeased | unhappy |

1. The street is very **shady**. _____

2. Mr. Axby is a **teacher**. _____

3. Mrs. Axby was **okay** for a long time. _____

4. Ralph is the **oldest** of the children. _____

5. John **likes** to study and to read. _____

6. She is in a habit of reading **rapidly**. _____

7. Dorothy was **happy** during last week. _____

8. She was **pleased** when she tried on the dress. _____

_____

9. Mr. Axby **does not look** for a place to park. _____

_____

10. The children are **worried.** _____

_____

VIII.   *Comprehension*

A.   Complete the sentence and add as many related sentences as you can find in the MODEL COMPOSITION.

>   Example: The street on which the Axbys live is called **Shadywood. It is called Shadywood because there are many shade trees there.**

1. Mr. Axby is a school teacher _____

_____

2. She loves studying _____

_____

3. Dorothy was ill during last week _____

_____

4. Mr. Axby often waits in the car _____

_____

5. Every week the Axbys go to the cemetery _____

_____

B.   Answer each question with a complete sentence.

>   Example: Why is the street called Shadywood?
>   **It is called Shadywood Street because there are many shade trees there.**

1. When did Mr. Axby become a widower? _____

_____

2. Why is John a good student? _____

_____

3. Why isn't Dorothy able to learn well? _____

_____

4. How long did Dorothy stay in bed? _____

5. Why is she doing some chores around the house? _____

6. For what occasion did Dorothy's father go to town?_____

7. What made Dorothy happy?_____

8. When does Mr. Axby come to wait for his children? _____

9. Why is Mr. Axby unable to find a place to park? _____

10. What does he do when there is no place to park? _____

11. How often do the Axbys visit the cemetery? _____

12. What is the reason for their visits? _____

IX.   Commentary on Model

A.   1. Describe the street on which the Axbys live.

   2. Discuss the result of Mrs. Axby's illness.

   3. Describe the children and their activities.

   4. Give an appropriate title to your composition.

B.   1. Discuss the points in the MODEL COMPOSITION that you like best.

   2. Discuss the points in the MODEL COMPOSITION with which you disagree.

   3. Explain paragraphs 1 and 2.

   4. Give an appropriate title to your composition.

X.   Composition

A. Using the key words and sentences from the MODEL COMPOSITION, write your own composition on a related topic.

the street on which we live	at the same time
there are many trees	he loves to study
after a long illness	he is unable to learn well
he is the oldest	she is doing some chores
she was ill	her father bought a dress
she vacuums the room	a place to park
on rainy days	they remember the good times
once a year	cherish their memories
she was happy	

B. 1. Rewrite paragraph 2 of the MODEL COMPOSITION in the **I** person. Make all appropriate changes.

   Example: **I** was ill during last week, etc.

   2. Rewrite paragraph 3 in the **past tense**. Make all appropriate changes.

   Example: Mr. Axby often **waited** in his car . . . .

C. Describe what you see in the picture below.

PART TWO

Writing the Paragraph

Chapter Six

Outlining

Words to Remember:

OUTLINE = *related items, ideas*

ORGANIZATION and ANALYSIS

TOPIC OUTLINE = *short phrases, single words*

TOPIC SENTENCE = MAIN IDEA

I. Model Composition

A. Winter Rain: A Fable

Even the hardest task is easier to accomplish with faith. A story I once heard will prove the point.

1. Once upon a time there lived a humble basket-weaver in a small town. He worked hard from dawn to dusk. His rewards were small. He had a wife and four children. Whenever he'd pity himself, he'd repeat the same old saying: "It seems like the poor must carry the burden of this world on their shoulders. The rich have fewer worries and less children to feed."

2. Listening to her husband's bitter complaints, the wife admonished him; "Quit your complaining and get on with your work. Keep the faith, and things will get better. Complaining never got things done."

3. The man was ashamed of having so little faith in himself. He turned his attention to the baskets waiting to be weaved and delivered. His wife and their oldest son helped with the work. Sometimes the man even whistled while he weaved the many baskets.

4. Winter arrived, and life came to a halt in the small town. All roads were covered with snow, and there was no way the baskets could be delivered to the market in the city. "If we could only manage till early spring, we'd be fine," the basket-weaver told his wife. "Keep the faith, believe, and things will happen," she repeated, as she went on with her work.

5. Their food supplies were almost gone, and the snow still covered the roads. There was no indication of a change in the weather. The basket-weaver worried silently because he was ashamed to complain to his smiling wife. She, too, was worried inwardly, but she knew that to complain would only worsen the situation.

6. The family got up early one morning, as usual. They were about to consume their last supply of food for breakfast. Suddenly, thunder was heard, and large drops of rain came falling. Everyone was so excited, they could not finish their breakfast. In the middle of winter rain fell! They ran outside and they drenched themselves in the falling rain. The roads would now be cleared. They could now travel to the city to deliver the merchandise! Everyone laughed and cried with joy. The woman clasped her husband's hand in her own. "Keep the faith," she said quietly. He understood.

B. **Composition by Degrees**

1. a. Copy the title of the MODEL COMPOSITION. _____
   _____

   b. Copy the sentence that tells about the topic of the composition. __
   _____

   c. Copy the phrase that tells about the man's vocation. _____
   _____

   d. Copy the sentence that tells how much the man worked. _____
   _____

   e. Copy the man's "complaint." _____
   _____

2. a. Copy the sentence that tells why the wife admonished the basket-
      weaver. _____
      _____

   b. Copy the phrase that expresses the idea related to the title of the
      composition. _____
      _____

3. a. Copy the sentence that tells why the man was ashamed. _____
   _____

   b. Copy the phrase that tells how the man behaved during work. _____
   _____

4. a. Copy the phrase that tells why "life came to a halt." _____
   _____

   b. Copy the phrase that tells what covered the roads. _____
   _____

   c. Copy the phrase that tells how "things will happen." _____
   _____

5. a. Copy the sentence that tells what "was almost gone." _____
   _____

   b. Copy the phrase that tells what "covered the roads." _____
   _____

   c. Copy the sentence that tells why the basket-weaver "worried
      silently." _____
      _____

   d. Copy the phrase that tells how the basket-weaver's wife worried. __
   _____

6. a. Copy the phrase that tells when the family got up. _____
_____

   b. Copy the sentence that tells what the family was about to do. _____
_____

   c. Copy the phrase that tells what "was heard." _____
_____

   d. Copy the phrase that tells what happened after the "thunder was heard." _____
_____

   e. Copy the phrase that tells why everyone was excited. _____
_____

   f. Copy the phrase that tells why the family was excited about the rain. _____
_____

   g. Copy the expression that concludes the story on the beginning theme. _____
_____

II.   *Words in Context*

A.   From the list of words and phrases preceding each section fill in each blank space provided in the text. You may use a selection more than once. Also, you may use more than one word in one blank space.

1. worked	dawn	lived	dusk	small
repeat	saying	seems	carry	pity
must	shoulders	have	less	feed

   Once upon a time there _____ a humble basket-weaver in a _____ town. He _____ hard from _____ to _____ . Whenever he'd _____ himself, he'd _____ the same old _____ . "_____ like the poor _____ the burden of this world on their _____ . The rich _____fewer worries and children to _____ ."

2. bitter	quit	work	listening
get on	keep	things	admonished

   _____ to her husband's _____ complaints, the wife _____ him; "_____your complaining and _____ with your_____ . _____ the faith, and _____ will get better."

3. turned	weaved	ashamed	waiting
faith	whistled	baskets	

The man was _____ of having so little _____ in himself. He _____ his attention to the baskets _____ to be _____ and delivered. It go so, the man even _____ while he _____ the many _____ .

4. way	delivered	city	manage
halt	covered	only	arrived
spring			

Winter _____ and life came to a _____ in the small town. All roads were _____ with snow, and there was no _____ the baskets could be _____ to the market in the _____ . "If we could _____ till early _____ we'd be fine." He said.

5. almost	indication	silently	roads
weather	ashamed	worried	supplies

Their food _____ were _____ gone, snow still covered the _____ , and there was no _____ of a change in the _____ . The basket-weaver worried _____ because he was _____ to complain. His wife, too, was _____ inwardly.

6. usual	food	thunder	got up	finish
middle	excited	rain	consume	laughed
cleared	travel	cried	woman	keep

The family _____ early one morning, as _____ . They were about to _____ their last supply of _____ for breakfast. Suddenly, _____ was heard. In the _____ of winter _____ fell! Everyone was so _____ , they could not _____ their breakfast. The roads would now be _____ . They could now _____ to the city! They _____ and _____ with joy. The _____ clasped her husband's hand in her own. " _____ the faith," she said silently. He understood.

B. Make the necessary change(s) when you substitute the new element into your sentence.

> Example: Even the hardest **task** is easier to accomplish with faith.
> (tasks)
> Even the hardest tasks are easier to accomplish with faith.

1. a. **He** worked hard from dawn to dusk. (we)

   _____

   b. **His** rewards were small. (our)

   _____

   c. **He** had a wife and four children. (I)

   _____

   d. **The rich** have fewer worries. (they)

   _____

2. a. She was listening to her husband's **bitter complaints**. (stories)

   _____

   b. **His** wife admonished **him**. (my)

   _____

   c. **Things** will get better. (life)

   _____

3. a. **The man was** ashamed. (we)

   _____

   b. He turned his attention to the **baskets**. (work)

   _____

   c. **His wife and their oldest son** helped with the work. (they)

   _____

   d. **The man** whistled while **he** weaved. (I)

   _____

4. a. Winter arrived, and life came to a halt **in the small town**. (there)

   _____

   b. All **roads** were covered with snow. (streets)

   _____

   c. There was no way to deliver the **baskets**. (merchandise)

   _____

   d. **You** must believe, and things will happen. (we)

   _____

5. a. **Their** food supplies were almost gone. (our)

   _____

   b. **The basket-weaver** worried silently. (he)

   _____

   c. **He** was ashamed to complain to **his wife**. (I, her)

   _____

6. a. **The family** got up early one morning. (they)

   _____

   b. **They** were about to consume **their** last food. (we)

   _____

   c. **Everyone was** excited because of the rain. (they)

   _____

   d. **They** could not finish **their** breakfast. (we)

   _____

   e. **They** could now travel to the city. (she)

   _____

   f. **They** cried with joy. (I)

   _____

   g. "Keep the faith." **She** said quietly. **He** understood. (He, I)

   _____

III.   *Structures (Key words [phrases] for composition)*

A.   Use the following key words [phrases] to form complete sentences. You may consult the MODEL COMPOSITION.

   Example: the task / is / with faith
            The hardest task is easier to accomplish with faith.

1. a. once / lived / basket-weaver _____

      _____

   b. rewards / were _____

      _____

   c. had / wife / children _____

      _____

   d. poor / carry / burden / shoulders _____

      _____

   e. rich / have / worries / children _____

2. a. listening / husband's / complaints / the wife _____

      _____

   b. quit / complaining / get on / work _____

      _____

    c. keep / faith _____

    _____

    d. things / get / better _____

    _____

3. a. man / ashamed / little / faith / himself _____

    _____

    b. turned / attention / baskets / weaved / delivered _____

    _____

    c. wife / son / helped / work _____

    _____

    d. man / whistled / weaved / baskets _____

    _____

4. a. life / came / halt / town _____

    _____

    b. roads / covered / snow _____

    _____

    c. no way / baskets / delivered _____

    _____

    d. manage / early / spring / we'd / fine _____

    _____

    e. she / went on / work _____

    _____

5. a. supplies / gone / still / covered / roads _____

    _____

    b. indication / change / weather _____

    _____

    c. basket-weaver / worried _____

    _____

    d. she / complain / worsen / situation _____

    _____

6. a. family / got up / morning _____

    _____

    b. they / about / consume / food / breakfast _____

    _____

    c. thunder / was heard / drops / came falling _____

    _____

    d. middle / winter / rain / fell _____

    _____

e. everyone / was / excited / finish / breakfast _____

_____

f. they / ran / drenched / falling / rain _____

_____

g. roads / would / be cleared _____

_____

h. they / cried / joy _____

_____

i. woman / clasped / hand / own _____

_____

B. Supply the missing preposition for each blank space. You may consult the MODEL COMPOSITION.

Example: The woman clasped her husband's hand (in) her own.

1. a. A humble basket-weaver lived _____ a small town.

   b. He worked hard _____ dawn _____ dusk.

   c. The poor must carry the burden _____ this world _____ their shoulders.

   d. The rich have less children _____ feed.

2. a. Listening _____ her husband's complaints, the wife admonished him.

   b. Get _____ with your work.

3. a. He was ashamed _____ having little faith _____ himself.

   b. He turned his attention _____ the baskets.

   c. His wife and oldest son helped _____ the work.

4. a. Life came _____ a halt _____ the small town.

   b. Roads were covered _____ snow.

   c. Baskets could not be delivered _____ the market _____ the city.

5. a. There was no indication _____ a change _____ the weather.

   b. He was ashamed to complain _____ his wife.

6. a. They were about to consume their last supply _____ food _____ breakfast.

   b. Large drops _____ rain fell.

   c. _____ the middle _____ winter rain fell!

   d. They drenched themselves _____ the falling rain.

    e. They could now travel _____ the city.

    f. They laughed and cried _____ joy.

IV.   *Grammar and Syntax [Points of Interest]*

Outlining is a necessary skill. It is useful in learning to read and write. An **outline** helps to understand the full meaning of written material.

A.   Form and Structure (What is an outline?)

An **outline** is prepared as a plan and structure of any kind of writing. It is basically a listing of ideas and important points. Items that are of similar or related nature are grouped together. In this way, it is possible to show clearly and simply the relationship of things in one group, and to distinguish group I from group II. For example, we can organize the names of various books into three groups:

   I. FICTION
     A. *Gone with the Wind*
     B. *All Lie in Wait*
     C. *The Winds of War*

   II. BIOGRAPHY
     A. *Memoirs*
     B. *Diaries and Letters*
     C. *The War Years*

   III. DRAMA
     A. *The Death of a Salesman*
     B. *Romeo and Juliet*
     C. *Oedipus Rex*

The above **outline** is called **topic outline**. All of the objects listed here are related to each other; they are books. The **outline** classified and organized the books according to I. **Fiction**, II. **Biography** and III. **Drama**. The **topic outline** is composed of short **phrases** or **single** words. Generally these phrases or words are numbered (I., II., III., etc.) or lettered (A., B., C., etc.) to show a certain order and relation of ideas as shown above.

[NOTE: There are basically three types of outlines: the **topic outline**, the **paragraph outline** and the **sentence outline**. They are related in their use, however. The **topic outline** is of major concern here, since it governs the order of **composition**.]

B. The Topic Sentence

The **topic sentence** expresses the **main idea** of a paragraph. It summarizes the whole paragraph, or tells the reader what the paragraph is about. The topic sentence is usually the first sentence of a paragraph. Some of the sentences that follow the topic sentence give it support. Other sentences in the paragraph expand the ideas expressed by the topic sentence and its supporting sentences.

> Example: **Even the hardest task is easier to accomplish with faith.** Once upon a time there lived a humble basket-weaver in a small town. He worked hard, and his rewards were small. He often complained about his fate to his wife. But his wife was cheerful. She encouraged the man to believe in himself. With faith things would be more easily done.

C. Exercises

1. *Outlining*—Arrange the following lists of items into outlines that could be used in writing a theme.

a. A theme about **well-known people**. Organize the following list of names according to two groups:

> I. Male
> II. Female

Alexander the Great, John Adams, Sarah F. Adams, Maxwell Anderson, Ethel Barrymore, Dante Alighieri, Francis Bacon, Lady Ann Bacon, James Balfour, Honore de Balzac, Charles Beaudelaire, Bernard Baruch, Charlotte A. Barnard, Samuel Beckett, Ethel L. Beers, Ludwig van Beethoven, Isabella M. Beeton, Alexander Graham Bell, Stella Benson, Cyrano de Bergerac, Leon Blum, Humphrey Bogart, Simon Bolivar, Louis D. Brandeis, Charlotte Bronte, Martin L. King, Emily Bronte, Robert Browning, Elizabeth B. Browning, Albert Camus, Miguel de Cervantes, Paul Cezanne, Agatha Christie, Confucius, Joseph Conrad, David Crockett, Harry S. Truman, Pearl S. Buck, Thomas A. Edison, Margaret Fuller, Cornelia O. Skinner, Carl Sandburg, Elizabeth Wordsworth

b. A theme about **food**. Organize the following items according to five groups:

> I. Meats, fish, poultry, eggs

II.   Breads and cereals
III. Dairy products
IV.   Fruits and vegetables
V.   Extras (sweets and desserts)

pork, wheat, bread, apple, potato, tomato, candy, sugar, salt, apricot, flounder, barley, beef, chocolate, pear, hot dog, cookies, rice, green beans, cherries, oatmeal, biscuit, cheese, milk, hamburger, bacon, creampuff, turkey, okra, eggplant, lobster, eggs, orange, veal, banana, corn, strawberry, beans, peas, chicken, squash, shrimp, ice cream, donuts, tuna, lollipop, dove, cake, pancake

2. *Topic sentence*—Identify the topic sentence (main idea) in each of the following paragraphs.

a. There are many ways in which our thinking is stimulated. To be productive individuals, we must think. When we study English, we think. We speak and create new thoughts. We write and think only in English. Thinking in one language, but learning another, makes it harder to progress creatively. When we study English, we must think in English.

b. The cosmopolitan nature of the English language is both an advantage and a disadvantage. On the one hand, its advantage is that it has drawn words from many sources. Also, each word comes with a precise definition. On the other hand, its disadvantage lies in the fact that these words are often very nearly alike in definition. To summarize, a writer not intimately familiar with their exact meanings will use them contrary to their correct usage.

c. It is important to use the right word in a given place. Therefore, the correct definition of a term must be ascertained lest one may regret having misused a word. For example, poor spelling is frequently the cause for misuse of words. Finally, unable to spell the effective word correctly, we will use a poor compromise, or an altogether wrong expression.

d. Advertising is an American way of life. Thus, Americans like advertising. Besides, people depend on advertisement in their daily life because they are consumers. The advertisers are manufacturers. Moreover, some advertisers are salesmen. Their merchandise needs advertising. Thus, every product is advertised. Most merchants buy ads for their products. In short, good advertising means success; bad advertising can mean failure.

V.   Idea Recognition

Copy from the MODEL COMPOSITION the sentences expressing:

A. what is easier accomplished with faith . . .

_____

B. who lived in a small town . . .

_____

C. why the basket-weaver repeated the old saying . . .

_____

D. what the poor must carry on their shoulders . . .

_____

E. what the rich have less of . . .

_____

F. why the wife admonished the basket-weaver . . .

_____

G. why the man was ashamed . . .

_____

H. why life came to a halt in the small town . . .

_____

I. why there was no way to deliver the baskets to the city . . .

_____

J. why the basket-weaver worried silently . . .

_____

K. what would worsen the situation . . .

_____

L. what followed the thunder . . .

_____

M. why everyone was excited . . .

_____

N. whose hand the woman clasped in her own . . .

_____

O. what the basket-weaver understood . . .

_____

VI. *Vocabulary Enrichment*

A. Paraphrasing

The following are **paraphrases** (rephrasing expressions or words without changing their meaning) of expressions or words found in the narrative. Write the expressions found in the MODEL COMPOSITION that correspond to the paraphrases below.

> Example. a task to accomplish   **a thing to do**

1. a person who weaves baskets ――――――――――――――――
2. worked from early morning till late at night ――――――――――
3. got little for his work ――――――――――――――――――――
4. is responsible for ――――――――――――――――――――――
5. told him to stop complaining ――――――――――――――――
6. he felt sorry about his behavior ――――――――――――――
7. everything stopped――――――――――――――――――――――
8. unable to take to town ――――――――――――――――――
9. don't lose hope ――――――――――――――――――――――
10. was worried secretly ――――――――――――――――――――

B.   Lexical Units

Select the word (or phrase) from the following list that best completes each of the sentences below. You may use one selection more than once.

> Example: The hardest task is easier to **accomplish with faith**.
> The most difficult task is more easily **done when you believe in yourself.**

all day long	little pay	poor	nothing to eat
clear	pity	turned	unhappy
deliver	show		

1. He worked hard **from dawn to dusk**. ――――――――he spent working.
2. His rewards were **small**. He received ―――――――― for his work.
3. The basket-weaver was **poor**. That's why he'd ―――――――― himself.
4. The rich have **fewer worries**. The――――――――people think so.
5. The husband **complained** bitterly. He was very ―――――――― .
6. He was ashamed of his **lack of faith**. He ―――――――― his attention to his work.
7. The roads were **covered with snow**. There was no way to ―――――――― the baskets.
8. Their food supplies were **almost gone**. They would have ―――――――― .

9. She worried **inwardly**, because she didn't want to _____ her concern to her family.

10. They **drenched** themselves in **the rain**. They were happy because the rain would _____ the roads.

C.   Related Words

Use related words to rewrite the following sentences without changing their meanings. Change the underlined word. Make further changes if necessary.

> Example: accomplished (v.)   accomplishment (n.)
> Even the hardest task is easier to **accomplish** with faith.
> Even the hardest task becomes an easier **accomplishment** with faith.

to work (v.)	to pity (v.)	to burden (v.)	to help (v.)
work (n.)	pity (n.)	burden (n.)	help (n.)
working (v.)		burdened (adj.)	helping (v.)

to admonish (v.)	to whistle (v.)	to carry (v.)
admonishment (n.)	whistle (n.)	carrying (v.)
admonishing (v.)	whistling (v.)	

1. He **worked** hard. _____
_____

2. The man **pitied** himself. _____
_____

3. The poor **carry** the **burden** of the world. _____
_____

4. The wife **admonished** the basket-weaver. _____
_____

5. His son and his wife **helped** with the work. _____
_____

6. The man **whistled while he worked.** _____
_____

VII.   *Steps in Writing*

A.   Add new words and revise the sentence, if necessary, to suit the changes indicated in parentheses.

Example: Even **the** hardest task is easier to accomplish with faith. (a)
Even **a hard** task is easier to accomplish with faith.

1. There lived **a humble** basket-**weaver** in a town. (many)

   _____

2. **He** worked hard **from dawn to dusk**. (they, all day)

   _____

3. **His** rewards were small. (their)

   _____

4. **He'd** pity **himself**, and **he'd** repeat the saying. (I)

   _____

5. **The poor** must carry the burden of this world. (we)

   _____

6. **The rich have** fewer worries. (she)

   _____

7. The wife admonished **him**. (her husband)

   _____

8. Keep **the faith**. (believing in yourself)

   _____

9. Complaining never got **things** done. (anything)

   _____

10. **The man was** ashamed. (we)

    _____

11. **He** turned **his** attention to the weaving. (I)

    _____

12. **His wife and his son** helped him. (the others)

    _____

13. **The man** whistled while he weaved. (they)

    _____

14. **All roads were** covered with snow. (the road)

    _____

15. **Their** food supplies were almost gone. (My)

    _____

16. **The basket-weaver** worried silently. (I)

    _____

17. **The family** got up early one **morning**. (we, day)

    _____

18. **Everyone was** excited. (we)

_____

19. **The roads** would now be cleared. (it)

_____

20. **Everyone** laughed and cried with joy. (we)

_____

B.   Opposites

Use the **opposites** to rewrite the following sentences. Make the necessary changes to suit the new sentences. You may use a word more than once.

> Example: easier–harder
>   Things are **easier** to accomplish with faith.
>   Things are **harder** to accomplish without faith.

better	fewer	hard	humble	inwardly	little
oldest	big	small	worsen	quietly	

1. There lived a **haughty** basket-weaver in a small town. _____

_____

2. His work was very **light**. _____

_____

3. His rewards were **big**. _____

_____

4. The rich have **more** worries. _____

_____

5. Keep the faith, and things will get **worse**. _____

_____

6. The man was ashamed of having so **much** faith. _____

_____

7. The **youngest** son helped with the work. _____

_____

8. Life came to a halt in the **small** town. _____

_____

9. The man worried **outwardly**. _____

_____

10. To complain would **better** the situation. _____

_____

11. "Keep the faith," she said **loudly**. _____

_____

VIII.   *Comprehension*

A.   Complete the sentence and add as many related sentences as you can find in the MODEL COMPOSITION.

Example: Even the hardest task **is easier to accomplish with faith**.

1. Once upon a time _____

_____

2. He worked hard _____

_____

3. Whenever he'd pity himself _____

_____

4. Listening to her husband's bitter complaints, _____

_____

5. The man was ashamed _____

_____

6. Winter arrived, _____

_____

7. Their food supplies were almost gone, _____

_____

8. The family got up early one morning, _____

_____

9. Suddenly, thunder was heard, _____

_____

10. Everyone laughed and cried _____

_____

B.   Answer each question with a complete sentence.

Example: What kind of a task is easier to accomplish with faith?
          Even the hardest task is easier to accomplish with faith.

1. Who lived in a small town? _____

_____

2. How did the basket-weaver work? _____

_____

3. What were his rewards? _____

_____

4. How many children did the basket-weaver have? _____

_____

5. When the weaver complained, what did his wife say to him? _____

_____

6. Does complaining get things done? _____

_____

7. What was the man ashamed of? _____

_____

8. Who helped the weaver with his work? _____

_____

9. What happened when winter arrived? _____

_____

10. What happened to the roads in the winter? _____

_____

11. When would the roads be cleared? _____

_____

12. Why did the basket-weaver worry? _____

_____

13. What was he ashamed to do? _____

_____

14. When did the family get up as usual? _____

_____

15. What was suddenly heard? _____

_____

16. Were the rain drops large? _____

_____

17. What was unusual about the rain? _____

_____

18. What would the rain do to the roads? _____

_____

19. How did this help the basket-weaver? _____

_____

20. What did the man understand at the end? _____

_____

IX.   *Commentary on Model*

A.   1. Describe the work of the basket-weaver.

2. Tell why the basket-weaver was discouraged.

3. Tell how his wife behaved.

4. Tell why the story is called "A Fable."

5. Give an appropriate title to your composition.

B.   1. Do you agree with the basket-weaver?

2. Do you agree with the basket-weaver's wife?

3. Tell why you agree or disagree?

4. Give an appropriate title to your composition.

X.   *Composition*

A.   Using the key words below and phrases from the MODEL COMPOSITION, write your own composition on a related topic. Organize an **outline**. Start the theme with a **topic sentence**.

once upon a time	he worked hard
small rewards	the poor carry burden
the rich have fewer worries	

B.   1. Rewrite section 1 of the MODEL COMPOSITION in the **we** person. Make all appropriate changes.

Example: Once upon a time **we** lived in a small town.

2. Rewrite section 5 in the **I** person. Make all appropriate changes.

Example: **My** food supplies were almost gone . . .

C. Make an **outline** for the following themes:

1. how to prepare for a picnic

2. how to celebrate New Year's Eve

3. how to go about getting a job

4. how to organize a rescue operation at sea

D. Write one **paragraph** about the picture below. Remember to include a **topic sentence**.

Chapter Seven

Elements of the Paragraph

Words to Remember:

Paragraph = *Topic Sentence*
Body
Conclusion (Transition)

Coherence

Topic Sentence = *Main Idea*
Body = *Development of Ideas*
Concluding Sentence = *End of Paragraph*

Transitional Phrases

consequently, therefore, likewise, however, yet, still,
moreover, furthermore, also, too,
first, besides, for example, as an illustration,
in conclusion, to conclude, in short, finally

I. Model Composition

A. The Town Fool: A Fable

The person who finds inner peace will discover happiness.

1. Everyone made fun of Clarence "the beggar." No one in town knew where he came from, consequently everyone was suspicious of this stranger. He simply appeared in town one day, and he stayed. Children ran after the haggard-looking man, mocking him both on and off the street. Likewise, some grown-ups jeered at him with contempt. However, there were others who permitted Clarence to earn a few coins by doing errands or manual work. In short, the town was learning to accept the beggar's presence as best it could.

2. The beggar's obvious contentment puzzled and annoyed almost everyone. Curious people regarded him as a kind of phenomenon. Therefore, they addressed the beggar in a sly way, trying to penetrate the shield of his contentment. Some of the people became angry at Clarence because he disregarded their attempts. It was all to no avail; Clarence kept his composure and also his friendly grin.

3. As time passed, the townspeople gradually became accustomed to the beggar's presence. They regarded him, therefore, with less curiosity. Many believed him to be unable to speak or to hear. "He's deaf and dumb," they said with a shrug, and they let the beggar be. Only the children still followed Clarence through the streets, although now with more amusement than hostility.

4. One day, the unexpected happened. It was going to be a day everyone would remember as long as they lived. The townspeople gathered in the market place. They were unhappy about the way the town was run by the Town Council. Likewise, they were not contented with themselves. They expressed their unhappiness in many different ways. Some shouted abuses. Others displayed posters with various slogans. Still others threatened with violence. Funny thing, there was not one voice heard in the defense of the Town Council.

5. Suddenly, the crowd grew silent. There were a few whispers heard here and there. "The fool, what does he want here?" "He ought to be run out of town!" "How dare he come here like this?" The cause of those remarks was Clarence "the beggar" who appeared at the scene with a large poster displaying only two sentences; MAN'S GREATEST LOSS IS THE LOSS OF HIS INNER PEACE! WHEN HARMONY PREVAILS WITHIN YOU, HAPPINESS COMES YOUR WAY. The words were printed in large letters with black paint on white cardboard. Clarence did not say one word, yet he spoke louder than all the shouting and threatening of the mob.

6. To make a long story short, it has been many years, and many generations have come and gone since those memorable events. Yet the townspeople
speak about Clarence to this very day. They remember the lesson of inner peace
and happiness as expressed by a humble beggar. No one remembers Clarence
as the "town fool." His name is among the most respected names of the town.

B.   Composition by Degrees

1. a. Copy the title of the MODEL COMPOSITION. _____
   _____

   b. Copy the sentence that tells about the topic of the story. _____
   _____

   c. Copy the sentence that tells about the main character. _____
   _____

   d. Copy the sentence that tells about Clarence's appearance in town.__
   _____

   e. Copy the sentence that tells about the behavior of the children. ____
   _____

   f. Copy the sentence that tells how Clarence earned some money. ____
   _____

2. a. Copy the phrase that tells why the people were puzzled. _____
   _____

   b. Copy the phrase that tells what some people did to penetrate the
   shield of Clarence's contentment. _____
   _____

   c. Copy the sentence that tells why some people became angry at
   Clarence. _____
   _____

3. a. Copy the sentence that tells what happened in time. _____
   _____

   b. Copy the phrase that tells how the people regarded Clarence in time.
   _____

   c. Copy the sentence that tells who still followed the beggar. _____
   _____

4. a. Copy the sentence that tells what kind of a day it would be. _____
   _____

   b. Copy the sentence that tells why the townspeople gathered. _____
   _____

c. Copy the phrase that tells what some people shouted. _____
_____

d. Copy the phrase that tells what some people threatened with. _____
_____

5. a. Copy the sentence that tells what suddenly happened. _____
_____

b. Copy the sentence that tells who was the cause of the people's remarks. _____
_____

c. Copy the sentence that tells what Clarence carried. _____
_____

d. Copy the sentence that tells how to become happy. _____
_____

6. a. Copy the sentence that tells how long it has been since the events took place in town. _____
_____

b. Copy the sentence that tells what the people remember. _____
_____

c. Copy the sentence that tells how Clarence is remembered. _____
_____

II. Words in Context

A. From the list of words and phrases preceding each section fill in each blank space. You may use a selection more than once. Also, you may use more than one word in one blank space.

1. simply	suspicious	consequently	made
stayed	ran	haggard	in short
learning	presence	could	knew

Everyone _____ fun of Clarence "the beggar." No one in town
_____ where he came from, _____ everyone was _____of
this stranger. He_____appeared in town, and he _____. Children
_____ after the _____ looking man. _____ _____ _____,
the town was _____ to accept the beggar's _____ as best it _____ .

2. sly	therefore	phenomenon	regarded
contentment	people	angry	penetrate

composure   grin

Curious people _____ him as a kind of _____ . _____ ,
they addressed the beggar in a _____ way, trying to _____ the shield
of his_____ . Some of them became _____ at Clarence. Clarence
kept his _____ and also his friendly _____.

3. gradually	regarded	passed	presence
therefore	believed	curiosity	through
speak	still		

As time _____ , the townspeople _____ became accustomed to
the beggar's _____ . They_____ him, _____, with less_____ .
Many_____ him to be unable to _____or to hear. Only the
children _____ followed Clarence_____ the streets.

4. likewise	shouted	still	violence
unhappy	gathered	place	run
unexpected	everyone	lived	contented

One day, the _____ happened. It was going to be a day_____
would remember as long as they _____ . The townspeople _____ in
the market _____. They were _____about the way the town was
_____by the Town Council. _____ , they were not _____ with them-
selves. Some_____ abuses. _____ others threatened with violence.

5. whispers	loss	peace	grew
harmony	happiness	within	there

Suddenly, the crowd _____ silent. There were a few _____
heard here and_____ . Man's greatest_____ is the _____of his
inner _____! When _____prevails_____you, _____ comes your way.

6. memorable	remember	peace	very
happiness	humble	yet	short
generations	gone		

To make a long story _____ , it has been many years and many
_____ have come and _____ since those_____ events. _____ the
townspeople speak about Clarence to this_____ day. They_____ the
lesson of inner _____and _____as expressed by a _____ beggar.

B.   Make the necessary change(s) when you substitute the new element into
your sentence.

Example: **The person** who finds inner peace will discover happiness. (he)

He who finds inner peace will discover happiness.

1. a. **Everyone** made fun of Clarence. (the children)
   _____

   b. **No one** knew where he came from. (nobody)
   _____

   c. Children ran after the **haggard-looking man**. (beggar)
   _____

   d. **The town was** learning to accept his presence. (we)
   _____

2. a. **Curious people** regarded him as a phenomenon. (they)
   _____

   b. **They** addressed Clarence in a sly way. (the people)
   _____

   c. Some of **the people** became angry at Clarence. (them)
   _____

   d. **Clarence** kept **his** composure. (I, my)
   _____

3. a. **The townspeople** became accustomed to Clarence. (we)
   _____

   b. **They** regarded him with less curiosity. (the neighbors)
   _____

   c. **Many** believed him to be deaf and dumb. (some)
   _____

4. a. It was going to be a day **everyone** would remember. (we)
   _____

   b. **The townspeople** gathered in the market place. (men, women, and children)
   _____

   c. They were unhappy about the way **the town was** run. (things)
   _____

   d. **They** were not contented with **themselves**. (we)
   _____

   e. **They** expressed **their** unhappiness in many ways. (she)
   _____

   f. **Some** shouted abuses. (many)
   _____

    g. **Others** threatened with violence. (few)

_____

5. a. Suddenly, **the crowd** grew silent. (they)

_____

    b. **He** ought to be run out of town. (she)

_____

    c. How dare **he** come here like this? (we)

_____

    d. **Man's** greatest loss is the loss of **his** inner peace. (our)

_____

    e. **He** spoke louder than all the shouting. (it)

_____

6. a. **The townspeople** speak about Clarence to this day. (they)

_____

    b. **They** remember the lesson of inner peace. (we)

_____

    c. **No one** remembers Clarence as the "town fool." (nobody)

_____

    d. His **name** is respected. (memory)

_____

III. Structures (Key words [phrases] for composition)

A. Use the following key words (phrases) to form complete sentences. You may consult the MODEL COMPOSITION.

    Example: person / finds / inner peace / happiness
              The person who finds inner peace will discover happiness.

1. a. everyone / fun / Clarence _____

_____

    b. in town / knew / came from _____

_____

    c. everyone / suspicious / of stranger _____

_____

    d. children / ran / haggard / man _____

_____

    e. grown-ups / jeered / with contempt _____

f. others / permitted / to earn / coins _____

g. town / was learning / the beggar's / presence _____

2. a. contentment / puzzled / annoyed _____

   b. people / regarded / phenomenon _____

   c. they / addressed / beggar / sly / way _____

   d. some / became / angry _____

   e. kept / composure / grin _____

3. a. they / regarded / loss / curiosity _____

   b. many / believed / unable / speak / hear _____

   c. only / children / followed _____

4. a. one day / unexpected / happened _____

   b. going to be / a day / remember _____

   c. townspeople / gathered / market place _____

   d. they / unhappy / the way / town / run _____

   e. expressed / unhappiness / different ways _____

   f. they / not contented / themselves _____

   g. displayed / posters / various / slogans _____

   h. others / threatened / violence _____

    i. not one / voice / heard / defense / Town Council _____

_____

5. a. suddenly / crowd / silent _____

_____

   b. there / few / whispers / heard _____

_____

   c. greatest / loss / inner / peace _____

_____

   d. harmony / happiness / comes _____

_____

6. a. has been / many / years / generations _____

_____

   b. remember / lesson / inner peace / happiness _____

_____

   c. no one / remembers / town fool _____

_____

   d. name / among / respected / names _____

_____

B. Supply the missing preposition for each blank space. You may consult the MODEL COMPOSITION'

Example: Everyone made fun   _(of)_   Clarence.

1. a. No one _____ town knew where he came _____ .
   b. Everyone was suspicious _____ this stranger.
   c. He simply appeared _____ town one day.
   d. Children ran _____ the haggard-looking man.
   e. They mocked him both _____ and _____ the street.
   f. Others permitted Clarence to earn a few coins _____ doing errands.

2. a. They tried to penetrate the shield _____ his contentment.
   b. Some _____ the people became angry _____ Clarence.
   c. It was all _____ no avail.
3. a. The townspeople became accustomed _____ the beggar.
   b. They regarded him _____ less curiosity.
   c. Only the children followed him _____ the streets.

  d. They followed him _____ more amusement than hostility.

4. a. They were unhappy _____ the way the town was run _____ the Town Council.

  b. They were not contented _____ themselves.

  c. They expressed their unhappiness _____ many ways.

  d. Some displayed posters _____ slogans.

  e. Still others threatened _____ violence.

5. a. He ought to be run out _____ town.

  b. The cause _____ those remarks was Clarence.

  c. He appeared _____ the scene.

  d. Man's greatest loss is the loss _____ his inner peace.

  e. When harmony prevails _____ you, happiness comes your way.

  f. The words were printed _____ large letters _____ black paint _____ white cardboard.

6. a. The people speak _____ Clarence _____ this very day.

  b. They remember the lesson _____ inner peace and happiness as expressed _____ a humble beggar.

  c. His name is _____ the most respected names _____ the town.

IV. Grammar and Syntax [Points of Interest]

A. Basically, an outline for a paragraph consists of one **summary sentence**. This sentence expresses the **main idea** discussed in the paragraph.

1. *Introductory sentence*—The **summary sentence** becomes an introductory sentence (topic sentence) within the paragraph itself. It expresses the **main idea** and it tells the reader what the paragraph is about. However, it does not include all the ideas to be developed in the paragraph. The **introductory sentence** is usually placed **first** in the paragraph.

> Example: "During the last ten years of the 19th century much progress was made in the field of psychology."

The rest of the paragraph will list and explain what this progress was.

2. *Paragraph coherence*—Sentences in a paragraph should **interrelate**. This means that each sentence ought to follow naturally from the force of the preceding one. In this manner, sentences within the paragraph are connected logically

(chronologically) and the reader is able to follow the thought easily. The paragraph shows **coherence**.

The harmony of a paragraph is generally secured by arranging certain ideas in a logical order. To help in the logical transition between sentences, one can use the following key words to express

    a. RESULT: consequently, therefore, thus, etc.

    b. COMPARISON: likewise, however, yet, still, etc.

    c. ADDITIONALS: first, moreover, also, too, furthermore, besides, etc.

    d. EXAMPLES: for example, as an illustration, etc.

    e. CONCLUSION: in conclusion to summarize, to conclude, in short, finally, etc.

3. *Body*—A well-written paragraph has a clear **central idea** stated in the topic sentence and a **body** that **supports** and **develops** that central idea. To be effective, the body of the paragraph must contain enough information pertaining to the topic sentence. It ought to deal only with subject matter that is related to the topic sentence.

> Example: "To make a telephone call from a public booth, follow these steps. First, remove the receiver and listen for the dial tone. Then put a coin in the slot. In most cases it will be a dime. Some calls will require additional coins. After you have deposited the correct amount, dial the number you want. When the call is completed, place the receiver back on the hook."

In the above paragraph, the main or **central idea** is expressed in the **topic** sentence. "To make a telephone call from a public booth . . ." The sentences which follow this central idea, enlarge and explain the topic sentence. All of the details mentioned in this paragraph deal with the process of "making a telephone call."

4. *The concluding (transitional) sentence*—This type of sentence is usually at the **end** of the paragraph. The **transitional** sentence does one of two things; it either concludes the paragraph or it prepares the reader for the following paragraph.

> Example: ". . . When the call is completed, place the receiver back on the hook."

"However, if the call is not completed, etc., etc."

[NOTE: The paragraph that follows the transitional sentence introduces a new idea; the possibility that a call **might not be completed**. The first sentence of this paragraph picks up where the transitional sentence left off, allowing for a logical sequence of ideas between paragraphs (Chapter 8).]

B.   Exercises

1. Each of the following paragraphs has a **main idea**, a **body**, and a **concluding** sentence. Identify these essential parts in each paragraph.

a. Advertising is an American way of life. Thus, Americans like advertising. Besides, people depend on advertisement in their daily life because they are consumers. The advertisers are manufacturers. Moreover, some advertisers are salesmen. Their merchandise needs advertising. Thus, every product is advertised. Most merchants buy ads for their products. In short, good advertising means success; bad advertising can mean failure.

b. The cosmopolitan nature of the English language is both an advantage and a disadvantage. On the one hand, its advantage is that it has drawn words from many sources. Also, each word comes with a precise definition. On the other hand, its disadvantage lies in the fact that these words are often very nearly alike in definition. To summarize, a writer not intimately familiar with their exact meanings will use them contrary to their correct usage.

c. It is important to use the right word in a given place. Therefore, the correct definition of a term must be ascertained lest one may regret having misused a word. For example, poor spelling is frequently the cause for misuse of words. Finally, unable to spell the effective word correctly, we will use a poor compromise, or an altogether wrong expression.

2. Each of the following "paragraphs" is incomplete. They are sets of sentences that lack either a **topic** sentence, a **body** or a **concluding** sentence. Read the "paragraphs" carefully and tell which of the essential parts is missing. Write the name of this element in the space provided.

a. On the one hand, its advantage is that it has drawn words from many sources. Also, each word comes with a precise definition. On the other hand, its disadvantage lies in the fact that these words are often very nearly alike in definition. To summarize, a writer not intimately familiar with their exact meanings will use them contrary to their correct usage.
Part missing: _____

b. Advertising is an American way of life. Thus, Americans like advertising. Besides, people depend on advertisement in their daily life because they are consumers. The advertisers are manufacturers. Moreover, some advertisers are salesmen. Their merchandise needs advertising. Thus, every product is advertised. Most merchants buy ads for their products.
Part missing: ───────────────────────────────

c. It is important to use the right word in a given place. Finally, unable to spell the effective word correctly, we will use a poor compromise, or an altogether wrong expression.
Part missing: ───────────────────────────────

3. Go back to EXERCISE 2. Insert one of the elements given below into its proper paragraph. Rewrite the entire paragraph.

a. In short, good advertising means success; bad advertising can mean failure.

b. The cosmopolitan nature of the English language is both an advantage and a disadvantage.

c. Therefore, the correct definition of a term must be ascertained lest one may regret having misused a word. For example, poor spelling is frequently the cause for misuse of words.

V. Idea Recognition

Copy from the MODEL COMPOSITION the sentences expressing:

A.   what no one knew . . .

───

B.   who was suspicious . . .

───

C.   where Clarence appeared . . .

───

D.   who ran after Clarence . . .

───

E.   what the children did . . .

───

F.   what some grown-ups did . . .

───

G. who permitted Clarence to earn a few coins . . .

_____

H. how Clarence earned a few coins . . .

_____

I. what the town was learning . . .

_____

J. what puzzled and annoyed almost everyone . . .

_____

K. how the people addressed the beggar . . .

_____

L. why some people became angry at Clarence . . .

_____

M. what Clarence kept . . .

_____

N. what the town became accustomed to . . .

_____

O. how the people regarded Clarence . . .

_____

P. what happened one day . . .

_____

Q. who gathered in the market place . . .

_____

R. who shouted slogans . . .

_____

S. who appeared suddenly . . .

_____

T. what Clarence displayed . . .

_____

U. what the poster said . . .

_____

V. how the words were printed . . .

_____

W. who speaks about Clarence . . .

_____

X. what lesson the people remember . . .

_____

Y. where Clarence's name is . . .

_____

VI. *Vocabulary Enrichment*

A.   Paraphrasing

The following are **paraphrases** (rephrasing expressions or words without changing their meaning) of expressions or words found in the narrative. Write the expressions found in the MODEL COMPOSITION that correspond the paraphrases below.

Example: to find inner peace   **to become peaceful inwardly**

1. people laughed at him _____

2. they didn't trust _____

3. they were cruel _____

4. shouted angrily _____

5. went to fetch things _____

6. they considered him _____

7. he was peaceful and satisfied _____

8. he kept his calmness _____

9. a smile on his face _____

10. they were delighted _____

11. everyone came together _____

12. threw insults _____

13. showed up at the gathering _____

14. would be remembered _____

B.   Lexical Units

Select the word (phrase) from the following list that best completes each of the sentences below. You may use one selection more than once.

Example: The person who finds **inner peace** will discover happiness.
Happy is the person who is **peaceful inwardly**.

contentment	ignored	defend	accepted	suspicious
remained	find out	composure	angry	fool

1. No one **knew where he came from**. Everyone was _____ .

2. He **came to town** one day. And he _____ there.

3. Children **mocked** the beggar. But he did not _____ himself.

4. The people were **puzzled**. The source of their puzzlement was the beggar's _____ .

5. They addressed the beggar in a **sly way**. The people wanted to _____ about him.

6. Some people were **angry** at Clarence. But Clarence _____them.

7. Gradually the townspeople became **accustomed** to the beggar's presence. They _____ his being there.

8. People tried to **make him angry**. But Clarence kept his _____ .

9. The people **shouted abuses**. They were _____ .

10. People remember Clarence's **lesson of inner peace**. No one remembers him as a _____ .

C. Related Words

Use related words to rewrite the following sentences without changing their meanings. Change the underlined word. Make further changes if necessary.

> Example: suspicious (adj.)   to suspect (v.)
> Everyone **was suspicious** of this stranger.
> Everyone **suspected** this stranger.

to appear (v.)	contemptuous (adj.)	to puzzle (v.)
appearance (n.)	contempt (n.)	puzzlement (n.)
curious (adj.)	to amuse (v.)	to be hostile (v.)
curiosity (n.)	amusement (n.)	hostility (n.)
angry (adj.)	to whisper (v.)	
anger (n.)	whisper (n.)	

1. He simply **appeared** in town. _____

_____

2. They regarded him with **contempt**. _____

_____

3. The beggar's contentment **puzzled** the people. _____

_____

4. Some became **angry** at Clarence. _____

_____

5. They regarded him with less **curiosity**. _____

_____

6. Children followed Clarence with more **amusement** than **hostility**. _____

_____

7. There were a few **whispers**. _____

_____

VII.   Steps in Writing

A.   Add new words and revise the sentence to suit the changes indicated in parentheses.

> Example: The **person** who **finds** inner peace will discover happiness. (people)
> The **people** who **find** inner peace will discover happiness.

1. **Everyone was** suspicious of the beggar. (they)

_____

2. **He** simply appeared in town. (I)

_____

3. **Children** ran after the beggar. (she)

_____

4. **Some grown-ups** jeered at him. (the townspeople)

_____

5. There were **others** who gave Clarence work. (people)

_____

6. The town was learning to accept **the beggar**. (Clarence)

_____

7. **Curious people** regarded him as a kind of phenomenon. (we)

_____

8. **They** addressed **the beggar** in a sly way. (she, him)

_____

9. **Some people** became angry. (I)

_____

10. **Clarence kept his** composure. (they)

_____

11. **Many** believed him to be deaf. (he)

_____

12. Only **the children** still followed Clarence. (we)

_____

13. The **townspeople** gathered in the market place. (they)

_____

14. **They** expressed **their** unhappiness. (we, our)

_____

15. **Some** shouted abuses. (they)

_____

16. **The crowd** grew silent. (she)

_____

17. **Man's** greatest loss is the loss of **his** inner peace. (our)

_____

18. **Clarence** did not say one word. (I)

_____

19. **They** remember the lesson. (we)

_____

20. **His** name is among the most respected names. (Clarence's)

_____

B.   Opposites

Use the opposites to rewrite the following sentences. Make the necessary changes to suit the new sentences. You may use a word more than once.

> Example: peace—unrest   happiness—unhappiness
> He who finds **peace** will discover **happiness**.
> He who finds **unrest** will discover **unhappiness**.

disliked	dissatisfaction	indifferent	many
unexpected	gradually	friendly	reject
accused	loudly	most	silent
unhappy	sly		

1. Everyone **liked** Clarence. _____

_____

2. Others permitted the beggar to earn **a few** coins. _____

_____

3. The town was learning to **accept** Clarence. _____

_____

4. The beggar's **contentment** puzzled the people. _____

_____

5. **Curious** people regarded him as a phenomenon. _____

_____

6. They addressed the beggar in **an open** way. _____

_____

7. Clarence kept his **unfriendly** grin. _____

_____

8. The people **suddenly** became accustomed to Clarence. _____

_____

9. One day the **expected** happened. _____

_____

10. The people were **happy** with the Town Council. _____

_____

11. Everyone **defended** the Town Council. _____

_____

12. Suddenly, the crowd grew **loud.** _____

_____

13. Clarence's poster spoke **silently.** _____

_____

14. His name is among the **least** respected names. _____

_____

VIII.   Comprehension

A.   Complete the sentence and add as many related sentences as you can find in the MODEL COMPOSITION.

> Example: The person who finds inner peace **will discover happiness.**

1. Everyone made fun of Clarence _____

_____

_____

2. No one knew where he came from, _____

_____

_____

3. Children ran after the haggard-looking man, _____

_____

_____

4. The beggar's contentment _____

_____

_____

5. Therefore, they addressed the beggar in a sly way _____

_____

_____

6. Some people became angry at Clarence _____

_____

_____

7. As time passed, _____

_____

_____

8. Only the children _____

_____

_____

9. One day, the unexpected happened. _____

_____

_____

10. The townspeople gathered in the market place. _____

_____

_____

11. They expressed their unhappiness in many different ways. _____

_____

_____

12. The crowd grew silent. _____

_____

_____

13. The cause of those remarks was Clarence _____

_____

_____

14. Clarence did not say one word, _____

_____

_____

15. To make a long story short, _____

_____

_____

B. Answer each question with a complete sentence.

Example: What will the person discover?
The person will discover happiness.

1. Who made fun of Clarence? _____

   _____

2. Did the people know where he came from? _____

   _____

3. What happened one day? _____

   _____

4. Who jeered at Clarence? _____

   _____

5. Who permitted him to earn a few coins? _____

   _____

6. What was the town learning? _____

   _____

7. What puzzled almost everyone? _____

   _____

8. How did some people address the beggar? _____

   _____

9. Why did they address him in a sly way? _____

   _____

10. Why did some people become angry at Clarence? _____

    _____

11. How did the townspeople regard "the beggar"? _____

    _____

12. What did the people say about him? _____

    _____

13. How did the children follow Clarence through the streets? _____

    _____

14. What kind of a day was it going to be? _____

    _____

15. Who gathered in the market place? Why? _____

    _____

16. How did the people express their unhappiness? _____

    _____

17. Did anyone come to the defense of the Town Council? _____

    _____

18. Why did the crowd grow suddenly silent? _____

    _____

19. What did Clarence carry? _____

    _____

20. What did the poster say? _____

_____

21. Do the people still remember Clarence? _____

_____

22. What do they remember about Clarence? _____

_____

23. How is his name regarded in town? _____

_____

IX.   Commentary on Model

A.   Using the key words and phrases from the MODEL COMPOSITION, write your own composition consisting of two paragraphs on a related topic.

suspicious of stranger	mocking the man
errands or manual work	peace and happiness
keep composure	unhappy with self
harmony prevails	respected name

B.   1. Rewrite section 4 of the MODEL COMPOSITION in the **we** person. Make all appropriate changes.

Example: It was going to be a day **we** would remember . . .

2. Rewrite section 6 in the **she** person. Make all appropriate changes.

Example: Yet **she** speaks about Clarence . . .

C.   1. Write about the **lesson** you've learned from the "Fable."

2. Write about the points you agree with.

3. Write about the points you disagree with.

4. Give an appropriate title to your composition.

X.   Composition

A.   Select three topics below and write one paragraph on each. Remember to

include an introductory (topic) sentence within the paragraph itself. Follow the
topic sentence with a **body** and the **concluding** statement.

1. how to change a car tire

2. how to climb a mountain

3. how to say "good night" to a date

4. description of the person you love

5. description of a flower

B. Write one **paragraph** about the picture below. Remember to include all
paragraph elements.

PART THREE

Writing
the Composition

Chapter Eight

Development of Composition

Words to Remember:

The Paragraph: Introductory

Main

Concluding (*Transitional*)

Interrelationship and Transition

Coherence and Proportion

I.   *Model Composition*

A.   World University Community: A Dream

1. All roads have one particular characteristic in common; they accommodate people of all nationalities, creeds and different physical and psychological features. All these people are constantly moving toward a goal that became dear to the heart of every striving individual: the road to a complete and lasting peace. Such peace, we believe, will be finally achieved by students of all nations uniting into a World University Community.

2. A Community composed of students of all nations throughout the world will be bound by one great goal: the proposition to maintain peace. The student is, after all, the life-giving substance for the world, as is the blood to the body. As the roads to peace become narrow and corroded through ignorance and misunderstanding among human beings, so do sick arteries delay the flow of blood.

3. The road to peace is filled with obstacles. These obstacles can be cleared with good will and enlightened action. The student of the world will realize that he is the future of all walks of life on earth: the statesman, the doctor, the lawmaker, the educator of tomorrow. A great responsibility rests on his shoulders, and he will be strong and faithful to the ideas expressed by the word: STUDENT.

4. Many travel to study in foreign countries. They come among strange people and new customs. Their reactions are varied. Yet, most students make a similar observation that people, wherever they may be, are identical in one aspect: they walk the road of life common to all mankind. Students have the opportunity to discuss and argue about various controversial issues. However, they soon find their place and walk side-by-side with others. They argue for the improvement of things rather than for their destruction.

5. The effect of the written and spoken argument has proven successful in the past. We remember the old saying: "The pen is mightier than the sword." Physical violence and brutality are replaced by the ability to walk the road to communication and understanding. We will repeat our attempts until the bonds of helplessness are torn and we are free to practice within the walls of the Universe that which was taught within the walls of the University. We take this road, although a winding and tiresome one, because just ahead of us lies our goal, the state of peace, love and understanding: WORLD UNIVERSITY COMMUNITY.

B. **Composition by Degrees**

1. a. Copy the title of the MODEL COMPOSITION. ＿＿＿＿＿＿

   ＿＿＿＿＿＿＿＿＿＿＿＿＿＿＿＿＿＿

   b. Copy the sentence that tells what "all roads have in common."＿＿

   ＿＿＿＿＿＿＿＿＿＿＿＿＿＿＿＿＿＿

   c. Copy the sentence that tells where "all people are constantly moving." ＿＿＿＿＿＿＿＿＿＿＿＿＿＿＿＿

   ＿＿＿＿＿＿＿＿＿＿＿＿＿＿＿＿＿＿

   d. Copy the sentence that tells how "peace can be achieved."＿＿＿＿

   ＿＿＿＿＿＿＿＿＿＿＿＿＿＿＿＿＿＿

2. a. Copy the sentence that tells what will "bind a student community."

   ＿＿＿＿＿＿＿＿＿＿＿＿＿＿＿＿＿＿

   b. Copy the phrase that tells what kind of "substance" the student is.

   ＿＿＿＿＿＿＿＿＿＿＿＿＿＿＿＿＿＿

   c. Copy the phrase that tells how the "roads to peace" become. ＿＿＿

   ＿＿＿＿＿＿＿＿＿＿＿＿＿＿＿＿＿＿

   d. Copy the sentence that tells why the roads to peace become "narrow." ＿＿＿＿＿＿＿＿＿＿＿＿＿＿＿＿

   ＿＿＿＿＿＿＿＿＿＿＿＿＿＿＿＿＿＿

3. a. Copy the phrase that tells what "the road to peace is filled with."

   ＿＿＿＿＿＿＿＿＿＿＿＿＿＿＿＿＿＿

   b. Copy the sentence that tells how the "obstacles and narrow passages" can be cleared. ＿＿＿＿＿＿＿＿＿＿＿

   ＿＿＿＿＿＿＿＿＿＿＿＿＿＿＿＿＿＿

   c. Copy the sentence that tells what the student "will realize." ＿＿＿

   ＿＿＿＿＿＿＿＿＿＿＿＿＿＿＿＿＿＿

   d. Copy the phrase that tells what "rests on the student's shoulders."＿

   ＿＿＿＿＿＿＿＿＿＿＿＿＿＿＿＿＿＿

4. a. Copy the sentence that tells where "many travel." ＿＿＿＿＿＿＿

   ＿＿＿＿＿＿＿＿＿＿＿＿＿＿＿＿＿＿

   b. Copy the sentence that tells what "observation" most students make.

   ＿＿＿＿＿＿＿＿＿＿＿＿＿＿＿＿＿＿

   c. Copy the sentence that tells what the students "argue about." ＿＿

   ＿＿＿＿＿＿＿＿＿＿＿＿＿＿＿＿＿＿

5. a. Copy the old saying. ＿＿＿＿＿＿＿＿＿＿＿＿

   ＿＿＿＿＿＿＿＿＿＿＿＿＿＿＿＿＿＿

b. Copy the phrase that tells what replaces violence and brutality. ___
_____

c. Copy the sentence that tells what the student will practice "within the walls of the Universe." _____
_____

d. Copy the sentence that tells what "goal lies ahead." _____
_____

II.   Words in Context

A.   From the list of words preceding each section fill in each blank space. You may use a selection more than once. Also, you may use more than one word in one blank space.

1. nationalities   goal   common   particular
   constantly   dear   physical   features
   accommodate   complete   striving

All roads have one _____ characteristic in _____; they
_____ people of all_____, creeds and different_____and psychological
_____ . All these people are _____ moving toward a _____
that became_____to the heart of every _____ individual; the
road to a _____ and lasting peace.

2. great   composed   world
   proposition   maintain   nations

A Community _____of students of all_____throughout the
_____will be bound by one_____goal: the_____ to_____peace.

3. obstacles   cleared   filled   passages
   widened   enlightened   spark

The road to peace is _____with _____ , natural and man-made.
_____and narrow_____ in this road can be _____ and _____
with each added_____of good will and _____ action.

4. foreign   new   travel   among
   students   reactions   opportunity   discuss
   argue   issues

Many _____to study in _____countries. They come_____
strange people and _____customs. Their_____are varied. They
have the _____ to _____and _____about various controversial _____ .

5. written   remember   effect   proven
  violence   ability   winding   brutality
  pen   past   mightier   communication
  peace   university   love   sword
  ahead   understanding

The _____ of the _____ and spoken argument has _____
successful in the_____. We _____the old saying: "The _____is
_____than the _____." Physical_____ and_____ are replaced by
the _____to walk the road to _____and_____ . We take this road,
although a _____and tiresome one, because just _____
lies our goal, the state of _____ , _____, and _____ :
WORLD_____ COMMUNITY.

B. Make the necessary change(s) when you substitute the new element into
your sentence.

   Example: **All roads have** one particular characteristic in common.
      (every)
      Every road has one particular characteristic in common.

1. a. **They accommodate** people of all nationalities. (it)

  _____

 b. **All these people** are constantly moving toward a goal. (we)

  _____

 c. **Peace** will finally be achieved by students. (understanding)

  _____

2. a. **The student is** the life-giving substance for the world. (they)

  _____

 b. The **roads** to peace **become** narrow and corroded. (road)

  _____

3. a. **Obstacles** can be cleared. (they)

  _____

 b. The **student** of the world **is** the future of all life. (students)

  _____

   c. A great responsibility rests on **his** shoulders. (our)

_____

4. a. **Many travel** to study in foreign countries. (she)

_____

   b. **They come** among strange people. (he)

_____

   c. **Their** reactions are varied. (our)

_____

   d. Most **students** make a similar observation. (of us)

_____

   e. **The students** have an opportunity to discuss many issues. (we)

_____

   f. **They** soon **find their** place. (she)

_____

   g. **They argue** for the improvement of things. (he)

_____

5. a. The **effect** of the written and spoken argument **is** successful. (effects)

_____

   b. **Physical violence and brutality are** replaced by understanding. (it)

_____

   c. **We** will repeat **our** attempts. (she)

_____

   d. **We take** this road. (he)

_____

   e. Just ahead lies **our** goal. (their)

_____

III.   Structures (Key words [phrases] for composition)

A.   Use the following key words [phrases] to form complete sentences. You may consult the MODEL COMPOSITION.

     Example: roads / have / characteristic / common
            All roads have one particular characteristic in common.

  1. a. they / accommodate / nationalities _____

_____

   b. people / moving / goal _____

c. became / heart / striving / individual _____

d. road / complete / lasting / peace _____

e. peace / finally / by students / all nations _____

2. a. students / bound / proposition / maintain peace _____

b. student / is / substance / world _____

c. roads / peace / become / ignorance _____

d. arteries / delay / flow _____

3. a. road / peace / filled / obstacles _____

b. narrow passages / cleared / spark / good will _____

c. the student / realize / the future / on earth _____

d. responsibility / rests / on shoulders _____

e. will be / faithful / to ideals / expressed _____

4. a. many / travel / study / foreign country _____

b. they / come / strange people / new customs _____

c. their / reaction / varied _____

d. students / make / observation _____

e. people / are / identical _____

f. they / walk / road / common / all mankind _____

g. students / have / opportunity / discuss / issues _____

_____

h. they / find / place / walk / others _____

_____

5. a. effect / written / spoken / argument / proven / successful _____

_____

b. pen / mightier / sword _____

c. violence / brutality / replaced / ability / communication _____

_____

d. we / repeat / attempts _____

_____

e. bonds / helplessness / torn _____

f. we / are / free / practice / walls / Universe _____

_____

g. we / take / road _____

_____

h. just / ahead / lies / goal _____

_____

B.   Supply the missing **preposition** for each blank space. You may consult the MODEL COMPOSITION.

Example: All roads have one characteristic ___(in)___ common.

1. a. They accommodate people _____ all nationalities.
   b. All these people are moving _____ a goal.
   c. It became dear_____ the heart of every individual.
   d. This is the road_____ a lasting peace.
   e. It will be achieved _____ students_____ all nations.
2. a. A Community is composed _____ students _____ all nations.
   b. This is the proposition _____ maintain peace.
   c. The roads _____ peace become narrow.
3. a. The road _____ peace is filled _____ obstacles.
   b. The student is the future _____ all life_____ earth.
   c. A great responsibility rests _____ his shoulders.

    d. He must be strong and faithful _____ the ideals which are expressed _____ the word: STUDENT.

4. a. Many travel _____ study _____foreign countries.

    b. They come_____ strange people and new customs.

    c. The students have the opportunity to talk _____various issues.

    d. They find their place side- _____ -side _____ others.

5. a. The effect_____the written argument has proven successful.

    b. Violence and brutality are replaced _____ the ability _____ walk the road _____communication and understanding.

    c. Just ahead _____us lies our goal.

IV. *Grammar and Syntax [Points of Interest]*

A. Types of Paragraphs

1. *Introductory*—The first paragraph is especially important in a composition. It serves a double purpose: while it tells the reader about the **subject** to be discussed, the opening paragraph also makes him want to **read on**. Thus, the introductory paragraph is an **interest-catching** device. It serves the composition in the same way a topic sentence serves the paragraph: as a summary of the composition.

> Example: Thieves found out they were wrong when they thought they could make some money by stealing a car from the Madrid Motor Co.

2. *Main*—Generally, the main paragraph of a composition further discusses the ideas introduced in the first paragraph. The main paragraph provides **support** for the general ideas expressed in the introduction; it is, therefore, related to the topic sentence. The main paragraph may be one of the longest of the composition; however, it is its **subject matter** that is most important, not its length. The main paragraph may also be considered the **body of a composition**.

> Example: Police disclosed Tuesday that none of the local car lots would buy the stolen car. And, Inspector Barry Salinas said, the thieves became so desperate they even tried to sell the car back to the Madrid Motor Co.

3. *Concluding*—The concluding paragraph can do several things: it can **summarize** the preceding material; it may **introduce** a new point while it re-

states the old; it may be a quiet ending to a composition or it may be made exciting and full of suspense.

> Example: When the Madrid Motor Co. refused to purchase the
> car, Salinas said, the thieves took it to Highway Ridge
> where they dumped it over an embankment.

B.   Arrangement and Order of Paragraphs

1. *Interrelationship*—Just as it is important to maintain a clear order within the paragraph itself, so it is within a composition where one follows a definite interrelationship of paragraphs. An effort must be made, therefore, to clearly state a **central idea** that bears a definite **relationship** to preceding as well as following paragraphs.

2. *Transition*—Oftentimes, an entire paragraph will serve as a transition. A transitional paragraph comes at a point in a composition where the writer wants **to start** on a new idea because he has finished with the previous **main point**. Various transitional devices are used to connect paragraphs. In addition to the transitional phrases introduced in Chapter VII, one may also use such transitional devices as **pronouns**, which make reference to items used previously, or the **repetition** of the very **item already mentioned**.

C.   Coherence and Proportion

In order to present a coherent picture of a composition the paragraphs are linked together by some common devices: **key words** are repeated, **pronouns** are used in reference to preceding nouns, **transitional connectives** are used (Chapter Seven), and reference is made to a common subject, event, or a significant idea that appears in previous as well as in the succeeding paragraphs. By using such devices, a writer weaves paragraphs into a unified composition.

There is no rule governing the length of a paragraph. Generally, a paragraph consists of more than one sentence but should not exceed a full page.

> Example: Thieves found out they were wrong when they
> thought they could make some money by stealing a
> car from the Madrid Motor Co.
>
> Police disclosed Tuesday that none of the local car
> lots would buy the stolen car. And, Inspector Barry
> Salinas said, the thieves became so desperate they
> even tried to sell the car back to the Madrid Motor Co.
>
> When the Madrid Motor Co. refused to purchase the
> car, Salinas said, the thieves took it to Highway Ridge

where they dumped it over an embankment.

D.　Exercises

1. The following paragraphs are part of a newspaper article dealing with one **main idea**: the rains came too late for the Midwest drought. Arrange the paragraphs **chronologically**, beginning with the **introductory**, followed by the **main** and **concluding** paragraphs.

The full effect of the drought, which some experts call the worst since the Dust Bowl days of the 1930s, has yet to come to light. But thus far it is clear that the drought will be felt around the world.

The long-awaited rains have fallen over the drought-parched midlands, rattling through the dried and yellowed leaves of what was to be a bumper corn crop but producing little more than mud on the heat-cracked farmland.

The great drought of 1974 appears to have ended with the rainfall, but consumers and farmers may have to live with its effects for years to come.

In many parts of the corn belt, the rains were too late to help the crops—in some cases the rain just made things tougher.

2. Arrange the paragraphs chronologically by placing the **introductory**, **main**, and **concluding** paragraphs in order. Give a **headline** title.

Police disclosed Tuesday that none of the local car lots would buy the stolen car. And, Inspector Barry Salinas said, the thieves became so desperate they even tried to sell the car back to the Madrid Motor Co.

Thieves found out that they were wrong when they thought they could make money by stealing a car from the Madrid Motor Co.

When the Madrid Motor Co. refused to purchase the car, Salinas said, the thieves took it to Highway Ridge where they dumped it over an embankment.

3. The following two newspaper articles lack either the **introductory** or **concluding** paragraphs. Select the missing paragraph from those given following the article. Rewrite the completed articles.

a. Pronounced dead at the scene was Shay Lessing, according to the Department of Public Safety investigators.

The mother, Mary Lessing, 20, of Castroville, was listed Monday in satisfactory condition at Methodist Hospital in San Antonio.

The DPS officers said the auto left the roadway and plunged down a bridge abutment to the bottom of a creek bed.

b. Reduced speed limits, triggered by the energy shortage, are getting more credit than they deserve for the reduction of highway deaths in the nation, according to the American Medical Association.

"We hope, of course, that the nationwide downward trend continues, but we believe that the savings in lives cannot honestly be attributed to any great extent to the reduction in the speed limit," Lee N. Hames, AMA director of safety education, said in an editorial in the current edition of the Journal of the American Medical Association.

While speed limits have been reduced to 55 miles per hour, Hames said that most traffic deaths occur at speeds under 55.

A two-year-old child was killed and the mother seriously injured in a one-car accident at 11 p.m. Sunday about one mile east of here on U.S. 90.

V.   *Idea Recognition*

Copy from the MODEL COMPOSITION the sentences expressing:

A.   what characteristic all roads have . . .

_____

B.   toward what people constantly move . . .

_____

C.   what will finally be achieved . . .

_____

D.   by whom it will be achieved . . .

_____

E.   who will be bound by one goal . . .

_____

F.   what the proposition will be . . .

_____

G.   what the student is . . .

_____

H.   why the roads to peace become narrow . . .

_____

I.   how the roads compare to arteries . . .

_____

J. what the road to peace is filled with . . .

_____

K. what kind of obstacles they are . . .

_____

L. what can be cleared and widened . . .

_____

M. how the roads can be widened . . .

_____

N. what the student will realize . . .

_____

O. what rests on the student's shoulders . . .

_____

P. what the student will be faithful to . . .

_____

Q. who travels to foreign countries . . .

_____

R. what kind of observation most students make . . .

_____

S. what opportunities the students have . . .

_____

T. what they argue for . . .

_____

U. what has proven successful . . .

_____

V. what we remember . . .

_____

W. what is mightier than the sword . . .

_____

X. until when the students will repeat their attempts . . .

_____

Y. what lies just ahead . . .

_____

VI. *Vocabulary Enrichment*

A. Paraphrasing

The following are **paraphrases** (rephrasing expressions or words without changing their meaning) of expressions or words found in the narrative. Write the expressions found in the MODEL COMPOSITION that correspond to the paraphrases below.

> Example: have a particular characteristic
> **they are similar to one another**

1. make space available _____
2. they are in motion _____
3. become fond of _____
4. countries getting together _____
5. having one purpose _____
6. a desire for tranquility _____
7. peaceful attempts become harder _____
8. they don't allow the flow _____
9. there are many difficulties _____
10. he has to do it _____
11. spoken thoughts _____
12. behave differently _____
13. find out the same thing _____
14. talk about things they disagree on _____
15. they get "with it" _____
16. discuss how to make things better _____
17. go on trying _____

B. Lexical Units

Select the word (phrase) from the following list that best completes each of the sentences below. You may use a selection more than once.

> Example: All roads have one **particular characteristic** in common.
> They all **accommodate** many people.

committed	misunderstanding	approaching
ignorance	unite	good will
enlightened action	destruction	strong

1. People are constantly **moving toward** a goal. They are _____ it.

2. Peace can be achieved by **students of all nations**. The students will _____ .

3. The students will be **bound** by one goal. They will be_____to this goal.

4. The road to peace becomes **corroded** and **narrow**. There is no peace because of _____ and_____ .

5. The **obstacles** can be **cleared**. Understanding comes through _____ and _____ _____ .

6. The student has a great **responsibility**. He must be _____.

7. The students argue to **improve** things. They want to prevent _____.

C. Related Words

Use related words to rewrite the following sentences without changing their meanings. Change the underlined word(s). Make further changes if necessary.

> Example: to move (v.)   moving (v.)
> People are constantly **moving**.
> People **move** constantly.

to strive (v.)	to last (v.)	to unite (v.)
striving (adj.)	lasting (adj.)	uniting (v.)
		united (adj.)

to propose (v.)	similar (adj.)	to discuss (v.)
proposing (v.)	similarly (adv.)	discussing (v.)
proposition (n.)		discussion (n.)

to improve (v.)	to observe (v.)
improvement (n.)	observation (n.)

1. The goal is dear to every **striving** individual. _____
   _____

2. This is the road to a **lasting** peace. _____
   _____

3. Students of all nations will **unite** into a World University Community.
   _____

4. This Community is composed of students who **propose** to maintain peace. _____
   _____

5. Most students make a **similar observation about** other people. _____

6. The students have an opportunity **to discuss** many issues. _____

7. They argue **for the improvement** of things. _____

VII.   *Steps in Writing*

A.   Add new words and revise the sentence to suit the changes indicated in parentheses.

> Example: **All roads have** one particular characteristic in common. (every)
> **Every road has** one particular characteristic in common.

1. **They accommodate** people of all nationalities. (she)

2. **All these people** are moving toward a goal. (every man)

3. **Understanding** leads to complete peace. (it)

4. **The student is** the life-giving substance for the world. (students)

5. The **roads** to peace **become** narrow. (road)

6. **He is** the **statesman** of tomorrow. (they)

7. **Many travel** to study in foreign countries. (the student)

8. **Their** reactions are varied. (her)

9. **Most** students make a similar observation. (all)

10. **The students** have an opportunity to discuss many issues. (I)

11. **They** soon **find their** place. (we)

12. **They argue** for the improvement of things. (she)

_____

13. The **effect** of the written argument **has** proven effective. (effects)

_____

14. **We** will repeat **our** attempts. (I)

_____

15. **We are** free to practice what **we learn**. (he)

_____

16. **We take** this road. (she)

_____

17. Ahead of **us** lies **our** goal. (him)

_____

B.   Opposites

Use the opposites to rewrite the following sentences. Make the necessary changes to suit the new sentences. You may use a word more than once.

> Example: particular–usual
> All roads have one **particular** characteristic in common.
> All roads have one **usual** characteristic in common.

successful	common	improvement	mightier	winding
faithful	lasting	delay	sick	long
strong	narrow	complete	natural	quickly
ignorance				

1. People have **different** physical features. _____

_____

2. All people are **slowly** moving forward. _____

_____

3. The road to a **partial** peace is **brief**. _____

_____

4. They want a **temporary** peace. _____

_____

5. The roads to peace become **wide** through **knowledge**. _____

_____

6. The arteries **quicken** the flow of **healthy** blood. _____

_____

7. There are **unnatural** obstacles. _____

_____

8. Man must be **weak** and **unfaithful**. _____

_____

9. They argue for the **destruction** of things. _____

_____

10. The written word has proven **unsuccessful**. _____

_____

11. The word is **weaker** than the sword. _____

_____

12. The road is **straight**. _____

_____

VIII. Comprehension

A. Complete the sentence and add as many related sentences as you can find in the MODEL COMPOSITION.

> Example: All roads have one particular characteristic in common; **they accommodate people of all nationalities, creeds and different physical and psychological features, in their walks of life.**

1. All these people are constantly moving toward a goal _____

_____

_____

2. A community composed of students _____

_____

_____

3. The student is, _____

_____

_____

4. The roads to peace become narrow and corroded _____

_____

_____

5. The road to peace is filled with obstacles, _____

_____

_____

6. The student of the world will realize _____

_____

7. Many travel _____

8. Yet, most students make a similar observation _____

9. The students have an opportunity _____

10. The effect of the written and spoken argument _____

11. Physical violence and brutality are replaced _____

12. We will repeat our attempts _____

13. We take this road, _____

B. Answer each question with a complete sentence.

Example: What has one particular characteristic in common?
All roads have one particular characteristic in common.

1. What do the roads have in common? _____

2. What do all people do? _____

3. Which goal became dear to every striving individual? _____

4. What do we believe? _____

5. Into what will the students unite? _____

6. Which great goal will the student Community be bound to? _____

7. What is the student for the world? _____

8. How do the roads to peace become? Why? _____

9. What kind of obstacles fill the road to peace? _____

10. How can the obstacles be cleared? _____

11. What will the student realize? _____

12. On whom rests a great responsibility? _____

13. How will the student be? _____

14. Why do students travel to foreign countries? _____

15. Where do they come to? _____

16. How are the students' reactions? _____

17. What are the students' observations? _____

18. What do the students argue about? _____

19. What has proven successful? _____

20. What do we remember? _____

21. Until when will we repeat our attempts? _____

22. What do we want to practice within the walls of the Universe? _____

IX.   *Commentary on Model*

A.   Using the key words and phrases from the MODEL COMPOSITION, write your own composition consisting of three paragraphs on a related topic. Make sure there is an **introductory**, a **main** and a **concluding** paragraph.

roads	people	different
toward a goal	lasting peace	all nations
road to peace	knowledge	ignorance
filled with obstacles	cleared and widened	constantly moving
future of all life	the student	faithful to ideals
strange people	reactions different	travel
common to all mankind	opportunity to discuss	side-by-side
violence and brutality	communication	understanding
bonds of helplessness	University	Universe
state of peace and love		

B.   1. Write about the **lesson** you've learned from the "Dream."

2. Write about the points you agree with.

3. Write about the points you disagree with.

4. Give an appropriate title to your composition.

X.   *Composition*

A.   Select one topic below and write a composition consisting of three paragraphs (**introductory**, **main** and **concluding**).

1. An intelligent person is biased.

2. An educated person has no prejudice..

3. People can achieve more through discussion than by fighting.

4. Having fun is more important than working.

5. Working is more important than having fun.

B. Write a short **composition** (three paragraphs) about the picture below. Remember to include all composition elements.

Chapter Nine

Types of
Composition

Words to remember:

Essay writing:

>*analytical*
>*interpretive*
>*knowledge of subject*
>*careful planning*

Correspondence:

>*formal – informal – business –*
>*heading – inside address – salutation –*
>*body – complimentary close – signature*

Term paper:

>*bibliography card – note card –*
>*outline – title page*

I.　*Model Composition*

A.　An Essay on Education

1. From the earliest days of our lives, we are involved, one way or another, in some type of education. As small children, we are taught "right" from "wrong" by our parents. The family circle is our first lesson in getting along with others.

2. When we reach school age, our parents enroll us in a public school. This event begins our "formal" education. It is called "formal" because we learn things in school that our parents were unable to teach us. We learn to read, to write and to count. This "formal" education continues throughout our lifetime regardless of the profession or vocation we select for ourselves.

3. Finally, there is a third type of education that everyone undergoes in one's lifetime. This education is based on the experiences of everyday living. Some people regard this type of education as the most significant. One fact remains true: the education of an individual is a never-ending process.

B.　Correspondence

1. *Formal*

> John Q. Citizen
> 782 Sandalwood St.
> San Antonio, TX　78226
> September 21, 1974

The President
The White House
Washington, D. C.

Dear Mr. President:

a. The enclosed headline in our local newspaper is the reason for my writing this letter. It is written without the presumption that my advice is being sought but in the firm belief that as a citizen I may be of help in a small way.

b. This letter is written in a sincere effort to lighten the burdens of the awesome task of the office you have assumed: the task of moral reconstruction, reconciliation and a beginning of a meaningful bipartisan dialogue. All this would be greatly served by your selection of a Democrat as your Vice-Presidential choice.

c. Your selection, I feel, would show the nation that a time of unprecedented cooperation on the political scene has come, nationally as well as internationally. This act will bring us a new era of reason.

d. In the final analysis, the decision is a difficult one to reach. Each man must decide the course of his own destiny. You, Mr. President, decide not only yours but that of our great nation. Congratulations and best wishes.

Yours very truly,

John Q. Citizen

John Q. Citizen

2. *Writing to a Friend*

August 30, 1974

Dear Jim,

a. *The most unusual thing happened this week in San Antonio. The rains came. We've had ten, yes, ten inches of rain in the last thirty-six hours. It certainly brings relief to the parched grass and other greenery. But the consistent rainfall has also created flash floods all over the city. As you know, we have no drainage, and the streets became rivers in no time at all.*

b. *You should have seen the cars floating in four to five feet of water at the intersection of San Pedro and Hildebrand under the railroad bridge! The drivers were rescued in the nick of time, but the cars were a total loss.*

c. *The downpour brought the only excitement to our otherwise easy-going life. We are all well and hope to hear the same from you. Can't wait for your Christmas visit with us. We are counting the days till your arrival. We all miss you.*

d. *Well, there it is. Best of luck to you, and don't forget to write. Keep well and enjoy yourself.*

As always,

Bill

3. *Applying for a Job*

Newspaper Advertisement: Wanted, English Editor, Southern Publishing Co. Indicate experience and salary expected. Vacancy beginning August 15. Write P.O. Box 547, Reston, Virginia 22090

> Isaac Salinas
> P.O. Box 711
> Lackland, A. F. Base
> San Antonio, TX 78284
> June 18, 1974

Southern Publishing Co.
P. O. Box 547
Reston, Virginia 22090

Gentlemen:

a. I saw your advertisement for English Editor in the *Library Journal* of June 6, 1974, and I wish to apply for the position. I have now completed three years of military duty with the U. S. Air Force, and I could start work in the immediate future.

b. During my term of duty with the Armed Forces I worked for the Information and Education Department. My formal training was in journalism and English and I have done a lot of work connected with news releases and military publications. I am very interested in editorial work and would like to pursue this line of endeavor. If I get the job you advertised, I would expect the salary that usually goes with the position of English Editor.

c. I am enclosing a personal data sheet with details about my educational background and work experience. I will be glad to furnish more information upon request, or come for a personal interview. I can be reached at the above address, or by phone at area code 512-342-8430, any evening after six o'clock. Expecting your kind reply.

> Sincerely,
>
> *Isaac Salinas*
>
> Isaac Salinas

C.   Mini-Term Paper

THE CASE OF THE HOT DOG:

A U. S. Favorite

by

Rachel Maya

1. It is a small sausage of finely chopped and seasoned meat, held in a cylindrical covering;[1] most people call this sausage the Hot Dog. Through the years, the Hot Dog has become a favorite with grownups and children of the U. S. of America. Its great popularity is due to the convenience it offers in its preparation.[2] Without much effort this tasty meal can be prepared for large crowds at big sport events or at sidewalk food stands.

2. The tasty sausage was originally called Hot Dog by the U. S. cartoonist Tad Dorgan in 1909.[3] The name was probably an allusion to the popular belief that sausage was made of dog meat. This sausage is served hot in a long, soft roll, with mustard, relish, etc.[4]

---

[1] *The Funk and Wagnalls Encyclopedia* (New York, N.Y. Unicorn Publishers, Inc., 1952), Vol. 29, p. 10797.

[2] Carl Cook, *The World of the Hot Dog* (Chicago, La Cuisine Publishing Co., 1945), p. 45.

[3] *Webster's New World Dictionary* (New York and Cleveland, The World Publishing Co., 1970), p. 679.

[4] *Ibid.*, p. 679.

D.   Composition by Degrees

1. a. Copy the title of the essay. _____

_____

   b. Copy the sentence that tells what we learn as children. _____

_____

   c. Copy the sentence that tells about our first lesson in "getting along."

_____

2. a. Copy the sentence that tells what happens when we reach "school age." _____

_____

  b. Copy the sentence that tells why school education is called "for-mal." _____

_____

  c. Copy the sentence that tells what we learn in school. _____

_____

3. a. Copy the phrase that tells us what the **third** type of education is.

_____

  b. Copy the sentence that tells what we base the third education on.

_____

  c. Copy the sentence that tells what some people think about the third type of education. _____

_____

E.   Exercises

1. The following is a mini-essay on a specific topic. Read carefully, then supply a proper title.

TITLE: _____

Mental health is as important to an individual as his physical strength. The secret of life lies in finding a way whereby the mental and physical can live in harmony within one individual. Only then can a person function without much difficulty and cope with daily problems effectively.

It has been said that the power of meditation gives a person the needed energy to become a well-adjusted individual. Therefore, one must devote a part of one's life concerned with the spiritual aspects of being. One must remember that food provides nourishment for a healthy body, but meditation elevates the spirit.

2. The following letters lack the **inside address**, the **forms of address**, and the **complimentary close**. Read the letters carefully then supply proper **inside address**, the **forms of address**, and an appropriate **complimentary close**. In doing so, identify the nature of the letters.

Rebeca Solomon
927 Mt. Kisco
San Antonio, Texas 78213
September 27, 1974

  a. _____

_____

_____

———————————————

———————————————

This is written in response to your ad of September 21, 1974, which appeared in our local newspaper concerning an opening for a position of executive secretary.

I have worked in this line of endeavor for over seven years, and I quit my last position only because my family moved to your city. The experiences of the last seven years have been great, and I feel that I want to continue the same line of work.

At your request, references will be forwarded to you. Attached is a personal data sheet for your convenience. Hoping to hear from you soon.

——————————————— ,
Rebeca Solomon

September 10, 1974

b. ———————————————

Though I haven't written for a long time, I've missed you a lot. I keep wondering how you are and how the world is treating you. Things are generally okay here; I only wish my rheumatism would stop annoying me.

I do hope you can come for the weekend of October 14th. We will be expecting you.

———————————————

———————————————

II.   Words in Context

A.   From the list of words and phrases preceding each section fill in each blank space. You may use a selection more than once. Also, you may use more than one word in one blank space.

1. help   enclosed   Dear   advice   letter
   way   belief   citizen   presumption   local
   reason

_____ Mr. President:

The _____ headline in our _____ newspaper is the _____ for
my writing this _____ . It is written without the _____ that my
_____ is being sought but in the firm _____ that as a _____ I may be
of _____ in a small _____ .

2. burdens   sincere   task   lighten
   presently   reconciliation moral   bipartisan
   choice   selection   greatly

This letter is written in a _____ effort to _____ the
_____ of the awesome _____ of the office which you have
_____ assumed; the _____ of reconstruction, _____ and
a beginning of a meaningful _____ dialogue. All this would be _____
served by your _____ of a Democrat as your Vice-Presidential _____ .

3. time   show   selection   cooperation
   nationally   act   political   reason
   era

Your _____ , I feel, would _____ the nation that a
_____ of unprecedented _____ on the _____ scene has come,
_____ as well as internationally. This _____ will bring us a
new _____ of _____ .

4. man   reach   final   great   congratulations
   destiny   decide   course   decision   wishes

In the _____ analysis, the _____ is a difficult one to
_____ . Each _____ must decide the _____ of his own
_____ . You, Mr. President, _____ not only yours but that of
our _____ nation. _____ and best _____ .

B.   Make the necessary change(s) when you substitute the new element into
your sentence.

Example: **She writes** a letter to a friend. (They)
         They write a letter to a friend.

1. a. The most unusual **thing** happened this week. (things)

   _____

   b. **It brings** relief to the grass and greenery. (they)

   _____

   c. The **rain has** created flash floods. (rains)

   _____

   d. **The streets** became rivers. (they)

   _____

2. a. The **drivers were** rescued. (driver)

   _____

   b. The **cars were** a total loss. (car)

   _____

3. a. The downpour brought **the only** excitement. (some)

   _____

   b. **I'm** waiting for your Christmas visit. (we're)

   _____

   c. **We're** counting the days. (she's)

   _____

   d. **We all** miss you. (I)

   _____

III. Structures (Key words [phrases] for composition)

A. Use the following key words (phrases) to make complete sentences. You may consult the MODEL COMPOSITION.

> Example: earliest days / we / involved
> From the earliest days we are involved.

1. a. saw / advertisement / *Library Journal* _____

   _____

   b. wish / apply / position _____

   _____

   c. have / completed / military duty _____

   _____

   d. start / work / immediate future _____

   _____

2. a. during / term of duty / Armed Forces / worked _____

_____

b. training / was / journalism _____

_____

c. have / a lot / work / with news _____

_____

d. am / interested / editorial work _____

_____

e. like / pursue / endeavor _____

_____

f. get / job / advertised _____

_____

g. expect / salary / goes / position _____

_____

3. a. enclosing / personal data / details _____

_____

b. will / furnish / information / request _____

_____

c. come / personal / interview _____

_____

d. be / reached / address _____

_____

e. expecting / reply _____

_____

B. Supply the missing **preposition** for each blank space. You may consult MODEL COMPOSITION C.

Example: I can be reached __(at)__ the above address.

1. It is a small sausage _____ finely chopped meat.
2. It is held _____ a cylindrical covering.
3. _____ the years the Hot Dog has become a favorite _____ grownups and children of the U.S. _____ America.
4. It's popularity is due _____ the convenience it offers _____ its preparation.
5. This tasty meal can be prepared _____ large crowds _____ big sports events or _____ sidewalk food stands.
6. The tasty sausage was originally called Hot Dog _____ the U.S.

cartoonist Tad Dorgan _____ 1909.

7. The name was an allusion_____ the popular belief that sausage was made _____ dog meat.

8. This sausage is served hot _____ a long roll.

IV. Grammar and Syntax [Points of Interest]

A. **Essay** writing requires the student to follow three basic steps:

1. decide what type of essay it is to be—**analytical** (determining the nature of an object), or **interpretive** (explaining the nature of an object).

2. have a **detailed knowledge** of the subject.

3. **plan** carefully and write with clarity without repetition and waste.

There is no rule governing the length of an essay. Usually, when there is nothing more to say about the **selected** topic, the essay ends.

Example: (Analytical essay)

On Playing Chess

Chess is played on a checkerboard set. The black corner is to the player's left. The pieces are arranged on the first and second rank facing each opponent. Each piece will face a piece of equal rank across the board. There are two sets of pieces: black and white. Each consists of a King, a Queen, a Bishop, a Rook (or Castle), a Knight and eight Pawns. The white Queen will be on white; black Queen on black. The board is the field of battle in a chess game.

Black

White

[NOTE: Because the King is designated "K" on the board, the Knight goes by the letter "N."]

The King is the most important chess piece. The game ends when the King is captured; this is called "checkmate." Usually, the King is the largest piece on the board.

The Queen is the most powerful chess piece. She is the second largest piece on the board. The Bishop wears a hat and is usually a little smaller than the Queen. The Rook (Castle) resembles a tower. He is usually as tall as the Knight. The Knight resembles the head of a horse. He is important in the game, because he is the only piece that can jump over the other pieces.

Finally, there is the Pawn, the foot soldier. He is the smallest of the chess pieces. However, when the Pawn reaches the opposite side of the board he can become a Queen, a Rook, a Bishop, or a Knight.

Movements of the different pieces vary. The **King** moves one square in any direction.[1] He must not move into a square where he would be in "check" for he might be captured by an enemy piece. When the King is attacked, he must defend himself by moving out of danger ("check"). If the King cannot escape his attacker(s) and he is lost, it is "checkmate," and the game is lost. The **Rook** moves back and forth, left and right, on a straight line. He can go as many squares as he chooses as long as he does not jump other pieces. The **Bishop** moves back and forth on the diagonal line as many squares as he chooses as long as he does not jump other pieces. The Bishop always remains on the field he occupied at the beginning of the game: black or white. The **Queen** can move like the Bishop or the Rook—any place in a straight or diagonal line as long as she does not jump other pieces. The **Knight** moves two squares in one direction and one square at right angles. He can jump over his own or his opponent's men. The **Pawn** moves forward one square at a time except on his first move when he can move two squares forward. The Pawn can capture his opponent diagonally one square to the left or right.

---

[1] Illustrations of the various movements follow the essay.

King Movement

Rook Movement

Bishop Movement

Knight Movement

Queen Movement

Pawn Movement

B.   Correspondence

1. **A formal** letter is usually written to someone not intimately known. It is written for reasons of introducing oneself or one's thoughts regarding a specific question. In writing a formal letter, one should always keep in mind the position of the person to whom the letter is addressed. The letter should be written in a sincere, easy-going and natural manner. The impression the writer will make upon the person to whom the letter is written depends to a great extent upon the appearance, form and tone of the letter.

The following is a sample of a formal (personal) letter:

a. (The **heading** gives the **date** and the full address of the writer.)

John Q. Public, Ph.D.
222 Shadwell Dr.
San Antonio, TX 78228
September 21, 1928

b. The Honorable John Tower
United States Senate
Washington, D. C.

(The **inside address** contains the name and postal address of the person to whom the letter is written.)

c. My dear Senator:

(The **salutation** addresses itself to the person receiving the letter. It sets the tone of the letter.)

d.   It has long been my understanding that all citizens are regarded as equals under the laws of our nation. Recent developments in Washington lead me to believe that my view has been based on a myth or mere speculation.

I am writing to you, as my representative voice in the affairs of our country, to act in rectifying some deficiencies of our judicial system. All citizens are counting on the honesty and sincerity of some public figures. The trust we have placed in your hands is a responsibility, not a privilege to be taken for granted.

(The **body** of the letter tells in simple, short sentences the thoughts the writer wishes to make known to the person for whom the letter is intended.)

e. Yours very truly,   (The **complimentary close** should be appropriate to the person(s) addressed.)

      John Q. Public

f. John Q. Public, Ph.D.   (The written **signature** is placed between the complimentary close and the writer's **typed** name.)

2. An **informal** letter is usually written to someone intimately known. It tells about people and events with which the writer and the person to whom the letter is addressed are familiar. One writes an informal letter when one feels the need to **converse** with another person. The letter, therefore, is more like a conversation than a formality; it is **sincere, original** and **easy-going**. It is usually written in **longhand**. The example is a letter inviting a friend to visit and attend a concert.

San Antonio, September 21, 1974

My dear Rosi,

Though I wrote you last night, there was one item I forgot to mention; this Friday night there is a guest concert of the Boston Pops at the City Auditorium. I bought two reserved seat tickets a month ago, so this is to invite you to come and spend the entire weekend with us. You've always wanted to hear this famous orchestra, and now you'll have the opportunity to do so.

After a week long fight with the flu, I'm finally getting better. Hopefully, by the time you get here I'll be well. Please call to let me know if you decide not to come. If I don't hear from you before Friday, I'll assume that you'll be here for the concert. See you soon.

Love,

Bill

REPLY:

Houston, September 23, 1974

Dear Bill,

I was sorry to hear about your illness, but happy to learn that you are almost well. Of course, I'll be delighted to visit with you for the weekend. I'm looking forward to the concert. It's a real treat! Just what I've always dreamed about. See you Friday. Thanks.

Love,

Rose

3. A **business** letter that is written with clarity tells in a **direct** manner what it is that the writer wants. The writing must also be **polite** and **natural** because it will tell the person(s) who will receive it much about the writer's character and personality.

Example:

April 15, 1974

(date)

William W. Flower
P. O. Box 1145
Stamford, Conn. 06904

(The **heading** gives first the **date** then the full address of the writer.)

Director of Sales
Meridian Publishers
P. O. Box 1495
San Antonio, Texas 78284

(The **inside address** gives the title and the full address of the person to whom the letter is written.)

Dear Sir:

(Salutation)

It has been one year and several months since the publication of my book *Technical Swahili* and there has been no quarterly sales report sent to me.

(The **body** of the letter tells clearly, in ordinary English, the writer's reason of forwarding the letter.)

This letter is written to inquire about the total number of sold copies thus far. You will find the clause covering this requirement on page three of our Publication Agreement.

Hoping to hear from you soon.

Sincerely yours,

(The **complimentary close** must be appropriate to the person re-

William W. Flower   ceiving the letter.)

William W. Flower   (The **signature** is written in hand
                                     above the **typed** signature.)

C.   Term (Research) Paper

A **term (research) paper** is simply a composition assignment. The term paper is usually longer than any other written assignment. The student selects the **main idea** for the paper, but the paper itself is based on what others have said about the subject. Therefore, a term paper requires **research**.

1. *Bibliography Card*—Research is carried out because facts are needed for the term paper. Each source of information must be recorded on a separate **bibliography card**. The collected bibliography cards will later serve as **footnotes** and bibliography. There are many types of bibliography cards. Here are examples of two such cards:

a. A book by **one author**:

Author	Mostar, Gerhart Herrmann
Title	*A Critical Profile*
Essential Data (give page unless the entire book was read)	The Hague, Mouton, n.v. Publishers, 1968

b. A book with **no author's name** given:

Title	*Webster's New World Dictionary*
Essential Data	New York and Cleveland, The World Publishing Company, 1970, p. 121

For more information about arranging footnotes and bibliographies the teacher will inform the students which **style manual** the students will use.

2. *Note Card*—It is important to take good **notes** when additional sources are found and consulted. The notes should be written clearly on cards similar to those for bibliography. The note is a **summary** of the source material, or a direct quote, which will be included directly in the paper.

The following is a sample note card:

Heading

Source

Notes and page reference in
left margin

> ***The Lively Art**, Payne*
> *200 "A note may be a summary*
> *in your own words of an au-*
> *thor's meaning or it may be*
> *a quotation taken directly*
> *from his work. If it is a quo-*
> *tation, it must be **exactly** as*
> *it appears in print and must*
> *be enclosed in quotation*
> *marks."*

The following is a **bibliography card** for the preceding **note card**.

Author

Title

Essential Data

> Payne, Lucile Vaughan
>
> *The Lively Art of Writing*
>
> Chicago, Follet Educational Cor-
> poration, 1965, p. 14.

After all notes are taken the student is ready to write the paper. Certain steps should be followed in writing the term paper.

a. Arrange **note cards** according to subject. Cards with information about the same subject must be together.

b. Prepare an **outline** following the **note card** arrangement.

c. Write the **first draft** of the paper.

d. **Reread** and **revise** the composition carefully.

D.   The **title page** presents a short, general statement containing information about the paper. The following is a sample TITLE PAGE:

THE VARIOUS WAYS OF

PREPARING SALADS

by

Katinka Mostar

Chemistry 406, Hour 5

May 3, 1974

E.   Exercises

1. Following are samples of **bibliography cards**. Examine them carefully and identify the missing item(s).

    a. A book by one author:

> Croft, Kenneth (Editor)
>
> *Readings on English as a Second Language.*
>
>   Winthrop Publisher, Inc.

    b. A book with no author's name given:

> *The Columbia Viking Desk Encyclopedia*
>
> New York, Viking Press

2. Arrange the "steps" for term paper writing in their proper order.

    a. Write the first draft of the paper.   ————

    b. Arrange note cards according to subject.   ————

    c. Reread and revise the composition.   ————

    d. Prepare an outline.   ————

V. *Idea Recognition*

Copy from MODEL COMPOSITION (I.A.) the sentences expressing:

A.   when our involvement in education begins . . .

_____

B.   what we are taught as small children . . .

_____

C.   what our first lesson in getting along with others is . . .

_____

D.   what our parents do when we reach school age . . .

_____

E.   what the enrollment in school begins . . .

_____

F.   when education is called "formal" . . .

_____

G.   how long "formal" education continues . . .

_____

H.   what the third type of education is . . .

_____

I.   what we base this education on . . .

_____

J.   how some people regard this education . . .

_____

K.   what fact remains true . . .

_____

VI. *Vocabulary Enrichment*

A.   **Paraphrasing**

The following are **paraphrases** (rephrasing expressions or words without changing their meaning) of expressions or words found in the narrative. Write the expressions found in the MODEL COMPOSITION (B.1.) which correspond the paraphrases below.

> Example: our local newspaper
> **a newspaper published locally**

1. that's why I'm writing _____

2. I don't suppose you want my advice _____

3. I strongly believe I can help _____

4. I sincerely want to help _____

5. the job of moral change _____

6. of making up _____

7. beginning a two-party conversation _____

8. it would help to get a Democrat Vice-President _____

9. a cooperation as it never before existed _____

10. not only at home, but also abroad _____

11. after all, it's tough to make up your mind _____

12. everyone has to decide what he wants to do _____

B. Lexical Units

Select the word (phrase) from the following list that best completes each of the sentences below. You may use a selection more than once.

> Example: From the earliest days of our lives **we are learning** right from wrong. We are **involved** in **some type of education.**

| "formal" | teach | get along |
| process | experience | each day |

1. The **family circle** is our **first lesson**. We learn to _____with others.

2. When we reach school age, we **attend public school**. This event begins our _____ education.

3. We **learn many things** in school. Our parents were unable to _____ us those things.

4. The "formal" education **continues throughout** our lifetime. Education is a never ending _____ .

5. What we **learn** in **life** is important too. We call this _____ .

6. **Experience** is a significant **part** of education. We add to this type of education _____ _____ .

C. Related Words

Use related words to rewrite the following sentences without changing their meanings. Change the underlined word. Make further changes if necessary.

Example: involved (v.)   involvement (n.)
We are **involved** in education.
Education **is an involvement.**

health (n.)	mental (adj.)	physical (adj.)
healthy (adj.)	mentally (adv.)	physically (adv.)
meditation (n.)	to adjust (v.)	to elevate (v.)
to meditate (v.)	adjusted (adj.)	elevating (adj.)
effective (adj.)		
effectively (adv.)		

1. It is important for an individual to be mentally **healthy.** _____
_____

2. A person must find a way to harmonize **mentally** and **physically.** ____
_____

3. One must find an **effective** way to function and cope with daily problems. _____
_____

4. When we **meditate**, we get the needed energy. _____
_____

5. He is a well-**adjusted** individual. _____

6. Meditation is **elevating** to the spirit. _____

VII. Steps in Writing

A.   Add new words and revise the sentence to suit the changes indicated in parentheses.

> Example: Food provides nourishment for **the body**. (us)
> Food provides nourishment for **us**.

1. **This is written** in response to your ad. (I am writing)

   _____

2. The ad appeared **in our newspaper**. (there)

   _____

3. **I have** worked as a secretary for seven years. (she)

   _____

4. **I quit my** last position because **I** was ill. (he)

   _____

5. **My family** moved to your city. (we)

   _____

6. **I feel** that **I want** to continue. (she)

   _____

7. At **your** request, **references** will be forwarded. (his, they)

   _____

8. Attached **is a** personal data **sheet** for you. (are)

   _____

B.   Opposites

Use the opposites to rewrite the following sentences. Make the necessary changes to suit the new sentences. You may use a word more than once.

> Example: least–most
> The King is the **least** important chess piece.
> The King is the **most** important chess piece.

largest	smaller	most	capture(d)

| always | important | smallest | tall |
| opponent | lost | beginning | different |

1. The game ends when the King is **liberated**. _____
_____

2. Usually, the King is the **smallest** piece on the board. _____
_____

3. The Queen is the **least** powerful chess piece. _____
_____

4. She is the second **smallest** piece on the board. _____
_____

5. The Bishop is usually a little **larger** than the Queen. _____
_____

6. The Rook is usually as **short** as the Knight. _____
_____

7. The Knight is **unimportant** in the game. _____
_____

8. The Pawn is the **largest** of the pieces. _____
_____

9. Movements of the **same** pieces vary. _____
_____

10. When the King cannot escape, the game is **won**. _____
_____

11. The Bishop **never** remains on the field he occupied in the **end** of the
game. _____
_____

12. The Pawn can **liberate** his opponent diagonally. _____
_____

13. The Pawn can capture his **friend**. _____
_____

VIII.   Comprehension

A.   Complete the sentence and add as many related sentences as you can find in the MODEL COMPOSITION (I.A.).

Example: The King is the most important **chess piece**.

The game ends when the King is captured; this is called "checkmate."

1. From the earliest days _____

_____

_____

2. As small children, _____

_____

_____

3. When we reach school age, _____

_____

_____

4. It is called "formal" because _____

_____

_____

5. This "formal" education continues _____

_____

_____

6. Finally, there is a third type _____

_____

_____

7. Some people regard this type _____

_____

_____

8. One fact remains true: _____

_____

_____

B. Reply with complete sentences. MODEL COMPOSITION (B.2.).

Example: What happened in San Antonio?
The most unusual thing happened.

1. What came to San Antonio? _____

_____

2. How many inches of rain were there? _____

_____

3. For how many hours did the rain fall? _____

_____

4. What does the rain bring? _____

5. What did the rainfall create? _____

6. Why did the streets become rivers? _____

7. Where were the cars floating? _____

8. Why did the cars float? _____

9. What was situated above the flooded streets? _____

10. How were the drivers rescued? _____

11. What happened to the cars? _____

12. What did the downpour bring? _____

13. How is life in San Antonio? _____

14. How is the writer of the letter? _____

15. What does the writer wait for? _____

16. What is the writer counting? _____

17. What does the writer wish for Jim? _____

IX. *Commentary on Model*

A. Using the key words and phrases from the MODEL COMPOSITION (E.1.), write a short composition on a related topic. Be sure to supply three bibliography cards containing sentences used in your composition. Give your composition an appropriate title.

mental health	secret of life
physical strength	live in harmony
function without much difficulty	cope with problems
power of meditation	gives needed energy
well-adjusted	be concerned with the spiritual
nourishment of body	elevate the spirit
individual	person

B. 1. Write about the **lesson** you've learned from MODEL COMPOSITION 1.A.

2. Write about the points you agree with.

3. Write about the points you disagree with.

4. Give an appropriate title to your composition.

X. *Composition*

A. 1. Prepare five **bibliography cards** of books you select.

2. Prepare five **note cards** from the above books.

B. Select one topic below and write a short (100 words) paper about it. Remember to include **bibliography** cards, **note** cards, and an **outline**.

1. jazz music	5. "the most typical thing I know about my country"
2. skyscrapers	
	6. American music
3. cowboys	
	7. American architecture
4. silent movies	

C. Rewrite the letter in E.2.b. in the **we** person. Make all appropriate changes.

D. Describe the activities of the individuals in the picture below.

Chapter Ten

Style,
Form and Structure

Words to remember:

Style: Formal—Informal

Simplicity — Sincerity — Directness

Form		Shape	
Poetry	*Prose*	*Triangle*	*Square*
Letters	*Dialogue*	*Circle*	*Pentagon*
		odd shapes	

Structure

simple sentence — compound sentence
beginning — middle — end
introduction — body — conclusion

I. *Model Composition*

A. Style is What You Make of It

1. Everyone has heard of "Ernest, the show off." From his flashy Cadillac convertible down to the polished tips of his expensive shoes, Ernest pretended to know how to live and spend his money. This was his style. His friends said that Ernest invented the expression "life style" so that others would imitate him. But that was only hearsay.

2. The truth was, no one really wanted to imitate Ernest. The language he used was like his flashy personality. He used cheap, vulgar words, even when he attempted to describe simple events. He was unable to think simply and directly. He lacked orderliness and sincerity.

3. Ernest did not realize that all his flashiness and money spending were fruitless habits. He tried in vain to impress those who would stay and listen to him till early morning hours. Ernest began to suspect that his "friends" stayed with him only to amuse themselves. The more aware Ernest became that his suspicions were true, the less capable he was of controlling his habits. Soon, because of the excessive spending, Ernest became a poor man.

4. It was only then that Ernest recognized the foolish ways of his past. He began reading with a passion. His job allowed him to spend his afternoons in the public library, where he became a familiar figure to all who worked there. His desire for knowledge was endless, as though he wished to make up for all the years of intellectual inactivity.

5. The change Ernest underwent was obvious. He dressed modestly and learned to be orderly and sincere. The economy car he drove was sufficient means of transportation. He became thrifty and less generous in spending his money foolishly. Ernest had fewer friends now, but those he had did not secretly amuse themselves at his expense. As his values changed, so did his style.

B. Composition by Degrees

1. a. Copy the phrase that tells about Ernest's character. _____

_____

   b. Copy the sentence that tells what Ernest pretended to know. _____

_____

   c. Copy the phrase Ernest "invented." _____

_____

2. a. Copy the sentence that tells how Ernest talked. _____

_____

   b. Copy the sentence that tells what Ernest lacked. _____

_____

3. a. Copy the sentence that tells about Ernest's habits. _____

_____

   b. Copy the sentence that tells what Ernest tried in vain. _____

_____

   c. Copy the sentence that tells why Ernest's friends stayed with him. _____

_____

   d. Copy the sentence that tells why Ernest was "less capable of controlling his habits." _____

_____

   e. Copy the sentence that tells why Ernest became poor. _____

_____

4. a. Copy the sentence that tells what Ernest recognized. _____

_____

   b. Copy the sentence that tells where Ernest spent his afternoons. _____

_____

   c. Copy the sentence that tells to whom Ernest became a "familiar figure."

_____

   d. Copy the phrase that tells about Ernest's "desire for knowledge." _____

_____

5. a. Copy the sentence that tells how Ernest dressed. _____

_____

   b. Copy the phrase that tells what type of car Ernest drove. _____

_____

   c. Copy the phrase that tells what the car was for Ernest. _____

_____

   d. Copy the phrases that tell how Ernest became in spending. _____

_____

   e. Copy the sentence that tells how his friends were. _____

_____

II. Words in Context

A.   From the list of words preceding each section fill in each blank space. You may use a selection more than once. Also, you may use more than one word in one blank space.

1. expensive	polished	pretended	heard
style	said	others	imitate
flashy	hearsay	spend	invented

Everyone has _____ of "Ernest, the show off." From his _____
Cadillac convertible, on down to the _____ tips of his _____ shoes, Ernest
_____ to know how to live and _____ his money. This was his
_____. His friends _____ that Ernest _____ the expression "life style"
so that _____ would _____ him. But this was only _____ .

2. wanted   cheap   language   truth
   flashy   simple   attempted   unable
   orderliness   directly   sincerity

The _____ was, no one really _____ to imitate Ernest. The _____
he used was like his _____ personality. He used _____ , vulgar words, even
when he _____ to describe _____ events. He was _____ to think simply and
_____ . He lacked _____ and _____ .

3. aware   suspect   realize   flashiness
   suspicions   amuse   morning   fruitless
   excessive   poor   controlling   less
   impress   listen

Ernest did not _____ that all his _____ and money spending were
_____ habits. He tried in vain to _____ those who would stay and
_____ to him till early _____ hours. Ernest began to _____ that
his "friends" stayed with him only to _____ themselves. The more
_____ Ernest became that his _____ were true, the _____ capable he was of
_____ his habits. Soon, because of his _____ spending, Ernest became
a _____ man.

4. ways   public   reading   recognized
   desire   familiar   allowed   passion
   endless   make up   intellectual

It was only then Ernest _____ the foolish _____ of his past. He began
_____ with a _____ . His job _____ him to spend his afternoons in the _____
library, where he became a _____ figure to all who worked there. His
_____ for knowledge was _____ , as though he wished to _____ _____
for all the years of _____ inactivity.

5. modestly   drove   orderly   change   generous
   means   thrifty   sincere   underwent   foolishly
   style   secretly expense   friends   values

The _____ which Ernest _____ was obvious. He dressed _____ and
learned to be _____ and _____ . The economy car he _____ was a

sufficient＿＿＿＿＿ of transportation. He became＿＿＿＿＿ and less ＿＿＿＿＿ in spending his money＿＿＿＿＿. Ernest had fewer ＿＿＿＿＿ now, but those he had did not ＿＿＿＿＿amuse themselves at his ＿＿＿＿＿. As his ＿＿＿＿＿changed, so did his＿＿＿＿＿ .

B.   Make the necessary change(s) when you substitute the new element into your sentence.

> Example: Style is what **you** make of it. (they)
>   Style is what **they** make of it.

1. a. **Everyone has** heard of "Ernest the show off." (They)

   _____

   b. **Ernest** pretended to know how to live. (she)

   _____

   c. This was **his** style. (our)

   _____

2. a. No one really wanted to imitate **Ernest**. (me)

   _____

   b. The language **he** used was flashy. (I)

   _____

   c. **He was** unable to think simply and directly. (we)

   _____

3. a. **His** flashiness and spending were fruitless habits. (their)

   _____

   b. **He** tried to impress **his** friends. (I)

   _____

   c. **He** was unable to control **his** habits. (she)

   _____

   d. Soon, **Ernest** became a poor **man**. (she)

   _____

4. a. **Ernest** recognized the foolish ways of **his** past. (we)

   _____

   b. **His** job allowed **him** to read many books. (my)

   _____

   c. **His** desire for knowledge was endless. (her)

   _____

   d. **He** wished to make up for all the years of intellectual inactivity. (I)

   _____

III. *Structures (Key words [phrases] for composition)*

A. Use the following key words (phrases) to make complete sentences. You may consult the MODEL COMPOSITION.

> Example: style / what / make / it
> Style is what you make of it.

1. a. everyone / heard / Ernest _____

   b. flashy convertible / expensive shoes / Ernest / pretended his / style
   _____

   c. friends / said / Ernest / invented / "life style" _____

   d. this / was / hearsay _____

2. a. no one / wanted / imitate _____

   b. Ernest / language / used / flashy _____

   c. he / used / vulgar / attempted / simple events _____

   d. he / unable / think / simply / directly _____

   e. he / lacked / orderliness / sincerity _____

3. a. Ernest / realize / flashiness / fruitless habits _____

   b. he / tried / in vain / impress _____

   c. friends / stayed / amuse / themselves _____

   d. he / unable / controlling / habits _____

   e. Ernest / became / poor _____

4. a. only / then / Ernest / recognized / foolish ways _____

b. began / reading / passion _____

c. job / allowed / spend / afternoons / library _____

d. became / familiar figure / to all / worked _____

e. desire / knowledge / endless _____

f. wished / make up / the years / inactivity _____

5. a. change / Ernest / underwent / obvious _____

   b. dressed / modestly / learned / be / orderly _____

   c. economy / car / drove / means / transportation _____

   d. became / thrifty / less generous _____

   e. Ernest / fewer / friends _____

   f. values / changed / did / style _____

B. Supply the missing **preposition** for each blank space. You may consult the MODEL COMPOSITION.

Example: Style is what you make ___(of)___ it.

1. Everyone has heard _____ "Ernest, the show off."

2. _____ his flashy Cadillac convertible, on down _____ the polished tips _____ his expensive shoes, Ernest pretended to know how to live.

3. He tried to impress those who would listen _____ him.

4. His friends stayed _____ him to amuse themselves.

5. Soon, _____ the excessive spending, Ernest became a poor man.

6. He recognized the foolish ways _____ his past.

7. He began reading _____ a passion.

8. He spent his afternoons _____ the Public Library.

9. Ernest became a familiar figure _____ all.

10. His desire _____ knowledge was endless.

11. He wished to make up _____ all the years of intellectual inactivity.

12. The car was a means _____ transportation.

13. He was less generous _____ spending.

14. They did not amuse themselves _____ his expense.

IV.   Grammar and Syntax [Points of Interest]

A.   Style

This book has guided the student through the initial steps of learning how to write. **Style, form** and **structure** are considered the finer points of writing.

Language changes from day to day. Words assume new meaning under different circumstances. Two commonly known levels of usage are Standard English (formal and informal) and sub-standard English (slang). Standard English is the kind of language spoken and written by most educated people in English-speaking countries. Sub-standard English is the language spoken in less educated social circles. Therefore, before experimenting with words and their varied usage, the student should try to follow the basic principles of Standard English.

Style varies from writer to writer, from one period to another, and from one subject matter to another. It is generally agreed that the most effective style of writing is demonstrated with **simplicity, sincerity** and **directness**. The simpler and more direct the writing, the easier it is for the reader to follow and understand it. Effective writing does not rely on tricks or adornments. It should be thrifty. The following thought expresses what is meant by "thrifty" writing:

WORDS

If I could express a thought in one word,
I would refuse to use more . .
Were I able to cut down a tree at one stroke,
I would strike but once . .
but
When running the risk of being misunderstood,
or leaving things unaccomplished,
I would spare neither words nor deeds . . .

From the style of the following excerpts, the reader should be able to identify their source:

1. And Pharoah said unto Joseph: "See, I have set thee over all the land of Egypt." And Pharoah took off his signet ring from his hand, and put it upon Joseph's hand, and arrayed him in vestures of fine linen, and put a gold chain about his neck. And he made him to ride in the second chariot which he had; and they cried before him: "Abrech"; and he set him over all the land of Egypt. And Pharoah said unto Joseph: "I am Pharaoh, and without thee shall no man lift up his hand or his foot in all the land of Egypt."

GENESIS, 41:44

2.   THE FOX AND THE LION
One day a fox who had never seen a lion was walking in the woods. Suddenly the king of beasts stood in the path before him, and the fox almost died of fright. He ran away and hid himself in his den. The next time he came upon the lion he merely paused to allow the majestic beast to pass by. The third time they met, the fox boldly approached the lion and passed the time of day with him and asked after his family's health.

APPLICATION: FAMILIARITY BREEDS CONTEMPT.

Aesop's Fables

3. When in the course of human events, it becomes necessary for one people to dissolve the political bonds which have connected them with another, and to assume among the powers of the earth, the separate and equal station to which the Laws of Nature and of Nature's God entitle them, a decent respect to the opinions of mankind requires that they should declare the causes which impel them to the separation.
---------We hold these truths to be self-evident, that all men are created equal, that they are endowed by their Creator with certain unalienable Rights, that among these are Life, Liberty and the pursuit of Happiness.----------

In Congress, July 4, 1776
The Unanimous Declaration of the
Thirteen United States of America

B.   Form and Structure

Form and **structure** are related; they are blood cousins. Furthermore, they cannot be separated from **style**, directly or indirectly. After deciding on a topic, the writer must make up his mind about the **form** of his writing. Is it going to be a **poem**? Is it better to express the thoughts and ideas in **prose** (narrative) form? Some writers have selected to write entire novels in the form of an **exchange** of **letters** between the characters. Others prefer the form of **dialogue**. There are many forms of writing. The most popular form is **prose** because it seems the easiest way to express thoughts clearly.

No matter what the form of a composition may be, to be complete it will have a **beginning** (introduction), a **middle** (body) and an **end** (conclusion); this is called the **structure** of writing. How **long** or how **short** a sentence is may also be regarded as the structure of writing. Simple, declarative sentences will be easier to understand, or to write, than the more complicated sentences.

Form is to writing what **shape** is to **space**. We have familiar shapes:

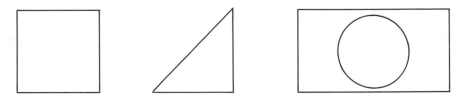

and we have some unfamiliar shapes:

Whenever the form of writing becomes unfamiliar, it is more difficult to understand than the more popular way of expressing the **same** thought.

Examples:

(Poetry)   *A GEM*
                A gem loses its value in its abundance,
                so does a word when misused --

demand and value are conversely consistent,
they both decrease when abused . . .

(Prose)   *A GEM*
When there are too many gems, they are worthless,
because the more we have of something, the less
we appreciate it. The same rule applies to words:
they are worthless when they are misused.

The following are two ways of expressing the **same** thought; the first is in the form of poetry, the second as a composite of shapes and words.

1.   *LIVE FOR DEATH . . .*

smoke . . . smoke . . . smoke . . .
fog . . . fog . . . fog . . .
smog . . . smog . . . smog . . .
pollution . . .
                    suffocation . . .
slow death . . .

danger is the staff
of life for
the new generation . . .

desperately seeking
nirvana, the magic wand
called weed . . . acid . . . LSD . . .

forgetting . . .

pollution . . . suffocation . . .
a gradual, but certain
escape in death . . .

2. *LIVE FOR DEATH*

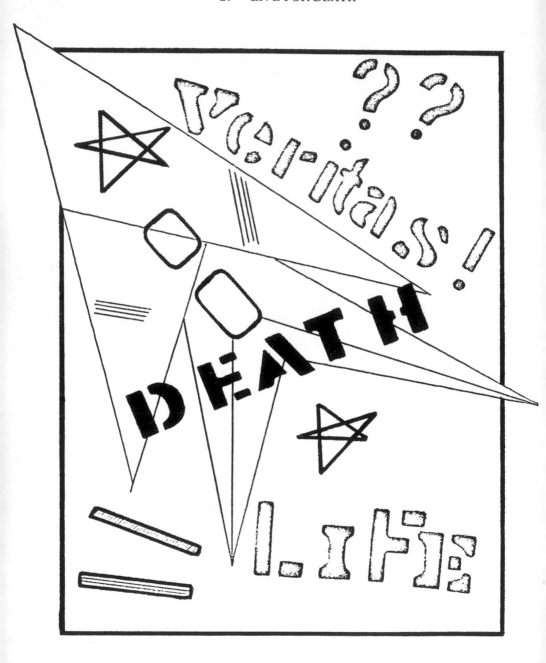

C.   Exercises

1. Following are short excerpts composed in different **styles** of writing. Indicate which of the passages is written in **formal** and which in **informal** English.

> a. Several nights ago, we went out to hear a musical performance. I was ill at ease and could not quite adjust to the situation. I did get to enjoy the evening eventually because the musicians were delightful. _____
>
> b. A couple of nights past, we got to go to a musical show. I didn't feel good. It was like I didn't fit into it. But finally I did have a good time because the music was great. _____
>
> c. Mary sat near the window contemplating the landscape. The sun was setting on the horizon, there was generally no noise coming from the outdoors, and the children were in bed for the night. Although she had never been to Europe, Mary would have liked to visit with her relatives there. They had not seen each other for over two years. However, with all the household duties and financial obligations, the outlook for an extensive vacation in the near future seemed very unlikely. She sighed heavily. _____
>
> d. Mary was sitting near the window thinking about the outdoors. It was sundown. It was quiet out there. The children were already bedded down for the night. Though she'd never been to Europe, she'd like to pay a visit to her relatives there. But she had too many things to do at home. With all her obligations, she couldn't see making plans for a long vacation. There'd be no chance for that soon. She felt sorry for herself. _____

2. Following are examples of several **forms** of writing. Indicate the **form** of writing for each of the examples. Rewrite examples a, b, c and d in **narrative** form.

> a.   SENSATIONS
> To experience sensations and feel
> emotions of the **other** sex
> is like trying to sense the desperation
> of a sparkling snowflake as it
> melts upon a warm surface . . .

b.   THE RING
women are the diamonds, men
the platinum which lends them support—
united they ornament one another,
apart, their purpose seems vague .. rather ...

c.   THE LIE
the truth spoken meekly
is less convincing than
a brightly colored lie
shouted from the rooftops ...

d.   VIRTUE
man's virtue lies not in his
recognition of the false
but in the service of the true ...

e.   HALFWAY MARK
enough enthusiasm in
any endeavor is a halfway
mark to achievement ...

f.   A FRAGMENT
The girl fought quietly but desperately against his searching, strong
fingers. Forster held her tightly with one arm around her slim waist.
With the other, he bent her over backward till she was prostrate on
top of the crate. The crate squeaked treacherously under the weight,
and Bronia continued in her attempt to escape from under Forster's
massive frame. Within the next few moments, in the quivering light
of the furnace we observed the most mystifying proceedings.[1]

g.

"Roman, Menasha was right," I whispered, "we build and they
destroy. Now we destroy as well. We *are* like them!"

"Don't be a fool. We fight the best way we know how," Roman
replied.

"It's not that simple," I insisted. "Seems like everything is crazy
and we are at the center of it!"

"Yes, so?" My brother cut off the discussion.

---

[1] Samelson, William. *All Lie in Wait*. Englewood Cliffs, N.J., Prentice-Hall, Inc.,
1969, p. 87.

"Good-bye, Tuviah!"
"Take care, Pinhas!"[2]

V.   *Idea Recognition*

Copy from the MODEL COMPOSITION the sentences expressing:

A.   who has heard of Ernest . . .

_____

B.   what kind of a car Ernest drove . . .

_____

C.   what kind of shoes Ernest wore . . .

_____

D.   what Ernest pretended to know . . .

_____

E.   which expression Ernest was supposed to have invented . . .

_____

F.   why others would imitate Ernest . . .

_____

G.   what kind of language Ernest used . . .

_____

H.   how Ernest's personality was . . .

_____

I.   what Ernest's personality was compared to . . .

_____

J.   why Ernest was unable to think simply and directly . . .

_____

K.   what Ernest did not realize . . .

_____

L.   whom Ernest tried to impress . . .

_____

M.   why his friends stayed with Ernest . . .

_____

N.   when Ernest became less capable of controlling his habits . . .

_____

O.   why Ernest became a poor man . . .

_____

[2]*Ibid.*, p. 211.

P.　when Ernest recognized the foolish ways of his past . . .

_____

Q.　what his job allowed him to do . . .

_____

R.　to whom Ernest became a familiar figure . . .

_____

S.　how his desire for knowledge was . . .

_____

T.　why his desire for knowledge was so great . . .

_____

U.　what was obvious . . .

_____

V.　how Ernest dressed . . .

_____

W.　what Ernest drove . . .

_____

X.　how Ernest became . . .

_____

Y.　how his friends were . . .

_____

VI.　*Vocabulary Enrichment*

A.　Paraphrasing

The following are **paraphrases** (rephrasing expressions or words without changing their meanings) of expressions or words found in the narrative. Write expressions found in the MODEL COMPOSITION which correspond to the paraphrases below.

Example: a way of life — **style**

1. a boastful person _____

_____

2. a very fancy car _____

_____

3. he made believe _____

_____

4. others would do the same _____

_____

5. not really the truth _____

_____

6. he tried to talk about things _____

_____

7. only to make fun _____

_____

8. to do what he wished _____

_____

9. he spent more than he had _____

_____

10. everybody knew him _____

_____

11. he wanted to learn _____

_____

12. for lack of learning _____

_____

13. the car took him places _____

_____

14. he saved money _____

_____

15. not as many friends _____

_____

B.   Lexical Units

Select the word (phrase) from the following list that best completes each of the sentences below. You may use a selection more than once.

Example: Ernest drove a **flashy** car. He was a **show off**.

imitate	cheap	style	vulgar
orderliness	controlling	excessive	amused
reading	sufficient	familiar	hearsay
impress			

1. Ernest **pretended to know how to live**. That was his _____

2. They **said** that he invented the expression "life style." But that was

only _____ .

3. He wanted people to do the **same** as he did. But no one really wanted to _____ his style.

4. The language he used was like his **flashy personality**. The words were _____ and _____ .

5. He was unable to **think simply**. He lacked _____ .

6. He **spent** a lot of money. Ernest tried to _____ his friends.

7. His friends **listened** and **laughed**. They _____ themselves.

8. The more **aware** he became of his friends' behavior, the less capable he was of _____ his habits.

9. Ernest became a **poor** man. This happened because of _____ spending.

10. Ernest had a **desire** to **learn**. He began _____ with a passion.

11. He **spent** many **hours in the library**. Ernest became a _____ figure to those who worked there.

12. He bought a **small** car. It was _____ means of transportation.

C. Related Words

Use related words to rewrite the following sentences without changing their meaning. Change the underlined word(s). Make further changes if necessary.

Example: to make (v.)   making (n.)
Style is what you **make** of it.
Style is of your own **making**.

to invent (v.)	to imitate (v.)	to use (v.)
invention (n.)	imitation (n.)	use (n.)
to attempt (v.)	orderliness (n.)	sincerity (n.)
attempt (n.)	orderly (adj.)	sincere (adj.)
to amuse (v.)	to desire (v.)	to spend (v.)
amusing (adj.)	desire (n.)	spending (n.)
to suspect (v.)		
suspicion (n.)	excessively (adv.)	
suspicious (adj.)	excessive (adj.)	

1. Ernest's style was his own **invention**. _____
_____

2. No one wanted to become an **imitation** of Ernest. _____

3. Ernest made **use** of vulgar language. _____

4. He made an **attempt** to think simply. _____

5. He wasn't **orderly** and **sincere**. _____

6. Ernest's ways were flashy and he was **amusing** to friends. _____

7. Ernest **suspected** all his friends. _____

8. He became poor because he would **spend excessively**. _____

9. Ernest **desired** knowledge. _____

VII.   Steps in Writing

A.   Add new words and revise the sentence to suit the changes indicated in parentheses.

> Example: Style is what **you** make of it. (we)
> Style is what **we** make of it.

1. **His** flashy Cadillac was expensive. (my)

2. **Ernest** knew how to spend money. (we)

3. This **was his** style. (has been, my)

4. **His** friends said that **he** invented the expression. (my, I)

5. **He** had a **flashy** personality. (she, good)

6. **He** used **cheap, vulgar** words. (they, nice, exceptional)

7. **He lacked** orderliness and sincerity. (she, enjoyed)

8. **They** listened to **him** till early morning. (we, them)

_____

9. **His friends** amused **themselves**. (we, ourselves)

_____

10. **He** became a poor **man**. (she, woman)

_____

11. **He** began reading many **books**. (I, stories)

_____

12. **He** spent **his** afternoons in the library. (she, her)

_____

13. **His** desire for knowledge was endless. (my)

_____

14. **Ernest** had fewer friends now. (Jane)

_____

15. As **his** values changed, so did **his** style. (my)

_____

B. Opposites

Use the opposites to rewrite the following sentences. Make the necessary changes to suit the new sentences. You may use a word more than once.

Example: flashy — modest
He drove a **modest** car.
He drove a **flashy** car.

vulgar	dull	spend(ing)	cheap	no one
less	early	lacked	simply	fruitless
poor	fewer	great	foolish(ly)	a lie
capable	sufficient			

1. **Everyone** has heard of Ernest. _____

_____

2. He wore **polished, expensive** shoes. _____

_____

3. Ernest pretended to know how to **save** his money. _____

_____

4. This was **truth**. _____

_____

5. He used **expensive, refined** words. _____

6. He was unable to think **in a complicated way**. _____

7. He **possessed** orderliness and sincerity. _____

8. His flashiness and spending were **fruitful** habits. _____

9. They stayed with him till **late** morning hours. _____

10. He was **incapable** of controlling his habits. _____

11. Soon, he became a **rich** man. _____

12. He recognized his **wise** ways. _____

13. His desire for knowledge was **small**. _____

14. The economy car he drove was **insufficient** means of transportation. _____

15. He was **more** generous in saving. _____

16. He spent his money **wisely**. _____

17. Ernest had **more** friends now. _____

VIII.   Comprehension

A.   Complete the sentences and add as many related sentences as you can find in the MODEL COMPOSITION.

> Example: From his flashy Cadillac convertible, **down to the polished tips of his expensive shoes, Ernest pretended to know how to live and spend his money.**

1. His friends said that Ernest invented the expression "life style." _____

2. The truth was, _____

_____

3. He was unable to think _____

_____

4. Ernest did not realize _____

_____

5. He tried in vain to impress _____

_____

6. Ernest began to suspect _____

_____

7. Soon, because of the excessive spending, _____

_____

8. It was only then _____

_____

_____

9. His job allowed him _____

_____

10. His desire for knowledge _____

_____

11. The change which Ernest underwent _____

_____

12. Ernest had fewer friends now, _____

_____

13. As his values changed, _____

_____

B.   Answer each question with a complete sentence.

Example: How is your style?

My style is what I make of it.

1. Who has heard of Ernest? _____
   _____

2. What kind of a car did Ernest drive? _____

3. What kind of shoes did he wear? _____

4. What did Ernest pretend to know? _____
   _____

5. Who said that Ernest invented the expression "life style"? _____

6. Was it the truth that Ernest invented the expression "life style"? _____
   _____

7. What was the truth? _____
   _____

8. How was the language Ernest used? _____
   _____

9. What kind of words did he use? _____
   _____

10. Why was Ernest unable to think simply and directly? _____
    _____

11. What did Ernest try in vain? _____

12. Why did his friends stay with him? _____
    _____

13. What happened when Ernest became aware that his suspicions were
    true? _____
    _____

14. What caused Ernest to become poor? _____
    _____

15. How did Ernest change when he became poor? _____

16. What did he begin doing? _____
    _____

17. Where did Ernest spend his afternoons? _____
    _____

18. To whom did he become a familiar figure? _____

19. Why was his desire for knowledge endless? _____

20. What was the change that Ernest underwent? _____

21. What type of car did he drive now? _____

22. How were his friends now? _____

23. Why did his style change? _____

IX. Commentary on Model

A. Write about the **lesson** you've learned from the MODEL COMPOSITION.

B. Write about the points you agree with.

C. Write about the points you disagree with.

D. Give an appropriate title to your composition.

X. Composition

A. Using the key words and phrases from the MODEL COMPOSITION, write your own composition on a related topic. Use the style of the MODEL COMPOSITION.

"show off"	pretend	spend	thrifty
"life style"	cheap	vulgar	orderly
fruitless	suspect	friends	amuse
control	habits	excessive	poor
library	read	knowledge	change
generous	simple	sincere	suspicions
recognize	economy	values	amuse

B. Select one topic and express your ideas about it in any **form** of writing.

1. Desire for knowledge comes to poor people.

2. The value of learning is great.

3. Ignorance is better than knowledge.

4. A tree is a beautiful thing of nature.

5. Nature is full of miracles.

C.   Describe the picture below in any **style** of writing you choose.

Appendix

I.   *The Principal Parts of Irregular Verbs*

A complete list of **irregular** verbs and their principal parts can be found in every good dictionary. Included here for the convenience of the reader are some more commonly used irregular verbs and their principal parts.

The first principal part of a verb is the **infinitive** (simple form of the verb), the second principal part is the **past tense** and the third principal part is the **past participle**. We don't ordinarily consider the **present participle** to be one of the principal parts because it is always regular and is quite simple to construct; i.e., be = being, go = going, have = having, do = doing, etc.

Infinitive	Past Tense	Past Participle
awake	awaked, awoke	awaked
be	was, were	been
become	became	become
begin	began	begun
bleed	bled	bled
blow	blew	blown
break	broke	broken
bring	brought	brought
build	built	built
buy	bought	bought
catch	caught	caught
choose	chose	chosen
come	came	come
deal	dealt	dealt
dig	dug	dug
dive	dived, dove	dived
do	did	done
draw	drew	drawn
dream	dreamt, dreamed	dreamt, dreamed
drink	drank	drunk
drive	drove	driven
eat	ate	ate
fall	fell	fallen
feel	felt	felt
fight	fought	fought
find	found	found
fly	flew	flown
forget	forgot	forgot, forgotten
forgive	forgave	forgiven
get	got	got, gotten
give	gave	given
go	went	gone

grow	grew	grown
hang	hung, hanged	hung, hanged
have	had	had
hear	heard	heard
hide	hid	hidden
hold	held	held
keep	kept	kept
know	knew	known
lay	laid	laid
leave	left	left
lie (recline)	lay	lain
lie (tell a lie)	lied	lied
lose	lost	lost
make	made	made
meet	met	met
pay	paid	paid
read	read	read
run	ran	run
say	said	said
see	saw	seen
sell	sold	sold
send	sent	sent
shoot	shot	shot
sing	sang	sung
sit	sat	sat
sleep	slept	slept
speak	spoke	spoken
speed	sped	sped
spend	spent	spent
stand	stood	stood
steal	stole	stolen
swim	swam	swum
take	took	taken
teach	taught	taught
tell	told	told
think	thought	thought
throw	threw	thrown
understand	understood	understood
wake	waked, woke	woke
wear	wore	worn
win	won	won
wind	wound	wound
withdraw	withdrew	withdrawn
write	wrote	written

II. *Parts of Speech*

This brief glossary serves the purpose of a rapid review of the parts of speech in their most common usage. Most of the material described here has been discussed in detail within appropriate chapters of the book. Some definitions are followed by typical examples of usage.

A.   The NOUN is a word that names a **person, place, thing, quality, state of being** or **action**. The noun has **number, gender** and **case**. It is used in every complete sentence as a **subject**. There are concrete (physical) nouns and there are abstract (idea) nouns. Examples: concrete = table, book, bread; abstract = happiness, love, thought.

B.   The PRONOUN is a **substitute for a noun** or a noun equivalent. There are several kinds of pronouns:

1. The Personal Pronoun—I, you, he, she, we, etc.

2. The Demonstrative Pronoun—this, that, these, those

3. The Indefinite Pronoun—anybody, somebody, many, each, one, some, etc.

4. The Relative Pronoun—that, who, which, etc.

5. The Interrogative Pronoun—who?, which?, what?, etc.

6. The Reflexive Pronoun—myself, yourself, etc.

C.   The VERB usually tells something about the **action** of the subject. The verb may also express **condition** or **state of being**. There are four types of verbs:

1. The Transitive Verb—tells what the subject does to an object, a person, a thing or a place.

2. The Intransitive Verb—does not need an object to complete its meaning. The intransitive verb tells something about what the subject is.

3. The Linking Verb—is a special kind of intransitive verb. It functions as a connection between a **subject** and a **predicate complement**.

4. The Auxiliary Verb—helps other verbs to express **action** or **condition** or **state** of **being**.

D.   The ADJECTIVE describes a noun or a pronoun. It is neither singular nor plural. The adjective can compare one noun to another. Adjectives are classified according to their function:

1. The Descriptive Adjective—**describes** the noun or the pronoun.

2. The Limiting Adjective—**limits** or **defines** the meaning of the noun or the pronoun.

E.   The ARTICLE comes in two forms:

1. The Definite Article—the

2. The Indefinite Article—a, one, an

The is used with a singular or plural noun; **a** is commonly used with a singular noun.

F.   The ADVERB modifies and changes in some way the meaning of a **verb**, an **adjective** or another **adverb**. The following are the most commonly used types of adverbs:

1. The Adverb of TIME—answers the question **when?**, i.e., **recently, soon, immediately, now, then, first, later, always, never, often**, etc.

2. The Adverb of PLACE—answers the question **where?**, i.e., **here, away, west, everywhere**, etc.

3. The Adverb of MANNER—answers the question **how?**, i.e., **quickly, slowly, badly, well**, etc.

G.   A PREPOSITION shows the **relationship** between a **noun** or a **pronoun** and another word. The preposition generally expresses the relation of one thing to another in regard to:

1. **time**—i.e. **before** noon, **after** the holidays, **until** midnight, etc.

2. **manner**—i.e. **with** happiness, **by** mistake, etc.

3. **position** or **place**—i.e. **at** the airport, **at** home, **in** the house, **on top of** the mountain, etc.

H.   A CONJUNCTION **connects** words or groups of words. There are two types of conjunctions:

1. Coordinating—joins equal grammatical units, i.e. Mary **and** Kip **and** Susan **and** Joe, Don **or** Sheila, etc. I'll tell you **if and when** I get ready. He'll do it at nine A.M. **or** after ten.

2. Subordinating—introduces a clause that depends on a **main** or independent clause; i.e.

   a. **time (as, before, when, while**, etc.)

   b. **reason** or **cause (because, since, why**, etc.)

   c. **supposition** or **condition (although, unless, whether. . . .or**, etc.)

I.   The INTERJECTION serves to express **emotion**. It is generally followed by an **exclamation mark (!)**, i.e. OH! HELP! HURRAH! etc.

Index

A

B

C

D

H

Hamlet, 6
Hebrew, 13
Houston, Sam, 46
Hyphen, 57, 68

I

Idea recognition, 49
Imperative, 31
Independent clause, 40
Indian, 13
Indicative, 43
Interrogative, 31, 41, 43, 46
Intransitive (verb), 41
Italy, 19

J

John, 2

K

Kernel

L

Latin, 13*ff.*, 19*ff.*
Letters, 231
Lexical Units, 4, 10, 51, 73-74, 101, 126, 148, 170, 194, 223, 247
Lie, the, 244
Linking (verb), 41

T

V

MAKE

THEM

CRY

ALSO BY SMITH HENDERSON

Fourth of July Creek

MAKE THEM CRY

A NOVEL

SMITH HENDERSON AND
JON MARC SMITH

ecco

An Imprint of HarperCollins*Publishers*

This is a work of fiction. Names, characters, places, and incidents are products of the authors' imaginations or are used fictitiously and are not to be construed as real. Any resemblance to actual events, locales, organizations, or persons, living or dead, is entirely coincidental.

MAKE THEM CRY. Copyright © 2020 by Smith Henderson and Jon Marc Smith. All rights reserved. Printed in the United States of America. No part of this book may be used or reproduced in any manner whatsoever without written permission except in the case of brief quotations embodied in critical articles and reviews. For information, address HarperCollins Publishers, 195 Broadway, New York, NY 10007.

HarperCollins books may be purchased for educational, business, or sales promotional use. For information, please email the Special Markets Department at SPsales@harpercollins.com.

Ecco® and HarperCollins® are trademarks of HarperCollins Publishers.

A hardcover edition of this book was published in 2020 by Ecco, an imprint of HarperCollins Publishers.

FIRST ECCO PAPERBACK EDITION PUBLISHED 2021

Designed by Paula Russell Szafranski

Library of Congress Cataloging-in-Publication Data
Names: Smith, Jon Marc, author. | Henderson, Smith (Joshua Smith), author.
Title: Make them cry: a novel / Jon Marc Smith and Smith Henderson.
Description: First edition. | New York: Ecco, [2020] | Identifiers: CCN 2019049282 (print) | LCCN 2019049283 (ebook) | ISBN 9780062825179 (hardback) | ISBN 9780062825186 (paperback) | ISBN 9780062825193 (ebook)
Subjects: GSAFD: Suspense fiction.
Classification: LCC PS3619.M58847 C66 2020 (print) | LCC PS3619.M58847 (ebook) | DDC 813/.6—dc23
LC record available at https://lccn.loc.gov/2019049282

21 22 23 24 25   LSC   10 9 8 7 6 5 4 3 2 1

MAKE
THEM
CRY

CHAPTER ONE

HARDBALL

Each breath was like ice water falling on hot coals in her throat, cold Michigan air turning to steam. But Diane Harbaugh didn't stop or slow down. She craved the pain. It was the entire point.

The burn toughens you, Hardball, she told herself.

She grimaced out a grin, remembering the nickname. She'd been Diane Hardball as far back as middle school. The track coach called her that. So did the crosstown rivals in high school. The debate team. Even her cohort 1Ls at UCLA Law. She liked it.

Run, Hardball. Run.

She pushed on through the grimy snow in the bottoms and frozen marshes. By spring the flies and mosquitoes would hatch in the millions from these Upper Peninsula bogs, but now the ice crunched under the pressure of her snowshoes like a saltine. Someone else might have pictured the crust as some sweet confection, a frosting or a sugar cookie, but to Harbaugh it was salt, a savory, she didn't go for desserts, not really, not even chocolate, why did men assume women loved chocolate so damn much, we don't, not all of us, not the strong ones. We like to feel the flume of our lungs too. We like to run up against something. We like good cold air, a good hurt, the tang of salt.

She'd been using herself up like this the whole time at the cabin. It was just her and Bronwyn, a true vacation, days of nothing on the schedule. She burst with every step, she couldn't get enough exercise, enough life. The sweat that soaked her thermals. The pride in the pushing through. The pain that made you recede within, and then you almost didn't notice the world out there until—

This tingling in her spine. A creepy inkling of being observed. Her legs wobbled at this new distraction. And for the first time in an hour, she slowed and clunked to a stop. She couldn't hear over her breathing or her heartbeat. Her vision wavered as she scanned the tree line.

Why would someone be out here in this country? Who'd she expect to step out of these woods? Some dude out on parole? Someone she mandatory-minimumed years ago?

Dufresne. This time it was Dufresne. Not the close-cropped GS-14 in charge of Southwest Task Force of the Los Angeles Division, but the bearded longhair he was before. The Dufresne who used to emerge from the shadows outside her Sacramento apartment, who'd come at all hours, whenever he needed a Sacramento County DA willing to file an indictment that the feds wouldn't touch. He'd tap on his horn as she passed. *Hey, Hardball.* When she finally got into Quantico and learned to put her head on a swivel, she always saw him on the bad-guy paper targets. That Dufresne.

Not that he was a bad guy. Dufresne was a very good guy. Her mentor. She adored him. She just *expected* him. Even there, somewhere in the woods.

She looked at her watch. Three hours she'd been out. Her legs shook, cold or exhaustion, she couldn't tell and didn't care. Spirit strong, flesh weak. This is the Upper Peninsula, after all. A white wilderness every which way, the odd contrail against the blue. She eyed the timber one more time. The steady thud of her heartbeat emptied out her ears, and she could hear the faint roar of a distant snowmobile.

Run, Hardball.

She couldn't help but smile when she spotted the smoke. *Bronwyn* had to be Welsh for *pyro*. She'd have laughed if she had the breath to spare. Christ, the man loved building a fire, balling newspaper and fashioning lattices of kindling and sticks. He'd wanted to saw the rounds with the chain saw himself, but she paid the Harrisons every winter to keep them stocked up, so he'd settled for splitting and stacking. She invited Bronwyn to run with her, but he passed, needing an objective, a task, a place to run to. He had a vanity about classic, useful manliness. And she liked it. This morning in the blankets she watched him sling on his Carhartt jacket and grab the axe from against the wall. He let it lay on his shoulder just so. The sight of him standing there sent a chain drive of desire wheeling inside of her, and she ordered him back into bed.

And then, after it was over, the same crank turned and sent her off snowshoeing, out the door before she had her coat zipped up. There was little to do out here but be an animal. She and Bronwyn weren't dumb together, just physical. No pretending otherwise. And maybe that was the state of the relationship now three, no, four months into . . . whatever this was. A few three-glasses-of-pinot dates, a Bay Area weekend, a Santa Barbara weekend, a brief campaign through Yosemite that left her more sore than she wanted to admit. And now the UP. Good sex. Very good, like, exceptional. High standards in that regard, the both of them. She and Bron were in a conjoined period of life-lust or something. That's how she'd put it, if anyone asked.

The chopping woodsman and the running snowrunner.

Perfect.

Well, almost perfect. At the edges, a niggling sense that he was getting a bit earnest by the fire in the warm blanket with wine. Inhaling her hair, sighing. She could feel him trying to *commune* with her from time to time. Dropping inmost sentiments, gauging her reaction. His hopes to live close to nature the rest of his life. A professed admiration for scrimshaw. She had to cover up her sudden laugh with a cough at that one. *Scrimshaw?*

She shouldn't be so hard on him, though. He was sweet, he was. And sexy. Just a bit corny.

Seeing the smoke from the fire he'd so carefully constructed, she suddenly realized something that stopped her cold: this setting, the weather, their easy companionship, would to a guy like him be perfectly romantic. He might propose. And she might say yes.

You would.

I might.

You fucking would say yes, you sap. Figure out the work stuff and the living arrangements, but say yes because maybe corny-becomes-cute, and good is just good enough, your mother's given up asking if you *even want* children, and Dufresne has been dropping hints that you gotta have a support structure, see, all these DEA people, they *need* their families. . . .

She pulled off her hat and let the steam rise off her head. Like the idea of marriage was smoking inside her skull. She trudged toward the cabin, a little lodge she'd inherited from her childless aunt and uncle. She clocked Bronwyn's footsteps all over the place, circling the house, trodden places at the windows, as if he had been measuring them. She'd mentioned a draft earlier. Looked like he'd tried to find it, the dear. She tugged her hat back over her chilled forehead and began to catalog. There would need to be repairs, new appliances, new windows, the tankless water heater Bronwyn said would suit the place—

Oh god, she'd thought, you're nesting.

She struggled with the shoes and poles, lost her balance, threw snow around every which way. Slow it down. Breathe. She pulled off her glove with her teeth and then the other one on the porch and undid the snowshoes. Two minutes before, she was bailing on the idea of settling for Bronwyn. Someone named Bronwyn. *Scrimshaw.* But now. Now it's almost inevitable. Waking every day to Bronwyn. Bron. Bronny.

Stock simmered in a pot on the stove. She went over without even taking off her coat and ducked her head into the pot and breathed deep.

"My god," she said, sensing him ease up behind her. "This smells professional."

He grunted and nudged her aside with his hip so he could put his handfuls of leek into the pot. Scrape of the knife's dull side against the cutting board. The stove's blue flame tossed against that draft.

"Entry-level, babe," he said. "Sear some bones, add a little water and fat, toss in some spices, whatever vegetables you got. I wanna cook like this every day."

That, right there. *I wanna cook like this every day.*

Every day with you.

He smiled at her, his white corn-cob teeth. She moved close to him, wished she'd taken off her jacket and bib already so she could better feel his body against hers.

"I'll take *this* every day," she said, clenching his ribs.

"Is that why you keep me around?" he asked into her neck.

"And to fix drafty windows." Harbaugh took him by the elbows and wrapped his arms around her. He pulled her tight. The knife still in his fist. She could feel the handle on the small of her back. She pressed herself against him.

"Okay," he said. "I'll get on it."

She put her lips against his cheek. She breathed against his skin and bit him.

"Take me out of these clothes."

She'd imagined him cutting her out of them, and when he set the knife down, she kind of wished he had. But he held her jaw with one hand and with the other quickly pulled off enough clothes to get at what needed to be gotten. She said things to him as he did this, but his body was the only answer he gave, a silence that thrilled her. She did the talking. She asked him to mark her skin, and he did. She asked him to lift her up, and he did. She told him to pull her hair. She ordered him to grab and take and weigh her down. She told him not to stop.

She ate in bed, practically guzzling the soup. She licked the bowl to get the last of it. Then she finally rose, donned her pajama pants and a sweater, and tied up her hair. Bronwyn had stirred up the fire (of course), and through the smoked glass the logs pulsed. She poked around in the kitchen for cinnamon to make mulled wine. The room was blue with evening, the cool of snow and diminishing light. So warm within, so cold without.

Bronwyn was saying something from the bedroom, she couldn't hear what. She didn't care what. Totally mean of her, and she knew it. But at times the man couldn't harbor an unexpressed notion. His plans for cabin renovations, kinds of dormers and shingles. When she left the room, he'd been on about kinds of joists, mortises, and tenons—

All at once, a flush of mild dread washed over her.

She couldn't say why, or where it came from.

The colors in the house hued dark, the air itself seemed bruised. She inhaled deliberately as though aiming a gun, absorbing the air like Dufresne had taught her, breathing in the warmth of the wine in the pot.

This was the same ill-at-ease she'd felt when she was running outside in the empty. She realized all at once that the footsteps in the snow under the windows weren't Bronwyn's—

As if on cue, a man walked through the front door.

She turned off the burner. She didn't say anything to him, this man who'd stepped his way brazenly inside. In fact, she actually moved toward him, because now she did recognize him and saw something lost and hurt in his face.

"Oscar," she said.

His eyes popped at his name. When she saw the pistol in his hand, she came to a neat halt.

His head tilted to the side. As if weighted down by what was happening now. Cold air slipped through the open door.

"Oscar," she said again.

He was tall, over six feet, and his face was drawn and wooden, as if its contours had been formed by years of running water. His peacoat could not be warm enough in this weather, his jeans were soaked through and snow-covered, he had to be freezing. He looked like a deer, liable to spring at any moment.

Harbaugh raised her hands, slowly, very slowly. She made sure he saw they were empty.

"Are you okay, Oscar?"

She knew he'd brought trouble, was himself trouble standing shivering in her cabin, but he was endangered too, this was plain.

"Do you want to sit? I can call—"

"Don't call nobody," he said softly. He made a gesture with the pistol. Not pointing it. More like reminding her of it. She nodded.

A thought came to her—*It's okay to feel what you feel*—and there was a comfort to it. Just like Dufresne told her before her first raid. She felt the fear, and felt okay about being scared, and she remembered again to breathe, and breathing reminded her to look the man in the eyes, so she looked.

Make how you feel your first observation. Pay attention to everything. What's possible and what is coming, both will reveal themselves.

His eyes, so jumpy and anxious.

"I'm gonna set my hands on the counter," she said, thinking, *Announce yourself.*

Oscar didn't speak.

Harbaugh put her hands palm down on the kitchen countertop.

"Just don't come near me," he said. His voice was soft and scuffed. Like he had a cold.

"I won't. And I won't do anything without telling you, okay? I promise."

He seemed scared. Almost like her. She observed his fear and her own fear like objects you could hold in your hand. She looked for what was next. Like Dufresne said to. *Don't try and do everything at once. You want that gun, but you won't get it in one move. Look for the adjacent possible. The next step you can take in the direction of getting that gun.*

There was only one adjacent possible: *Listen. Listen to him.*

Oscar shut the door with his foot. He said nothing.

Get him to talk. That's your move.

"Thank you," she said, willing kindness into her eyes. "You must be freezing."

He nodded. He agreed, and, agreeing, began talking, almost comfortably.

"My family went all over Arizona, Texas, Califas, Idaho. Picking the fields."

"Yes, I remember. You told me before."

"I'm telling you again." He was confused, his eyes shunting about. "What the fuck was I saying?" He turned his face upward, as if trying to steer his thoughts back on track.

Just listen, damnit.

"Some of those towns were pretty goddamn cold. At night especially. We'd sleep in the car all together. I remember you could put your breath on the window. Didn't want to get up in the mornings. Not ever. But it was never cold like this."

"Your whole childhood, right? The migrant work?" she asked.

He shook his head, dismissing the question.

"We had a trailer back then, before we moved to Pedro, a . . . I can't remember the name. Old, chrome. It's called a wind something something."

"An Airstream?"

"No."

She resisted the urge to disagree with him. *Listen.*

"It was . . ." He touched his temple once, twice, three times. "Something. I wanted to say something about it, but I can't remember the pinche name."

He looked up again. She wondered what he was on. Her stomach clenched, and a sudden urge to move tickled through her. She gritted her teeth, resisting what her body wanted. She wanted to *run.* But that was not the next step. She couldn't get to the adjacent possible on foot. She swallowed, breathed. Examined the urge to run.

Fear?

No, not fear. Revulsion.

The sight of him here, of all places. Thin and dark. He looked sick, broken, cracked.

"Oscar," she said, using his name to make herself stay put.

And he said "Diane" back to her. A warmth in his eyes. Like everything might be all right—

A loud bang startled them like a shot. The light was changing, and Bronwyn was saying from the living room that they should move the lamp, he keeps knocking the damn thing over when he leaves the bathroom.

Bronwyn just slowed at the puzzling presence of Oscar before stopping completely at the sight of the gun. Then he went rigid. Edged against the wall, flush, in a valence of fear. The lamp he'd kicked over slowly rolled along the floor, light spoking through the shade.

Oscar had turned in the direction of the noise, and now he made some kind of strange involuntary sound, a slipped groan. She couldn't see his face, his back to her now.

A step in the wrong direction. Get him back.

"That's only Bron," she said. "Can you look at me again, Oscar? He will stay there, won't you, Bronwyn?"

Bronwyn didn't move, but she yearned for him to say he'd stay put.

Tell him you're cool, Bron.

He just looked at her.

Fucking say it.

His lips parted, but nothing came out.

"He's gonna stay right there. You don't have to worry about him, Oscar," she repeated.

Oscar turned back to her. "Bet that," he said. He didn't look confused anymore. He'd found a focus, something to be pissed about.

"This is Oscar, Bronwyn," Harbaugh said, pleasant but flat.

Bronwyn's gaze bore down to the floor, into it.

"We—"

"We *what*, Diane?" Oscar barked, working the nape of his neck with his free hand.

Shit. She'd seen him like this before. Inconsolable. At odds with himself.

"We who? You and me?" he asked. "You and him? You and all your DEA? Who the fuck you talking about?"

"I'm telling Bronwyn how I know you," she said quickly, no time to think how it would land.

"Brawn-win," he said, trying out the name. "You want to tell Brawn-win. Well, that's easy, man." He spoke over his shoulder, looking at her. "Diane knows me from when she ruined my life."

She'd felt it even before she saw him, in the ghostly dread that had preceded him. She'd known somehow, the light telling, the feeling in her chest. He'd come for her. He'd come for revenge.

Three years ago. Oscar is picked up on an anonymous tip. Sitting in a Cadillac in Koreatown, waiting on his side piece getting her nails done. Rollers roll up and snatch his ass. It's quick, he's not sure he even locked the 'lac.

He's soft-spoken, quiet, but asks for his lawyer right off. He's a gentleman, as polite as can be to Harbaugh when she walks into Interrogation. *Ma'am, no thank you, yes please,* all that shit.

She's all business right back at him, short and snappy at first, white-lady voice, but then she gets a little spark going at him with her eyes. The idea isn't to flirt per se, but to dangle an opportunity. Could be anything. A roll of hundreds on the floor, a cold Coke set in front of him. It doesn't matter what it is, the idea is to give him the sense of a choice, a chance. Give him adjacent possibles.

So he can feel the loss. So she has something to take.

Her partner, Russell Childs, hangs back, just dropping in twice to say they are trying to reach Oscar's lawyer. By now, she and Childs have their routine. He leaves her be, and she sits with the guy until it's comfortable, until the tension isn't legal in nature.

This is stupid for me to say, Oscar, but I'm going to do it anyway. You're like a famous person to me.

Fuck outta here.

I'm for real, Oscar. You're a big deal.

She pulls a notebook out of her bag, places it on the table. His notebook. His face drops for just a second, though he recovers quickly. She starts idly flipping through the notebook.

I know you're not going to admit it, but this—this is a payout ledger. Well, more than a payout ledger. It's got all those trucks you're not personally affiliated with, and the DL numbers of your drivers. And your routes that change randomly. It's all very tight. But that's not what impressed me.

She turns the book around and points to an item. He flinches, just so, but he flinches.

Forty thousand dollars to a store in the garment district.

Not mine.

Okay, sure. I'm gonna keep going, though. So we got a subpoena for every joint in the garment district, right? All these purchase orders for Under Armour and Levi's and Nikes for retail outfits in Baja, paid for in cash, in Los Angeles. By you, Oscar. Financial forensics worked forever to figure out how you got the money back to Mexico. But the mistake we made was following the money! They should've been following the T-shirts and shoes. Because Baja hasn't paid for the T-shirts and jeans yet, have they? No, they give nice clean pesos to your broker, who takes a little cut and passes your money on to the cartel in Sinaloa. A little tariff fraud in the meanwhile to sweeten the pot. That's how you get your money to Mexico.

She taps the notebook.

And it was all your idea.

I don't know nothing about that. About the money. I'm just a low-level guy.

Low-level guy! Oh my god, that is so not you. You're amazing, I'm amazed. This is next level! It's really very sophisticated.

He closes the notebook and pushes it away. He gazes at the ceiling.

A sophisticated dude wouldn't have lost the notebook, he suddenly says.

But you even handled that right! You were suuuuuuper cool. For nine months you laid low. For nine months I watched you sip beers on your front porch and go to the boxing gym and eat dinner with your girl. Girls.

He shakes his head at that. At all of it.

So nine months you drive the speed limit and drink club soda when you go out. I was worried you wouldn't come back. Because you knew this notebook was out there. I was worried you'd just drop out and live on whatever capital you got stashed away.

Where'd you get it?

Hotel housekeeper. Her brother got picked up by ICE. She thought it might help him. And it did. But it helped us even more.

He closes his eyes, breathes deep. Counting his remaining chances.

I'm not saying shit. I'm not some wab just across don't know he got rights.

Okay, Oscar, forget I said anything. I should just go. You've got a lawyer coming—

No! Sit down! Óyeme! Sit down!

He's begun to see a few moves ahead, what few moves he has left.

His lawyer will come, he'll get out, he'll go home, his phone will be silent, no one will talk to him, he'll bed down with his pistol, jump at every sound, he won't sleep, he'll nod off, startle awake . . . all his adjacent possibles trending in one awful direction.

Please, he says. *Please sit. I'm asking you please.*

He swallows. He blinks. He's seeing that it's all come down to her. She is his adjacent possible.

Oscar, your lawyer will explain—

He shakes his head. *Theirs, not mine.*

Right, the cartel lawyer. She knocks on the two-way mirror for Childs, knowing for damn certain no one's called a lawyer yet. *The call might not have even gone out yet. Let me check.*

He keeps folding his hands together. They writhe.

I can't be here. I'm a dead man.

You're fine—

Alive ain't nothing but a mask I'm wearing. ¿Sabé?

She sits. Crosses her arms. Time to take the last chance away. Now that he's naked.

But you were saying you're just a low-level guy. Right? Isn't that right?

We don't need to do that bullshit no more. I'm not playing here. This is the real now. You know what I am. And you know I'm fucked.

She sticks it in: *Oscar, you can't even see fucked from where you are.*

Please, he says. *Help me*, he says.

She stands. His arms hang at his sides, his head lolled back in the attitude of someone freshly shot.

He stood totally still, no movement. Like his whole body was driftwood. He'd changed so much. The stress, the wire he'd been compelled to wear, the lies he was made to tell. The waiting for the end, the outcome. He had no cool, no dominance about him anymore. He'd been rotted out.

"Hey. Oscar. Remember when we first met? You thought you were a dead man. But look. You're here. You're not dead."

"I could've died like a man," he said, moving finally, a grim shaking of his head. "Gone out with pride. But no. I'm just one of your snitches instead."

"But it doesn't have to end like—"

"This is never gonna end," he said, leaning his face forward, saying *obviously* to her, *are you dumb, are you retarded*, light from the lamp on the floor catching him for a moment before he moved back again into the blue dark.

"We're just in a pause, Oscar. I was gonna call when I got back."

"No. *No.*" The snap of his voice like a switch. "You trapped me. You made me weak. You *liked* me weak. Chingá, you actually got me to beg you. You had me so twisted up . . . and you made me think you cared about me. You put this dream in my head. You asked me to follow you, and I did. I am so stupid."

His grip on the gun was loose, wrong. He didn't handle a gun, had never been a killer. He was a manager, not some sicario.

Maybe he'd miss. Was it down to that? Bad aim?

"Oscar. This is normal. The stress, the feelings, they get intense. I feel them too."

"No, no, you did it on purpose. This is your way. You made me dream this bullshit dream."

She was no good at shit like this. She took options away. She cornered people. Doors, she closed. She didn't give people a choice, choices, a chance. Not really.

Spin it. Spin this.

"*You* chose to cooperate, Oscar," she said, and he winced at the truth in it. "And that was a brave choice, a good choice. You did the right thing."

She yearned to believe what she was saying. She had to. She had to hope he could see the candid sympathy in her eyes.

"The right thing." He shook his head. "No. *This* is the right thing."

He pressed the gun barrel to his own temple.

The gun flashed, and he dropped.

She gasped so hard it hurt. Her ears rang and hurt and her head tilted dizzily and then she realized she was stumbling toward Oscar on the floor. She kicked the gun away from his hand and knelt and felt for a pulse and then stopped. There was no remedy for this. The ringing slapped and syncopated in her ears, and she realized it was her own heart.

She raised her eyes to Bronwyn. He was still stuck there at the wall, as though something iron and strong held him fast.

CHAPTER TWO

GREEN LIGHT

The day she shows him the ledger, she leaves Oscar for the observation room. He needs to come to terms with what he's committing to, how his days will be made more and more of lies. He'll be a traitor, the old ways and connections gone forever. He won't sleep. A nervous flutter will overtake his left eye, ulcers will burn his gut. Innocuous things—parked vans, strangers in his local bar, the sounds of the Pacific wind in the eaves of his house—will startle him. A life of small, incessant torment. But he has to choose this heedless leap himself. And he needs to know that he's the one who chose.

But to the agents watching and taking bets in the observation room, that's not what's most important: they are waiting for tears. They stand in front of the two-way mirror. Dufresne in the back. Childs in a folding chair right by the glass. Urlacher, Hemmings, Grant, Rivera, Watson, and almost all of Group 11 watch Oscar consider all the important things, and the coming ruin of his life, but the only thing they're really watching for is tears, his face wet, pink, stained.

Good job, Childs says when she comes in. *You got this dude.*

She sits down. She watches Oscar too. When he obliges them,

first with a single long track down his left cheek and then with a wet sob, a racetrack cry goes up in the observation room, and they say *Goddamn, every time, how does she do it, every motherfucking time.* And he's really bawling now, hyperventilating, holding the table and then holding his head, running his hands over the black stubble of his skull, snot issuing out his nostrils, *Good god, this one's a gusher, they're all gushers from Harbaugh, fuckin' A.*

And from the back of the room Dufresne clears his throat. Says, *He's just been born.*

Born? The fuck you mean born, D?

Like a baby in the cold world.

Cold world, my ass. This one's a little bitch.

Nah, not a bitch, Urlacher. That spanking new CI is as crafty as they come. Harbaugh pulled him into a whole new place and whapped him on the ass to let him know. He's born again, I tell you.

Gentlemen, Childs says. *The cash.* He has his palm out.

Harbaugh doesn't even turn around. Truth is, she can't stop watching Oscar cry.

Don't know how she does it, Urlacher says, handing over his bills.

She's the Midwife, Dufresne says, and she turns around to look at him, she wants to see the man's face after he's named her like this, but he's already gone.

It took the Michigan State Police an hour to arrive on the rutted back roads to the cabin. Harbaugh had walked three miles in the direction of civilization for cell service to try them, and then she'd called Dufresne, quickly and calmly telling his voice mail what had happened. She rode back to the house in a highway patrol car, explaining who she was, who Oscar was. She showed them her credentials. When the police said they needed recorded statements, she ran to Bronwyn's rental car without her coat. Dufresne had left messages returning her call. It had rung when they arrived at the station. She'd kicked it to voice mail and texted him: I'm walking into the police station now.

He texted back.

where

Sault Ste. Marie.

the hell is that

Practically Canada. Michigan.

Bronwyn went to the front desk and then beckoned her into the back with him, where they sat by a detective's desk.

you okay? Dufresne asked.

A little spooked. But ok.

are you with anyone

Yeah.

whose your trauma team contact?

Dunno. I'm fine. Really.

I'll look it up

She barely heard Bronwyn and the detective decide he would give his statement first. She sat alone, regarding the scarred tile, the humming fluorescent lights, watching her phone. It buzzed with Dufresne's new message:

it's me.

Oh. I filled the contact form out when I started. Before you became my boss.

hang in. there soon.

You don't need to.

Of course there was no response. When Dufresne made up his mind, it stayed made.

Oscar's body had been taken to the Chippewa County Medical Examiner's Office, but no one did anything about his blood on the floor, the walls. Bronwyn brought her coffee in the bedroom, he touched her knee, her neck. She let him. She smiled at him and leaned her head to his gentle handstrokes and took it back when that seemed all right to do.

"You wanna talk?" he asked.

There was nothing she wanted less. She shook her head *no*,

registered how helpless this made him, but she felt no obligation to do anything about that. She tucked her lips together and tried to grin in gratitude.

"What can I do?" he asked.

"Nothing," she said and immediately regretted because it sounded like she couldn't be helped. But she didn't need help. She only wanted to close her eyes and wake up alone. But he needed to be needed. Because he'd just stood there when he spotted the gun, because he'd been helpless, pinned to the wall. She felt for him, she did, but there was nothing to be done—by him for her or by her for him.

"Let's just sleep," she said.

Dufresne arrived the next evening as Bronwyn was cleaning up the blood. At the knock Bronwyn lurched up, rag in hand, asking who was at the door. She was by the fire, looking at the flames.

"It's my boss," she said, having looked through the window as she crossed the room.

"You didn't say anyone was coming."

She shrugged in a kind of non-apology as she opened the door. Dufresne was there, hunched against the cold in his thin jacket. He'd gone bloodshot. The man couldn't sleep on planes. He hadn't shaved, and his thin gray hair was flecked with snow.

"Hey, Hardball," he said.

"Hey, old man."

She let him in and let him hug her and have a look at her. His eyes were kind and tired and a skosh worried. She smiled to put his mind at ease. Tried to, at least. She then turned around to introduce Bronwyn, who was wiping his hands on his jeans as he came to shake Dufresne's hand.

"This is Bronwyn. He was here too. When it happened."

They all stood quietly like this a moment in Dufresne's calculated reticence. He never said the first thing. Bronwyn shifted in place.

"Well, I don't know what to say either!" she blurted out.

Dufresne laughed. Bronwyn cleared his throat, nodded succinctly at each of them, and started back for his bucket.

"Bronwyn," she said too sharply.

"What?"

He turned around and looked at her, and Dufresne did too. She still didn't know what to say.

"Booze," she said, as if she'd just then invented the concept, and fetched a bottle of Maker's Mark from the cupboard and poured three messy splashes into three mismatched glasses and handed them around the butcher's block where they'd gathered.

Bronwyn took the glass, looking quizzically at her, as if to ask her a couple different how-comes and what-fors. *Why is he here? What's happening?*

Dufresne looked into his glass. "To you two being okay," he said. They clinked. Dufresne drank last.

"Oh Bron," Harbaugh said, "you got blood on you."

He looked at the pink line around his wrist, at the bucket, and then at the floor where there was still more blood, watered down, but yet to be sopped up. She wasn't sure what kind of move to make. She wasn't going to wash his hands for him. If they were engaged, though, would she wash his hands? Chide him into it, maybe?

They weren't engaged. That idea was from before.

"I'm okay," Bronwyn said, sipping the last of his whiskey, setting down the cup.

She started to pour another for him.

"I said I'm okay." That quick grin at Dufresne again. "I'm gonna take a walk."

He tossed the rag into the bucket of pink water and whipped his coat and hat off the peg and swept outside. The shallowness of the nothing she felt didn't upset her, just sounded off like an alarm behind a closed door.

Bronwyn's footsteps receded away in the new snow. In the fresh silence, Dufresne swirled the remainder of his drink and looked around, lightly taking the place in.

"This is nice."

"Family cabin. Spent a lot of summers and winter breaks up here."

He nodded in the direction Bronwyn had gone.

"Is he family or . . ."

"Or."

"Or?"

"What? He's . . . Bronwyn. You want to know if we're getting married or something?"

"You have this tendency, Diane," he said, "to think your mind is easily read." He took a sip. "Just populating the cast of characters here."

"He's a lumberjack," she said.

"A local, then."

"From Santa Barbara."

"A Santa Barbara lumberjack," Dufresne said with a touch of smarm.

"I mean he's a lumberjack at heart. His dad's a lawyer and his mother's a banker, but he won't soil his neck with a white collar. He makes these tables that are almost sculptures, kind of functional, I guess. He runs a recycling center. That fill it in enough?"

She could feel Dufresne seeing into her with his soft brown eyes somehow, coaxing her. He'd always had her number, even as far back as Sacramento. He didn't say a word.

She finished her whiskey.

"Who am I kidding?" she said. "He's slumming. It's all daddy money."

"This is hardly a slum," he said, softening his searching eyes.

"I don't know," she said, helplessly. "This was supposed to be a romantic weekend. But now with, you know . . ."

"About that. Where's Bronwyn when it goes down?" he asked, nodding toward the blood.

"There. He came in from the bedroom and saw him and just stood against the wall."

"And he doesn't do anything else that spooks Oscar? Besides simply come in?"

She sighed.

"What?"

"He just stands there. He wishes he had done something, done *anything*, other than freeze. Which is why he's stomping around in the snow."

Dufresne thought whatever he thought about that, and then looked everything over. He set his cup on the butcher's block. She poured them both another, and they drank. She worried her forehead with her fingers.

"What?"

"I don't love him," she blurted out. "I was *this close* to thinking, I dunno, that we were going to be together, but I don't love him. When it was happening, all I needed was for him to protect himself. Just be cool. But he was rooted in place, scared shitless." She couldn't tell what Dufresne was thinking. She went on talking. "And now I have to protect his ego. His whole deal, the lumberjack act, the wobbly tables, scrimshaw . . . it's all a performance."

Dufresne's face darkened, and she stopped talking.

You shouldn't say these things to him.

"Goddamnit, Diane," he said.

"What?" she asked, alarmed at the sudden frustration on his face. He was looking at his empty glass. He was going to say one thing, set it aside, and said this instead: "Childs should be here. Your partner."

"I filled my Trauma Plan paperwork years ago," she said, stepping back from him. "You're down as my primary because you were my mentor."

"I'm your supervisor, and—"

"I told you not to come!"

Dufresne hadn't moved. But his jaw was set, and he was breathing audibly through his nose like he'd exerted himself and didn't want to show it. And then all at once, she knew what he was thinking.

"Within two minutes of us being alone, you're telling me you don't love this guy."

Now she was sure.

That night.

That fucking night.

One too many drinks, the two of them in the abandoned coat check, her fingers on his lapel. Claudia Dufresne calling for her husband, the two of them stumbling out to her withering gaze. Dufresne spurred by his tremendous Catholic guilt, leaving her instantly and gliding to his wife. Harbaugh standing there in a spotlight of Claudia Dufresne's gaze. Nothing to say because nothing happened, but something might have, but nothing did. That nothing fucking night.

Dufresne leaned away from the butcher's block and turned to get a glass of water from the tap. He was looking out the window.

"Why would your informant track you all the way to the Upper Peninsula of Michigan just to blow his brains out?" He wiped his mouth on his sleeve and did not turn around.

She was still too stunned to speak.

"How'd he know you were here?"

He turned around.

She managed a shrug.

"Diane."

"I don't know," she muttered. "I don't know." This time firmly.

"What did he—"

"He said I ruined his life."

Dufresne pondered this a moment. He went to the marked spot on the floor. He toed the blood–water outline.

"I looked at the case you were building. You were setting up a sting with him?"

"A Sinaloa peso broker."

"Stalled out?"

"Just tricky timing. I didn't want to rush it. He was anxious."

"Anxious?"

"Yeah."

"He was trapped. CIs are always trapped," he said, his eyes gone sad. Like he was the one who was trapped. "I should've been more on top of this one."

He came over and screwed the lid back onto the bottle. He looked old.

"I quit drinking," he said, smiling, though she could tell he was serious.

"I won't tell," she said.

"I know," he said. He gestured toward the outside, where Bronwyn had gone. "You gonna be all right?"

She nodded. He buttoned up his coat.

"There a motel around here?"

"Rudyard. You probably drove right by it on the way in."

"Okay."

"Dufresne."

"What?"

"I never wanted to make trouble for you. It was a little work crush is all, nothing more. I wish—I wish we could go back to how it was before things got weird. I wish that so much. I wanted this job back when I was a DA, and it was because of you. You made me want to be an agent. You know that. I owe you everything. And that's *all* I feel. Gratitude."

He nodded, acknowledging what she'd said.

"Get some rest," he said and left her alone.

She waited and waited for Bronwyn to come back, finally going out after him in the dark. He'd trudged out into the meadow under the naked moon.

She walked along his tracks deep in the snow. She didn't break through like he did; she was slight from all her coursing these woods, she was a slight thing right now, light in her footing, a ghost.

She felt herself slip free of Bronwyn and a little bad for it, for sidling up so close. Did she lead him on, did she play with his heart, did she play with Oscar, did she play with Dufresne, was she Dufresne's middle wife, his work wife, did she play too hard, try too hard, did she make all the boys cry?

Did she know her own heart? Did they? Was her heart just a hard ball of stone?

She stopped. She turned back toward the cabin. The cold was fine, she would not die out here. She didn't even shiver. But there was no reason to stay, not a minute more. *Should I go, all I want is to go.*

She looked up and caught a ribbon of the northern lights, a greenish pennant softly shimmering.

A green light, she thought. *Go.*

CHAPTER THREE

THE RACES

Harbaugh pulled into the Santa Anita racetrack lot and parked remarkably close to the front, only remembering as she walked through the nearly empty gate that it was a Tuesday. The last time she'd been to the famous track, for the Breeders' Cup, the place had been stocked with California's horse-racing elite. It had taken her twenty-five minutes to get in, shoulder to shoulder with the well-heeled and well-hatted throng. No such trouble today, though. She stepped up to the only ticket window open for business, paid the extra $10 for club level access, and passed right through the turnstile.

She wiped her palms on her pants, more like she was getting set to breach a front door and clear rooms than meet her partner to observe a target. Her pits too, Jesus Christ. Her first day back on the job, and she felt like a panicked seventh grader, confined within her own hideous skin.

She headed for the women's restroom, which was totally empty, wiped herself off, breathed, looked at herself in the mirror. Told herself it would be okay, to just get back to work. To just not touch anyone with her sweaty palms.

She bought a schedule and made her way to the observation gallery to watch the weekday bettors survey the first-race horses and jockeys. A group of about thirty men. Guys dressed like programmers bearing headphones and backpacks mingled with professional poker players, grinders who counted excursions to the track as exercise. A few mid-functioning alcoholics in football jerseys and sweatpants sipping Bloody Marys like cartoon mosquitoes.

There was only one other woman anywhere about the grounds. She sat on a bench waiting on someone with her eyes closed and head thrown back to absorb the sun through the Pasadena haze. The woman seemed to feel herself being observed and opened her eyes, alighting on Harbaugh immediately. She squinted and then lifted her chin as if they shared a secret intelligence about this place and the men who congregated here. Which they did. Harbaugh had been going to the races since she was knee-high to her daddy—

Her phone buzzed. Bronwyn. Not Childs or Dufresne or anybody else from work, no, not people she actually wanted to hear from, just Bronwyn *again*. She let it ring. She'd been back in LA for two days—or, if you were measuring time in Bronwyns, nine calls and a dozen texts. She'd left him a note at the cabin, curt and clear: *This is tough, I need some space, I'll check in later. xoxo.* It felt bad, but only just, and less so every time a message from him lit up her phone.

After Michigan, Dufresne had told her to take some PT. In a massive display of self-control, she'd texted him exactly twice about coming back on time. He demurred on the second try. She stopped bothering him. Couldn't have him measuring time in Dianes. Shit was weird, though. She'd expected to be called in to talk to him and his boss, Cromer, the Los Angeles office assistant special agent in charge. But nada.

She'd killed a few days jogging in her Fairfax neighborhood, taking stupid hikes up Runyon with the actors and models and WAGs and their little dogs, every text from Bronwyn curbing her own urge to pester Dufresne. At a rock outcropping under an umbrella she sat listening to an old hippie play surprisingly competent Hendrix on a Fender through a Pignose amp and was overcome by the thought that this was, in fact, where she was right now. Alone. The women she knew here—a real estate agent with two kids, a costume designer, an orthodontist—were all friends of friends from Sacramento, law school, and fucking Facebook. Los Angeles friendship was catching up at lunch every three to nine months, apologizing to each other for having to cancel so many times. Los Angeles friendship was a requisite holiday party. Los Angeles friendship was a boring-ass Saturday at the LACMA looking at Mapplethorpe's butthole. Truth was, she'd only moved here to do cases, and even the small investment in nominal friendships felt like a horrible chore. And to be stuck in this jittery holding pattern had been a perfect torture.

Her phone trembled again in her pocket. Childs, thank god.

You here or what?

She smiled. She started to type, thought better about what would sound just right. What wouldn't sound like someone counting time in Bronwyns. She looked around.

Scoping the ponies right now, partner, she wrote.

Addict.

Where are you.

Parked. Walking in.

Hit the ATM.

I'm working.

Obvi. Me too. But I'll make you rich bitch.

Harbaugh began flipping through the racing schedule, looking for the right race to make the best bets, the trifecta—boxed, always box it. Riding on her dad's shoulders out of the beer garden, weaving through the crowd at the county fair, she'd learned to bet. *Only play the trifecta, boxed*, he'd said. *Two favorites, you choose the long shot*. She always took a filly, picked names that sounded heedless and fraught: Juanita's Gambit. Baby's Long Dive. Becca's Chance. Madame Kinetic.

She set the program aside as the bettors observed a large chest-nut colt that was primed to race, anybody could see that, eyes rolling around like small pool balls as he urged against the trainers man-handling him by the halter.

A shadow fell across her lap.

"Sit," she said, waving a hand. "*Sit.*"

An old joke. Childs had read in *Military Times* that sitting eight hours a day would reduce his lifespan, so fuck sitting. He'd always squat or pace in place. Or kneel like a quarterback drawing up a play, which was what he did now. She glanced at him in his wrap-around sunglasses, a toothpick in his teeth.

"Those shades are a real douchey."

"These shades are dope."

"God, is that an *ivory* toothpick?"

"My dental hygienist said the wood ones are fucking up my gums and enamel."

"The ivory won't?"

"I dunno. It's a work in progress."

"You're the only person in the world who'd call a toothpick a work in progress."

"The toothpick is an oral fixation. The work in progress is this," he said, running his hands down the length of himself. "My temple."

He was as fit as an orchestra of fiddles.

"You're gonna live forever, Russ."

"Not without the work, baby," he said. He looked over his shades at her. Her shirt.

"It's a vintage tee," she said.

"People take care of vintage things. That's disintegrating."

"The sight of bra strap really throws you, doesn't it?"

"You got two speeds, girl. Legal eagle and meth dealer."

A yelling commotion in the stalls saved her from having to con-jure a retort. Handlers were struggling with the chestnut Thoroughbred, keeping him from rearing up, turning him in the narrow stall. With an explosive bang the horse kicked the wood enclosure.

She looked it up in the guide. "Islands in the Stream," she said.

The handlers began their staggered departure, with racehorses, owners, and jockeys hastening subtly toward the racetrack. A few bettors jogged ahead, stirred to hedge or capitalize by this latest aggression on the part of Islands in the Stream.

"You spooked him," Childs said, reaching down to pull her up.

"You're the one looks like a cop." She snatched his toothpick from his mouth as she came to her feet. "I hate this thing."

She inspected the toothpick, the delicately filigreed handle end, the entire thing like a miniature cane for a miniature dandy. She looked at Childs.

"Don't do it," he said, half grinning because he knew it was too late.

She flicked the toothpick into the air, where it vanished into the white sunshine, and started for the track.

They took seats in the Turf Terrace section, the place already set with linen and a pitcher of water. The shade was cool, but the heat was beginning to build on the track. Childs put his sunglasses in the front pocket of his dress shirt. Something he'd wear out dancing, she thought. Something he'd ironed this morning.

"You're right," Harbaugh said, impressed by her plush seat and the silverware and plates. "I am underdressed."

"Up top's even more chichi." Childs gestured to where several idle cocktail waitresses chatted on the patio outside the Chandelier Room. She could just make out an ice sculpture past the waitresses. Cooks wheeled out steam tables.

"All that stuff for Lima?" she asked. Group 11, their team in the LA office, had been coordinating with San Antonio, tracking the distributor for the Cartel del Golfo on what appeared to be a little money-washing tour of his southwestern properties. So far, the Texan had shown a not-so-novel interest in California wine collections, real estate, and Thoroughbreds.

Childs shrugged.

"These fucking guys. He might not even show. And all that is gratis."

"You know the only thing you ever bitch about is what these guys get 'gratis'?"

A good portion of Childs's psychic fuel was resentment. He hated guys like Lima for what they did, what they were, but what really pissed him off was the free shit they got from civilians.

"Doesn't it drive you nuts?"

"I don't give a shit how narcos split the check. Or don't split the check. I just like the chase."

"You're like a dog that way."

"Dogs are too happy to get bogged down in the injustice of it all."

"It's fucked."

"Woof."

"Seriously," he said, pouring them glasses of water and gazing up at the patio.

"Look, I don't hear you complaining about senators or actresses or brokers getting free shit."

"I don't have to watch them eat free lobster all day," he said, taking a swig from his water.

"But you don't get to arrest them, either."

Harbaugh took in the vast grandstand. Much of the action was still inside, people getting their first beer, studying the program over a coffee, already yearning at the bank of televisions broadcasting races in New Jersey and Florida. A weekday languor here, the crowd thin, the odds less volatile. An almost scholarly vibe, with so many pure horse people, cowgirls, and vaqueros. And the shady operators in white sport coats or tennis sweaters who knew how to fine-tune Thoroughbreds like Formula One engines with injections right up to the edge of the rules. Racing always brought out the simplest things: cheating, trophies, cheating trophy wives. People with cash to burn. Or in Lima's case, clean.

"So the track is brokering Lima's horse deal?" she asked.

"I'm not even sure he's here to get one. He's been buying horses and houses in San Antonio, Dallas, Tulsa, Taos. And that's just the past month. Dude's got so much capital, he just throws it at whoever the hell will take it on. I think Santa Anita knows he's on a spending spree. But more important, they know he can bring other whales to the pool."

"Explains the ice mermaid."

"More than mermaids. Lookit this now."

The patio started to fill with colorful had-to-be prostitutes, glittering eyes and big laughs. Judging one another in long sidelongs, clustering like tangled Christmas lights.

She sank back in her seat and sipped her water. Took in the track, the warming breeze. It was good to be back at work.

The waiter returned.

"I'll just have coffee," Childs said, before he could go through the specials. Harbaugh looked at him over her menu. Another thing she teased him about: he didn't drink. Not that she wanted a drink now either. But Childs was so tight he wouldn't even order dry toast here.

"You're not having anything?" she asked.

"I'm *having* a four-dollar coffee," he said.

Harbaugh rolled her eyes for the waiter. "I'll have a coffee too," she said. "But leave a menu."

Childs sipped his water.

"Not gonna bet either, are you?" she asked.

"I cannot participate in unjust shit like this," he said. "This whole circus is rigged to screw these addicts."

He nodded toward the stands filling below them, the shambling track junkies, a thin weekday parade of souls atingle. The screenwriter in a Hunter Thompson Hawaiian shirt, the Armenian playboys, the old Chinese lady digging in her fanny pack. She liked Childs personally—he was loyal, on time, and less of a patriotic swinging dick than the other ex-military. Guys like that meathead Urlacher. But Childs had been an MP. He was deeply, essentially protocoled.

"Not one little bet?"

"I only play poker," Childs said.

"That's gambling, hon."

"No, poker is war. No house, no rigged odds. It's just you and the enemy. Battle royale."

"Semper fi," she said.

When the coffee came, Childs stirred in two sugars and sipped it hot, glancing at the landing for Lima. He picked at a stray bit of lint off his sleeve and then slid her a pair of small binoculars.

"He's not up there," he said. "Check the track."

She eyed the infield with the glasses. A crew positioned the starting gate on the far side of the grass. The tires didn't leave deep marks in the green. She watched the men unhitch the starting gate. The horses and jockeys began making their way. The wet turf gleamed.

"Looks fast today," she said. "No good for mudders. My dad loved mudders. But today's gonna be for hot starters, early leads."

"You gonna tell me about it?" Childs asked. He meant Oscar.

The anxious chestnut Islands in the Stream hopped restlessly in the two circles of her vision.

She set down the binoculars to look straight at him. "He came in out of the cold. Stood in my doorway. Said some shit." She creamed her coffee and took a sip.

"Well, don't go on and on."

"And then he shot himself."

Childs pinned her with his penetrating, cut-the-shit MP gaze.

"In the temple," she said. "I don't know what else to tell you, partner. It wasn't pleasant. But at least he did it quick."

"What'd he say?"

"That I'd ruined his life," she said softly. "Things like that."

He sighed, looked off and back at her. "Fuck him," he said. "Laying that on you and then offing himself?"

"I did okay, Russ. I was cool."

"Of course. But how are you now?"

"Okay."

"I'd have shit my pants and gone to church. I'd be fucked up." Childs's eyes narrowed. "How'd he find you?"

"That's the scary part. He must've been following me."

She took up the binoculars again. The sun shone off the white paint of the starting gate. The horses loped and trotted and some threw their heads. All was anticipation.

"He's lucky he's dead, else I might kill him again. I never liked that dude."

"He was freaked," she said. "You know how some CIs get."

He took the binoculars from her eyes. "Last time we saw him was ten months ago," he said, nonchalantly sweeping up and over to get a look at the landing for Lima, then back onto the table.

"Sounds right."

"Dufresne had me look it up. Me and you met him down in San Pedro."

She could tell he was waiting for her to say something about that.

"He fell *hard* for you," Childs said.

"Meth-addict me or the legal eagle one?"

"I was there."

"So was I."

"There for him eye-fucking you every time we had a sit. For him hitting you up a dozen times a day. *And* I was there for him bawling his eyes out the day we brought him in. The little bitch."

"They all bawl. You shitheads call me the Midwife, remember?"

"I never call you that. You know I don't. And that's not what I'm saying. Oscar was . . ."

"Was what?"

"I'm just saying"—he peered around like someone could be listening—"If it was the other way around, and some fine-ass Juanita was hitting me up all hours—"

"You'd tap it."

He showed her his wedding ring. "I'm married. I could *never*," he said, nodding his head enormously as though he were wearing a wire.

She didn't quite laugh, but his smile took her partway to it. Talking to him like this felt good, normal.

"Thanks, but informants from San Pedro aren't exactly my type," she said.

"Don't get it inside out. I'm saying *he* had feelings for *you*. And then he offed himself. Look, I couldn't give Dufresne a good answer on why we hadn't talked to Oscar in so long. I had that family shit in San Diego and then got up on this Lima thing. I just kind of mumbled to Dufresne that it hadn't blipped my radar for a while now."

She sipped her coffee. "Same."

"So did Oscar, like, ever threaten you? Back then?"

"No."

"Or freak you out?"

"The case was in the same place last week as it was ten months ago. Nowhere. We were trying to set a meet with Oscar's peso broker. But Oscar was scared of tipping him off. So we were just holding."

The public address blared over them, announcing the first race. The stands had become populated, people at nearby tables. The address ended, but there was a new buzz all around.

Childs had his phone. A weird look on his face.

"You get this?"

She pulled her work cell out of her pocket.

"No bars."

"Dufresne wants you to come in."

Childs showed her the message, his face a frankness of concern.

The roar from the meager crowd of bettors and track junkies was startling. The day's first race had begun.

"Give me a pen."

She went through the form quickly, marking the first five races.

"Bet these," she said. "Trifectas, boxed." She stood. "Seriously. These are good picks, Childs. All yours. Gratis."

CHAPTER FOUR

THE 210

The 210 West was an unusual shit show, a fiery crash that funneled everyone into Pasadena and had Harbaugh wondering again about her egress out of the metropolis, fireball or earthquake, disaster scenarios that she helplessly entertained in standstill traffic. She peopled the chaos. Imagined getting out of her car, taking her gym bag and her service revolver, and just walking into the Angeles National Forest. She'd have no reason to stay.

God, your job is all you got.

So?

So this is good? You're good with this?

Ask a man that question.

Point taken.

She ended up making downtown in a personal worst of ninety-three minutes with both her work phone and her personal phone on the seat next to her alternately buzzing. She shoved the latter into her glove box as she answered the call from the downtown office with the other.

"On my way," she said.

"I'm sorry? Is this Agent Harbaugh?"

"Yes. Tell Dufresne I'll be there soon."

"This is Finn at the duty desk. I have a Mr. Travis on the phone for you."

"Who?"

"Mr. Travis."

"Am I supposed to know who that is?"

"Right. I'm sorry, Agent Harbaugh. He said you wouldn't know him. But he keeps calling, over and over, six times already. From Tampico, that's where he is. Mexico."

"Tampico? Look, I'm about go into the parking garage." She pulled off the street, flashed her badge at the security guard, and descended into the cool shade. "Can you take a message? I'll call him back."

Her tires squeaked and echoed off the walls. The duty desk cut out. Harbaugh watched the CALL ENDED alert appear on her screen.

She parked in the open spot, got out of the car, and stopped. *Shit.* She promptly got back in. She opened the glove box and just looked at her personal phone, wondering if Dufresne would ask for it. If she could give it to him. If this was where things were headed.

Put it out of your mind.

But why'd he call you in, then?

She left it.

She glanced through the pane on Dufresne's door. He was on the phone, the only one in Group 11's section of the tenth floor. Silence in the Federal Building wasn't exactly rare—one area or another often emptied out, everybody in the field—but the way Dufresne sat behind his desk, hand to temple, listening to the other end of the line, gave the emptiness an uneasy tenor. A murmurous undertone of trouble.

He saw her and gestured to come take a seat, mouthing *Sorry*, as whoever was on the phone—probably Cromer, the ASAC and his immediate boss, judging from his scant *Sure thing*s and *Monnit*s—buzzed away in his ear. She sat up in the chair, which had been further deepened over the years by Urlacher, the team fat-ass, who lived to waste time brown-nosing Dufresne with disgusting stories that usually took place on his boat on Lake Arrowhead.

There was an open manila folder in front of Dufresne, but she couldn't make out the contents from her seat, which was notoriously low-slung, an obvious power move that everyone teased him about. She looked at the framed newspaper articles of past busts and convictions on the wall. The Israeli who ran the pill mill. The sting that ruined a certain film financier and world-class prick.

Then this: the picture of Dufresne's wife and kid, a little tow-headed six-year-old who had his mother's small nose and Dufresne's brown eyes. Claudia, a sweet thing who inspired nothing in Harbaugh, not shame or sympathy, maybe just the nagging sense that she ought to feel guilty but didn't, because nothing had happened. Nothing. Not in the coat check that one time, or anywhere else at any other time. Nothing had happened, ever. So if she didn't feel guilty, why the fuck did she keep thinking about it?

Because he does, she thought, catching his eye. Because of the things you did for him, the things he did for you—

Dufresne said, "All right, I gotta go," which was probably him telling Cromer that she'd arrived and whatever was in that file in front of them would soon be broached. He hung up. Fixed her with a curt preliminary grin.

"Childs said it was pretty dead today. Where is everybody?"

"OG-3 needed some more manpower out in Ventura. The ASAC asked for able bodies." He flipped through some paper on his desk. "I had some more questions about the CI . . ."

"Oscar."

"Oscar. Yeah. You okay with me asking now?"

"As opposed to?"

"In this setting."

Weird.

"Dufresne, it's me. Of course."

He slid the folder aside. Opened a drawer, got some kind of file out, thought twice about it, put it back in. "So about how long did you and your CI talk before Bronwyn came in?"

"A few minutes?"

"He—Bronwyn—corroborates that, but of course he wasn't in the room when Oscar came in. That's why I'm asking."

"Yeah, a few minutes. Like five. I mean, time moved kinda slow, so maybe less."

"He had the gun out?"

She nodded.

"And what did you talk about before Bronwyn came in?"

"I was startled, so I just said whatever I thought would keep him calm."

"Like?"

"Like I told him that I was going to put my hands on the counter. Announcing myself. Stuff like that. Just trying to get some control of the situation."

"And then what?"

"Let's see, I asked him or he said something about how cold it was. Not much. He didn't seem upset until Bronwyn surprised us. But I think he knew Bronwyn was there. There were footprints by the windows outside. He scouted the place."

He wrote this down, nodding.

"About that. How'd he know where to find you?"

"No idea. None. I've racked my brain."

Dufresne sighed and pursed his mouth like a teacher asking a pupil to show her work. "You didn't talk to him before you left?" he prodded.

"It'd been a while."

"I mean, talk at all to him. Before you left town. You might've let something slip then."

"No."

"Because I subpoenaed his phone records."

He looked sad saying it. He started tapping on the folder.

"Okay."

"You still don't know what I'm talking about."

He waited. Palms down now. Serious.

"Is that a question?" she asked.

"There are messages sent to your number."

"So? He was my informant."

"Your *personal* phone."

She sat up, was promptly sucked back down. Fucking fat-ass Ur-lacher.

"You know how spotty our service is. A lot of my CIs use the other number."

Dufresne leaned forward. She could smell his breath. Coffee. Cigarettes. His nerves.

"Okay," he said. "I need both phones."

"I have personal messages on that phone—"

"A CI follows one of my team members out of state and then pops himself, I gotta be sure I know why."

"You do know why. You said it. He felt trapped."

"I need to verify the nature of your relationship."

"This is overkill. I'm not gonna let the Agency comb through phone—"

Dufresne shoved himself away from his desk. "All right, I have to turn this over to the Office of Professional Responsibility. You're not special, Diane."

She gripped his desk, close enough to look into each of his eyes.

"Dufresne. *Dufresne.* Look at me. This is ridiculous. This is me."

"And this is me. Your *boss.* Not your mentor, not your primary—"

She saw him wonder what he was going to say, and then she realized what this was all about.

"My what." She said it flat, like she wasn't asking.

He pinched the bridge of his nose like he always did when he was furious.

"Your work crush," he said. "You need to follow the rules."

"Oh, I see," she said. "When did this kick in?"

"It's always been this way—"

Fuck it.

"You used to like it when I broke the rules," she said. She hardly believed the words were coming out of her mouth, but they kept coming. "All those bullshit indictments I filed so you could rattle some cages. The wiretap applications I set up so you didn't have to go to federal court."

"The OPR officer will be in touch," he said, slapping closed the folder. He was alarmed, trying not to show it, trying to hold a flat affect.

"And then, when I couldn't file the Mann indictment, when I said 'This could get me fired on a Brady disclosure violation,' what did you say, Brian?"

She could see that she was right, the kind of bashful look-away he pulled, like all those times it was just the two of them. Him coming by her Sacramento place for a drink and to complain how full of shit the AUSA was for not filing a federal indictment. That office, what a bunch of cowards they were. How much balls *she* had, and only state DA. If only she was a US attorney. But what a long shot that was. How you practically had to be royalty to get one of those gigs. A dad who was a judge at least—

He got up suddenly and closed the door. Dropped back into his chair.

"I asked for your help," he said. "Whatever you were comfortable with."

"That's right. And I kept exculpatory evidence from defense attorneys so bad men who would've gotten off went to prison. I was comfortable with that. You know why?"

He looked away again and then back at her.

"Because you said 'Look, Diane, you really should be at the DEA, Diane.'"

"There was no deal."

"Quid pro fucking quo, and you know it. I helped your career, Brian, and I did it at great risk to mine as an ADA."

"You're saying things you shouldn't say."

It was true. Even she couldn't believe her mouth right now. But the gates were open. The horses were loose. Her eye alighted on the kid, the wife. He followed her line of sight, knew what was coming.

"I'm *sorry* I made shit weird at home. I'm *sorry* you feel like you can't trust me. I'm saying things you need to hear—"

"I know when I'm being threatened. I know exactly what you're saying. That if I find anything weird between you and your dead CI, you've got leverage on me."

Holy shit. That's not what she meant. *Jesus.*

"No, that's not it at all! I did good work for you! How do you think those indictments made it past my boss? On such flimsy fucking evidence? I put *garbage* in front of the court for those cases. Why? Because even if it was wrong . . . it was right. What I'm trying to tell you is, you needed someone to do the things I did. Brian, I do the things."

Dufresne shoved the manila folder at her, papers spilling everywhere. He stood up and said, very slowly, "That's why I want your phone. Because you *do* things."

He literally quaked in a rage she'd never seen before.

Except she *had* seen it before. Dozens of times. Times they brought in a guy like Oscar. Times they put her in there with him, because of her knack. Times she sat down with the guy, got him to feel a little special and then took away his choices, one by one. She knew this moment. This is what Dufresne looks like when he runs out of choices, she thought. This is what Dufresne looks like scared. He's calling his lawyer as soon as I leave.

She pushed herself up so she was at eye level with him, leaning forward over the desk. "I wish you trusted me," she said. "But you can have my phone when you get another fucking subpoena."

CHAPTER FIVE

LUCKY

She could only make it as far as the elevator bank before she began sobbing.

Fucking fuck. So stupid. So weak. Blowing up like that.

She paced down the blurry hall to the bathroom, banged into a stall, and sat down.

You daffy bitch.

The quiet emptiness of the bathroom, the building, made her bawl the more. She wasn't threatening him. She fucking wasn't. She was trying to explain why he could trust her. All her life she just wanted to be where she mattered, where her choices carried weight. And Dufresne was pushing her out now, she could feel it, that deep lonesome, that pit that made her restless to be in the action, to be at the center of something, anything, *just use me, make me useful*, and the only answer is the quiet and nothing and nothing means nothing—

"Agent Harbaugh?" came a voice outside the stall, hard off the tile. "Are you in there?" The voice softer now.

Harbaugh spun some toilet paper into her hand and wiped her face and nose.

Get it together, woman.

"Yeah. Yes. Who's asking?"

"I'm sorry, I saw you go in and was waiting, but well, after a little while I came in and . . ."

"Hon. Out with it."

"There's a call."

"No. Not now."

"It's just that he keeps calling back over and over."

"Hold on."

She looked at the snotty paper in her hand and she shuddered out the last of her urgent angry lonesome tragic sadness—*put that shit in a box!*—and stood and straightened herself and stepped out. A woman in a long pencil skirt was just inside the doorway, halted mid-departure. Strawberry hair. An awkward sympathy, a sympathetic awkwardness, something, whatever.

"Get in here," Harbaugh said.

"He's on the landline, actually."

"He keeps calling over and over, you said, get in here."

The woman stepped inside, and Harbaugh went to the sinks. The woman stood behind her and watched Harbaugh in the mirror as she scrubbed her face, tied up her hair. Harbaugh looked her in the eye the whole time.

"What's your name?"

"Cynthia."

"Want some advice?"

The woman looked at the door and then back at Harbaugh. Kind of a rube, this one. Citizen of NorCal?

"I feel like I should?"

"Stay at the track," Harbaugh said.

"I'm sorry?"

"It's a nice day. The horses are ready to run. Get a beer and bet the ponies, Cindy."

"Cynthia."

Harbaugh nodded. "So who is it?" she asked.

"Huh?" Forget NorCal, probably Nevada. You could see tumble-weeds in the thought bubble over her head.

"On the phone, hon."

"Oh! A Mr. Travis? From Mexico? Says he'll only talk to Agent Diane Harbaugh."

"Right. Mr. Travis," Harbaugh said wryly, wiping her eyes again. She adjusted her T-shirt, which was bunched up on her shoulder. She had a look at herself. Her flushed face, her blue eyes gone puffy.

"You like this T-shirt?" she asked. Cynthia wore a cardigan against the air conditioning, small pearl earrings, and a nice thin watch. She looked relieved, even pleased, to have an answer to this question.

"Oh, I do," she said. "I love Jane's Addiction."

Tumbleweeds, trailers, whiskey Cokes. Reno. A hundred dollars says she's pure uncut Reno.

She didn't want to see Dufresne again or anyone from the team, so she took the call at the duty desk. Two desks with a shitty view southeast of down-town. Helicopters hovering. News and PD both. She figured she'd take the call and then . . . well, what? Something. Could take your own advice and go bet the ponies. Could fly somewhere. Throw a dart at a map.

But—and the thought came suddenly—who would she go with?

Her father dust and ashes set loose by her one summer day five years ago on Mount Elbert. Her mother with maybe not even six months sobriety this time. Camping out in her guest room wouldn't help her stave off the jones for vikes and vodka. Her stepfather, fuck that. It'd been at least a decade. Her exes, double-fuck that. Thinking about any of them made her want to laugh.

Meaning, you got nobody.

Which's nothing new.

So pick up the phone. Do the thing, you bad bitch you—

"Hello," she said. "Mr. Travis?"

"Is this Agent Harbaugh?"

"Yes."

"*Diane* Harbaugh?"

"Yes."

"You don't know me," he said.

No shit.

"No, I don't."

"I'm not calling at random. So I'd appreciate it if you didn't hang up on me again."

"This is the first we've spoken."

"Yeah, but I've been disconnected more times—"

"Sir, I'm on the line. I'm here now."

Christ.

"Right," he said, clearing his throat. "So this gentleman came by my office, and he asked me to call you. Well, more like demanded."

"What gentleman?"

"Now, that I don't know exactly. He will *not* say his name. I've tried to get it over and over."

"Okay, that's a little strange."

She took a pen from a cup of them and slid a notepad in front of her. Flipped to a blank page.

"What I think, too. But he is sitting right here across from me, still shaking his head no."

"Okay, fine. Can I talk to him then?"

"I'm sorry, ma'am, but he won't take the phone."

She scoffed. *What the hell am I supposed to do, dude?*

"Okay, well, what are we doing here?"

"I'm calling from Tampico, Tamaulipas, Mexico. He says . . ." She could hear him muffling the phone, then bringing it back. "Says, 'El Capataz necesita su ayuda. Está listo.' That make sense, or you need me to translate?"

El Capataz. The Foreman. She didn't need a translator. But it didn't make sense either.

"No, I got it."

"Ma'am? What he's asking is, do you remember him?"

"Hold on, Mr. Travis," she said.

She pressed the space bar on the woman's computer and the LCD display lit up, but of course she wasn't logged in.

"I've been on hold for a good while already—"

"I'll stay on the line. I just need a second. All right?"

"Okay, but hurry."

Rather than risk disconnecting him with the hold button, she set the phone down on the desk. She got up and looked down the hall. She found Cynthia standing in front of the open refrigerator, sniffing and discarding old takeout.

"Cindy? *Cynthia*. Do you have access to TILLER?"

"I don't even know what that is."

"Come here."

They were a few moments logging Cynthia out of her machine, logging Harbaugh in, opening the TILLER database. Cynthia bent over the keyboard, Harbaugh sitting on the desk, her hand over the receiver.

"Type in 'El Capataz.'"

"In the Known Aliases field?"

"Yep."

"Didn't sound like a given name."

"Nope," Harbaugh said, and then picked up the phone. "Mr. Travis?"

"I'm here."

"Just another second, okay?"

She watched the database load. Several names. Nothing familiar.

"He wants you to come down here," Travis said.

"I'm sorry?"

"He wants to meet face-to-face."

"In Tampa— Where again?"

"Tampico. Tamaulipas, Mexico."

She covered the receiver.

"Cross-reference Tampico, Mexico," she said to Cynthia, then into the receiver, "Tamaulipas?"

"Yes. Tomorrow."

At that she laughed outright. No way she was going to fly down to Mexico off of some random call. She couldn't.

"Call me back at this number with your flight information, and I'll get a car," Travis said.

Or could you?

"Hold on now. There's a protocol for this sort of thing." Loads of protocol. Approvals. Dufresne would have to—

Cynthia turned the monitor around for her to see. No names.

"And I'm not empowered to simply meet with, well, who? And I don't even know what this is regarding."

"Hang on," Travis said. He was holding the phone away. She heard some muffled talk. "He says you gave him your card. He says you should remember him."

"What's his actual *name*, Mr. Travis?"

Cynthia looked at her, hands over the keys, ready to type in whatever Harbaugh heard.

"He says to come alone. Tomorrow. I have to go."

"I need to know who he is."

"Please just call me back with that flight info," Travis said, "and I'll take care of the rest. I'm being told to hang up now."

"Wait!"

The line went dead.

"Hung up?" Cynthia asked.

Harbaugh looked out the window at the helicopters at their stationary positions in the sky, motionless save for their blurred rotors. At the end of the chase.

"What do you want to do?" Cynthia asked.

She thought about going to the airport, the idea of it, of getting on a plane, of leaving for Tampico, of leaving for anywhere. The traffic. How long things take.

She couldn't remember meeting the guy. But meet, they did. She set the phone back in its cradle and stood.

"Let's pull some files," she said, setting the phone back in the cradle. "I'm feeling lucky."

CHAPTER SIX

NO RIDER

Harbaugh was back at Santa Anita in time for the penultimate race. All that remained of the crowd was a smattering of old Mexican cowboys in faded jeans and Chinese men and women perched over stat sheets in front of the bank of televisions. She got a tallboy of Budweiser (Bud Heavy, full flavor, no lite shit today) from the enormous bar on the club level. The California sun glowed pink on the mountains, and she plopped down across from Childs right where she'd left him. She chugged the beer. He looked at her with a little alarm.

"Goddamn," he said. She grinned. He called the waiter over for a club soda. A father of two, Childs had a gorgeous, witty wife who was awfully grateful he wasn't a soldier anymore, yet he remained too vain to let a beer calorie pass his lips.

"I'm in the penalty box," she said, burping and grinning. "OPR got me by the dick."

"The hell for?"

A twentysome-minute monologue explaining the whole thing to Childs. From the very beginning. At times she felt like a fool explaining it all, circling back into background, like some idiot who didn't know how to tell a story, how to start a story, but screw it, she told it anyway, there was no way to understand if she didn't give every detail.

Every detail except the shady stuff, the Brady violations, the end-around-the-federal-court wiretap applications. She did tell about her coming over to DEA at Dufresne's urging. And about the button-hole moment in the coat check, the work crush of it all, the double standard of it all. Then onto the things he already knew: Michigan, Bronwyn, that suicidal piece of shit Oscar. And finally telling how she ended up crying in the stall alone, foolish and panicked that she'd never be able to work again.

Childs sipped his drink the whole time, listening sincerely, as far as she could tell.

"I'm not perfect in this," she said, burping like a codger, "but what the actual fuck?"

"The actual fuck?" He waited for Teetering Bridges to beat Bee-keeper at Play by a half-length, the horses urging one another for-ward, oblivious to anything but each other. "The actual-actual fuck is that when superiors and subordinates have any kind of thing, the subordinates are the ones get screwed over. Just like the army."

"Dufresne, though?"

"Dude is cool. But a boss is a boss, covers his own ass. Don't forget that."

She drank her beer and looked over the track, the shadows of the infield stands lengthening, the San Gabriels as dry and angled as folded butcher paper.

"You didn't bet, did you?"

"I should've. You were more right than wrong."

"Told you. Let me see your program," she said. "Gotta get in on the last one."

He looked at her beer, the cash she already had in hand, and shook his head. "Girl, you pretty much a hot mess. Go home, get some sleep."

She grinned and took the program. "Oh, but we haven't even talk-talked yet."

At the upstairs bar she scanned the names and odds. A guy on the phone next to her was doing a pill deal, loudly announcing to some bro that he had five Percocets "not fifteen minutes from there." She slapped her badge on the bar for him to see. He looked annoyed, and then his expression slackened in sudden understanding. He edged away, the idiot.

She ended up choosing the two odds-on favorites, Cheshire's Smile and Scarlet Street, both at 3 to 1. And an Irish long shot by the name of Molly's Revenge. Not one a mudder, from what she could divine from their past races, all clean and fast horses.

When she returned with her slip, she inquired after Lima.

"Only seen a couple white boys in fedoras getting manhandled out of the Champagne Room. He's got a suite at the Langham. We'll put eyes on him tomorrow. So what's this other thing?"

She sipped her new beer.

"Remember when I was just starting out, how I'd give my card to everyone got pinched?"

"Yeah, seed the room."

"Right, give 'em all the same line: 'Look, man, one day you're gonna want to talk to someone. It should be me.'"

"Heard you with that bullshit a billion and one times."

"Well, that bullshit worked." She took the binoculars out of their case and watched for numbers 3, 5, and 8. Her ponies. "One of those dudes called *me*."

"Really."

"Remember that raid in La Palma, like, five, six years ago?"

"Those Mara motherfuckers."

"Right. But there were a bunch of dudes we picked up that day, non–Mara, had nothing on them. Weren't on the list, no priors, no cause, we couldn't keep them without calling ICE."

"Yeah."

"Do you remember that proud motherfucker would only give his name as El Capataz? The Foreman?"

She slid a printout of the file from the deconfliction database. Set up by Homeland Security shortly after 9/11, TILLER cross-referenced data from every federal agency.

"Fuuuuuck. He's basically a number two now? In the CDG? Is this for real?"

She nodded, and Childs whistled at the image of a very high-up man in the Cartel del Golfo—El Capataz, Gustavo Acuña Cárdenas.

"I don't know exactly where he sits on the org chart, but Acuña is El Capataz. It was a bitch to find him, though. I had to get deep in the manila, but I remembered seeing 'El Capataz' in some wire transcript. I finally found it—he was ID'd there as Acuña."

"But there's no mention of Acuña as El Capataz in TILLER?"

"That's the weird part. He doesn't have a jacket here or in Mexico."

"A guy that senior?"

"So he's managed to stay out of trouble, he's connected, whatever. But then I saw that *no one* has searched his file. Not once. I mean, isn't the whole point of TILLER deconfliction? So we can know who else has been watching a guy like this?"

"Right, there should be a dozen DEA agents listed here, at least. ATF, FBI . . . even the Coast Guard could've pinged his file at least once."

"But look here." She pointed to the Date Created field.

"His file was created two days ago? Well, that explains why no one's searched it."

"But it doesn't say *who* created it. He calls me out of the blue two days after he mysteriously appears in TILLER? Something's going on."

"It's weird," he said, sliding the printout to her. "But there could be a lot of explanations."

She watched the horses being led out through the binoculars. Scarlet Street was a feisty bay taking lunging steps. A promising sign.

"So what'd he want?"

She watched Cheshire's Smile surge sideward like he might sun-fish like a rodeo bronc. "Me," she said.

"What do you mean, *you?*"

She pulled down the binoculars and gave him a *get this* look. "To meet him in Tampico," she said. "Alone."

Childs blew out a considerable breath and laced his hands behind his head. "Alone?"

"By tomorrow."

"That's—"

"Impossible. I'd have to get Dufresne's okay, just for starters."

"That ain't happening. Not after today."

"Right."

"Besides, Dufresne'd have to clear it with the ASAC," she said. "Who would then go to the SAC."

"And the SAC in Mexico City would have to get the State Department's okay."

"And Mexico City would have to notify our 'Mexicans partners.' Federales. Local policía."

She looked through the binoculars again. Spotted her other horse, Molly's Revenge, an angry filly tossing her piebald head, skittish. Good girl.

"I have a feeling El Capataz doesn't want this done the normal way," she said. "He doesn't trust the Mexican cops, so he's going way back to an old connection with our side."

"I buy that," Childs said.

"But why's his TILLER file brand-new? And why can't we see who created it? Something's up."

She resumed watching through the binoculars, the horses enter-ing the starting gates, the jockey struggling to get settled on Molly's

Revenge. She had a feeling these were the right horses. When she put the binoculars down, she saw that Childs had slid the printout back to her. Like he didn't want to touch it.

"So, what? You want to go?"

"Don't worry," she said. "Even if Dufresne didn't hate me now, there's no way we could set this up inside a week, let alone a day. And if I just popped down there on my own? On top of all this trouble I'm already in?"

Bettors filed down to the fence along the track to watch the last race. The air had cooled some. Beer in hand, she shivered in the shade.

"Oh, don't play," he said as the race started.

"What?" she asked.

"We both know what you're gonna do!" he said over the staccato barks of the race announcer.

She looked at him to say more, but the magnetic valence of the race pulled their attention back to the track. She took up the binoculars, the horses vibrating in her shaking hands. Cheshire's Smile and Scarlet Street dashed out to a competitive lead in the first three furlongs. Molly's Revenge was stuck somewhere in the back third, and Harbaugh found herself losing heart as she fell farther after the turn. Maybe she was wrong about the filly.

"I'll just call Mexico City myself and let them handle it!" she shouted.

Molly's Revenge was dead last, but surging around the second turn. *C'mon girl*, Harbaugh urged. The horse sped into the middle of the pack, finding her rhythm as Cheshire Smile and Scarlet Street traded the lead.

"The hell you will!" Childs yelled.

The PA blared, the crowd roared and pleaded and swore, but Childs was as clear as a church bell. She let down the binoculars from her eyes to look at him, to make him repeat it. But then Molly's Revenge suddenly surged in the thronged middle of the final lengths, riderless and wild, finishing somewhere near to third. All around them erupted alarm and surprise and questions. She couldn't make sense of it.

"What the hell happened?"

"A horse lost a rider," he said, and she followed everyone pointing at a commotion of trainers and officials running on the dirt, some trying to catch the loose horse, some directing the ambulance rolling toward the jockey, others waving and talking in walkie-talkies. She took in everything, all at once, the confusing spectacle.

"You're going down there," he said in the buzzy stillness, and for a moment she thought he meant the spectacle before them. "You'll see what this guy has and be back before supper. And if you come back with a little something Dufresne can't resist, something that'll smooth over this Oscar bullshit, well, all the better. I know you. You've already looked into flights."

"Am I that transparent?"

"When are we leaving?"

He was serious. It was sweet of him, but she couldn't allow it.

"Oh partner, you can't go AWOL too. Can't have Dufresne gunning for both of us."

"You're not going to meet a cartel underboss without backup, Diane."

"I need backup *here*. Dufresne and OPR are gonna have questions. For you. Besides, this Capataz wants me to come alone."

"I'll wait in the goddamn car! He doesn't have to know—"

"Russell. Enough. You know you gotta stay."

She expected more resistance, but a shout went up as the final announcement rang out. He looked at her ticket and then the scoreboard. He shook his shaved head.

"You won," he said. "And one of your goddamn horses didn't even have a jockey."

"I'm having a helluva day," she said, watching the replay on infield monitor. She finished her beer and stood. "I better go get my money."

He grabbed her wrist.

"Every one of these fool gamblers has days like this." He wasn't looking anywhere else, though. Just right at her. "There's no telling which way your luck's actually running till the whole thing's been played out. And by then . . ."

"By then what?"

"It'll be too fucking late."

CHAPTER SEVEN

THE ONE TWIN

*I*t was the ninth month of the siege. Windrows of corpses littered the stone roads. All the children had long since perished. No dogs, cats, or kine. Every man in the keep verged on cannibalism.

The large warrior sipped the cold horsebone broth from his pot and surveyed the archers and pikemen sleeping behind him, piled up for warmth. He was not native to these lands. These were not his brothers. He was known as the Twin, no one asked him why. He weighed as much as two men—

Cough.

—but his drawn sad eyes yet gave credence to the idea that he lacked his other half—

And another.

—despite the absurd mass such a pair would necessarily make.

Fucking cough.

Tomás Jiménez Quiñones set *The Twin Dawn: A Tale of the Novena Land* on his lap. He regarded the faded cover, a loin-clothed swordsman in the classic airbrushed-on-an-Econoline mode: sword overhead flashing with some unknown thrumming power, a three-breasted goddess affixed to the Twin's thigh, the Frazetta-esque landscape, the sky a gyre of planets spinning off into the void.

"Ahem. Hey. *Bro*. When's this El Codo coming home, eh?"

Tomás lifted his gaze to the American. Name of Sam. White-boy dreads, a neat pair of Dickies, Man U jersey, wallet chain, fattie behind his ear. So much chill tailored to broadcast the pot plantation millionaire he'd become.

Not that Tomás ever submitted to first impressions. He read people true. Beneath the cultivated patina of a quasi-rasta pot dealer, Sam was just another gabacho from the suburbs. His couch slouch from two decades at the Nintendo, the little baby fat jowling at his twenty-six-year-old neck—these gave up his Glencoe, Illinois, pedigree to Tomás. He was like that white boy—what's his name?—on his day off from his day off.

"What's that movie about that dude takes a day off?" Tomás asked.

"*Ferris Bueller's Day Off*?" the dreaded one asked back, sarcastic as fuck.

"Ferris," Tomás said, snapping his fingers.

"Next you gonna ask me what's the karate movie with that kid?" Dude laughed and laughed. "Or what's that star movie about the wars?"

It was damn hard to accept a guy like this sitting on such a stellar grow. But sit he did.

And now he was sitting here to kill a guy. A guy by the name of El Codo, a Sur 13 boss who distributed stateside for the Golfos, in particular to this gabacho Sam here. Now that medicinal weed was legal and Sam had his own grow, he didn't need El Codo's muscle. He was smart enough to keep kicking up to the Golfos in Mexico, but it didn't make sense to give an additional 15 points to Sur 13 no more, so he appealed and the Golfos sent Tomás to sort things out.

"Seriously, though," Sam said. "When's this chode supposed to be back?"

Americans hated to wait. They wanted what they wanted the moment they wanted it. Even ones like the dreaded Glencoe here, thinking he's sitting in El Codo's house to get the jump on him. But that's not what they were actually waiting on. Tomás needed a Golfo ruling before going ahead, so they were waiting on a callback.

"Sometime," Tomás answered.

He looked at his watch. A Timex he got in Juárez. Scratched to hell. Took a licking, all that. He had his own scars, of course. A couple of nasty indentures on the meat of his palms where a garrotte sliced him the time he forgot his gloves in Matamoros. The meter-long track across his stomach from that fool with the stiletto in Saltillo. The burns on his right thigh, like melted pink wax stuck to his skin, still weirdly tender, aching a little every time he sat down.

"These fuckers," Sam said. "Never on time. And El Codo not even to his own funeral, right?"

Sam smiled and tossed his eyebrows at his joke, but what he'd said wasn't funny, and Tomás didn't laugh.

"I guess that's just how they do," Sam said, winding himself up. "Make like they're all important and you're not. That was always El Codo's play for getting a piece of my shit. Be the big dude tells me how things go."

"El Codo was your direct connect for a long time, no?"

"Shit," Sam said, dismissive. "I mean, sort of. I mean, yeah, but that stopped, like, literally years ago. Now he's just middle management. Meaning he don't do shit. Sur 13's an unnecessary layer. Time for layoffs, know what I mean?"

Sam waited for a response from Tomás, who didn't give him one. Sam went on anyway.

"Weed's medical now, and El Codo thinks he gets fifteen points for nothing? My entire op's aboveboard and clean. El Codo don't do shit for me." Sam turned his head up and pushed some kind of whiteboy grito at the ceiling. He seemed to be proud of how untroubled he was.

Tomás wasn't particularly impressed. "Sur 13 made your grow possible," he said. "They are part of the business."

"Sur 13 are leeches. Like the goddamn government. It's all the same shit racket."

Sam looked at Tomás again as if expecting something, agreement maybe, or at least acknowledgment he'd made a good point.

Tomás simply crossed his hands over his lap like a patient priest.

"Anyways," Sam said. "El Codo don't know I can call guys like you up."

"You didn't call me," Tomás said, regretting it as soon as he said it. He wanted this conversation to end. He wanted to read.

"I called the dudes who called. I called my *actual* investors, and they sent you up."

Tomás nodded, slightly.

"I'm paying cold, hard for your services," Sam said, tapping a pocket of his crisp jeans. "Don't forget."

Don't forget, I bought you—the huevos on this gabacho.

Tomás tried to let it drop. It wasn't like him to let some bro get on his nerves. But shit had been gnawing at him lately. He'd even popped off to El Rabioso, the plaza boss, the other day. Tomás was definitely off his game, no idea why. Or maybe it was the game was off.

Outside, a rooster cockadoodled, even though it was 11:37 in the morning. LA roosters, late risers like all the wannabes on the other side of the 101. Or maybe this rooster was already famous. Who knows? Tomás had just seen una chica muy famosa down here in Silverlake. The starlet who'd wrapped her car around a tree. Or maybe she'd knocked down all those parking meters. Something. She'd fucked up her fancy Audi—he remembered seeing it all smashed on TV. Then seeing her in real life walking out of some pipirisnais white-girl shop that used to be a TV repair joint.

Sam sank into the couch opposite Tomás, looked around. There wasn't much to look at. A couch, leather chair, floor lamp, nothing matching. Two walls of bookshelves. Sam drummed his hands on his knees like they needed a video game controller. All those buttons, how did these dudes even play on them? Then Sam took his pistol from inside his jacket and tapped it on his knee. Antsy for a stoner.

Probably toked the sativa when he needed the indica.

Probably was nervous.

Probably hadn't done anything like this before.

So ignore him.

Tomás began to read again.

"Why you reading that?"

¡Chingale! Este güey just will not stop talking.

"It's from that package on the table," Tomás said, gesturing at the open Amazon box and another couple of paperbacks there, turning back to the book.

"Just helped yourself, huh?"

Tomás shrugged.

"Looks pretty stupid," Sam said.

"There's a woman with three chichis on the cover."

Sam scoffed. Got up and touched through the shelf of books. Paperbacks, all of them.

"Everything here's swords and wizards," he said, lifting up a vintage issue of *Heavy Metal* and an Elfquest graphic novel. "What a fucking tool. I'm surprised he reads at all. What kind of gangster reads this shit?"

Tomás set *The Twin Dawn* back down.

"What should he read, then?"

"I dunno, real stuff. Definitely not what an author just made up sitting behind a desk."

"Real stuff like . . ."

"Philosophy, fucking theology. Something *deep*. Like Carlos Castaneda. *That* will blow your ears back. Dude changed my whole perspective."

"On what?"

"On reality, what the fuck else? I've discovered that this"—Sam gestured at all the books—"fictitious bullshit is just a waste of brain-power. Authors are like . . . what is it they call those dude witches?"

"Warlocks."

Snapping his fingers. "Yeah, that. Warlocks. Hella cool word."

Tomás stared at him.

"Writers get their power making stuff up," Sam continued. "And that's power over *you*."

At that, Tomás couldn't help but smile. "Me?"

"The person reading. See, I don't read nothing fictitious, nothing somebody just made up. But, hey, you want to, go ahead. Seriously. Don't let me stop you from tearing through El Codo's library."

"You can tell him when he gets here," Tomás said, picking up the book again. "And then maybe recommend a few titles before we kill him."

"For real, though. You actually think that book's good?"

"What I actually think," Tomás growled, looking for his place, "is no one should tell me what to do."

Sam slumped down in the bean bag. Wouldn't look at Tomás now. Just glared at the books. Knew better than to keep arguing, though.

But why hadn't Tomás just let it go first? Something had really gotten into him, arguing with this gabacho about *books*. Some kind of cloud was darkening his way. Like a spell put on him. Maybe the white boy wasn't wrong to be talking about witches.

Sam took the joint from behind his ear, lit it, sighed. Again and again he kept on sighing. No talking, thankfully, but now all this pinche noisy sighing. The guy doing it just to be annoying. Same as Tomás's big brothers would when sus mamá told them to leave him alone. They'd fart and burp, try to distract him by just sitting there being bored at him. His brothers *hated* him reading.

And they really hated what he read. Coming up in Monclova,

that wizard shit was weak. It'd get you beat down. Definitely he should've grown out of it at the first wisp of a mustache. But then Mamá kept buying D&D setups and Tolkien books, hoping to coax him into a proper education. Sure enough, his English got better. And he was staying home off the streets.

But she wasn't keeping him out of trouble by keeping him el niñito. And when his brothers—ignorant dumb-asses, each one— found his stash. . . . ay chingao. Drawings of shirtless warlords and dwarves! Self-portraits as a knight! Love letters in sloppy medieval script to damsels and wenches!

Soon enough his brother Santiago started calling him El Frodo. At first Tomás played it off and didn't react, but then, one day while playing fútbol in the street, all four of them started saying it over and over. *El Frodo, El Frodo.* He was terrified the nickname would stick. Which of course it did. In Monclova, you couldn't get away with that. The magic in those books seemed so literally gay. Tights and elves. Fairies and hobbits. So British, so soft. He might as well have been an actual joto for having such books. Zero-percent-nothing is cool about *The Chronicles of Prydain.*

El Frodo. The name still burns.

So he tossed out all the books and comics and posters and dice and figures. Just fútbol, all day sometimes, and then basketball and baseball too. He started lifting weights, he got faster. He learned the politics of friendship. He took chicas, the Abriles and Mercedeses and Gracielas, to the Observatory and Xochipilli Park and became a real cherry popper.

One day he heard someone say it behind his back, or maybe he just thought he heard *El Frodo El Frodo El Frodo* and he lost it. He threw chingazos at the first fucker he saw and then at any fool wants some. Broken noses, bruises, kicking dudes when they fell, he kept kicking, he fucked up like five putos by himself. And then everyone says *Tomás está bien loco, he don't give no fucks, a este güey le vale madre.*

He'd rather die than get shit-talked.

So he turned himself into something no one would even think to talk shit about *ever*. He watched Bruce Lee and Freddy Krueger. He watched bootleg tapes of motherfuckers actually dying, bootlegs way better than *Faces of Death*. He studies the bloodiest tabloids—la nota roja—like they were homework. He found pics of encobijados and stared hard at these bodies wrapped in blankets covered with messages, the skinned skulls, detached limbs. He came to understand the deep codes these deadly men always spoke in. He looked until gore didn't push his gaze away, weaponized his mind to better weaponize his body. He learned to box properly and went 13–1, four KOs. For a minute, he was even scouted for the Olympic team. But his project wasn't sport. He was making himself as death-dealing and hard as those badass characters he grew up reading about. But for real-real.

And then one hot summer day he rode his new motorcycle to the recruiting station, and signed his life away with ejército mexicano.

His mother wept. But no one—*no one*—ever called him El Frodo again.

Tomás read on. The Twin got himself in trouble when he went AWOL from the keep. Joined up with a new crew, the Horde, having to prove himself in one-on-one combat. Chapters ending with him passed out facedown and suffocating in the mud or otherwise on death's brink, revived or healed by magic a few pages later.

The writing was crazy, a fantastic hardcore bloodbath. The "corded gouts of blood" from the "pulsating neckstem" of his foe. The "volcanic waves of his roar" that set the wolves of the mountains "howling in winsome brotherhood."

It was silly.

It was awesome.

Tomás flipped to the back cover to have a good look at the author. A black-and-white photo of a dandy with a thin mustache, his mouth full of pipe smoke. An arched, amused eyebrow. As though he knew sooner or later you'd want a look at him, wondering what kind of sadistic genius you were dealing with. *This one*, the author photo said. *Julian Renfield at your service, you sick fuck.*

Tomás flipped to the front pages. Published in 1973 by Darkling Rose Press. He was surprised he'd never seen it before. Because this was his kind of shit. The titillation, the gore, the fancy wordplay, which honestly, he dug, he'd always dug, the way these British guys had a million words and expressions. But the Twin too. His kind of hero. Irresistible and murderous. A mysterious past. His initiation into the Horde where the motherfucker thought he was dead rang true—the Zetas did recruits like that now. Pretending they're about to kill you, taking you all the way down before lifting you up, born anew, back up to the light. Renfield knew what he was talking about. *With a hearty swallow gulping down the distilled grain, he'd earned another day through strength and cunning . . .*

Tomás could go for a drink himself. A bump, a blunt. Something.

He could feel the kid looking at him. Meaningfully. Wanting to talk. Again.

"What?" he asked, his eyes still on the page.

"Thanks for doing this, man."

Tomás vaguely nodded.

"Things just had to come down to this. I known a long time El Codo wasn't gonna negotiate. Had to go to the Golfos."

Tomás nodded again, tried to read again. But he could sense Sam getting ginned up to share yet another notion.

"So," Sam asked, "what happens with his house, you think? Like, after we kill him. When he ain't around no more."

"*This* house?"

"Yeah. 'Cause El Codo'll be a rich corpse, owning this. Place'll be worth a fortune in a couple-few years."

Tomás let the book fall in his lap, Sam's blather now of interest. "Go on."

"Silverlake, man. Hood's blowing up."

"Nah. This the wrong side of the 101, compa."

Sam snorted. "You don't see all the hipsters down here eating tacos and buying cobijas? I been to cool-as-fuck house parties down here. Shit's on Cobrasnake. It's 2007, dude. I got partners already scoping business-zoned spots for the dispensary."

Tomás looked around as though taking in the house for the first time.

"I did see somebody the other day, walking around. Somebody famous."

"Who?"

Tomás shrugged. "Dunno. The chica who crashed her car. But I seen her on TV or billboard or something before."

Sam nodded. "A million dollars. At least. Knock out that wall, open-floor-plan this casa, put a patio out back? It'd be dope." He laced his hands behind his head. "Hell, just throwing out this wizard shit would add five K to the place."

"It's all junkies on Sunset," Tomás said. "And chickens and used cars here in the hills." The rooster called out on cue. "See? No está chido, güey."

"Dude, there's *tons* of gays out here already. Pretty soon be lines for brunch."

"What you mean? Like breakfast?"

"Benedicts, bro. That's when you know there's beaucoup cash to be made."

It was hard to tell if the Glencoe kid, so far from the big green lawns of the Chicago exurb where he'd grown up, was right about the LA housing market. Zetas like Tomás were all ex-military, and working for the Golfos, Tomás didn't learn shit about distro or logistics, let alone real estate. Zetas got paid to kill. What Zeta understood real estate? But maybe Sam did. The kid had made a good wad growing medicinal weed. How the fuck did he know when and how to do that? Some kind of gabacho superpower that let him see into the beating American heart of these things?

Maybe that's what had been eating Tomás. That he didn't know a damn thing about business or the real world, besides deleting people who existed in it. Books and killing, that's all he knew. And what kind of shadow life was that? You set down your book and escort people out the door.

"How shitty's that novel?" Sam asked.

"Enough, cabrón."

"Jesus, man. You actually grok it. You're killing me."

Keep talking, Tomás thought, and I might.

Sam scoffed, leaped up, went over to the fridge. Even after smoking the whole joint and quasi-napping, he was still anxious, wasn't calming down. What was taking El Rabioso so long to call? Tomás and the Glencoe kid would come to blows before this was over.

The kissing sound of the fridge opening, jars ringing against one another on the door. The kid's voice redounded out of the empty fridge. "El Codo don't even have no beer. What kind of person has no beer?"

The kid didn't have no superpower, he was just an audacious brat. Always needing to have something in his hand, something in his mouth. Like a baby, pacifying himself. Pinche mamón. What was so bad about Sam's life that he had to get all fucked up? White. American. Young. Knows how to run a grow. Money. Could drop out of this business and go to college, get a straight job. Could get into real estate tomorrow. The kid was made of options. These gabachos, they never knew how good they had it. Most guys like Tomás *had* to get pedo all the time—mota, coke, roches y pildoros, crystal—just to cope. Their lives were too much the things they had to do for the bosses. The blood and bodies, the screams. But Sam, Sam had it pretty—

The cell phone in Tomás's pocket buzzed. It was El Rabioso, Tomás's direct superior in the Golfos, the plaza boss of Reynosa. Tomás went into the kitchen with it vibrating in his hand.

Sam shut the fridge. "Who is it?" he asked, excited.

Tomás shooed Sam out with his chin. He was about to answer but glanced out the kitchen window at the dying pomegranate tree, the dirt yard. Thinking, a person could cut down that tree and then put in a little grass. Be a nice view. The reservoir, the houses on the opposite hillside. He could picture a patio, too. Saltillo tile. A chimenea, a fountain or pond, maybe. That'd look good. More like somebody's home.

"¿Bueno?"

"¿Estás en Califas, no?"

Tomás told him yes, he was still in California.

"El mero patrón te necesita en Tampico." The man's voice was raspy, impatient. Like he'd been up all night on the phone. "Ándale pues."

Tampico? He'd never been there, never heard of any cartel business there. He was going to ask what for, but El Rabioso was already telling him to round up an estaca and go there. El Esquimal, the boss, wanted Tomás specifically to take care of this. There was an impatience in El Rabioso's voice, like someone was watching him make the call or a meeting was held up for it. And he hadn't said anything about this LA job.

"¿Y que hago con el asunto de Los Angeles?" Tomás asked.

Now El Rabioso sounded pissed to be answering questions, barking "Sí sí sí, finish the thing in LA and then get down to Tampico." Finish it how? Tomás wondered, but El Rabioso was on about Miramar, near the refineries. La Plataforma y Válvula Petrolífera. Una compañía owned by an American, name of Travis Moman. He wrote it down.

When Tomás asked what was so urgent, El Rabisio hesitated, and his voice dropped.

"Gustavo," he said, as though a single name was sufficient to explain it. Tomás flipped through a mugbook of Gustavos in his mind. Most of them dead. "¿Gustavo El Chuco?"

No, El Rabioso told him, not that Gustavo. The boss's nephew Gustavo. The one who builds the things. Gustavo El Capataz, Gustavo the Foreman, Gustavo the Nephew. *That* Gustavo. A major dude, higher even than a plaza boss, right there one rung down from the big boss in the flowchart. The one who built stash houses with safe rooms and secret passages in all El Esquimal's places in Mexico. Gangster real estate with getaways and torture chambers and lairs and all kinds of shit.

Sounded like now he was making his own getaway. Tomás wondered what he'd done and what they wanted done to him.

"Digáme," Tomás said. "¿Quiere torturarlo?"

He wasn't really asking if he should torture him, he was probing to see why he was running, what the trouble was, what was the scope of the damn thing.

"No, cabrón," El Rabioso growled. "Si él muere, tú mueres."

Fuck. They wanted him alive. Which meant he'd need guys. A whole other level of complication. Wresting a man from place against his will would take force. Shit like this always went sideways. And Tomás could tell he wasn't being told everything, and with El Rabioso it was pointless to ask. Pointless to ask why the boss's nephew was on the run. Pointless to ask who he was running to. Pointless to ask what kind of trouble this put everyone in. The whole thing was such a setup to fail.

"¿Entiendes, Tomás?" El Rabiso shouted. "Es muy importante. No lo mates."

He'd been quiet. Fretting too long.

"¿Comprendes, soldado?"

"Sí," Tomás said, thinking, No, I don't comprendo. "Claro."

"¿De verdad?" El Rabioso was pissed at the little sigh Tomás let slip, and he started going off, asking him did he have nothing else to say, was Tomás the one gives the orders now, was he the boss, was that how it was, did he want to share his thoughts about that.

"Nada más, señor," Tomás said.

El Rabioso hung up. Before he could get clear on the Sur 13 and the Glencoe kid. Who was now lingering in the doorway to the kitchen.

"Who was that?" he asked.

Tomás didn't say. He just looked at the kid.

"What?" Sam asked.

"You ever kill someone?"

"We've fucked some fuckers up. Humboldt County's no joke. People try to run up on the crop all the time." Sam bit his lip, nodded at a fake memory. "I've beaten some dudes down. And we might've killed one guy once."

"Okay."

"We probably did."

"Okay."

"I know how the game goes, what I'm saying. You need pros for a problem like this. That's why I called the big guys in to take care of Sur 13."

Tomás felt suddenly, profoundly dry inside.

Like his heart and lungs would blow away in a strong wind.

Like he was a papel-maché piñata stuffed with dead grass.

Like you could maybe just poke your finger through him.

A spell had been put on him, and he didn't know when.

Tomás turned around away from the kid and pulled a glass from the cupboard and filled it with water and looked out the window into the backyard. Badly laid paving stones churned up by the growing palm. Holes in the dirt dug by some animal. Weeds and dead grass. Fixing a sad yard was a problem he didn't know how to solve. It was okay that it looked sorta budget. It reminded him of Monclova, in a way.

"I have to go," he said.

"Whaddya mean? I just said I need pros. At least you and me. Where you gotta go?"

Tomás looked at him. This kid. Did he even know how stupid it was, asking a guy like Tomás his business? Huevos, man. No, he was just dumb. Either way, he decided to tell him. What the fuck, the sun wasn't about to set or nothing. There was some day left.

"First, Sam, I must go get some men from a prison."

"What? Like break 'em out?"

"I would call it more like borrowing."

"In Mexico?"

"Yes."

"Cool. *Borrowing.*" Sam nodded his approval. "To fuck up these Sur bitches?"

"The nephew of the cartel's boss is hiding in Tampico."

"Tampico? Where the fuck is that?"

"On the Gulf."

"Shit. Why's he hiding?"

"I don't know."

"He's probably turned snitch on the jefe, right? Like gone to the federales."

"Perhaps."

"So you gotta smoke him. Tight. I get it."

He gripped his own gun a little too much like a toy.

"No, I have to bring him back alive. Which makes it difficult."

"No doubt. Way harder to make a dude go somewhere than off him."

Tomás sighed. He looked at the kitchen window. Maybe he could do something about that yard. But for now, there was work to do.

"That is why you must handle things here yourself."

"By myself? I never—"

"Look, güey, you wanna be in business with CDG, you gotta pull your weight."

Tomás pulled from his pocket a bag of coke and a knife. He opened the bag and scooped a bump onto the blade.

"This'll help," he said.

Sam took the hit and did one more, and then Tomás did two.

"You want more?" he asked.

Sam shook his head no. Tomás shrugged, snorted another two himself.

Sam took the pistol out and took a deep breath and gripped the thing.

He leaned against the sink.

"You just wait in here. Those steps out front are steep. He always comes in here for a glass of water."

"How do you know?"

"You follow your target, Sam. It's a hunt. You learn about the prey."

"All right. I can do this. All right." He bobbed his head to some private hype-music, a soundtrack in his head.

"You stand over there, near the pantry. When he turns around, he'll see you pointing your pistol at him. You come into the middle of the kitchen, like this. He'll move over this way in front of the door behind you. Open it."

"This door?"

"Yes."

"That a basement down there?"

"Yes."

"So I shoot him from where you're standing. Then he falls down here?"

"That's the idea."

"All right. Pretty slick." Sam was impressed. "What's all this plastic up in the doorway?"

"To keep all your blood from spraying onto my wall."

"*My* blood?" Sam asked.

"I don't want blood on the walls, Sam. This house gonna be worth something someday. Even with all my shitty books in it."

Tomás fired and Sam spun and he fired again and the kid fell backward. He tangled in the clear sheeting and was sucked down the stairs, plastic and all. He'd fallen in exactly the way Tomás said he would. Which was good.

He went downstairs to finish up. He was relieved to see the Glencoe kid's bewilderment still intact in his dead eyes. Tomás didn't like it when they were scared. He hardly ever had anything against them. Even the ones who talked shit about his books.

CHAPTER EIGHT

TAMPICO

E ven after Harbaugh looked up the *World Factbook* basics on Tampico (Mexican Navy shipyard, "sundry" pipelines, Pemex refineries, et blah cetera blah), she still couldn't put her finger on why she felt like she'd been there before.

This vague sense of foreknowing vexed her all the way from her apartment to LAX, then through the red-eye flight. She finally quit trying to figure it out in the back of the Tampico cab. She had to concentrate on her Spanish, and even then it came out stuttering and stupid as she told the driver to go to La Plataforma y Válvula Petrolífera in Miramar, just south of the refineries. It seemed like the driver understood, though.

As soon as he put the cab in gear, she realized she hadn't asked him anything about price. "Wait," she said. "How much?"

He looked at her in the rearview mirror and tilted his head to the side.

"Oh, lo siento," she said. "Perdón, perdón. Pero, uh, ¿cuánto cuesta?"

The driver kept looking at her silently. There were three

wristwatches clipped around the mirror, two digital, one a dial. As if so many watches gave him more time.

"Cuarenta," he said finally.

She had no idea whether or not forty pesos was a fair price, but she nodded and said gracias.

The cabbie nodded back, picked up a T-shirt from where it lay on the passenger seat, and began tucking it into the driver's-side window against the sun. Though it had rained earlier and low areas were swamped with standing water, the sun was out and hot. When the cabbie situated himself, he took off with a honk, and Harbaugh leaned back in her seat to watch the city go by. They passed boxy, flat-roofed buildings, pink and lime green and orange and purple, exteriors alternatingly weathered and fresh. And so many trees, palms and lemons and mangoes and figs and others she didn't know, trees all along the roads and twisting through the gates and spilling out of courtyards and springing from every edifice.

The answer to why she felt like she'd been here before arrived with a visceral force that shuddered her upright: *Frida.* Of course. Harbaugh had written about Tampico in a college paper on Frida Kahlo. Honors English at Santa Clara University.

Or was it honors history?

Maybe both. She was honors everything back then. She could still remember the Tampico passage she gussied up for the paper, something about these baby blues and sea greens, the wrought-iron balconies and galleried facades designed to imitate Spanish lace. Even then she wanted . . . well, what? Not recognition, not that exactly. To be worldly. To possess cosmopolitan urbanity. Something.

Whatever the reason, Kahlo had been Harbaugh's go-to topic for the better part of undergrad, at all the debate tournaments and the dorm hangs with earnest, stoned dorks. How on-and-on she'd go about Frida's folk-art anticolonialism, her magical realism, her undaunted self-promotion in an art world that couldn't harbor a single woman genius. Her polio, her car accident, her lifetime of pain. Diego Rivera, seriously *fuck* Diego Rivera. The Mexicayotl movement, socialism, communism, Trotskyism—

Trotsky.

Frida's affair with Trotsky.

Riding out in a government cutter from Tampico to meet the Russian revolutionary, beckoning him to safe haven, she was a vision, no doubt: tight ornate braids haloing her face, earrings of dangling jade. As exotic to the Russian as agave spikes or cactus flowers. Trotsky's plain Russian wife, Natalia, didn't have a chance.

Their affair, it started right here, in Tampico.

Well, not *here*, stopped in traffic on the way to the Zona Industrial under a web of power lines, idling next to a yellow-and-red Oxxo.

No, the Tampico where Frida had introduced the Trotskys to Mexico was a few miles back, at the Catedral de Tampico, the fluted Corinthian columns and cantera stone, the clock chimes lifting the pigeons en masse like a palm. It was weird to remember this place in such a contrived way, and to be here now, doing some clandestine shit, and in that, to feel like she knew the revolutionaries. Frida on a trajectory to international fame. Trotsky faring worse by a Stalinist's ice axe. But their brief affair. Back in college, Harbaugh kinda had a thing for a Trotsky.

Dufresne resembled Trotsky now, just a touch, come to think of it. That goatee he grew a few years ago, his caffeinated mushroom cloud of hair.

All she did was straighten his collar after he pulled on his coat. And she looked at him. He paused in her tipsy gaze. Everything moved slower and with an intentional heft. He didn't say anything, and neither did she. He leaned in and she leaned back into the coats and laughed and he pulled them aside to get her or get to her and she looked at him *come here already give us a kiss*. He began to or seemed to begin to . . . Then the fast voices outside broke the spell. He helped her out of the rack and both of them emerged from the coat check. The only suspect thing with his wife was that he had the wrong coat,

Harbaugh's instead of hers. Or both coats, she couldn't remember. She more or less bolted.

That was the end of it, any inkling of a work crush, older men in general. And the moment itself, it was nothing. How many dozens of passes made at her, stone sober. Guys on her own team. Urlacher every other day. The coat check was nothing, so stop rehashing it. It was nothing.

A nothing so big I'm down here in Mexico?

Something like that.

And that's gonna get me back in Dufresne's good graces, like Childs was saying at the races?

It couldn't hurt to get somebody like El Capataz. A source at that level? Could make Dufresne's career.

And your own.

Which is why she was here sitting in no-breeze heat, breathing sour exhaust. For her career.

She leaned out the window a little bit, hoping to get some fresh air, but that didn't help much. Still so steamy. Just sitting in the cab she was soaked, sweat on her back, her legs, her lips, everywhere. She felt like the sunflowers in the median looked—drooped and downcast from the morning shower.

Finally the traffic broke and they got up to pace. There were pedestrians everywhere, catching up with the day's work after the rain, she guessed. The cabbie kept tapping the horn at someone he knew walking, at intersections, at another cab. He worked the horn in a kind of crude Morse—warnings, touts, and acknowledgments.

They closed in on the beach, where roadside fruit sellers chopped watermelon and pineapple. Men on bikes towed carts full of inner tubes, swimsuits, goggles. Hawkers held shells and shook towels in the air. They were right close to the water now. She could smell salt spray and yesterday's shellfish and melon rinds and meat smoking on grills. Playa Miramar, even the name was pretty. She craned her head, hoping for a glimpse of the water, but all she saw was a light-house, white and green with streaks of rust.

She texted Childs. **Landed. Going to the place. I'll be in touch.**

It was her work phone—she'd left her personal phone in the glove box, waiting on a subpoena. It wouldn't come to that. Dufresne would come around, she'd come back with this cartel underboss. Something good would come.

The cab turned up a street that evolved into a long boulevard that took them away from the ocean and tourists. A tinge of polymer now, chemicals. Looming concrete walls topped by razor wire. Cranes and towers and grids of pipes and stairs and smokestacks. They went into the Zona Industrial, past a long line of Pemex oil tankers sitting idle on the railway tracks, gated parking lots full of trucks. Jumpsuited workers chatted idly in spangled reflective vests.

They turned into an oil-slicked gravel drive and came to a gate with a security guard who halted them. The man took a miffed interest in Harbaugh in the back seat, as though she were the latest of the day's outrages. He called on the phone in his little station. He inspected the trunk, and the car grew hot in the forced stillness. He finally let them through.

A large American—tanned, late fifties, wearing Brooks Brothers and a silverbelly Stetson—came out of a trailer and waved them on ahead toward a building the size of an Arkansas Walmart.

When the car pulled in front of a set of huge open bay doors, she paid the cabbie, got out, and stood there with her black duffel, watching the man labor under the heat toward her. Travis Moman. She'd asked Childs to do a background check on him. No priors. Divorced, a house in Houston, mid-six-figure income, permanent-resident status in Mexico. Nothing hinky.

The cab pulled away as he came up. He took off his hat. He had the welcoming eyes of a natural salesman.

"You're Agent Harbaugh?"

"Diane," she replied, shaking his outstretched hand. Soft. Fat.

"I'm Travis Moman," he said with a Texas-gladhander accent that matched the open road he repropped atop his head. Underneath his manners, she could see he had all kinds of things on his mind, her presence just the latest. He took her bag and headed toward the door next to the open bays and threw it open, beckoning her to go first. He was watching the fence and she looked too, but if there was anything beyond the palms to see, she didn't.

"Welcome to Tampico," he said, in a helpless and wry way.

She nodded and stepped inside. Her eyes adjusted to the dimness. A sweet tang of solvents. Long rows of pipes and fittings. Crates on high shelves. An idle forklift parked against the wall. It felt like the depot where her father maintained the school buses. A feeling of hidden things. Daddy's liquor in his tool locker. A feeling she had on cases that found her in auto shops and outbuildings. Bales of coke in hidden compartments. She realized this was such a case, that a narco was tucked away somewhere in this warehouse. An inevitable aptness, a kind of bloodhound déjà vu.

"What do you do?" she asked, her voice swallowed in the warehouse's vastness.

"I sell refinery equipment mostly," he said as he beckoned her into a side door into a reception area. A few chairs, magazines. Air conditioning.

"So where's our guy?"

"I gotta give you something first," he said, setting her bag behind the counter, leading her into a hallway through an open door. They passed a lavatory, a supply closet, stopped at an office door, vertical blinds closed against the floor-length window. He unlocked the door, stepped inside, and stood in front of his own desk, hands on his hips. He pointed with his belly and belt buckle at the bricks of cash stacked under the lamp.

"What's that?" she asked.

"The way it works down here is, *I* pay. Customs. State, municipal, Pemex, the Finance Ministry. They all get something. No one buys *me* off."

"That's a lot of money."

"Back in my day a phone call was a dime."

"What else is he paying for?"

"My everlasting silence, at the very least. A sum like that, I assume he feels entitled to an array of services."

"Right."

He waved a hand in the direction of the money. "So take it."

"Take it where?"

He stepped over, licked a thumb, and pulled off a bill and held it up. "Tell him no problem for the phone call, we're square. And then give the rest of the twenty-five Gs back." When she didn't make a move for it, he sighed. "I don't want any trouble. I didn't ask for this."

"I get it," she said. "But I'm not gonna open with 'Your money's no good here.' Let me get the lay of the land first."

"You came alone," he observed.

"Just like he asked."

Moman looked at the ceiling. The floor. Then over her shoulder at the doorway.

"Do you have a plan?" he asked. A thing he wouldn't have asked a man. But a fair question.

She did not have a plan so much as a few . . . *options*. For contingencies. If things broke right in any of a half-dozen ways, she'd get Dufresne on the phone and explain and make nice. After all, El Capataz had jumped into her lap. What was she supposed to do? It was better to ask for forgiveness than permission. She could only imagine what an informant at his level could bring in. Operations. Conspirators. Dirty money, dirty banks, dirty authorities. Who knew? Maybe he was just making contact, would have to head back in, would turn informant.

"Of course I have a plan," she said. "Why don't you show me where he is?"

Moman led her down the wide middle of the warehouse and then hung a left at a row of shelves, unmarked metal objects arranged on them according to some obscure method.

"There's about ten refineries just north of here," Moman said. "Petromex and so on in the Zona Industrial. I move odds and ends for the tankers that come in and out of the port, but most of the stuff here is for refineries. The old man was a wildcatter, so I reckon I come by it natural."

Harbaugh listened as the heat and the light streaming in from the high clouded windows in the distant ceiling gave the vast space a cloistral quality. Like summer mass. Stained glass. Smoke from the censer.

"So he just appeared at your doorstep yesterday without warning?" Moman tipped back his hat and let out a thoughtful sigh.

"Naw. He called ahead, made an appointment with the receptionist to see me. But then I got hung up, ran late. He sat here a few hours at least. I figured he'd blow out and didn't really give a damn, not knowing who the hell he was. But there he sat, pretty as a prom date. Decked out in the spiffy Western-cut sport coat and the pressed denim jeans and the real silver on his black leather belt. Only thing missing was his boutonniere."

"You know he's a narco."

"First impression was only that he was norteño. But him wanting me to call the DEA kinda telegraphed it."

Travis slowed their pace in a canyon of shelves, the gloom and heat and odor of metal growing more hellish with every step in this hot warehouse. A true cathedral of the Americas. Not a church—a warehouse. Her head swam. Sweat beaded on the Texan's neck, ran down his shirt collar. He breathed heavy, this air like a fever.

"He's way back here?" Harbaugh asked, sounding more wary than she wanted.

Travis looked over his shoulder and stopped before a heavy steel door, industrial beige like the walls. Lever handle, key lock. He took off his hat, his hair pasted like a decal to his forehead.

Then she felt it. A cool stir of air. A smile broke across his face. Then hers. She tilted back her neck to the cool breeze.

"This joint can get hotter'n a Willie Fourth of July picnic," he said softly. "Times we're really busy in the warehouse, I work in there." He pointed a thumb over his shoulder at the door. "Doubles as a temperature-controlled storage space. There's a leak in the duct, makes a nice little pool of cool right here."

"He's inside?" she asked, patting the sweat from her neck.

"Never thought someone would rack out in here, but there you go."

"You're whispering."

"Installed a jam bolt yesterday can only be undone from inside." Moman said this as though it were a sly secret, almost a playful thing. "Why we're not going in yet. He might could shoot us, we're not careful."

"He's armed?"

"Yeah, he's armed all right," he said, amused by the question.

The heat had been oppressive a moment ago, but now she was freezing. She started to cross her arms, but stopped. She didn't want Travis thinking the cold bothered her, thinking that any of this bothered her. She buttoned her blazer, as if in preparation to meet the man.

"Three quick, two slow, three quick. A pause and then do two quick, three slow, two quick. And step back for him to open up. He don't come out. You gotta go in." He performed the knocks. "You just make sure he knows I ain't taking that money," he said, stepping away from the door. "I don't want no trouble."

Ten minutes, and she found she still couldn't enter the room. It wasn't fear so much as dread, the same dark-hued knowing feeling that preceded Oscar. Like *she* was the door.

She just kept standing there shivering, air-conditioned air pooling at her stationary feet.

The fuck are you doing.

After the long flight, she'd had the urge to take off running through an empty alone place. She wanted to feel her muscles straining, sweat stinging her eyes, her lungs thrumming. Instead she was here, standing still, suddenly freezing. No backup, no middle ground between sweltering and freezing, and nothing to do but knock.

CHAPTER NINE

MAN IN THE BOX

The door sealed behind her with a heavy thump. Gustavo Acuña Cárdenas—El Capataz, the Foreman—stood before her on a worn grass mat, his hands open at his sides as if to show her he wasn't armed. An embroidered brown suit jacket, tan piping. Cowboy angles, gold-and-black untucked Versace button-down, designer jeans with a straight-edge crease broken in places, like a man back from a night out at the dancehall.

"Buenos días," he said. "¿O tardes ya?"

"No, it's morning—mañana, Señor Acuña," she said.

"Llámame Gustavo, por favor," he said. He pointed behind her. "Cierra la puerta."

She looked at him, unsure what the word meant.

"Lock it," he said.

She nodded and popped the bolt in place and he thanked her. It was cold in here too. She resisted a shiver, took stock of the room. His musty musk. A floor lamp with a naked bulb that burned too bright to look at. A 1950s metal desk against the wall, a faux leather office chair and a newer mesh-back one. Filing cabinets, a cot, a cooler, and a rather large television. A greasy paper sack, a sixer of empty Jarritos bottles. Through an open door in the back she could see a toilet and sink. And atop a rumpled sleeping bag on the cot lay two semiautomatic pistols. A Taurus 9 mm and a FN Five-Seven, looked like.

"I left them over there," he said of the guns, "to put you at ease."

"All right."

"To say to you I can be trusted. See?"

"Yes, I understand. Thank you."

He lifted his chin as if to say *You're welcome, of course*. He wasn't handsome, but he wasn't plain or ugly. His appeal lay in the sense of importance he radiated. Like a beloved mayor or corrupt bureaucrat.

"I'm a bit surprised you had my card all these years."

"I didn't. We all put them in the trash." He made a dramatic pause. "But I got a good memory." He smiled. His veneers glowed.

"Why'd you memorize it?"

He pulled over the faux leather chair for her and sat on the cot, springs squealing. He asked her if she wanted anything to drink. *Don't take anything from him.* She passed. He nodded, and took up with her question.

"First time I got arrested in El Norte, I was muy joven, twenty-one, something. Cops on purpose put me in a cell with a bunch of Los Trece Locos. Me, I'm no Loco, they knew I wasn't, they knew I knew it. Some bad shit."

Gustavo held up his fingers. They looked like they'd been broken and glued back together many years ago. He pointed to his left eye socket, which she saw now was out of shape, his nose a bit bulby.

She nodded, letting him know that she understood.

"I broke everything defending myself. I bled like an animal." He popped out his front dentures and sucked them back in. "Went to the dentist, mmmm, five times? Something like that. Some puto finally kills me someday, they gonna get rich with all the gold out my mouth for sure."

"That's terrible. I'm sorry."

"Eh, American cops are like that. Pero you, you"—pointing at her—"weren't like that. You gave me my own cell, made sure I got some food."

"I did?"

"Yeah, it was you. And after you left, even one guard start calling me Mister before they deport my ass. Not saying I was treated like no boss. Just like a man, same as others. But that mattered to me, that these things changed after your visit." He shrugged. "So I remember you. I make sure I remember your number from your card, 'ey."

Harbaugh nodded, didn't say anything. She waited to let him talk. That was the whole point of giving out her card all the time—maybe someday someone would have things to say. Maybe even then she saw it in him. A seed of a notion of a desire to talk.

But now he sighed and stared off.

"You never worked in Mexico before, right?" he finally asked.

"No. California mostly. Virginia, Louisiana, all in the States."

"Nobody yet touched you."

"Touched me?"

He laughed. Stopped to look at her—was she serious? foolish?—and then laughed again.

"What's so funny?"

"I never seen your name. ¿Entiendes? I never heard Diane Harbaugh mentioned. Never found it wrote down. Nobody down here know you."

Was he actually trying to diminish her? *You called me*, she wanted to say.

"Mira, I know the books, and there's names all over," he said, solemnly. "Many many many names. You got no idea all of them. They keep so much records of things—híjole, ustedes don't even know."

She realized what he was on about.

"You mean dirty cops," she said.

"Dirty anybody. Dirty peónes to dirty presidentes. I'm talking everybody that's got touched."

"You don't know who to trust."

"These days, everyone been touched. Todos. That's why you are special."

"You trusted Mr. Moman."

"I *paid* Señor Moman."

"A pretty penny too."

"Pretty penny?"

"Twenty-five grand."

He smiled.

"What?"

"Are you—what you call it? 'Shaking me down'?" He tugged at his sport coat, popped the sleeves.

She sat up straight, noticed right away what her own body was unconsciously telling her: she needed leverage. A foothold. It ached, in a way. And she'd fucked up, mentioning the money, putting him in the position to give and take.

So flip it. Find out what he wants. Grant him a wish, so you have something to take away.

"I'm not shaking you down. Only you can tell me why I'm here now, Señor Acuña."

"That is three questions."

"Is it," she said, a touch of tough bitch in it.

"Por qué you. Por qué here. Por qué now." He counted these off on his broken fingers. "You? Because you give me your card. And you're not in the books." He folded down his ring finger. "Here? Because in this box"—he folded down his middle finger—"nobody can fuck me up."

"So why now?"

He regarded his index finger aloft and then tapped his temple with it.

"Because what's in here."

He smiled.

Those front teeth were stunningly white. Enamels like tiny tile. His nails, long crescents, almost delicate. He might have been broken, but he'd been put back together, groomed and perfected. He looked as though he hadn't a need in the world.

"I got a big secret," he finally said. "Enorme."

Don't ask. You don't give a shit. Let him know you've heard this a million times before. And you don't want a secret. You expect a pipeline of secrets.

She crossed her hands on her lap.

"About the Cartel del Golfo," she said, flatly.

"Claro. That's why you came right away, no?"

He was still smiling. Joy in this sense of leverage. *You came right away, you came running.* Not in the books. A nobody. An errand girl. *Calm down. Choose your words and level the playing field. Find out what he wants . . . and then withhold it.*

"What can I give you for this?" she asked, slightly emphasizing "give," the gift, her gift to him.

"A lot. Big help from you is what I want. Enorme."

Good. He needs something enorme. Wait for it.

She held up her palms as though to ask what.

"First, I got to get a new face so no one knows me. I mean *no one.* Even God on his throne shouldn't recognize me when I sneak into heaven. No me identificaría."

She nodded as if to say *This is nothing, no problem, I'm made of favors.*

"What else?"

"I want a full American life. Social security, ID, retirement, what they call it? The golden parachute. I leave with very little. I could not arouse suspicion."

"I understand. What else?" she asked.

"I need this deal on paper."

Bingo. A guarantee, a promise. She leaned forward, doubt fixed in her expression.

"Hmm," she said, thinkingly. A way of saying *That could be tricky.* "What else?"

"Not gonna be in no Supermax the rest my life. I don't leave this room without that paper in my hand." He held out a palm, tapped a finger on it.

She sighed, shook her head.

"Señor Acuña. You didn't expect me to bring some kind of legal agreements to this meeting?"

"You know who I am, sí?"

He wanted a face, money, a deal. It was time to put him in debt for these things.

"I know you're a member of the Cartel del Golfo," she said. "And I came right away like you asked. *Alone* like you asked. It would've taken days, a week, to get approval for a sit like this. But to meet you, in this way, in the time frame you asked me to . . . I had to ignore protocols. But I decided to make a good faith effort and come right away. *By myself*, like you asked."

He searched her face for deceit. She let him. Because there was none. In fact, she had already given him so much. Just coming. Being able to come.

"Like you were saying, I'm not in the books," she said. "This visit is off the books."

He grinned again, this time sadly.

"Everything ends up in books, mi querida."

She stood. He appeared small, smaller somehow than a few moments ago.

"But if I knew what this was all about, then I could begin—"

"You would be in as much danger as me."

"Danger?"

"I am the only one who knows," he said.

She looked closely at his face, his stubble, his jet-black hair. Those bloodshot eyes. He *was* harboring something big. Or many things. Operational things. Hideouts. Laundering methods. But also something that ate at him, his conscience. Something he needed to get away from, if his haggard expression was to be believed. Something hounding him.

"You're on the run," she said.

"It won't be long."

"What won't?"

"Before they all come."

"Who? The cartel?"

"Everyone wants what I know," he said. "Everyone."

She suddenly felt like she did in Michigan, like she was being watched from the trees.

Why?

His TILLER file.

Whoever looked at it would see who accessed it, would see one name—

Diane Harbaugh.

Whoever had created it three days before—

That's who's watching from the trees.

"Get the paper. Take me to America. Then I will give you everything."

She closed the heavy door behind her and then heard the thick and immediate click of the bolt as Gustavo locked himself in. She locked it and pocketed the key. Her every instinct was to take flight.

But there was really no choice. She'd have to get that paper.

CHAPTER TEN

BLUE LINEN

She shivered in the cold blast of the AC and rubbed her arms under her jacket. It took two steps to arrive in the heat of the warehouse, warming, soon sweltering. She opened her phone. No signal. Then a deluge of text from Bronwyn: **Just call me. Jesus. I don't know what I did—**

She toggled to Childs's number. He picked up on the first ring.

"I'm with him. El Capataz. And he has something big," she said. "You remember that walk-in, the lawyer tight with the Aryan Brotherhood? He was all spooked to talk to us because he knew about all those murders in Chula Vista? Same thing here."

"Okay, okay," Childs said. "Hold on."

The sound of him shuffling down the hall to the corner break room with the funny smell. Windowless, something horrendous in the drain back there. Where no one ate, a good place to talk.

"He's nervous, thinks he's in trouble, but I don't have any evidence of that per se. If we cool him out, I bet he goes back inside and we get the works. Even now, he's *dying* to tell me *something*. But he won't until he gets to the States. I'm thinking if we get him on the phone with someone in the Southern District DA's office—"

"You gotta get out of there," he cut in. "Like, now."

"That's what I'm saying! We gotta move on this."

"No. I'm talking about you. *You* need to leave."

"What? Why?"

"They know you're there."

"They who? I just got here."

"Dufrese said DC called. State Department."

"What? DC? How the hell—?"

"Cromer was chewing Dufresne's ass about you a few minutes ago. Then Dufresne comes out, *pissed*, yelling at me. Did I know you were in Mexico? The fuck kind of partner am I? For a second I thought we might have to throw down."

"This is really weird, Russ."

"Much worse than just weird," Childs said.

"No, I mean, it's shady as hell that *anyone* knows I'm down here."

"I didn't tell."

"I know—it's gotta be TILLER, Russ. Somebody created that file two days ago. I'm the only one who looked at it. And now everyone from DC to LA knows I'm down here?" The line was silent. "Russell?"

"Look, whatever's going on ain't good. You gotta come back."

She saw the sense of it, but also wondered how it'd make a difference at this point.

"Stop being such an MP for a minute. It's too late for me to get out of trouble."

"You're already in deep shit as it is over Oscar. Now this? Cut bait."

He was right. But she knew she wasn't going anywhere.

"Look, do me a favor. Reach out to the San Antonio office—"

A racket of voices from somewhere in the warehouse.

"Diane, I can't. I'm sorry I told you to go down, but Dufresne and Cromer—"

Something was going on.

"Hold on," she said.

"You have to listen to me," Childs said.

She took the phone away from her ear to hear the voices. Men. Growing closer. Her hackles rose and she looked around, half wondering if she should go see who it was, other half wondering if she should hide.

"Shit, someone's here," she hissed.

"Who?"

"I don't know. The cartel? What do I do?"

"What the fuck, Diane? You get out of there! Just leave!"

"Okay, okay, I'll call you later."

She hung up, jammed her phone in her back pocket as two men rounded the corner. They halted, silhouettes against the daylight of the big bay doors, she couldn't make them out, couldn't see if they were narcos or policía, and her stomach dropped when they stepped forward because they were Americans.

The one in front wore an off-the-rack navy-blue suit with a red tie, and she could tell, even from her remove, that he was a paunchy blue-blooded middle Ivy.

Right.

DC.

He looked almost apologetic.

She could see something stronger than irritation on the other one's face. Not quite anger, something more like anguish. He wore a blue linen short-sleeve shirt and tailored pants. Dark aviators. He tapped an unlit smoke against his thigh, letting the cigarette pay out between his fingers like a nail.

"Can I help you?" she asked.

Blue Linen hung a few steps back as Middle Ivy approached. This felt prearranged.

"We're from the embassy, Agent Harbaugh."

"You know who I am." She said it plain, matter-of-fact.

Blue Linen kept fiddling the cigarette against his leg, flipping it, tapping his fingers flush again. She fingered him for the one lurking on TILLER. What did he want with Gustavo?

"You have ID?" she asked.

"I'm the special assistant to the ambassador," Middle Ivy said.

He reached into his jacket, pulled out his lanyard ID badge for her to inspect. She took it from his hand, the thing still around his neck. John Robert Quincey, special assistant to the American ambassador to Mexico, sure enough. He even gave her that Foggy Bottom down-the-nose look. She knew these guys. Carrying on like the upper crust of government. Even as voices on a speakerphone they oozed the arrogance of an elect, like they were endowed by the presidential line of succession with a special status.

"I assume this is legit," she said, letting the lanyard fall against his chest. "I've never seen one. And you," she said to Blue Linen, "you're what, human resources?"

"Department of Blow Me," he said.

"Coming in a little hot, this one," she said to Quincey. "What's so code red to get State on the scene?"

Blue Linen sucked his teeth impatiently like he had a powerful toothache and looked past her, over her head. She had a powerful urge to kick him in the nuts.

"He's back there, Quincey," Blue Linen said, pointing behind her to the heavy door.

"We'll take it from here," Quincey said.

"Take what from here?"

"Fucking Acuña," Blue Linen barked.

Yes, his balls. They were in need of a swift kick.

"He called *me*," she said to Blue Linen.

A blur of light-blue shirt, steel-gray pants, sunglasses, as he strode right over to her. Somehow she managed to stand her ground in the midst of his jawline level with her eyes. His shoulders. The volatile nearness of him. His withering contempt.

"Oh, I bet the piece of shit did," he said. "But the only relevant factors are: (a) this is Mexico and (b) State has jurisdiction and (c) State says fuck you. Oh, and fucking (d) I don't like saying the same goddamn thing over and over, so (e) beat it, bitch, because (f) he's my asset now."

She exaggerated her open-mouth shock into a cartoonish, mocking O as if to say *Ooooooh, what a big meanie you are!* but thinking, Asset? That's intelligence parlance—

Fuuuuck.

"Asset?" She stepped back, looked at Quincey. "So this one's CIA, then?"

"Has he left? Did you fucking fuck this?" Blue Linen asked.

"*Who* are you? What's *your* goddamn name?" she asked.

Nothing. Stone face. Shaking his head, pinching the bridge of his nose under those aviators.

"Ian Carver," Quincey said to her. "I assure you he is with the ambassador's office."

"Ambassador's office, my ass." She said to this Ian Carver. "You went fishing in TILLER. Saw me in there, didn't you? Flagged me for travel notifications? You fucking followed me here!"

"Quincey," he growled.

"It *would* be best if you returned home, Agent Harbaugh," Quincey said.

"The fuck are you two to order me around?" she barked.

"Bitch," Carver said, "this is the chain, or as much as you've ever seen of it. Quincey ranks you, ranks most everyone in this country but for the ambassador, who, if you don't know, is the legal arm of the president of the United States."

"Let's ask the US attorney for the Southern District of Texas about that."

She took out her phone. Carver ripped it out of her hand as soon as she entered the passcode.

"Hey, what the fuck!"

She lunged for it and then he had his hand on her neck, firm and with an astonishing ease, like it was commonplace for him to wrangle someone like this. She tried to knock his hand away, and he gripped her trachea *hard*. She tried to pull in a breath, but her throat couldn't catch it. He thumbed through her phone, calm as someone waiting for dry cleaning.

A grinding, panicked sound escaped her, and then a surge of adrenaline quickened through her and she launched a fist into his underarm and wrenched herself out of his grip. She coughed and turned aside so he wouldn't see her gag.

"Please, Agent Harbaugh," Quincey said, without terrific sincerity.

"I don't have time for this!" Carver bellowed at no one, clicking through her phone, reading messages.

Blue tossed the phone back at her. It fumbled out of her fingers, clattered to the floor. She snatched it up. She clocked the annoyed look Quincey shot at him. Carver picked the cigarette up off the floor, where he must have dropped it. Resumed tapping it against his thigh.

When she looked up at Quincey again, his mouth had fallen open. He looked at her like she was bleeding from the ears. Then she realized he wasn't looking at her at all. He was looking past her. As was Carver.

She turned around, still holding her sore neck. The door was open. Gustavo stood before them. He had no coat, and his shirt sleeves were unbuttoned, the stiff cuffs hanging oddly open, large and starched like cardboard takeout containers. She didn't see the gun until he put it up to his head.

"I am leaving with her." He wagged the pistol by his ear. "Or I leave alone, like this."

BAGRAM AFB, PARWAN PROVINCE, AFGHANISTAN

MARCH 19, 2004, 19:07

POLYGRAPHER: I've started recording, Operative Carver. Are you ready?

CARVER: I guess.

POLYGRAPHER: You guess?

CARVER: Shipley didn't administer these in the field. I only had a couple during training at the Farm.

POLYGRAPHER: And after you were at Tora Bora.

CARVER: Yeah, that's when the Company first came calling.

POLYGRAPHER: You were the tip of the spear at Tora Bora.

CARVER: Fifth Special Forces went in right after the daisy-cutters.

POLYGRAPHER: Something happen there that made you want to quit the army?

CARVER: More like what didn't happen.

POLYGRAPHER: Catching UBL.

CARVER: We warned the brass the back door to Pakistan was wide open. General Franks had eight hundred Army Rangers just shitting in diesel drums and sipping cocoa. We couldn't even get them to drop Gator mines into Pakistan, it was fucking derelict—this is what you wanted to talk about? Ancient history?

POLYGRAPHER: You tried out for the SEALs in 1998.

CARVER: More ancient history, huh?

POLYGRAPHER: You didn't make it.

CARVER: I did not.

POLYGRAPHER: Why?

CARVER: They're the best of the best. Statistically, pretty much nobody makes it.

POLYGRAPHER: Guys with your scores do. Was it a medical issue?

CARVER: No.

POLYGRAPHER: Psych?

CARVER: Fuck no. Are you trying to catch me in some kind of lie? About this of all things?

POLYGRAPHER: About this of all things I'm just trying to get an answer. Why didn't you make the cut, Operative Carver?

CARVER: They hold a fucking vote. Every week, anyone still in the running picks four guys. Two they want in battle with them. And two . . .

POLYGRAPHER: And two who . . .

CARVER: They hope'll wash out. They didn't want me. The other guys didn't. Which is lucky for you.

POLYGRAPHER: Why is that?

CARVER: Because no one quits the SEALs to join the CIA.

TOPO CHICO

The writing in this pinche book had gotten too dense. Tomás wanted to rip *The Twin Dawn* in half and set fire to the pages. It wasn't the sentences. It was the goddamn girth of the world, the bottomless mythology Julian Renfield had created. As soon as Tomás thought he had the lay of the land—lands—Renfield would unveil another kingdom or secret order or astral dimension, and Tomás had to read yet another dozen pages of clan genealogies or ancient wizard wars.

But the bitch of it was this: he couldn't quite quit the thing either. When they emptied Visitación in the Topo Chico prison for him, Tomás didn't mind being cooped up—the clouded chicken-wire windows, the cigarette smell, the little red phone—because he had the book. There was a sweet regicide in the offing. When the Twin tossed an infant king off a parapet, "extinguished with no more racket than an egg slipped from a maid's skirt," Tomás had to set the book down.

Goddamn. That was *so* good.

Didn't matter it was backstory. Didn't matter it was sidestory or digression. Shit like that stopped Tomás cold. Renfield somehow knew exactly how death conducted itself, and page on page kept evoking things Tomás had done or seen done. Like the jefe de policía thrown to the boss's tiger in Morelia. The thing with that Sinaloa mistress. Those teenage snitches lit afire at the gas pumps—

He looked at his watch. Thirty-five minutes now, like some peasant for a bus!

He berated the penal functionary, demanded fresh air and a view from the tower.

Once inside, he dog-eared his place. Regarded the unfinished aggregate concrete, looked out the big windows onto the yard. He went out onto the observation deck that overlooked everything within the walls and the depressing vista beyond, empty countryside the same pale shade of the sky. A cage of steel fencing and razor wire, waves of noise from the teeming mass below, as loud and varied a racket as an El Tri match. Prisoners yelling, laughing, talking shit. Dozens of weight lifters on plywood benches hefting wrought-iron pipes attached to bumper plates of concrete repurposed as weights. Corridos bounded from a sound system somewhere, accordion, bajo sexto, synthesized drums, vocal harmonies, but overlaid with the dull roar of the crowd, it was impossible to make out the tune. The scene was almost like a saint's day or Carnival, except everyone was male, all in the same baggy prison-issue jumpsuits. Brown skulls and black hair in a sea of orange. Dudes could barely walk around, they were so packed in. Reminded him of Rensfield's Horde. To be honest, the Twin's run with that jodido crew was getting a little tired. Sure, war and plunder were cool—Tomás was a soldier, after all—but it was all hack and slash. In the real, soldiers wind up in a place like this. Caged. There was no way he could do real time in a place like this. Rather be dead.

He tilted his head back to feel the sun through a thin skin of cloud cover. Remembered one of Renfield's digressions in *The Twin Dawn* about a sky god. Said to appear in multiple forms—a cloud, whispering rain—the sky god was usually chill and gentle, though sometimes he'd get pissed and turn into a scorching sunray on a cloudless day, hurtling spears of lightning from on high. Legend was, a league of knights went around doing deeds and shit for him. Tomás hoped the Twin was headed for that crew. A sky god was something you could lay it all down for.

The door inside banged open. El Supervisor at last. A white polo shirt and khakis, his hair slicked back. Tomás left the deck and met him inside the tower. He ignored his outstretched hand and sat in the chair.

"Señor." El Supervisor grinned sheepishly. "I'm sorry I'm late. I came as fast as I could. You see some men out there you want?"

"In the yard?"

"I assume you are here for men, yes?"

"I came for Zetas. Not these losers."

El Supervisor listened, grinned. He smelled a little of alcohol, and his shirt was sweat-stained like a greasy paper bag.

"What's wrong with you?"

"Señor?"

"Why you grinning like an asshole?"

El Supervisor swallowed and flattened his expression. It was petty to scare this peon, but fuck it. Tomás felt not a little like the Twin. Huge. Imposing. Badass and mean.

"I thought they told you."

"Told me what?"

El Supervisor tried to gather his words.

"Speak, man!"

"The Zetas and El Motown, they are—"

"El Motown?"

"Their leader. El Motown and his men, they are holed up in Fallujah."

"What Fallujah? Like Iraq? You're telling me they're in Iraq?"

"Block D!" he stammered. "It's called Fallujah, and I cannot get to them."

"*El Motown? Fallujah?*" Tomás shook his head. "I'd like you to concentrate, speak clearly, and make sense now."

El Supervisor held out his palms plaintively, a gesture that seemed to come all too naturally.

"What I am trying to say is that between here and Fallujah are three cell blocks. A and B are no problem. Everyone housed there is in the Commons on recreation break." The words spilled out of him now. "But C Block is the problem. It is no-man's-land. Los Trece Locos, Los Caballos de Hierro, and a few others run that block. They are all at war with Zetas. The whole prison is, really."

"Ah, I see the problem now," Tomás said, smiling, "Why didn't you say so?"

El Supervisor visibly relaxed.

"I'm sorry. You make me very nervous—"

"Yes, the problem is very clear," Tomás said. "You think this is a *prison.*"

"Señor?"

"But it's not a prison. It's a *bank.* And you know what the Golfos deposit in this bank? Convicted Zetas. They spend a lot of money in bribes to make sure that their best men are put *here* in Topo Chico. And now you're telling me that I cannot make a withdrawal. Which is no different than stealing."

"It is not so simple to get them," El Supervisor said, panicked. "See for yourself how easy it is!"

Tomás scowled at the man's tone, and he cowered and pressed his hands together. He had the look of someone who knew he'd made things worse and was used to making things worse and knew that he would go on making things worse. Especially for himself.

Tomás, still holding the book in both hands against his lap, remained seated as he had the entire time. "What do you do here?"

"I am very sorry," El Supervisor said.

"I did not ask if you were sorry. What do you do?"

"I am the supervisor," he said quietly, as if it might be an insult to say something so obvious.

"I know your title. What do you *do*?"

"I keep the prisoners inside," he said. "The deposits, I mean."

"The *walls* keep them from leaving the prison. Am I talking to a wall? I asked what you do."

Tomás sat still, waiting for the answer they always gave.

"I don't know," El Supervisor said, surrendering. "You tell me."

"Exactly. You do what I tell you." Tomás opened his book. "Get your men together. Take me to this Fallujah, this El Motown."

He watched the guards don their riot gear, and even helped them cinch their body armor, tighten their helmet straps. They were, to a man, scared shitless. They were not warriors, and they knew it.

Tomás was, though. Soldiering, warring—that's what he loved. Being part of something greater than himself. The simplicity of every day ordered and leveraged. He was a natural fit as soon as he enlisted. It was obvious he'd be promoted quickly, and soon enough he was in Las Fuerzas Especiales, the Mexican Special Forces. He even went to Fort Bragg for nine months' training with the Americans' Delta Force. Learned the latest ways to subdue and kill. How to manipulate chaos, to work in silence. How to end a life quietly, painlessly, bloodlessly. How to make someone talk. How to make a terrifying spectacle of ordnance.

And that's how pinche Tomás cabrón, straight outta Monclova, became one of the baddest motherfuckers to walk the earth. Cocksucking wizards and elves could daydream him.

He got fifteen confirmed kills his first year hunting narcos, more if you counted the chopper strikes he called in to obliterate their strongholds. Soon he and his team were keeping trophies from these monsters. Pistolas del oro. Jewelry. Jacked-up F-350s and Silverados. Soon the Fuerzas Especiales started collecting narco ears. Wearing bandoliers of them into battle. Finishing off a room and locking the door and doing all the coke. Soon they were pocketing the cash. Taking the weapons. Selling the drugs.

It wasn't long before the Golfos flipped the colonels in Fuerzas Especiales. Understandings were reached, agreements brokered. That's how it worked. Pretty soon they just paid you outright, put you to work for services rendered. Running security. Taking out rival cartels. They made double their yearly wages in a weekend. Not a one turning down mordidas, not ever. It was like living under a spell, magic words uttered, and they'd all been transformed. Soon they were just doing hits for the cartel, rolling up in the DN-IV Caballo to shoot up a house, a car. The orders coming from who knows where, for whatever reason, nobody can tell, nobody cares, you were paid to do this, the answer is cállate and take the money, pendejo. Cash is the chain of command. Money gives the orders.

Pretty soon everyone quits the Fuerzas Especiales, joins a new Golfo army: Los Zetas. Dudes who used to be real soldiers, special forces gone over to the dark side to work for the Cartel del Golfo. *Me vale madre, you're a sicario, bro*. Straight-up working for the worst hijos de la chingada in the country. It wasn't like in no book, not like the Twin walking out of the castle to join the Horde. It was more like the Horde absorbed you.

Which is what was happening to these prison guards. They thought they were workaday dudes, held the keys, guarded the joint, poked the laundry carts for escapees. But now, looking Tomás in the eye as he tightened and slapped their helmets, they realized that they worked for Golfos, they were in now and there's no getting out.

El Supervisor locked the exterior doors after they'd bunched into the access room, then unlocked the door and let Tomás and twelve armed guards into A Block. It was empty, quiet save the creaking of their belts and gear, the clomp of their boots. They passed rows of cells, watched by a few wary stragglers who'd stayed inside during rec time. Tomás marched with the men in riot gear, conspicuous in his shirtsleeves. They passed through A Block and entered the guardhouse and then into B Block unmolested. This one much the same. Mostly empty, mostly quiet, utterly subdued.

When they entered the guardhouse before C Block, El Supervisor locked the door behind them, stowed the keys on a retractable cord inside his pocket, and pointed.

"Los Stop Signs," he said.

Eight prisoners waited for them in front of the guardhouse. Arms crossed, some craning to see who was in the guardhouse. El Supervisor looked like he expected Tomás to see this and turn around.

"Open it," he said.

El Supervisor swallowed and hemmed and unlocked the door, and Tomás shoved the men into the block. Though they outnumbered the prisoners, the guards halted. Despite their clubs and armor. As though their bodies would not allow them forward.

"Don't stop for them!" Tomás yelled. "Go on!"

The men looked at El Supervisor, who struggled to see them from under a helmet askew and too large for his head. No one moved.

Tomás walked up to Los Stop Signs, addressing the thin man up front.

"Who are you?"

"You can't go any farther," the thin man said.

"Your name. I'm not asking again."

"Armando Araya Hernández."

"Maybe I recognize you," Tomás said. Dude was probably CDG. Everyone in here was, or in a subsidiary. "I have Golfo business in D Block."

"No one goes there."

"I do."

"You a Zeta?"

"I am."

The man looked at the others, back at Tomás.

"Then you can't go."

"A Zeta goes where the CDG sends him. And anyone in my way dies."

Araya shrugged.

Tomás looked at everyone, the guards and these men blocking their way both, as if to canvass their hearts and daring. All were scared. What they would do with that fear was the question.

"We are together, Zetas and Golfos," Tomás said. "The bosses will not like to hear how Armando Araya Hernández is sowing division between us."

Araya looked at his men now in much the way Tomás had, as though taking a vote.

"The bosses can fuck a goat."

Tomás lifted his shirt so they could see the pistol in his belt.

"Stand aside."

Araya shook his head and stepped to the side and the men parted, but hardly.

There was an irritating hesitation on the part of the guards, and Tomás reached back and yanked the nearest one forward.

"Go!"

Tomás shoved another guard forward, and another and another. He continued manhandling them ahead, and a melee began and escalated quickly, predictably, the Stop Signs descending on them, fists flying. The guards huddled in groups of two or three, batons rising and falling in terror as they beat the men back. Tomás kept pulling the men forward until the last, and they finally found their courage and lurched ahead, swinging and missing and hitting. The prisoners dodging or falling, some bleeding and crabbing backward, more coming, appearing from everywhere, cells disgorging men with shivs and bats.

Tomás drew the pistol on the prisoners, and they yowled like outraged dogs. The guards in their fear began to jog ahead in a rough formation. The block exploded with noise, utter rage.

"Move!" Tomás shouted as the men bunched and then spread out, bunched again. "MOVE!"

El Supervisor hid inside the chevron of guards cleaving ahead, batons now hissing in the air at the japing prisoners who lurched out at them in improvised charges. The march devolved into a headlong flight, burning and curling toilet paper rolls and heavier items wrapped in flaming sheets coming at them in long arcs. Tomás walked ahead as if in a dream, as if he'd been here before, wondering where he'd seen this before, and realized that it was like a scene from the book.

Renfield knew his shit.

The block filled with men and noise. The guards bunched again and swiveled and swore and halted and started in a herd. Full panic now. Fire raining down. Chaos.

Tomás fired his subcompact 9 mm up at the higher levels. The bullet whanged off the railing. A shout went up and the fire ceased falling, save a few red ashes. They moved on, running now. A prisoner lunged out from under a stairwell, and Tomás put a bullet in his forehead and the man's head tossed back and he toppled down. Another came out of the new smoky murk in front of them and the now frantic guards clubbed him down and strode over him, stomping. Tomás saw lighters flicking above and ahead of them, and he fired several rounds into those upper reaches again, scattering the pyros for another moment.

Spotting the guardhouse, El Supervisor yelled "There it is!" and the men broke ranks like the abject cowards they'd become and sprinted and clustered at the door. Tomás hung back in the smoke like a specter and found a spot along the side wall between two empty cells as prisoners dashed past him and in packs of three or four began to drag off individual guards, screaming. It was as if he were invisible, prisoners looking right at him as they took their quarry into cells.

A single flaming projectile arced down like a small comet and exploded in a spray of pure fire in front of him, igniting guards and prisoners alike, who fought flame and one another, slapping and punching and wiping fire and blood from their eyes. One such man ran toward Tomás, a guard, and he shot him in the chest and stepped aside from the man's dying burning momentum. He strode through the guards, who were now clubbing at bodies in ridiculous windmill swings. He addressed El Supervisor, fumbling with his keys at the door, told him calmly, "Open the door."

The idiot couldn't seem to get it right.

Tomás took the keys.

"Is this the key?" he asked.

The man's eyes were wild and darting as in a songbird's skull, like a small animal whose great ambition was to be overlooked.

"Is this the key!" he shouted this time.

A large battery struck El Supervisor's naked forehead, and blood poured into his eyes.

Tomás shoved the key into the lock and it had started to turn open when a hand clapped onto his. He fired into the man who'd grabbed him and the hand clung harder and Tomás fired again and the grip weakened and Tomás opened the door and pulled El Supervisor inside the empty guardhouse. He grabbed at two nearby guards who were screaming and swinging clubs. With arcs of fire exploding on the walls around him he felt no fear, only marveled at the Renfieldian quality of the scene as he stepped inside. The last of the guards budged after in twos and threes like terrified cartoons, and Tomás fired once more out the door before the last man swung it closed with a bang.

Seven guards slumped against walls, sat on the floor. Breathing heavily. Crying. Mumbling, bleeding, and drooling. One guard puked. The rage outside pounding the door, all attention warily turning to see if it would hold.

"You bastard," El Supervisor said through a bloody face to Tomás. "You have killed all of us! We're not getting out of here!"

The guards' faces clenched and soured. They might have even killed Tomás were he not armed and they not exhausted and fundamentally coward. Tomás for his part looked through the meshed reinforced windows into the cell block ahead. The windows were covered with cardboard.

"Let's go see this El Motown," Tomás said.

El Supervisor held a wrist to his head, his hand bloody, looking at Tomás like he was crazy. Tomás hefted him by his chest armor to his feet. Then he addressed the men.

"If you would like to live, get up."

They walked into a fenced-off area past a generator roaring like a jet engine, so loud they couldn't even hear it exactly, just felt it beating their organs. Guards wept and prayed. El Supervisor ran ahead and opened the iron door. The grateful men went through.

They passed now into an altogether new space, the sound of the bootheels rising as the noise of the generator diminished behind the closing, now closed door. The Zetas of Fallujah stood quiet, fiercely still like a tribe. The guards, missing helmets and gloves, were momentarily baffled by this apparent peace. No waves of corridos from the commons, no cries and calls from bestirred and vespid prisoners, no war. Not even the flat-screen televisions or refrigerators issued a sound. Just a ring of faces, eyes glazed at them, calmly taking in this foolish band that had somehow made its way to them.

Tomás took in the place. Kegs. Freezers. Bags of dried food. Pallets of beer and Jarritos. A huge gas range constructed out of corrugated metal, house turbines, and grill irons. The smell of soup and beans cooking and cigarettes. Men sat on couches and beds, holding glass pipes, cigars. Some held pool cues. A few with hand towels draped over their shoulders in the large kitchen among the propane tanks, blue-flame stoves, and outtake chimneys spiderwebbing up into the ceiling. All of the prison Zetas regarding Tomás and the guards with remorseless eyes. Far fewer men than he expected. Not a hundred, not many more than fifty perhaps.

No one came over to them. There was neither greeting nor defiance.

"Where is El Motown?" he asked.

It was as if he hadn't even spoken. Tomás scanned the crowd for the Zeta lieutenant. He didn't know who he was looking for—he wondered if he was called El Motown because he was dark-skinned. Or maybe it was that he'd been in charge of cocaine distribution in Detroit.

They watched like animals watch. With interest. Without apparent emotion. Their stillness entered like smoke, made a man wonder and speculate and dive deep into the horribles of his imagination. Tomás couldn't help but be somewhat proud of that. Even these hemmed-in prison Zetas holding beer bottles and glass pipes made you a victim before the fact.

"They're going to kill us all," El Supervisor hissed.

Tomás leveled his pistol at the man's head. This was no time for manifest anxiety.

"Shut up?" he asked. "Please?"

A man near the kitchen wiped his hands on a rag, yes, darker than everybody else, a little more fit, his arms swollen with bench presses and curls, a pot belly like a drum. Completely bald. The others parted for him. El Motown, presumably.

Tomás stepped forward.

"Commander," he said, not knowing the man's old rank. Not knowing what ranks existed in here.

The man's face was pitted with scars that couldn't be seen until he was close up. He looked closely at Tomás.

"Fuerzas Especiales?"

"How'd you know?" he asked, returning the man's handshake. His hands, his grip, were tremendous. The room went at ease, after that. Talk. Games. Music. Tomás was one of them. He belonged.

"Come on, brother," El Motown said, jutting his chin. "Follow me."

They stood on a thick Persian rug, among framed pictures of classic cars, a decent-sized TV, a fridge and microwave, a butcher-block table splotched with white paint. Lightbulbs in wire baskets on the wall.

"Whiskey?" El Motown asked.

"If you are."

From a cupboard on the floor in the corner, El Motown took a handle of Jim Beam, poured some into coffee cups. They drank. Tomás sat in a folding chair, El Motown on the bed.

"I need some men," Tomás said.

"There are plenty of men on the outside."

"Zetas."

"Again, there are plenty. But you come here."

"Topo Chico is on my way."

"Why do you need Zetas?"

Tomás hesitated. He'd never been asked such a question. Zetas did what they were told. But this El Motown was acting like these men were his to dispense. Unbeholden to the cartel. How strange that would be, to question the orders. Not that he didn't think about it, not that he didn't bitch to himself. But he never questioned an order. He could hardly imagine it.

El Motown waved him off before he decided how to answer.

"It doesn't matter," he said. "We don't work for the Golfos anymore."

"What are you talking about?"

"I'm not talking about anything," El Motown said with a wry grin.

"No one quits the Golfos."

El Motown took a drink of whiskey. He seemed to be considering how to respond. He had to know that Tomás would relay whatever he said back to the cartel. This strike or insurgency or whatever it was. He had to know that once the Golfos found out, they wouldn't stand for it.

Assuming he let Tomás go.

He didn't dwell on the thought. Death was always around the corner. Or perhaps sitting right in front of you, drinking whiskey.

"You know I have to tell El Rabioso about this. El Esquimal won't allow it."

El Motown smiled, though his eyes remained humorless. "You might be here one day."

"Or dead. No one knows the future," Tomás said. He sipped and the whiskey burned too hot in his throat to be the real thing and he held the cup in his lap.

"I know the future."

"Then you know what happens," Tomás said.

"More Zetas," El Motown replied.

"You say that like it's a bad thing."

"Isn't it?"

"Compared to more doctors, maybe."

"Soldiers make doctors necessary."

"So does malaria."

El Motown laughed. "This is true. But we are much more dangerous than malaria," he said, looking out the door of the cell.

All Tomás saw was Zetas moving about, and El Supervisor and the guards in a little separate huddle. "It doesn't have to be this way," he said.

El Motown laughed again. He drank and poured more whiskey into their cups, even though Tomás no longer wanted his.

"What happened here? Why did the others try to stop us from coming?"

"They aren't keeping you out of here. They are keeping *us in.*" He watched to see how Tomás would react to this. "They are afraid you will open the gates and let us devils out."

"But how do you survive? What do you eat? Where do you get the whiskey?"

"They bring us what we want."

"Why?"

"Because otherwise we would kill them."

"But *why?*"

"Because we are Zetas."

"You're making no sense to me."

El Motown set his cup down on the butcher block. He turned it slowly around with his finger as if it could be oriented in some meaningful way.

"Let me show you something."

He rose, and the two of them walked through the block. Zetas played pool, dozed in the splash of rotating fans, opened beers, and played dominoes. They walked over broken glass. Somewhere a tattoo gun buzzed, and he looked into a cell where a man tied off and shot up. These soldiers had all gone to seed. A lorn aura of the shipwrecked hung over the place.

El Motown led him through a curtain made of shower rods and bedsheets. A half-dozen green oil barrels. Traces of black and burgundy seepage from the sealed lids. A pungence that made his bones, his balls, ache. El Motown held his palm out, like a showman introducing a magic trick.

"Those Golfos would sneak into Fallujah, kill us, steal from us," he said. "They even planted a bomb once. We'd kill them whenever we caught them, of course, but when we did this, they came to heel."

He realized what he was looking at. He'd heard of the practice, but never seen it. He'd cut people, beat people, shot many people . . . but he'd never burned a man alive in an oil drum.

"You stewed them," Tomás said.

"And we sent video over to the fuckers." El Motown stated this as if it were the obvious strategy. "Now there is peace, you see."

Tomás imagined the Stop Signs watching their comrades being burned alive in these drums. Even hardened men had a tough time seeing such things, someone you knew, someone who could have been you, who could be you, suffering in that way. No wonder they tried to kill him and the guards.

El Motown thumped his fingers on the barrel idly. The fumes were visible, and the man shimmered in Tomás's vision.

"So you've turned on the Golfos."

"This is the future. Zetas in charge. What happens here will happen out there. You'll see."

"A civil war?"

"How many Golfos did you kill on your way to see me?"

"There was no choice," Tomás said.

"Spoken like a Zeta. That's exactly what I've been saying to you, 'mano! No choice. Your mind doesn't understand yet, but your mouth already knows. You were made for this, you were trained for it. There's really no choice . . ."

Tomás grew suddenly dizzy and could not listen. The fumes. This talk. El Motown now going on about chaos and war and how in the future chaos wouldn't be just a tool but the norm. The war coming from President Calderón and the Americans, the Always War, a world of soldiers and soldiers only. It was all churn, he said. New players and old. Cartels and gangs and bosses and alliances. He talked Tijuana, Sinaloa, Beltrán-Leyva, fucking Juárez, Golfos, Zetas. Tomás reeled.

"Please—"

"There is even rumor of a group nobody knows anything about except that they are called El Problema! The *Problem*? They are naming names like that now?"

A fucking Renfield story. Realms within realms within realms, as inside so outside, and so hard to understand.

"Please, may we . . ."

Tomás rubbed his eyes, started coughing. El Motown led him

into an open area, patting his back, and Tomás breathed deeply and held his knees and then stood and looked up at the sun coming through the milky skylight. No clouds or sky gods, just the weak light of an occluded sun.

"The Golfos have been around for a long time, friend," he said. "But Zetas are newer, stronger, and more vicious. As are you. One cannot hide from his nature. Not for long."

Tomás couldn't get the smell out of his nose. He rose, taking deep breaths. They stood there against the wall for a while, watching the guards tend to their wounds, the Zetas getting high. One group of soldiers on the battlefield, the other on some kind of shore leave. El Motown handed him a slip of paper like a waiter handing over a check.

"What's this?"

"Call this number when you need help," El Motown said. "Now let's get you some men."

Tomás looked at the number and at El Motown. Maybe the fumes had made him stupid. But none of this made any sense.

"Why are you helping me, when I'm working for the Golfos?"

"I must help you," El Motown replied, as if the answer were obvious, slapping him on the back of the neck, squeezing with his massive hands. "You're a Zeta, compa."

From the passenger seat of the van, Tomás looked at the road, pissed he'd forgotten the book somewhere in the prison. On the last page he'd read, the Twin had boarded a trireme with the ragged remainder of the Horde, and when they set off into the placid waters of the Loch, he'd marched up to the deck and beheaded the captain and quartermaster, announced that he would be commanding the vessel, and set course for the purple thunderheads, heading right into the storm.

Apt, that. He didn't need a book. The Zeta driving took a long hit from the meth pipe and held it out for Tomás, who declined. He'd never much liked speed. The driver shrugged and passed it to the back of the van, where his fellows were cleaning their guns and chattering and laughing. They'd come from a prison within a prison, they were ripping high, they were headlong for trouble, they were the trouble itself. As they headed to Tampico, the sunset behind them was blood red in the side mirror. And the air had a bloody tang as well, and to Tomás, it felt electric and bristling, it smelled like death and rain.

LA NADA

She's on the moon now. She doesn't yet know she is dreaming, so it's all unnerving, the moon is perilously small, she could walk the circumference in minutes, but her body is stuck to the thing, pressed into the rock by an immense gravity. As the moon spins, she has the strange feeling of being pinned down and going head over heels, and she is grateful at least to be hard-pressed into the dusty surface. She seems to know intuitively that if she stood she would fly free.

It won't be long now, he says.

Who says?

She turns to look. She is holding his gloved hand in her own gloved hand, and she knows when she looks that it is Oscar and he is dead. She knows that she is not dead, that a craft is en route for her, she will go home, but the stars spin above them and she wonders how it will all play out, how long she will have to wait. Because he is going the other way because he is dead.

Oscar sits up. The moon continues rotating backward. The stars rifle overhead. She has an urge to put her foot on the floor, like she would do if she'd had too much to drink. To stop the spins. But the moon is the floor.

Oscar lets go of her hand and stands.

She can't see his face, just his boot as he leaps and floats away and toward the horizon as the moon turns. He is at the horizon so quickly. No resistance in space. The sun flashes through her visor. The quiet is total. She is alone and afraid.

Wait, she says, sitting up. Standing up now. She crouches and leaps. The moon falls away. She knows how cold it is outside the foil of her suit. She looks up (but what *is* up?). He's turned to face down at her (what *is* down?), and she floats to him. In the cold vacuum, they turn slow. For a while together they tumble.

And tumble.

Where are you going? she asks, knowing already she cannot go with him.

To finish.

To finish dying?

No answer. His breath on his visor. Their suits are vivid silver and flash as they rotate in the darkness, the spotlight of sun, the soundless hum of the heavens. She imagines the vibrations of the rings of Saturn, the rungs of Jacob's ladder, she remembers his tattoo, the one of the Virgin Mary on his chest, el corazón inmaculado floating in between her perfect palms.

They arrive at an edge of overwhelming blackness.

La Nada.

He extends his hand and it disappears into the black and he turns to look at her and nods gently inside his helmet, his breath frosted all around the visor, nodding as if to say *I gotta go, cielito*, and she holds his hand yet as he goes in and allows him to pull her hand in too and in the startling shock of La Nada she lets him go. He is gone.

A pane of blackness like still dark water inches from her face.

Oscar. Oscar.

There is no fear. Only wonder. That vast finality.

She puts her head inside.

Big mistake.

A terrific blast of Pure Noise, a malevolent horn, a distortion, a terrible quake to make her eyes shudder, water, and close.

She is out. She looks down through blurry eyes, the plane stretching forever, reflecting nothing, not even starlight, taking everything.

The Pure Noise again. She kicks and swims and spins around. Stars. She wants stars, those lights, however far, however cold those lights.

Silence. Her breathing.

The Noise again. . . .

Her eyes flutter open.

Someone shouting in Spanish. The box. Mexico.

The Noise again. Like a buzz on metal. A filing cabinet.

What cabinet?

Where you put your phone.

Gustavo.

Tampico.

Buzzing again so loud. *Fuck.*

More Spanish spilling out, so fast she cannot follow. Her eyes are open. She's in the box.

"My phone. It's my phone, Gustavo."

Curses, mumbles, his pillow over his face.

"I'm sorry."

No reply.

"There, it's off now."

Just looking bullets at her.

"I'm gonna go out now. Sorry, I'm sorry. Can you get the door?"

He nods, finally.

The warehouse—midday-hot but fluorescent-lit—was empty. Her steps slapping on the concrete, echoing off the walls and floor. Her heart raced yet, a little rabbity stutter to it. No one around. Good.

But lonesome.

The disorientation of waking up didn't dissipate. No, not disorientation. Worry.

She read the screen to see who'd called. Of course. Bronwyn.

Not Childs. Not Dufresne. No one from the DEA. No one she needed.

Goddamnit. She stopped walking wherever she was walking. *Orient yourself. Work backward.*

She'd fallen asleep.

Before that, hour upon hour just sitting with Gustavo, just trying to keep him from Oscaring himself. All night. Waiting for Dufresne to call her back. Before that, waiting for Childs to call her back. She'd pretended this was all normal, to be expected. Told Gustavo her supervisors were following expedited protocols, but protocols nonetheless. Things could only move so fast. He'd fought sleep, tossed and grumbled, but then his breathing grew steady and she sat down. His snores were outrageous. She didn't think she could nod off. But she did. Deep sleep, deep space—

She shook it away. She didn't want to go back to that dream.

She fired a **WTF?!** to Childs and another to Dufresne and went in search of coffee. She found an empty break room in the office area. Just cigarette butts in the small metal ashtray and a few empty Jarritos bottles.

The fluorescent light pinged above, and one of the bulbs went out. She looked in the cabinets for coffee. Nothing. Her head had begun to throb. She rubbed her eyes and swept out of the break room and down the hall, passing offices, trying to clear this foggy head of hers. She stopped at the sight of Travis at his desk, doing something on the computer, figures on a spreadsheet. Tongue out like a kid at algebra. Noticing her, he sat up. The cash still on the desk.

"Agent Harbaugh."

"Mr. Moman."

"Where's El Capataz?"

"Asleep. Or was. My phone rang. Is it really six p.m.?"

He didn't have a clock or watch, and he peered at the corner of his Dell.

"So it is."

"Jesus."

Travis leaned back in his chair. Fixed his hands over his belly.

"Y'all don't seem to be in much of a rush," he said, with a grin indicating that she had better be.

"It's all in hand," she lied. "Should have an exfil plan soon. Just waiting on the paperwork from Mexico City. Approvals and such. You know."

"Probably I don't." He squinted, took a slow deep breath, and paid out a sigh through his nose.

"I'm sorry," she said.

"For what exactly?"

Sorry she'd come down here half-cocked. Sorry she couldn't raise anyone on the goddamn phone. She had no plan, that's what she was sorry about. Embarrassed really. And she was sorry she was lying to him about it.

"The inconvenience?" she suggested.

"I don't want to know what's afoot," he said. "I wanna be as see-no-hear-no as possible. So don't feel like you actually gotta answer this." He paused, exhaled ostentatiously. "But can't y'all just leave?"

Despite Moman's request otherwise, she had half a mind to explain everything. To tell him that she was doing this all by herself, that she'd come down to get a big win and whisk herself out of trouble. But there was no support, it was just her, alone, having to figure this shit out, and she and Gustavo couldn't just take a commercial flight or walk across the border, no one was waiting for them. She wanted to tell him that she'd thought it would've all been sorted by now, though. That someone would've called. She couldn't really imagine what was in store, what the conclusive event would look like. The CIA guy. Blue Linen. Carver, if that was really his name. What was behind him. The mind reeled. The might of State or the Defense Department or the Mexican police. Would this end in a raid? With Gustavo shooting himself before anyone else could? Him dead? Her dead. Everybody dead. Maybe a boat would do the trick. She wanted to ask Moman if he had one—

He was watching her ponder these things. Perhaps dimly aware of the scope of her problems. Instead of answering, though, she just ended up asking a question back at him.

"What happened to those assholes from State?"

"No idea. I'm just sitting here wondering who's gonna take this money off my desk," he said. "You ever heard of a man having so much trouble getting rid of cash?"

"Kind of, yeah," she said, looking at her phone. "It's hard to move money."

"You're not gonna get anything in here."

"Anything what?" she asked, sounding more alarmed than she wanted.

"Your phone," he said. "You'll wanna be on the loading dock to get any bars."

The sun was hidden behind cranes and smokestacks. The sky overcast, the air a heavy and wet astonishment in her nostrils. She started sweating as soon as she stepped outside. How the fuck does anybody stay dry here?

She held up her phone, watched two bars and two new text messages appear—Bronwyn again—when she heard someone behind her stepping up, coming out. She whipped around. Carver emerged from the shade of the loading bay. She shoved her phone in her pocket.

"Jesus," she said. "Nice tradecraft, bro. Cool use of shadows."

"It's the shade, hon. You've been in an icebox all day, so maybe you didn't notice that it's hotter'n balls out here."

"Where's your pal?" she asked, running a hand through her hair, composing herself.

"Mexico City. Trying to explain this charlie foxtrot to the ambassador."

"*Charlie foxtrot?* Are you twelve? Or—oh fuck—you were a jarhead, weren't you?"

He ignored this, asked, "Where's the narco?"

"Why are you so interested in him?"

"You first."

"You know why. He's a lieutenant in the CDG. And he only wants to deal with me."

"Oh, I know." His eyes softened sadly. "You're handcuffed to the sumbitch now."

Sumbitch. He didn't have a southern accent, but there was a touch of the rural about him. His baggy pants. He was compact, but had rangy movements, eyes that darted and discerned. A hunter. Midwestern probably. Kansas or something. She didn't have his number, but she had a few of the digits. Farmer, hunter, soldier, spy.

"Why you, though?" he asked.

She told him about the card. The call.

"Now answer *my* question," she said.

"It's classified."

"Is it now."

"You figure out how to get out of here yet?" he asked.

"I have irons in the fire."

"Irons in the fire. Right. Wheels in motion. Forces gathering."

"Why are you still here?"

"You sleep?" he asked.

"Why are you still here?" she asked again.

"I racked out in the SUV. I can sleep anywhere." He grinned, openly, warmly. None of that keyed-up threat-assessment hardness to his face.

"What. Are. You. Doing here."

"Awaiting word. Like you."

"From?"

"Mom and Dad," he said.

"Mom and Dad?"

"Condi Rice and whatever dipshit is running the DEA. State and DEA have to hash this one out."

"Sure. And maybe Langley?" she asked.

His face did a little shrug at her. Like he was trying to shake off some worry or other. No, more like he was telling her this wasn't a big deal, that she didn't need to worry. Jesus, his whole affect was different now. This wasn't the same guy who'd throttled her yesterday. He was too cool now. Calm. Which was annoying, considering what a psychopath he'd been the day before. He shouldn't be able to stand there all calm. She wanted to *bother* him.

"This isn't gonna go your way," she said.

"Yeah, it's gonna get real gnarly before it's all over."

Her phone buzzed, startling her. Carver didn't even perk. He just turned sideways in a gesture of giving her the space of privacy. Raw consternation discomposed her face—she could feel it curling up her cheeks and forehead. Who the fuck was this guy today? Stubbornly baffling.

She closed the message she'd started to Childs and opened up the longest single text in history, broken up into a bunch of different messages. It began with Bronwyn telling her to sit down and read the whole thing. That he'd worked out a lot of his thoughts, and she owed it to him to listen—

Closing the phone, she muttered "Jesus" and sighed.

He looked up at that.

"What?" she barked at him.

"It's that guy? Bronson?"

"You had my phone for thirty seconds, and this is what you read?"

His eyes all furrowed. As if vaguely concerned but personally untroubled.

"Tell him the chemistry was off. Or that you got back with an ex. But give the guy closure."

"Yeah, this is a ton of your business."

"Nature abhors a loose end."

Loose end. Interesting.

"Is that why you're here?"

"To give you fantastic advice? Hardly."

"You're the one created Gustavo's TILLER file, aren't you?"

He put his hands on his hips and looked at the ceiling in approximation of someone working out an answer, an answer she knew would be mostly smoke.

"Why didn't you just call me?" she asked. "Or maybe he pulled my card because he's running from you?" She wasn't going to let him off. "You're here to tie up a loose end."

He scoffed.

"What's so funny?"

"That dude's main ingredient is loose ends," he said. "A couple hundred at least. Not someone you wanna room with. But you do you."

He looked hard at her, almost urging her to listen. He meant something specific by "a couple hundred," but she wasn't sure what. Murders, she assumed, like that was supposed to shock her. What was Carver's agenda? He had come at her so explosively off the bat. In fact, a theory had gripped her as soon as he'd grabbed her by the throat: Gustavo was involved in some shady intelligence operation. Like the shit she'd pulled with Dufresne. Different scale, but the same kind of thing. She'd reckoned with this idea so much last night that it had slowly acquired more credence and had actually become a fact in her mind. But now, she wasn't so sure, looking at Carver shaking his head and rocking on his heels. He seemed worried. Gustavo could be something far worse than she'd imagined. Maybe the man in the box wasn't just a narco, maybe he was something she didn't yet understand.

"I have an idea," she said.

"Can't wait to hear it."

"How about some interagency cooperation? Unless you're just waiting for another chance to choke me out."

He didn't say anything back. Not right away. She perceived his regret, maybe it was even shame, but only in a slight and softening way. His eyes, that's where it came through. As though he were actually thinking of her for the first time. He had clouded things barging in and trying to take control yesterday. She'd thought his purpose was to thwart her, dispose of her. When a man grabs you by the throat, your first thought isn't that this is a rash act of panic. But maybe Carver had less power than she assumed. Maybe she'd been fooled by the neck grab, by his whole fiery aspect.

"You have an inflated opinion of my control of this situation." He walked back to where he'd been hiding among the racks, where he picked something up off a shelf. When he reappeared, she saw he was holding a dripping-wet plastic sack and a paper one, stained with grease. He held out one of the bags toward her. An offering.

"What's this supposed to be?"

"Interagency cooperation. You two gotta be starving."

He nodded toward the back of the warehouse. His face was soft and open. Handsome, even.

She took the paper sack. A warm aroma of hominy and cumin when she opened it. Tamales, salsa tied up in Saran wrap, napkins. He pulled a beer out of the plastic bag and gave it to her.

"Run this back to him," he said. "There's plenty more if you change your mind."

She stood outside the box right under the vent, the AC blowing straight down on her. Outside, a plane passed overhead, the sound of it echoing in the warehouse. Somewhere deep within, a forklift engine kicked on and beeped, backing up.

She realized then that she was ringing too. She set the beer and tamales on a shelf, dug out her phone.

Dufresne.

"*Finally.*"

"You need to come back."

"I can't."

"You can, and you have to."

"You can help me, Brian."

"Help you?"

She could hear him breathe. She could just see his pained grimace. She had to try a new tack.

Revise the past. Relitigate that shit.

"Okay, listen. I'm sorry I said . . . *those things*. About everything I did as DA. I did all that on my own. If I gave the impression that I expected a job—"

"Stop."

Don't stop. Negotiate. Give him things.

"And the trouble with my CI? You can have my phone. I'll manage OPR, it'll be fine—"

"Let me assure you, it will not be fucking fine with OPR."

Shit. New tack. *Just listen to him.*

"Cromer and I just got off a conference call with the State Department asking how in the hell we have an agent who goes to a sit in Mexico without following a single fucking protocol."

She heard him seesaw a pencil on his desk between a thumb and forefinger. A thing he did when he was frustrated. She knew this about him, knew a lot about him.

"Let me tell you what I got," she said. "I have a lieutenant in the CDG who wants to come to America and spill everything he knows. The reason why anyone knows I'm here is because the CIA wants him too, but he only wants to deal with me. All I need is a plane. None of the brass will give a shit what we've done once this dude strolls in and we debrief and proffer him. Please. Brian, it's me."

She'd never begged him for anything. He just had to see she was for real. He'd quit tapping the pencil. She could hear the casters on his chair move as he leaned back and turned around to look out the window.

"I'm not going to help you," he said softly.

She took the phone away from her ear. Hearing that hurt, and there would be more pain if she kept listening. Everything all gone to hell. He was still talking and she didn't know what the words were but they all meant the same thing. She was done.

"You hate me," she said.

"I hate that you didn't tell me you were going," he said. "I hate that you didn't come to me when the call came in. I hate that Childs told you to go. I hate . . . I don't hate you. I hate what's happened."

He sounded like someone on the stand. Like someone in a pre-trial deposition, in an interview with the DA. Parsing. She could hear him breathing, and that was all. She couldn't imagine what he was doing. She couldn't see him.

Then he hung up.

EXCULPATORY EVIDENCE

A slender moon shone in the evening sky. Beneath a grove of palm trees Carver sat on the bumper of an open black Explorer. A wooded spread of pecans and figs and bastard scrub and more palms stretching behind him. Deep shadows there, the sun falling quickly. She turned her face into a small breeze.

"These aren't bad," she said, handing Carver two empty corn husks. She swallowed the last bite of tamale. "I could use a beer."

He smiled and pulled a can of Modelo out of the plastic bag sagging with ice and beer, offered it to her. She cracked it open, took a sip. She sighed. The things on her mind.

"If anybody other than me knocks on that door," she said, "he's gonna blow his brains out. You appreciate that, right?"

"I do."

"I meant, do you care?"

"A great deal, actually," he said.

"That's hard for me to believe."

Her phone buzzed. Bronwyn again, surely. She looked to confirm it: Call me. I want you. I don't want to lose your love please call. I'm so mad at myself more than ive ever been. please

She typed: **Not now. Stop.**

She put the phone away.

"Him again," she said.

"Persistent."

"We saw my informant kill himself. *He* saw my informant kill himself."

Watching Carver not quite spit-take, but stopping mid-drink and wiping his chin, she wasn't sure why she'd told him this.

Though she did know, of course. It was time to talk about it.

"Less than a week ago," she said.

"Holy shit, that's . . ." He trailed off, took another sip of beer. "Civilian, right? This Bronwyn?"

She nodded.

"That's tough. Man."

"He followed us all the way to the Upper Peninsula."

"Michigan? Your informant tailed you?"

"I must've told him about the cabin at some point, I dunno."

"I'm sorry," he said. "I didn't mean to tease you earlier . . . and get all up in your business like that. Or I did mean to get in your business, but now I feel bad about it."

She laughed. "You do that a lot?" she asked.

"Get in people's business?"

"Feel bad."

"No. Can't say that I care for it."

They stood in the silence, in the lee of the palms where the air was cool. They drank their beers. She rather liked his new, chastened demeanor. Maybe that's why she'd wanted to tell him. To see of what else he was made.

"My boss came out to investigate—he actually flew up to the Upper Peninsula—and was instantly suspicious about the whole thing, and then he and I had a blowup—"

"The guy or the boss?"

"The boss. It was . . . *stressful* isn't the right word for what I felt. I said things."

"Impossible not to say shit to bosses," he said. "I literally can't *not* say the worst things to them."

She laughed again.

"So then this call comes in"—she pointed over her shoulder toward where Gustavo was sealed up—"and I get here last night and it's like, fuck, here's another one's gonna blow his head off."

Carver's turn to laugh. A full-on astonished one. "I thought I had a bad week going."

"Your week can suck my week's dick," she said.

They both laughed. He settled against a few duffel bags in the back of the Explorer. She noticed his boots, thick black soles, some kind of mesh, plated. High-end, military-contractor issue.

"And so this Bronson," Carver said, "he's worried about you and contacting you all the time."

"Bronwyn. Not that it matters. But you were right about him. He's pining."

"It does make sense he'd be worried about you. I were him, I'd worry."

He was trying to revise what he'd said, tell her maybe she was a little bit right, make her feel better. It was sweet.

"After it happened," she said, thinking how exactly to put it, "I felt this really unfair feeling."

"Unfair?"

"He's a good guy, actually," she continued. "He's handsome and strong and not dumb. He's nothing like the guys at the office, the cops and jarheads. But when Oscar showed up and killed himself like that, I . . . this is awful to say, but I couldn't stop seeing Bronwyn standing against the wall, just scared shitless. One minute I was imagining every Thanksgiving at his parents' place in Montecito, and then the next . . . I was just *out*."

She paused to hear herself. It was the first time she'd even put these thoughts into words. She wasn't talking to see Bronwyn clearer. She was talking to see herself clearer, and she knew she could only do that with someone else listening.

Carver crushed his beer can on the ground and fetched out another. Quietly, unselfconsciously, he burped. He started to apologize, but she waved him off. She was *talking*.

"I didn't want to see him. I didn't want him to touch me. I knew that pretty much *instantly*. I guess I just expected him to know how to handle something like that without shrinking away. God, is that awful of me? It is. I'm awful."

Carver shook his head. "I've seen guys panic in firefights, and afterward? Everyone in the FOB knows. No one has to say a word. The survival instinct is amoral. A whole platoon will unattach from someone who ain't gonna make it. It's brutal."

"Yeah, all right," she said. So he *was* military. Or ex.

He cracked his beer and drank. She wondered what else he thought. What else he would think about what else she was thinking. What she could tell him. What she couldn't.

"So the informant, what was his malfunction?" he asked.

"Oscar?"

"Yeah. Why'd he off himself?"

She'd been on the other side of these situations often enough to know what happens. If she went on just a little bit more, she knew she would spill everything. She'd seen it so many times, that moment when the men she arrested decided they'd tell it all, round and true.

You don't decide anything anymore after that, after you tell.

"He went crazy," she said. She was going to keep on talking. She knew she shouldn't, not with somebody she didn't know, with somebody who had just fucking choked her, but she was going to talk. It was stupid, but she'd always been stupid in this way—Dufresne, Bronwyn, Oscar, too much quick intimacy with all of them—but he was here and he was listening and she needed that.

"When he showed up," she continued, "he didn't look like himself. I didn't even recognize him. I'd seen him be really brave, but I'd also seen him bawl his eyes out."

"You were close," Carver said softly. Kindly, without any reservation or judgment in his face. She felt intense, almost profound relief. And fear. He was a strong listener. She couldn't hide things in words.

Is this what it's like?

To sit across from me?

To let all the defenses down?

To be open?

She sat next to him on the back of the vehicle, the sun almost gone beneath the city behind them, the sky a deep pink down to a bruised darkness swelling on the eastern horizon somewhere over the Gulf. Gulls called and swarmed. He didn't say a word. He sat still, letting her gather her thoughts.

"We were going after the money," she said. "Oscar would go to the garment district and buy a boatload of T-shirts, Nikes, hats, whatever. Tourist shit, mostly for the Europeans and Asians and Americanos going down to Tijuana. He'd pay five hundred K for the stuff and have it sent to one of the commercial distributors down in Mexico. Now the distributor is on the hook for five hundred K's worth of goods, right? But instead of paying Oscar back, they pay Oscar's peso broker for it. In pristine pesos. Which the peso broker would then deliver to the cartel, minus his fee. That's how Oscar got his money to the cartel."

"Like a cutout for money."

"And all his invention. This dude from San Pedro in a little stucco house with a view of the Port of Los Angeles. Even after we busted him, he was still plotting. We'd watch the ships come in loaded with illicit shit from all over, drugs and stolen cars, and he had it in his head that he'd be working those dirty Harbor Department guys in no time."

"Denial."

"And he wouldn't set up a meet with the peso broker! And I have the *perfect* guy for a sting. This Orange County retiree. Ex-biker, strictly old-school, who—get this—just happens to own a T-shirt company. All we gotta do is have the peso broker meet with our guy, do a few runs for smaller amounts. Once our biker is in everybody's good graces, we'll arrest the peso broker in Mexico. We'll have more than enough to extradite. Which should be enough to get him to flip."

"But Oscar won't set up the meet. Why?"

She looked at him, telegraphing the next bit.

"I'm not supposed to even *see* a CI without my partner. But inside of a few weeks, Oscar's only texting me. I'm the only one he'll communicate with. Asking, can I come over? Can we talk privately? He gets butt-hurt when I won't meet him at his place or when I won't stay. Fixing me these rum and lime and coconut cream things at his place."

"Ah."

"And I'm Windex-clear that it's not in the cards, not in this life."

"Right."

"But maybe I'm, you know, *even then*, saying or suggesting or hinting that it could be? If the situation were different? If our world wasn't the world?"

"Give him a dream to jerk off over."

"I'm thinking, let him tire himself out trying to get into my pants. Let him drunk-text me at three a.m. or send me pics of his bare chest and tell me how hard it is to be a gentleman. Let him send me apologies the next morning, say he's ashamed, his mama didn't raise him like this. He's just spinning, that's what I'm thinking. And he's gonna tire out."

"Right."

"But then we got made."

He looked over at her.

"By who?"

"So I'm at Oscar's. It's late. The usual. Rum drink. Him trying to make a move. Not make a move. Figure out what he's supposed to do with all this fear and energy and most of all his boner. He wants to fuck his way out of this, you know? Not gonna happen, of course. Of course, of course. But still, I'm letting him be persistent. I'm letting him . . . I'm letting him touch my arm, I'm letting him sit close."

"Okay."

"Then there's this knock."

"Shit."

"Oscar leaps up and peeks through the Judas gate and his face goes real scared. Like terrified. But he's opening the door. He's too scared to *not* open the door. So it's bad."

"Who is it?"

"The peso broker."

"Fuck."

"I never felt so scared in my whole life. Oscar opens the door, and this guy Hector kicks it wide and stands in the doorway and I'm like, it's over, I'm about to die. The way this Hector is looking at me, he *knows* who I am. He knows."

"Fuck."

"But he says 'Who the hell is this?' to Oscar. And there I am with my sweater in my lap . . ."

"You're dead."

"I'm so dead. And you know what Oscar says?"

"What?"

"He says, 'This is Beth. Or Becky or some shit? I dunno, dude. Just come from the bar with this bitch. What do you want?'"

"Hector buys it?"

"They go into the kitchen. They talk. The guy's gone in ten minutes. Less."

"Holy hell. So you're good."

She turned to look at him. He, back at her. Open, clear-eyed. Not a scintilla of judgment. A knowing.

"I think I'm gonna need another," she said, handing him her empty. He took her can, stood, and crushed it. Then reached into the sack and cracked a new one open and handed it over in a fluid transaction, never breaking eye contact.

"So when the guy leaves, Oscar slides down onto the floor by the door, and he loses it. And then I did too. We held each other on the couch. He didn't try . . . anything. We just stayed like that, next to each other all night."

She sipped her beer and the alcohol warmth spread to her face, she could feel her face redden, there was a euphoria building because she'd almost told it all, she was going to tell everything. It was the alcohol, but also the way Carver was there, quietly, hearing her, waiting to hear her . . . she felt relief, gratitude, an exquisite exhilaration.

This is what it's like. The telling, the feelings, the giving yourself over.

"The investigation was dead," she said. "I couldn't go forward. We couldn't set up the peso broker."

He almost seemed to know. About her. About people.

"If Hector has even a halfway decent lawyer, he's gonna ask what I'm doing at Oscar's that night. Shoes off, sweater off, cozy on the couch with drinks. A good lawyer will hammer me on these things, question after question about broken or bent regs. I'll have to explain this misconduct, mitigate it, fucking maybe lose the jury over it."

"Really?" he asked. "That seems a little extreme."

"I was an ADA. I know what a team of attorneys can do for a syndicate. Every case I ever worked could be reopened. I can't have that. And lots of bad motherfuckers possibly getting walking papers."

"Because you weren't wearing shoes? Who the fuck cares?"

"You have no idea." She shook her head. "I was a DA too, in my past life. Cases I prosecuted? Cases I helped prosecute? In particular, cases I worked with my current supervisor."

She watched him figure it out.

"You two pulled some stunts," he said.

He was a very good listener. There was no holding back now.

"We did things. I did things. Flimsy indictments to rattle suspects. Buried exculpatory evidence from the defense."

"Shenanigans," he said. "Whatever."

"I obstructed justice. It could be argued that I am now in the employ of the DEA and under the direct supervision of my coconspirator on those cases. A good lawyer would argue that my curious change of employment was in exchange for these misdeeds. This peso broker might not just be the end of my career, it might be the undoing of any conviction I ever touched."

Carver slid out of the SUV and stood in front of her.

"This is so fucked up."

She didn't argue. She didn't even really disagree with him.

"Anyway, you wanted to know what was Oscar's malfunction. He was stuck on a case I had to let die," she said. "I let him languish. I put him off. I ignored him for months and months."

He paced there as she spoke, waiting for her to finish.

"Don't. He killed himself because his conscience told him he was a piece of shit. Accurately. Don't you dare blame yourself." He shook his head and sighed and leaned against the SUV. "I'm serious. We're out here dealing with a level of wickedness nearly impossible to fathom. So you worked in some gray areas. No one gets to judge you. Not the lawyers, not the bosses. Nobody."

"But they do, actually. And now, with this situation . . ." She gestured toward the warehouse, trailed off.

"He called *you*. You had the huevos to enter the situation!"

He cracked open two more beers and handed one to her, though she wasn't finished with the one in her hand.

"I get the exact same shit at Langley," he said. "I have an actual polygrapher. A personal lie detector assigned just to me. So I have to spend a black-site-worthy number of hours answering questions about reports I filled out six months ago. Reports inevitably consisting of me saying the same motherfucking thing I always say. How the Gulf Cartel is deeply embedded with Mexican paramilitaries. Christ, you'd think a multibillion-dollar criminal organization in league with the military of our southern neighbor would garner—"

He stopped mid-rant. Shook his head and scoffed at himself. It was like a switch had flipped, and his manic energy had returned in force. Work. Bosses. His issues with authority.

"Sorry," he said. "I'm glad we're talking like this. Honestly, I wanted to reset with us. I came in here with a rage-on, and I apologize."

"Thanks."

Purple had spread like spilled paint across the sky. She wanted to forget what she was doing here. Cool evening wind blowing off the chemicals. Palms soughed, gulls called. She could smell charcoal supper fires somewhere not too far away. Dusk, odor of salt and the ocean. She thought of the smell of sunshine when she was a little girl, which was the smell of her father's cigars and his shaving cream and pilsner and the racetrack.

"I already placed my bet," she said. "I took his call, and then I came down here. It's not an obligation exactly, but after Oscar . . . my conscience is lit up. Gotta see it through."

Carver tossed his half-finished beer over his shoulder and went into the back seat of the Explorer. He returned with a laptop. Tapped an enormous password into it, propped it on a duffel for her to see.

"Gustavo, if you're inclined to make a judgment on him, is what you might call la peor de todas. The fucking worst. Dude's notches have to be in the hundreds." He pointed at the laptop screen. "And he's responsible for this parade of horror."

Photos of dead people in an excavated mass grave. Some very clear, though at strange angles, probably taken from a concealed body camera. Fuzzy video screen grabs. Multiple pics of buses half uncovered in the dirt, bodies inside. Various stages of decomposition. Dark blotches of soaked blood. Some ligated, some sprawled like cut-down double-jointed puppets.

"Four full buses. Dozens and dozens of construction workers. We found kneepads, tools, boots, shit like that, too. Gear, work clothes."

He left the laptop open as he talked. She couldn't turn her eyes away from the slideshow.

"These men were an entire subcontracting company created and funded by your El Capataz in there. All skilled laborers, all dead. And there's more. Truck drivers, cooks, suppliers . . . basically anyone had dealings with this outfit was *deleted*. Including several of his direct underlings. And the one left standing?"

She got out and stood. Arched her back. She felt a little drunk, the sky now dark purple and red as a battered eye.

"Why? Why kill everyone and then run?"

"Sounds crazy, don't it? Like an act of sustained madness. Something that would make a person want to run away. Or kill himself."

She let her body rest against the truck. Birds swooped and dove and her thoughts stirred and whirled too.

"Construction workers," she said.

"They built something."

"A tunnel?" she suggested.

"That's a theory. This crew had the right skill set."

"Which is why this is a national security problem."

A phone rang. His.

"Your turn," she said, relieved it wasn't hers. Then she realized that his phone calls could affect her too. That whatever was coming would almost certainly call him first. That she had no one looking out for her, no shield.

He glanced at the screen but didn't answer. His eye was trained on a vehicle idling outside the gate. A black SUV she hadn't noticed before.

"Who is that?"

"I dunno."

They watched the SUV until it pulled out, as though forced away by their attention.

He closed the laptop and went and slipped it in a pocket behind the driver's seat. He put the phone back in his pocket unanswered.

"I gotta run."

"Wait."

He hopped in the cab but left the door open.

"Seriously, who could that be?"

"I don't know," he said. "But the thing is, you're never gonna feel like the coast is clear, so if you're waiting for that, forget it." He sighed and rubbed his face with his hands, and when she saw his eyes again, he said, "He trusts you. Which means I need you . . . even if the DEA doesn't. Hold tight, all right? I'll be back as soon as I can and we'll figure this out."

"Fuck."

"It'll be fine."

She nodded. She didn't have a choice.

"Shit," she said. "I told you everything about me."

"Yeah," he said smiling. "You did."

She sat outside in the lazy breeze and quiet. When she went into the empty warehouse, everyone had cleared out, no sounds of a remote forklift or even trucks on the roads. Maybe an hour had passed. She leaned, a little tipsy, against a huge pipe. She wished she had a cigarette, though she hadn't smoked since college. She felt entitled to one. Like someone headed for the firing line.

Her phone was plugged into a wall socket, and lit up where she'd set it on an overturned bucket. A message. She stood away from the pipe and heard footsteps in the darkness. She stepped forward, wincing at the noise her feet made.

The footsteps continued, closing from the dark.

"Hello," she said firmly. Deep dread at the nonresponse. She scanned her immediate area for something handy. A wrench, a crowbar, but there was nothing. Just a man coming on into the light. Black jacket, dark black hair, jeans. Mild, sleepy eyes. Something neat about him, nothing extraneous. Like a lizard or beetle or maybe it was just the sheen of his hair. She wished she wasn't so tipsy. She straightened herself.

"Hello," he said. "My name's Tomás."

BAGRAM AFB, PARWAN PROVINCE, AFGHANISTAN

MARCH 19, 2004, 19:49

POLYGRAPHER:	So after Tora Bora, you went to the Farm.
CARVER:	Earned my Agency lanyard and then straight back here. Then joined Counter-Terrorist Pursuit Team 796.
POLYGRAPHER:	In ███████.
CARVER:	Officially in ███████, yeah. But that first stretch had us all over the map. In ████ and ███████ and in ███████. Trying to get good intel, find competent locals to train into militias. Bagged a few dopes for Guantanamo. But nobody that gave us UBL. The Pakistani army was a worthless backstop. Tora Bora just proved al-Qaeda could swoop in and out at leisure.
POLYGRAPHER:	Why couldn't the Agency pursuit teams secure the border?
CARVER:	The border? Seriously? The border isn't even a concept in ███████. No one in any of those border provinces gives a shit about Pakistan or Afghanistan, they're so wrapped up in their tribal scraps. All the villagers see themselves as Pashtuns first. You can't secure a country that doesn't even believe it exists.
POLYGRAPHER:	So what did you do?
CARVER:	Run over IEDs. Get ambushed with rockets. We'd shoot back, of course, pound the hell out of them, chase them deep into Pakistan, but we couldn't secure shit.

POLYGRAPHER: What about coalition support?

CARVER: As if. Whole battalions banked up in the Green Zone playing Xbox. A dozen times we called in air support and got cockblocked by the brass. You're asking why couldn't we secure the border? The brass. To them, it was a mortal insult having CIA Ground Branch teams operating in their battlespace. I know these fucking guys. They wanted us to fail.

POLYGRAPHER: But then Shipley took over the pursuit teams.

CARVER: Thank Christ.

POLYGRAPHER: You're loyal to him.

CARVER: He was the one who picked me, you know? Saw something.

POLYGRAPHER: Something the SEALs didn't.

CARVER: I'd have been in Fallujah clearing blocks if it weren't for him. Holding handfuls of my guts sooner or later.

POLYGRAPHER: What I'm getting at is—

CARVER: I know what you're getting at. That Shipley finger-banged my insecure little heart.

POLYGRAPHER: You knew that it was extralegal activity. The stuff you guys did in ▮▮▮▮ took a degree of fealty.

CARVER: How's that?

POLYGRAPHER: So you were always okay with supporting traffickers, poppy warlords, using American manpower and resources?

CARVER: I don't decide what works. We were actually making progress. Catching terrorists, stabilizing the region, so the NGOs could teach girls to read and fix cleft palates and vaccinate babies. Peace. That's what winning looks like, don't it?

EL PROBLEMA

The man followed her to the door, a few steps behind.

"He's in there?"

Over her shoulder, she looked at him.

"Yes."

The man stepped in front of her and ran his fingers over the doorway and painted walls. He crouched and looked where the room met the concrete floor and then stepped back and took in the entire box. Then he climbed the storage racks on the right to get a view of the roof, and she saw the holster under his jacket.

When he dropped down, he softly wiped his hands and nodded like an inspector.

"Tell him I have a message from the Eskimo."

She took this information without comment, utterly pliant. She performed the series of knocks on the door and looked over her shoulder again to see the man several yards back, leaning against the racks. He tipped his head as though he'd done this exact thing before. He was expert at it, and she was doing just fine. When Gustavo opened up, he had the gun to his own chin, and he let her in this way and bolted and locked the door behind them.

"There's a man out there," she said.

Gustavo's hair was askew, and he straightened it in the little bathroom mirror. When he was done, he kept looking at himself. "He is not American," he said, as if he knew already who it was waiting for him.

"No. He says he has a message from the Eskimo. Who's that?"

"Es mi tío," he said in contempt. "El Esquimal."

"The head of the CDG."

"The man waiting is a sicario. A Zeta."

He reached into his dopp kit and took out a baggie of cocaine. Did a bump in each nostril, then splashed water on his face and smashed down his hair with his bare wet hand.

Wanting something to do with her hand as well, she took out her phone.

"There's no one to call," he said, drying his hands on a washcloth. "He is outside the door now?"

"Yes."

"And the Americans?"

He did another bump.

"Gone."

"Señor Moman?"

"I don't know."

Gustavo did another bump. Nodded and blinked. "This man is only one?"

"Yeah," she said. "One man. Tomás, he said his name was."

He cleared his throat. "You should have ran," he said.

Harbaugh wedged her hands into her pockets to hide them shaking. The man showed up and simply ordered her to get Gustavo, and he did it gently and firmly like a shepherd or a horseman.

"I'm sorry," she said.

He wiped water from his wet head off his shoulder. He'd shed his shirt, and his belly pooched out under his white tank and over the handle of the pistol. He'd gone grimy, wired. His jaw moved around. An agitation rising within him.

"He said he had a message," she said. "Maybe he's just delivering it?"

Gustavo was looking at her like one might a card trick, his tongue out the side of his mouth. Then some thought anguished and angered him and he began pacing. "You were supposed to get me away from here!"

She didn't know what to say. She just looked at the ground. She wanted to tell him she wished she'd been able to make it work, but that seemed too small of a thing to say. Little and late. Her hands were at her sides, balled in fists. She was useless. She couldn't help it. She couldn't help anything.

Breathe.

She uncurled her fists, spread her own fingers as wide as she could.

"Let's think," she said, more to herself than to him. "Tell me why they want you, exactly."

"They don't want me! They want what's in here." He tapped his head.

"Which is what?"

He grabbed the nine and the cocaine and seemed to be weighing shooting himself against doing more blow. "What I built for them."

"And what did you build?"

He shoved the nine in his belt and tapped out a portion of coke on the desk and rolled up a bill and spread the coke around and just inhaled it.

"Fucking everything. First I build houses in America to clean money. Mansions paid with cash. Easy, no problem. Then I think I can maybe do more. So I start to make safe houses with secret rooms. For hydro, for cash, guns, whatever shit we need to be secret. Rooms for our guys to hide out. So then I come down to Matamoros to make getaways for the boss, escapes . . ." He sat heavily on the cot and it cried out under him. He massaged his head and began shaking his legs, bouncing the springs. "You should have took me north," he said. "Pero it's not your fault, right? I am the stupid one called you."

Her head began to throb. The beer she'd drunk. The springs. This room. This man.

"Did you kill all those workers?" She asked without thinking it through, just saying it because her head pulsed and she was as scared as she'd ever been in her life. "The men who built for you?"

He bounced all the more.

"I saw pictures, Gustavo. The American showed me. Stop that."

The springs cried under him as he pressed his head in his hands. The springs screamed.

"Stop that!"

He stood. The sudden quiet like a shot.

"If I'm gonna die," she said, "at least do me the honor of telling me just how much of an idiot I am. That I came down here to save a mass murderer—"

"I had no choice about them," he hissed. His face glistened with sweat or the water he'd splashed on it or both. He leaned forward, and his pinned eyes bored into hers. "Many of them, I knew for many years. Their families. They were the best. And they did the best work of their lives for me."

A hard thrum behind her own eyes, a coming headache as clear as a thunderhead. *Get a drink, Hardball.* Her father always said to stay wet if you're drinking. At the track, he'd order a water with every beer, carry the program under his arm, and throw back the water, hustling to the betting window or trackside. His straw hat. His furry neck—

"We built a tunnel."

A tunnel. You were right.

"The best tunnel," Gustavo said. "Many millions of dollars. Electric rails. Silent. Deep. The biggest project the Golfos have ever made. Top secret, I'm in charge."

She pinched the bridge of her nose, closed her eyes, trying to stanch the headache, to listen.

"I tried to protect them. I took precautions. Their buses had no windows. They lived on the jobsite. These men, they don't know where we are. They only know me, they're my guys, not cartel guys. Nobody was going to the police, nobody. But El Esquimal, mi tío, he don't care, he don't want to take no chances. When the work is finished, he says to me, 'Delete them.' Everyone, all the men. I tell him no, maybe we kill just the drivers, only the men maybe who know how to get to our location, how does that sound? But El Esquimal says 'No, everyone, kill them all.' Because no person can know. Take no chances. That is the most important part. Keep secret. Silencio. Nadie lo sabe. Word get out, the tunnel is worthless. It must be secret or the tunnel is just millions of dollars thrown away. So I got no choice. I delete them. He orders me. Kill them all."

She took her hand from her face and looked at him.

Do you believe him?

I don't know. I need water.

Does it matter even if he's telling the truth?

"I need water," she said. She walked past him into the little bathroom. A sink to blanch at, the bowl dirty red. Rust the color of blood. His dopp kit. Razor and deodorant and toothbrush and pomades in one side. Baggies of coke in the other. She turned the tap and a burst of gray aerated water spewed out. She cupped her palms under the flow. Potable, if dank.

Gustavo sat on the desk, where he could see her.

"I tell everyone we are going to celebrate, get on the buses. But they don't go to a party. They meeting Zetas in the desert. But I don't even see it! I'm not even there!"

Do you believe this?

Maybe. I don't know.

"Mi tío kill my best workers and maybe he don't like me complaining about that, no? Maybe he'll kill me, tambíen. That's why I run here, away from them. I called you for help. *You*."

She looked at herself in the little mirror over the sink, the circles under her eyes. She pulled her hair out of its tie and shook it out and gathered it in her shaking hands. Understanding didn't help. She looked at her own face with something like pity. She'd really done it this time.

"I'm the only one alive know where this tunnel is."

She stuffed down a sob and turned to look at Gustavo. "What do you want to do?"

"Ay chingao, abre la puerta," he said, letting loose from his mouth something like a whistling sigh and pulling the pistol from his jeans. "Let him in."

For a few moments, time did not move.

As she rose from her chair.

As she took one step to that heavy door.

As she took another heavy step to that heavy door.

That shepherd was out there and time did not move.

Everything was at once.

This headache.

The program folded under her father's arm.

The back of his neck, his ear seen from below.

Oscar on the floor crying. Dufresne tapping his pencil.

Her pet turtle, a crayon melting on a pie tin in the sun, a finger-written message on a frosted windshield, a cigarette in eighth grade, a stick of gum, frothy rum drinks that tasted almost too good.

This heavy door swinging open.

The shepherd shooting her in the face.

La Nada.

But Tomás did not shoot. She was still here. There was light yet, she was alive, so she hadn't been shot or killed, not yet. Not yet.

The man stepped inside and inventoried the space. He sniffed at the close, cooled air, which couldn't circulate enough to evict the smell of Gustavo's cologne, his body odor, his food, the persistent kept reek of him.

She backed up against the file cabinet. Gustavo put his own Taurus 9 mm to his temple. His FN was stuffed in his pants, in back. The low ceiling loomed like the lid of a tomb. He grinned harmlessly.

"No tienes que, no es necesario," Tomás said about the gun Gustavo had to his head.

"¿Quién es?"

"No importa." He tilted his eyes down, a subtle show of respect. "Pero soy Tomás Jiménez Quiñones."

"No, you a pinche Zeta." Gustavo turned to Harbaugh. "He's a sicario."

"All right," the sicario said to both of them. "Let's calm down. No dramatics, please. Today, I am just a courier."

"Courier?" Gustavo shook the pistol at his head. "I'll courier myself, cabrón."

"All I came here for is to talk," Tomás said, reaching very slowly into his own coat, withdrawing his .40 Smith & Wesson, and handing it grip first to Harbaugh. "So put that down, please. Mira."

Harbaugh's hand shook as she took the pistol. She grabbed it tight. Wondered if either man noticed how scared she was.

The sicario, this calm shepherd named Tomás, again gestured for Gustavo to hand over his gun to Harbaugh. "Solo quiero hablar," he said. "De veras."

Gustavo sniffed and filled his chest up, and she felt her own breath leave her body. But then he reached back and pulled out his FN and handed it to her. She set it on the cabinet when he handed over the nine, and kept the .40 and the nine in her hands, where they dangled heavy in her grips.

"Ta bueno," Tomás said to both of them.

"How El Esquimal know where I am?" Gustavo asked.

Tomás shrugged. "No se."

He stepped to the side and leaned against the wall, his neat leather jacket falling open as he propped a foot behind him. Like he was only here to observe.

"What do you want?"

He nodded again. "After we talk, then you'll come with me."

"Why the fuck I do that?"

"Because I'll convince you," Tomás said.

"Psh," Gustavo said, shaking his head. "No me chingues, güey."

"I won't hurt not a hair on your wet head."

"You a liar," Gustavo said.

Harbaugh wasn't so sure. Something straight about him. Or maybe he was just convincing. Maybe she was just primed to hope, to believe that Gustavo would leave with him. To believe that she'd make it out alive. Every trouble she'd gotten into up to this moment had shrunk down to such a scant size, her entire life now so preciously quaint.

Gustavo pivoted around and hooked a pinkie into the bag of blow. Thought better of it and tapped the small amount against his thigh and brushed it off.

"Look, everything's okay, man," the sicario said. "Your family just wants you to return home. Nothing more than that."

She looked at Gustavo, who was smiling now and nodding. "Órale, güey, you don't got any idea what he want me for?"

"Not at all," Tomás said.

Gustavo turned to Harbaugh. "Tell him why El Esquimal want me."

The sicario stood away from the wall, laced his fingers together beneath his belt buckle, and tilted his head forward to hear her out.

"Go, tell him," Gustavo said, uncrossing and then crossing his arms.

"He built a tunnel for his uncle," she said. She cleared her throat. "For the cartel. He's the only one who knows where it is. The men who worked for him were killed to keep it secret. And Gustavo thinks that his uncle will do the same to him. So he ran."

The Zeta looked up to see if she was finished. A fresh kindness in his eyes.

"Ah, well there, you see?" he said. "A misunderstanding! This is not a problem. I was told not to harm you. You are family, El Capataz."

"Family," Gustavo said, snorting back a laugh. "Un pinche Zeta cabrón talk to me about family! Family don't matter when we all narcos. All of us, yo"—thumping his chest with a finger—"la policía, los políticos, la Iglesia, los soldados"—he pointed at Tomás—"todos nosotros!" He turned to Harbaugh. "Los bosses, El Esquimal and the others, they got bankers and brokers to wash money and be all legal. They got oil rigs, lawyers, governors. They got everything! Consultants, that's what it is now." He started shaking his head, getting more upset. "Pinche consultants, chingados! El problema!" Now he did turn around and take double snorts of cocaine in each nostril, continuing to mutter about a problem, the problem. He kept saying that over and over, *El problema, el problema.*

"The only problem," Tomás said finally, "is that you won't do what you need to and leave with me."

"No no *no.* 'La Empresa,' 'El Asunto,' o algo así," Gustavo said. "En inglés, 'the Concern.'"

The Zeta sicario looked at Harbaugh, amused. "What is this? The Concern?" He lifted his chin to acknowledge the confusion on her face. "See? We don't know what you're talking about."

"Big players." Gustavo was also looking right at Harbaugh. It was as if both men were trying a case before her. "Globalistas. Their networks. Security. Insurance. *The Concern.* Means I am expendable now. The tunnel was my last job."

Gustavo was at her side, and now he put a soft palm on the back of her neck. She shuddered at his touch. The sicario stepped in front of the door. She trained the pistols on him and he stopped and raised his hands, and she felt a terrible certainty that something terrible was about to happen. That events were about to spin hard.

"But maybe you're right. Maybe it was a misunderstanding. But I called her to save me," Gustavo said. "And she DEA."

She wanted to knock his palm away, but there were guns in her hands, and instinct told her she didn't want to see what would happen if she took them off the sicario.

"Do you think El Esquimal be happy we together with this secret?"

The Zeta squinted, pondering this.

"This tunnel is perfect," Gustavo said. "It can move millions of dollars of product every minute. Quiet as a submarine. Es un secreto muy precioso para El Esquimal."

She felt him leaning in, close to her ear now, she could feel his breath. "Sos Automotriz, Piedras Negras," he whispered to her. "To Eagle Pass, Texas. Martinez Auto Works."

She popped her head back. A pleased grin spread across his face.

what has he done, what has he done, what has he said, what has he said

Her whole body tingled as though he'd shocked her with a live wire.

"You son of a bitch," she said to him.

He'd just told her where the fucking tunnel was. In front of the man sent by the cartel to bring the secret back, safe, sound, and otherwise unknown. She fought a wave of nausea to a draw somewhere in the middle of her throat and kept the nine and the Zeta's .40 trained on him.

"Please sit down," she said.

The man raised his palms slowly, almost gently, showing her that he wasn't going to do a thing.

"What's going on?" he asked.

"She know where the tunnel is," Gustavo said.

All the Zeta did with this information was nod. As if he understood immediately what this meant, all the fallout. He seemed to be grinning slightly, or maybe now it was a grimace, she could not tell. She tried to parse this expression for his intentions, but she could not. Maybe he didn't have any yet.

"I need you to sit down," she said to him.

"Where?"

"On the cot. No, on the chair."

He kept his hands up until he turned the folding chair around, and put himself on it backward. To hide behind it? To have a chance? To use it? To throw it?

"This is not your fault," the sicario said to her.

She felt Gustavo take the nine out of her free hand and she let him, concentrating on the sicario, the shepherd, this Tomás.

You're fucked. It doesn't matter who has a gun.

"I'm fucked, right? You can't let me go now," she said to him.

"You're giving the orders," Tomás said. "Not me."

"Bullshit. Answer me. You have to stop me now."

He made a face that this was correct as far as it went.

"Su teléfono," Gustavo said to Tomás, holding the nine on him.

The Zeta frowned, reached into his pocket, and held out the phone to them.

"Toss it," Harbaugh said. She quaked within as the simple flip phone skittered over. She slowly lowered herself to pick it up.

"I'm going to kill you," Harbaugh said to Gustavo. Her breathing was ragged.

He shrugged helplessly.

You're so fucked.

She had to concentrate.

With gestures Gustavo maneuvered the Zeta into the bathroom. She endeavored to breathe deep and her head pulsed as Gustavo noisily budged the heavy metal desk against the door.

"We must hurry," he said, kicking the desk tight against the door.

"You bastard," she said. "You son of a bitch."

SOFT STEPS

Harbaugh and Gustavo ran through the darkened rows of piping and gear, their footfalls echoing in the dark like the steps of the headlong idiots they were. *Run, you idiot*, Harbaugh kept saying to herself.

The light in this part of the warehouse was so dim that she nearly collided with a beam. The sicario's heavy pistol swung in her right hand and threw off her stride, but Gustavo receded behind her nevertheless, and in a moment she realized that she could outrun the pudgy Mexican, leave him to his fate, find her way to a car, to the airport, a motel, a hideout, American soil.

She could call for help yet. She could try to rectify these grave errors she'd made.

Don't think. Just fucking run, idiot.

She arrived at an intersection of rows and slowed, halted to see her choices. Right, and deeper into the brooding dark of the warehouse, the shadow-shapes there. Straight ahead to the offices, toward the scant light of a lamp from one of the rooms. Or left toward the loading bays, the open doors, the overhead lights.

Gustavo was stomping in his boots, almost upon her. She shot left to the dock, her feet light on the pavement, her breath ragged, her vision blurred and blurring. *Run.*

Figures up ahead in the light. Men in her teary vision like elongated mirages. As she ran, she began to make them out. Uniforms. Badges glinting in the pooled light of the loading lamps. Police caps. Jackets that read POLICÍA FEDERAL. She could cry.

"Hey!" she screamed. "Necesito ayudar!"

She was maybe two hundred feet away in the vast warehouse, Gustavo clomping behind her.

The police turned at her call. They shielded their eyes from the lights overhead, the better to see her in the warehouse's inner murk. A couple of them stood up from where they'd been squatting. They set down bottles like men at a party interrupted. They did not otherwise move.

She slowed to a jog. She called out again, was almost walking now, trying to catch her breath.

When a pair of men in white tank tops hoisted rifles and shotguns, she stopped. She could make out the ink on their naked collarbones and shoulders.

Fuck.

She stopped. Dread pricked and drew at her skin.

Not cops, she thought, standing there. Those are not cops, you idiot—you fucking fool—you are dead, Tomás's Zetas have killed you.

These men dressed as cops arched and tilted their heads. To hear her better, to smell her better. They swiveled their arms in their sockets like prizefighters. She stepped backward as though the darkness could swallow her back, as though time could rewind itself, as though there were a near place, a choice that didn't lead to this pass.

"¡Quiubole, mami!" one of the men called out. Laughter and low murmurs carried over the metal and concrete and rebounded all around like thrown voices. The pistol somehow still dense in her grip.

The next thing she heard was Gustavo, his footsteps—his receding footsteps. He'd already turned back into the darkness.

The men tore off after her, no shots, not yet, but she could hear their feet, nylon jackets, the metal buckles of the nylon straps on their submachine guns jangling, the fall of their boots coming for her.

She made it to the dark intersection, she could hear that she'd outpaced them, and she turned, whispering to her feet—*soft steps! soft steps!*—toward the dim light from the hallway there. A simple unpromising maw. She jogged inside and again halted. The close narrow air here still possessing the day's warmth. Her breathing was panicked, not winded. She made herself inhale through her nose. She'd never get through this if she gave herself away.

She sprinted to the end of the hall to the side door that surely egressed outside.

Fucking locked, *fuck fuck fuck*.

To her left, she clocked the break room, the door to the front office. Ahead to her right, the door to Travis's office, the light from there giving shape to the hall. The restroom door beyond that. No sound here. No sign of Gustavo, fucking bastard. She tried the door again. The handle rattling. *Too loud. Too loud.*

She spun around. Listened.

Someone coming.

She stepped inside the office. Travis sat upright in his chair, his arms splayed, his head thrown back, his brains and blood on the wall behind him. Gustavo's money that had been neatly stacked there was gone.

She choked off her gasp at Travis's body. His desk lamp had gone out of kilter and aimed at the doorway, and she knew she'd occluded its light and revealed herself to anyone approaching from the warehouse.

Fuck.

She padded light-footed to the desk and crouched behind it. Pooled blood at her feet in the nap of the carpet. She checked the sicario's .40 in her hand and wondered when she'd lost the nine.

How could you have lost it? How could you?

Calm down. Don't get upset. If you're like this, they'll get you.

The wall in front of the desk was made of glass, but the vertical blinds were closed.

The other gun. Fuck.

Stop. No past, no more unforced errors, idiot. Be quiet, be invisible.

The light. Use the light.

She put her knee in Travis's blood and set her forearm on the desk as a rest for her gun hand and aimed at the open doorway. She was behind the desk and the lamp, and the man was all the way in the room before he saw her.

"Don't," she growled.

He had a submachine gun slung over his shoulder, and he made a slow demonstration of raising his hands up and away from it. She stood. She motioned for him to lose the gun, and he lowered his arm and shook. It clattered to the ground. He did this like he'd done it before.

She nodded toward the window and he stepped over the gun he'd dropped and went in front of the window, both hands raised. Again as if this action were somewhat rote. He had dark deep-set eyes, and even from here she could smell the beer on his breath. He worked his jaw around in an aborted yawn or some kind of chewing tic.

"Don't move," she said softly, and then "No te," but she couldn't remember the Spanish so she just said "No te mover."

She opened the desk drawer, feeling for keys. She felt pencils, coins, paper clips, nails, she felt a pack of cigarettes.

No keys.

She was making a lot of noise, and she glanced down to look and then immediately up at him again and the man's gaze cut back to hers the moment she did so.

"Fuck," she said.

"Sí." He nodded. "Fuck."

"Shut up," she hissed. "None of this is my fault."

His dark eyes seemed to harbor small question marks at that.

"I didn't do anything to get me this far into this," she said.

"¿Mande?" he asked, leaning forward, and it was the last move he'd ever make as his head leapt open. Gustavo was in the room, off to the right, and her ears were ringing at the abuse the nine-mil round had done to the air. He was pointing at Travis, speaking, she didn't know what, what about.

This is a nightmare.

A circle in hell.

A horror-show trap.

Gustavo kept pointing at Travis, talking. She finally realized, after some inconceivable unknowable amount of time had passed, that he meant *Pockets. Check the pockets.*

The man's keys were in his jeans, and by the time she'd fished them out, Gustavo was popping off the nine down the hall and into the warehouse, unloading shots, calm and almost metronomic.

She crouch-dashed into the front office. Shadows of the Zetas appeared at the window like paper puppets. When someone tried the door, she dropped to the floor behind the counter. Then the windows erupted, bits of drywall and glass raining down. Gustavo was crawling down the hall, and she scrambled over him to unlock the side door, expecting any moment to be shot dead. She got the door open and fell into it and made it outside on her knees and elbows. He followed her and she stood and rounds punctured the door and she left off locking it behind them and then they were both running over the ragged asphalt and grass of the side lot into a small Hyundai, the only car parked on the side of the building.

She felt for the key with the heavy plastic logo and shoved it in the ignition. Another burst of submachine gun fire inside the warehouse disguised the sound of the car starting, and she put the Hyundai in reverse and backed away from the building in a long mad arc and then put it in drive and kicked up a bucket of gravel pulling away. She swerved to the open security gate, past the dead guard who sat palms up in the corner of the gatehouse.

"Piedras Negras," she said. "Eagle Pass. Martinez Auto Works."

"SOS Automotriz," he added.

She gunned the engine.

"Goddamnit," she said. "You motherfucker."

It was quiet inside the Elantra. It smelled like new car and the cigarettes Travis Moman had smoked in it. Who was dead now, who'd done nothing but try and help the assholes in his car.

They swept by houses packed together, closed storefronts in gray blurs, the occasional blast of neon.

"I am sorry," he said. "But you needed motivation."

She swerved to miss a dog that in her rearview hunched up, seemed to shake its head at the close call and tiptoe away. The road bent, gave onto a larger boulevard, divided by a median of palms.

"Pero you gave no choice," he said.

She looked over at him, settling back in the seat.

Fuck him. He deserves nothing.

She slammed the brakes, and the sedan slid to an angled stop in the middle of the street.

"Get out," she said. She removed the .40 from where she'd jammed it under her leg.

He ignored her, looking out the back window.

A distant whine, the plaint of a small engine like a model plane. No, not model planes.

She swung all the way around to see several motorcycles bursting out of the curve, cutting across the boulevard in a braiding swarm, wending heedless of the palms like loosed hounds, which, of a sort, they were.

TUNNELS EVERYWHERE

The truth? If the bathroom didn't smell as badly of the man's cologne and tamales and the shits he took, Tomás would have been content to sit on the rusty throne and just read until the prison Zetas drinking on the loading dock ran out of mezcal and beer and came looking for him. But the shitbox *did* reek, and he didn't have his book. So Tomás jammed the flathead screwdriver on his multi-tool into the door hinges and used his boot to hammer out the pins. That's when the shots started. Then more gunfire. The nephew's nine, the Zetas submachine guns firing back. Ni modo.

In moments, he had the door free of the hinges. He was climbing over the heavy metal desk when two Zetas burst in, one of them firing wide into the wall before the other stopped him from killing their boss. Tomás paused in his climb over to sigh at these fools. Then he sat on the desk lacing his boot as they waited for an explanation, an order, but he really had neither. This was such an entire mess, the whole thing gone to la chingada. Un desastre. Un problema.

El Problema. El Motown had said that, and then this stupid nephew of the boss said it too. And him with a DEA agent. Telling her about a tunnel. Realms burrowing into realms. What the fuck was he talking about, globalistas and consultores? It was messy. Muy messy. Shitty. Tamales and cologne.

He watched the prison Zetas who'd almost killed him pass a little joint in the doorway. This is how it'd end for him. Something like this. Today or someday. But probably worse.

More gunfire. Automatic. What would the bosses do with a dead DEA agent? That kind of heat? They'd turn him over to the Americans. His house in Los Feliz wouldn't hide him then. No, the Americans would search it and pull up all those dead bodies. And then he'd fry in an American death chamber. But he'd already be doing that for the dead DEA agent. Even pinche gringo barbarians can't kill a man twice.

And what would the bosses do if she got away and gave up the tunnel? El Esquimal would barbeque his ass for letting that secret go.

"Where's the phone?" he asked.

The prison Zetas shrugged.

Worthless.

He walked through the warehouse, breathed the comparatively fresh air. The coolness of the night. They were waiting on the motorcycles when he made it to the loading dock. He told them to hold on. They rocked and urged like fighting dogs.

He got in the van and fumbled around the dash, the glove box. A phone in the cupholder. He dialed. He yelled at the men to kill the engines, he couldn't hear. He waited for them to gutter out.

"It's Tomás."

"El Rabioso's not here."

"I don't give a fuck. This is urgent."

"Not here," the guy said, and hung up on Tomás.

El Rabioso should've told him there was a tunnel. That the nephew was running to America. He would've approached it differently. He looked at the useless phone.

He got out of the van and nodded. The Zetas pounced on the kick-starters, the pickups roared to life.

He walked back to the warehouse as their engines screamed in the night and diminished away. The front office windows absent, the door all shot up. He went inside and over the shards of glass into the hall and then into the office where he had killed the owner of this place. He regarded the dead Zeta there. It would be a wonder for some cop to identify him, try and piece together how a convict with a military record from Penal del Topo Chico had to come die with this gabacho businessman in Tampico. They would puzzle over that one.

Puzzle pieces. Everything was enmeshed, everything could touch everything else. No one was out of reach. Nothing could be locked away. Realms within realms. Tunnels everywhere.

THE DEAD END

Three motorcycles buzzed the Hyundai, riders kicking the doors and slapping the hood, surging in front of the car, speeding ahead, braking, speeding ahead again. They slowed, fell back, then ripped past like guided missiles, engines screaming and then whining almost dolefully as they shot by and into the scant cross traffic. They wound through parked cars and utility poles and the few unfortunate pedestrians. Red lights, green lights, it didn't matter, they were heedless of wreckage or death.

Harbaugh gripped the wheel, tried to keep the car moving. But she knew these men would soon kill them. These men would not give up.

Gustavo had climbed over and now slouched in the passenger seat, melting into the door. A stopped motorcycle waited for them to pass and then fired into the street and pulled alongside. Two men on the bike, making Halloween faces. The driver kept them upright when Harbaugh swerved to miss what turned out to be a plastic bag. The man in back reached inside his jacket for a garish silver pistol. The filigree shone in the moonlight as he tapped it on the window.

Gustavo scarcely moved. He would not budge. She braked. The pair zoomed ahead.

"Where do we go?" she asked.

"Ahead," he said.

"To where?"

He just waved his hand vaguely onward. As though he'd heard this story before, seen this part of the episode.

"You gotta do a little better than that, asshole."

She swerved again, testing the new pair of riders, but they simply swept onto a sidewalk, their engine noise blasting in intervals from behind the parked cars like horns.

She dialed Childs. Straight to voice mail. She shoved the phone back under her thigh.

Think. You're still alive. You still have some kind of a chance—

Another motorcyclist appeared at Harbaugh's window, scraping the side of the car with something. He shouted. He spat. He smiled at her.

They headed south in the Hyundai, traveling out of the Zona Industrial to the airport and the city proper. Screaming through the night. The three bikes kept them in this lane of the roadway, a hellish motorcade, a fury of popped clutches and backfires, swerving in mad helixes in front of the car, sideswiping in delight. It was a wonder none had crashed. They dodged her lurches right and left, her accelerations and brakings. She couldn't turn or stop. She sensed a dead end. A trap. She didn't dare be too evasive for fear of the same. No unforced errors, no mistakes.

There were two more bikes trailing behind, five total by her count. A Toyota pickup with a deep purring engine and a jacked-up Ford F-150 that bellowed and brapped on a set of giant off-road tires. Farther back, she clocked a white van that had to be part of the convoy, the caboose of the train. Ten, maybe, twelve guys.

"There's about a dozen of them," she said. "We can't . . . I don't think we can . . ."

Gustavo watched out the window as she trailed off. In the intermittent streetlights he looked old, almost senile, disinterested. Like it didn't matter what was happening outside. Which was right, she realized. It didn't make any difference how many men were trying to kill them.

Run, idiot.

She slowed at an intersection, scanned right then left and sped through.

"We gotta think of—" she started. A loud crack startled her. And then another. "The fuck's that?"

The thwacks continued, like a hatchet or axe. She didn't want to take her eyes off the road, the motorcycles veering and converging ahead of them but she glanced into the rearview. A bright headlight sent hard coronas of shine into her eyes. She blinked, tried to train her eyes on the roadway. Thwack. Thwack.

"Es un antena del carro," Gustavo said as the motorcycle pulled alongside him. As though it were a mere curiosity, this rider on the motorcycle striking the car. The next blow actually broke the sideview mirror, and Gustavo patted his shirt pockets. The rider kept at it till all the glass fell out.

"Chingao," Gustavo said.

"What?"

"I had cigarettes," he said sadly.

"Jesus Christ, you motherfucker. Cigarettes? We need a plan to get out of this!"

The bike jerked forward a bit, and the driver jammed the antenna into the hood's air vent. It twanged back and forth, right in front of Gustavo. Yet there he sat, inert. In a bray of exhaust the bike spun ahead, swerving right in front of the Hyundai and then on up the road, quickly out of sight. The palm trees were painted white at their bases, and the headlights gleamed off them. She jumped a bit whenever they leapt out.

A lull for a dozen panicked thoughts. Where they could go. What they could do. *Run*. But where? To who? She glanced down at her phone, wedged between her legs. She wished she'd gotten Carver's number.

They were gonna have to run and shoot their way out. She glanced over at Gustavo. First to see if he had his gun and then to just silently rage at him. His fault. All his fault. This man just staring straight ahead.

"Slow down," he said.

Carrizo Springs, Texas. Martinez Auto Works. Fuck, she still remembered. This asshole—

"Slow down! Stop!"

Red lights suddenly reared up in front of them. She slammed on the brakes, braced herself with rigid arms against the wheel. Gustavo's head hit the dash before he flopped back into place. There was no time to savor that. An accident or roadblock. Flashing lights.

She looked in the rearview. The F-150 pulled up behind the smaller Toyota. Both vehicles flipped off their mounted roof lights. The cars in front of her moved forward, slowly. She could see a cop up ahead, palm up, halting the cars ahead of them.

"Did one of the bikes wreck?" she asked, before she realized that was impossible. An ambulance wouldn't be on the scene already, all these dark blue police cars—

Of course. The cops. She began to power down her window. Gustavo gripped her leg.

"No."

She stopped the window halfway down.

"Why?"

"You talk to him, they kill him."

"You actually want me to roll by like nothing's wrong?"

"They will kill him. And all these other cars, la gente estará muerto tambíen. All the people." She looked over at him. He gazed ahead. "Don't say nothing."

In the rearview, she watched the shapes in the cab of the Toyota. Just shapes of men. No intentions to read save general menace.

"So where are we going?"

"We just go," he said.

"Fantastic." She turned her head around. "What happened to the bikes?"

"Why you think I know?"

"Goddamnit! You caused all of this!"

The cars were stopped for the ambulance to pull out. She remembered the way in, a straight shot back the way she'd come. It was a small airport, not much in the way of security, but maybe enough.

"They aren't shooting up the cops," she said, "maybe they won't shoot up the airport security either."

"They will take us to a little room."

"Good. Better than being out here."

"No, the policía will come."

"*Good.*"

"No good! It is them will give us to the Golfos."

Traffic wasn't moving at all. Neither were the shapes in the Toyota. No motorcycles. Eerie stillness. This was madness.

"We're not gonna outrun them, no way," she said. "And we can't just go till the gas gives out."

"Claro."

"Fuck you. I'm trying to talk it out."

"The airport will not be what you think it is."

"All right, all right," she said. "You have any ideas?"

Gustavo clucked his tongue. "No tengo más. Never. Nothing. No more."

Throw him out of the car right now. Feed the beasts. Maybe somehow get away.

He just shook his head, eyes still closed, skin squeaking against the window.

She scrolled through the contacts on her BlackBerry. Dufresne. Held her thumb above the green phone icon. She did not expect him to answer, but at every ring she let herself hope.

His voice mail clicked on. She hung up.

The bridge had burned. She was out here alone.

The traffic started moving, the cop circling his arm. They rolled past him and the scene of the accident. Two ambulances. Three cars. Gnarled metal. Smithereens of glass. She navigated between the deep pink flares, feeling a sudden rich unreality that recalled a fundamentalist Christian haunted house she'd gone to. The tableaus of abortions and drug addictions and one for drunk driving. Except this was worse for being so very actual. The Toyota purred, the F-150 growled.

She took a moment to consider leaping out. *Run.* But she stayed at the wheel.

This is the fastest way to run right now.

The traffic around the accident thinned out and they gathered speed, passing shuttered shops and gas stations. Darkened billboards. Palms serried in the medians. Parallel to the road a canal with little footbridges. They could have been puttering along any Gulf Coast thoroughfare in the States. Concrete buildings, bright paint, American fast food joints. The breeze, the humidity, the familiar smell of ocean. She could not imagine anywhere they could go.

Because there isn't anywhere.

In the sky a small twin-engine plane taking off. They weren't far. The airport couldn't be more than five minutes away now. She scanned for the tower. She didn't want to miss the turn.

The airport is all we have.

Two motorcycles had pulled alongside them now, one on each side. One in front. She could hear the Toyota rumbling close by. Out of the corner of her eye, she saw Gustavo raise his pistol toward her. She instinctively leaned back, grabbed the barrel, and as the motorcycles raced ahead again, saw his wild and bewildered expression and realized he'd been aiming out the window.

He threw open his door.

"What are you doing!"

He seemed to consider the roadway blurring beneath him, the pistol in his hand.

"Jump out if you want to end it!" She let off gas. The Toyota was on her bumper. "Do it!"

He raised the pistol to his head.

She swerved the car suddenly to the right and caused the passenger door to swing shut, not out of a desire to save his life or even to avoid something in the roadway. She had simply felt something. A startle from nowhere that made her yank the wheel before she realized that it came from between her legs: the phone. When it vibrated a second time, she picked it up and held it in front of her face. An unknown number.

She answered.

"It's Carver."

"Holy shit, what?"

"I've got eyes on you. You need to listen closely, and we'll get you out of this."

"Good god, roger that," she said. "How'd you—No, sorry, I don't care. What's the plan?"

"Are you the one driving?"

"Yeah. Gustavo's with me."

"Who is that?" Gustavo asked.

"Shut up." She couldn't hear Carver talking. "Sorry, what did you say?"

"I said I got you."

"What am I supposed to do?"

"Just keep going like you are."

The Toyota truck motor was rumbling like the sound of a battalion behind them. The F-150. She couldn't see any of the bikes.

"Can you see the bikes?" she asked.

Carver didn't answer. Neither did Gustavo.

She thought she heard shouting, even over the traffic and the Toyota engine, and the sound of the F-150 peeling. The Toyota pulled to her right bumper.

"Who you talking with?" Gustavo asked again.

The Ford pulled up onto her right. She knew immediately that it was going to force her into the Toyota, edge her into the grill guard, and the two trucks would send the little sedan into a sideways skid. She set the phone on the seat and gunned the gutless engine, but the Toyota matched her speed, stayed on her corner. The Ford squeezed over.

"Fuck."

The Ford a few feet from her shoulder, her face. The Toyota on her ass. She tapped the brakes, the Toyota clipped her, braked and skidded. She wrenched the wheel right, swerved free and in front of the Toyota, and sped on. The Ford hung up behind an old pickup in the right lane, the Toyota raced up on her rear. She reached over and grabbed the phone.

The bikes had appeared again, veering ahead and behind, not doing anything yet, waiting.

She looked down. Unknown. She toggled to speaker, hit it.

"I'm here," she said. "Forgot to put you on speaker. They were gonna run us off the road."

"I saw. Nice driving."

"I missed the turn."

"It's okay. Stand by."

They were coming up on a slow-moving van now.

"On my signal, pass this van on the right side," Carver said. "Now."

She accelerated in the non-lane between the van and the sidewalk, heard the whoosh of a motorbike's evasion, and wished she'd knocked the motherfucker over. Tilting the wheel to the left, she cut in front of the van with very little to spare, the antenna in the air vent whipping around like trash in a tornado.

"It's open. Gun it."

She pushed down the gas and the Hyundai did what it could, not much, but something.

"Go all the way to the left lane."

She drifted over, smooth and swift.

"When I say, you brake hard. We're gonna pop you over the median."

"Really?"

"You'll head back the other way."

"Shit, shit. Okay."

"Not quite yet, though. Get past these cars."

Three vehicles in this lane. She caught and veered around them, and then cut back quickly. Behind her, squeal of tires, honking. The Toyota swerved. A horn. The Ford maybe. She sped up.

"Now what?"

Gustavo had turned around, was looking out the back window.

"They gonna shoot," he said.

"Hold it, hold it . . . ," Carver said.

Gustavo was blocking the rearview. She shoved him out of the way. She could make out the passenger in the Toyota leaning out his window, the unreal shape of a submachine gun. There was another car in the lane. She was heading straight for it.

"Hold it . . . don't slow yet . . ."

Gustavo said something she couldn't hear. She kept on right ahead, heading straight for the car less than fifty meters away.

"And . . . NOW! CUT! *NOW!*"

She braked hard, spun the wheel, and the car lurched up onto the grassy median, clipping a palm but bouncing through and across, skidding all the way into the far right north lane, facing back in the direction they'd just come from. Stopped. She watched in awe as the Toyota driver locked eyes with her going the other direction.

"Punch it!"

She shoved her foot on the gas, making sure not to hold the wheel too tight, let it find its own high-speed equilibrium.

"Las motociclistas," Gustavo said.

The bikes leapt over the median in front of them, jarred their riders, swerved. Some stalled as the sedan passed through them. And then already there was one outside Gustavo's window, another buzzing around next to her, yet another right behind them. But she wasn't scared anymore.

"Keep going," Carver said. "You're all clear ahead for the next little bit."

"What about the bikes?"

"You're gonna make the turn this time. Get ready."

Holding the car steady, she slipped around two cars and then got the car up to 110 kmh. When she heard the Toyota's engine loud and getting louder very quickly, she gripped the wheel tighter.

"The small pickup's coming up behind," Carver said. "Hang on. Don't decelerate—"

A sudden crash threw them forward, her shoulder smashing into the wheel, the phone flying onto the floorboard. The car swerved, she regained control, righted it. In the rearview the Toyota. Fucker had rammed her. She yanked her seat belt on. As did Gustavo. A wonder they hadn't done so yet.

"The phone," she said to Gustavo.

"What?"

"The floor. The phone! We gotta make a turn. I need to know when!"

He unlatched his seat belt and bent to find it.

"It's down near my feet!" she shouted. In the mirror she saw the truck coming hard. "Shit, get up!"

She shoved herself back into the seat again and braced as much as she could.

The blow pulled her into the seat belt, tight against her breastbone. She could feel her organs bouncing as her head flew forward. The car wobbled and careened. Her vision blurred. She blinked and pressed the gas. Gustavo was gone.

"Take it!" he said from the floor, handing up the phone. He climbed back into his seat, pulling on the seat belt.

"I'm back. I dropped the phone," she said.

She jammed the phone into her bra strap.

"You still hear me?" she said, turning her chin to the side.

"Keep driving. Stay in this lane. It's not far."

The Hyundai was still handling okay, but in the side mirror she could see a panel of the car's tail razoring in the wind like a flame.

"We lost one of the bikes," Gustavo said. "And the Ford, tambíen, I dunno."

"This car can't take more hits like that," she said.

"Just listen to me and drive," Carver said.

"I am."

"Truck," Carver said.

She looked in the rearview. It was urging up on them again.

"Don't lose speed. Let it come."

"I just said we can't take a hit!"

She braced—for nothing. The truck lunged, and then it dropped back. A few seconds later, did the same thing. Sped up, got right on her tail, backed off.

"He's trying to make you lose control. Don't."

"Okay, sure, no fucking problem."

"Don't brake until I tell you. Pass this car."

She cut around the slow vehicle in front of her. She glided back into the center lane and accelerated. They were coming up on a light, changing, yellow, now red. She let off the gas.

"Can I go thr—"

"Go! Go! Go!"

She hit the gas and raced through the light and felt her belly surge with the car. She looked in the rearview to see the Toyota and Ford and motorcycles all ignore the same light.

"We didn't lose them."

"That's fine."

"Why?"

"Turn right when I say."

"Then what?"

"One thing at a time."

The phone was slipping a little under her bra strap. She was sweating. She worried it would fall, but she was going too fast to take her hand off the wheel and adjust it.

"You're about to take a hard right into an alley."

"Okay.

"There's a car dealership and then some kind of store. You see?"

The phone slipped, she felt it slide down under her armpit. She had to let go of the wheel with one hand to get it, pull it out of the bottom of her shirt, yank it up to her ear.

"Don't slow down! Why are you slowing down?"

"I lost the phone," she said, loudly, but trying not to panic or yell. She had the sudden stupid thought that she didn't want him to think she was scared or out of control.

"Do you see the store?"

She squinted. It was all just buildings blurring at her.

"Yeah, I think," she lied. Scanning the road. "You said paint store?"

"Roger, the paint store. A hard right."

She got ready. Trying not to grip the wheel too tight. She had no idea what the paint store looked like.

"Is it this one—?"

"Now! Turn!"

She cut hard right, fishtailing into an empty dirt and gravel lot. The car momentarily slid, the headlights panned across the alley and onto the corrugated fencing before she passed the wheel hand under hand leftward and gunned it down the pitted dirt road. Fences of different sizes. Barrels, garbage cans, flashed by. An orange cat shot across the road in the headlights. The car dipped and bounded over the uneven broken asphalt, the pure dirt and sand.

She heard the motorcycles and looked to see their headlights emerging from the dust cloud, two right behind, one farther back with the Toyota truck, its roof lights flipped on, a huge iridescent cloud in the dust. She kept looking for the F-150 in the juddering mirrors, and then it finally popped up in the rearview too. A strange counterintuitive relief at that. To know what was coming after you.

"Your seat belt on?" Carver asked.

"Yeah."

"Take it off."

"Off?"

"Yes."

"On my mark, I want you to slam on the brakes."

"They're right on top of us."

"You're among friends now."

"What?"

"When you come to a halt, shut off the car, duck down. Count to ten. And then get out and run left. Stick to the wall. Got it?"

"Count to ten. Run left."

"The narco hear this?"

She glanced over. He was wedged against the door in the corner of his seat. He nodded. Winced as the car jounced over a pothole.

"We got it," she said.

"All right. Get ready."

She kept the phone in her hand. The motorcycles were in a train behind her, the lead jolting forward as if to get by, but it couldn't in the narrows of the alley.

"When do we stop?"

Nothing. Silence on the line. The ping and punch of gravel.

"Carver?"

She looked at the phone, then at the corrugated fencing sliding by in a blur behind Gustavo, at the off-road lights of the pickups filling the mirrors. Flash and racket. Engines rumbling in chorus in these rusted and concrete confines. She smelled their yellow dust, watched the cloud of roar and chug bearing down on them. The narrow alley ahead lifeless as a moonscape in the naked headlights.

"Carver!"

She worried that the phone wasn't working and then suddenly Carver yelled "Stop now *STOP!*" and she hit the brakes and the phone dropped away or she let it go as in a dream and the braking car turned slightly like a person turning her head at the sound of her name.

A motorcycle clipped the front bumper. The rider ragdolled over the headlights in front of them, the bike careering riderless into the wall they were facing quarterwise. A second bike skidded past the same left side, avoiding the car and wall, but then he flew off his bike too in a loud pink mist.

In the skidding din of the bikes and pickups behind them, she saw moving shadows, two, then three, then more in black fatigues and helmets and ballistics masks, parting like matadors for the second riderless motorcycle to fly past. Red laser sights hitting the windshield as they jogged forward, one of their number pausing to execute the first rider, still motionless on the ground. They converged around the car.

"Duck!" the phone shouted from the floor.

There was so much noise and light, she did not need to be told.

In the sustained gunfire she heard bootsteps on the hood. Then a suction and a whoosh and an explosion, the interior of the car inundated with light. She could see Gustavo's face, his wide eyes, his gritting teeth, the veins on his temple and neck. And then new darkness, the heavy quiet that is having gone deaf. In the ensuing moments a steady clattering. Like fingernails on a Formica table. Like falling poker chips. This is more gunfire. A person went steadily past the driver's-side window, casings casting dark butterfly shadows in the light flash of the barrel. The fight was moving behind the car.

Within her it was quiet right then. It was still. She wasn't running anymore.

Gustavo opened her door. She looked behind her, expecting him to be on the floor where she left him, but his door was open and he was saying "Ten, remember?" and her ears rang, flooded with more percussive pops. He pulled her out and they were running along a wall, they were stepping over something—was that an RPG launcher?—and then they were stopped. She stepped in place, tingling all over.

Gustavo was looking within an empty building behind them, a darkened auto shop from the smell of it. More men in black assault gear, firing into the alley. They peeked through a broken window. The Toyota was blackened. A burst from one of the large-calibers. The Ford bouncing up, the last of the roof lights going out.

A full silence.

She could hear Carver's voice—his deep rapid cadence, almost joyful—and three men talking about thirty feet away. She couldn't make out what they were saying. She could hear their voices, though. She didn't understand why she didn't understand. Her head felt heavy, like someone had dumped sand into her brainpan and then watered it down. Her heart raced yet.

"No es inglés o español," Gustavo said.

She looked at him.

"They not Americans," he said.

"Or Mexicans?"

"What I said. That ain't no Spanish." He shook his head. "No lo sé."

He stood away from the wall and walked back out to the car.

"Where are you going?" she demanded. She looked into the building, where Carver and these men still conferred, then went after Gustavo. The alley was lit by the fire of the burning Toyota, and nothing else. And then the lights mounted on their weapons flickered on, and she could see the dark figures, almost ghosts, moving along the alley walls. The lights aimed at the ground. The men crouching. Gathering.

"Well done," Carver said, sweeping by them to the Hyundai. He flipped on his own gun light and inspected the back of the vehicle. Satisfied, he opened the back door and began to undress, pitching his helmet, face mask, goggles, and gloves in the back seat. He slammed the back door shut and stood over the opened front door.

"They didn't even get off a fucking round. This car, minus whatever you did to the chassis, should be good to go."

The men were still at their task in the alley.

"What are they doing?" she asked.

"The fellas? Gathering up casings. We like to keep it neat."

She watched them working their way up the alley. Pinching the ground and putting the casings into sacks on their belts like sharecroppers, like a new kind of migrant farmer. It felt like a dream.

"Keys?" Carver asked from behind the driver's-side door.

"What?"

"The keys," he said.

"In the ignition," she said, looking around. The smoke and dust. The silence.

"Guys, let's go."

They got in the immaculate sedan and left the scene.

LA PALOMA

Tomás had been sitting in the doorway of the Iglesia Pentecostal Unida a la Paloma for the better part of the day, drinking drip coffee the church secretary had made before she and the preacher left him there alone. They hurried away, neither one looking back as they departed, lest they turn to pillars of salt. An unmistakable menace about him.

The church had a smooth concrete facade, sky blue with bright gold trim. A huge steeple, three stories, with windows, rooms, probably they even did church shit up there, looking out over the earth like Christian owls. And now this incongruous man had propped open the door of the church and sat so he could see what little there was to see through the wrought iron spike fencing that surrounded the property and yet remain in range of the fan the secretary set up for him.

He ran a hand over his head, sniffed the odors of the ambush still clinging to his hair. Burnt rubber and paint, gasoline and rocket exhaust. Smoking flesh. Maybe even some tattoo ink from those dead prison Zetas whose bodies lay a few hundred meters away, on the other side of the cinder-block residences and shops and empty lots. He wiped his hand on his pant leg. What a disaster. The sun was hot and high, making the smell worse probably. He needed a shower.

Across the street a crowd of bystanders edged the yellow tape and barricades to observe Tampico's entire law enforcement community, crime-scene techs in khaki, morgue workers in white. They'd never seen a spectacle like this, everyone enthralled—men in pressed shirts, orange-vested municipal workers, women with umbrellas against the sun. Straw-hatted fruit peddlers at their carts. Everyone just edging for a glimpse of blood and death. And they couldn't see shit. Fucking stupid, fucking weird. Crowds always gather for violence and wreckage. For things like this, perpetrated by men like him. As if all this bearing witness might be a kind of inoculation against what might come for them someday.

Which it wasn't. Obviously. There was no protecting yourself against the future. He wanted to go tell them that, be a wise man talking some wise shit, but he knew they wouldn't listen. Plus it was a stupid thing to talk about at all. Nobody'd listen to a wise man these days. They wouldn't know what to do with one.

Tomás took a phone from his shirt pocket and texted the boy.

Talk to me. Tell me what you see

Behind the church he'd found a kid and his brother kicking around a half-deflated fútbol. He'd palmed the older boy several large bills, sent them to a store for burners. Sent one up in the church steeple, another one on the ground. Told them to observe and report to him.

cops and army still here, the boy wrote back.

The kid was quick. Tomás was impressed.

How many?

Lots of them 20 maybe? nobody leaving more keep showing up too

Be fast when things change, Tomás texted back. **You need to tell me instantly.**

okay

When they look like they're ready. You hit me RIGHT THEN.

Ready for what.

To do something new.

yes sir

Keep out of sight, both of you.

okay good we will

Tomás put the phone back in his pocket. He could use more kids like those two. More useful than those pinche prison Zetas. Such a far cry from the soldiers they'd been trained to be. But those dudes were doomed. The ambush was that perfect.

He'd been a block behind. The pickups followed the motorcycles into the alley. His gut told him to hang back. The way the Hyundai had somehow found a slot in the palms on the median and whipped around was like another driver had taken the wheel, and had his men on the hook. Right then Tomás should've radioed them to hang back.

But they wouldn't have listened, he knew that. The fools had been high since Topo Chico, galloping and carnivorous, so game they didn't see the danger of a blind alley. So they died. Astonished and probably crying like curs bellying the ground and they'd asked for it. The blood they ultimately sought was of course their own.

Their stupid bloodlust saved him, though. They'd gotten ahead and given Tomás a chance to see the red laser sights cutting through the airborne dust. He'd killed the engine and headlights and was gliding to a stop when the RPG ripped into them. Then the guns opened up, and he cranked the ignition so hard he bent the key. He'd backed the fuck out of there, expecting any second for the windshield to spiderweb with sniper fire.

What those badasses had pulled off was amazing, and apparently without a casualty. The concentrated violence of it all. He was truly in awe. Troubled only by the mystery of it. He didn't feel a lust for vengeance, not at all. He just wanted to *know*, his ignorance like a wound he couldn't stop worrying, fussing, and touching. They'd set a trap, destroyed some dozen psychopaths, and then vanished. No trail, no way to even start smelling one out. He was stuck here in Tampico. Knowing nobody, no contacts, no knowledge of this territory, nothing to tell El Rabioso—

He pulled out his phone, texted the kid again.

You see that earlier? The battle?

it woke us up. didn't see anything.

Okay. You talk to anybody saw anything?

people said there was motorcycles. then just the dead men and some cars sped away

what kind of cars?

Don't know.

I'm wondering what the people looked like who attacked

dunno i only heard them

Alright. It's okay. You're doing good. Stay out of sight.

yes sir.

But keep your eyes open for me.

can I ask something, sir?

Go ahead.

are you a narco, sir?

Why do you ask?

because you have money for us and are concerned with these men.

does that make me a narco?

Are you police.

I'm not a narco or police, Tomás wrote. I'm a knight.

He looked at the phone, the kid's nonresponse, and wondered himself what he meant. Wondered was this for the kid or the kid in himself who still read about wizards and swords even as he tussled with narcos and an American DEA agent. He wished he had that fucking book. Even to be in Fuerzas Especiales, on the other side again. Simple. Working with the federales, probably the DEA—

Of course.

The DEA woman.

Tomás realized with sudden galling clarity that he'd surely underestimated her. She seemed so afraid when Tomás showed up, but when El Capataz told her where the tunnel was, she knew exactly what to do. The bitch was the one driving the car, after all. Had led them right into an ambush. Some kind of killer-killers. Realms in realms. Tunnels everywhere. And now the nephew and the DEA woman were long gone.

Hey, he wrote to the kid, **do you see any gringos?**

The badasses were probably Americans. SEALs, Delta, CIA.

I don't think so, the kid wrote back.

like American uniforms maybe?

I will ask joselito

He had to find them. Not for the tunnel. He didn't give a fuck about the tunnel. That was a problem for El Rabioso and El Esquimal. The ache, the churn in his gut, was embarrassment. This DEA woman had lured his men right into the crosshairs of a death squad. He should've gotten her name. He'd been outdone.

joselito says he sees police, the kid wrote, **and ambulance workers, soldiers, but not any gringos he can tell.**

Alright.

we don't know the other stuff. whether american or officers we don't know stuff like that

I know, it's okay. you see any military walking around?

Maybe the ambush was just Mexican military. Some new Special Forces unit.

don't know, the kid wrote back, **everyone is in masks**

I know. But maybe some asshole with ornaments on his shoulders or a fucking beret or something.

not that I see

okay. keep watching

He needed to find her. He needed to learn what kind of world he'd entered. The new rules.

Fuck, it was so hot, even with the fan. How did these tampique-ñas live like this? Tomás stood up, let himself inside. He walked up some steps and then down to the church's baptismal pool. This was some kind of American Christianity, where they dunked adults in the water. He saw churches like this from his time in Texas. Big as arenas, lots full of pickups. They spoke in tongues, they preached wealth, wasn't no peon Catholic church, they had a big-dick American God.

Yeah, it was Americans who shot the Zetas up. He was sure of it.

He undressed and folded his clothes onto a pew and got in the perfect water. He dunked himself and slicked his hair back and sprayed water from his mouth and went under again and started rubbing his skin, washing himself. He let his eyes float on the surface like a crocodile.

Did this mean he was saved now? As in salvation, go-to-heaven, all that? That's what these weird Christians believed, right? You go under, you're born anew, no? Maybe somewhat saved, a percentage, half- or quarter-saved? Did his soul get at least some little bit of profit from this church water?

Probably not. Even Tomás wouldn't let a guy like himself in a place with all those good people. Wouldn't be fair. Tomás had never read the Bible, never listened to homilies, never paid attention, but he knew that Christianity had some pretty strict rules. A ticket to paradise cost more than a bath. Maybe you got less time in purgatory. Probably it was something like that. A thousand years off his infinite sentence or some shit.

But these church folk didn't believe in purgatory. They baptized anybody, adults, old men, not just babies. They didn't believe in a holding-cell-place after death, that complicated Catholic shit like his mom and the priest taught. With these people, you were just cleansed or not. Pretty good loophole, that. Sin up until the last breath, just get baptized at the end.

The water felt so good. He gazed at a big carving on the wall of a dove flying through fire. No stained glass, no jewels, no big gold crosses for him to guess how much they were worth, no sad-ass Jesus pictures where he's all skinny and fucked up, no saints, not even the Virgin. Just this dove. Maybe this wasn't no Christian church at all. Birds carried messages from wizards. Watched over travelers and seekers. Giant ones like this dove here let select badasses hitch rides. Funny to think of this as some kind of bird-god joint. Him in a giant birdbath.

Tomás dunked his head once more, slicked his hair back, and walked up the stairs out of the pool and down again to the floor. He rubbed his feet dry on the cheap carpet, sat naked for a while thinking he'd probably be killed soon. Just had that coming-to-the-end feeling. Couldn't place it exactly. Like the shot-up Zetas were an alarm. Time was up.

He put on his socks and then his pants and shoes. He went outside, propped the door again with the chair. He sat there shirtless in the sun and texted the boy.

hey

yeah, the kid wrote back.

Still nothing?

nothing but I am watching close

Alright, Tomás wrote, listen up.

yes?

I am a narco, okay. I just want you to know that.

are you famous?

No, nobody knows me. But maybe you heard of El Esquimal?

no I don't know maybe then why's he called that?

I don't know anymore

Is he your boss

He's the big boss. He keeps a low profile. I understand you don't know him. I answer to El Rabioso.

Who is he?

The plaza boss.

is that what they call the one who oversees knights?

Tomás smiled. **I suppose so.** Then, **i'm telling you this so you know to watch out.**

For what?

More of like what happened last night.

Tomás moved his chair out of the sun. He held a hand above his eyes, squinted. The sun hammered down on the crowd across the highway. Afternoon just starting, and it still hadn't thinned out at all. What was the point of the crowd? Or of even warning the kid? Some false hope that you could manage the chaos. Same as wondering who exactly killed his men. Who the DEA woman was. He didn't know shit, maybe never would. So don't fucking worry about it.

He closed his eyes, tried to enjoy the air on his wet skin.

A text came in.

an ambulance, the kid wrote.

somebody's alive? Tomás wrote back. Some luck maybe. Maybe his Zetas got a shot off.

I think so

You see who?

some hurt dude

Is he in armor, maybe a uniform?

not sure let me check

If one of the ambushers was wounded and still alive, then Tomás could find out who they were, maybe even catch up to his quarry. Could be a good thing. Maybe things could be understood after all.

Or maybe a new problem: a prison Zeta. The cops would interrogate him, and he could very well give everything up. Topo Chico. What the CDG had loosed him to do.

That would be very bad. Tomás was the one here on scene, boots on the ground, the one giving orders to children now. When it ends all fucked up, he's the one gets zeroed. He wasn't under the zero yet, but from where he sat he could definitely see that motherfucker.

His phone buzzed.

i can't tell what he's wearing

okay thank you, Tomás texted back.

Things could maybe still be salvaged. There were possibilities. If the guy was an American, things could be learned. If he was a half-dead Zeta with prison tattoos and a long story, well, Tomás could handle that as well.

He stood. For a last moment he felt the fan blow against his skin. Then he pushed the chair inside, let the church door fall shut behind him, and put on his shirt.

On the edge of the yellow tape a couple of expressionless uniformed police made sure no one got through. Tomás still couldn't see much. The wreckage from the ambush—bodies, bikes, cars—was too far away. He had a view of the morgue van, although they hadn't started loading the dead into it yet. He could see the front of the ambulance pointed toward the street. He yearned to see what was going on with the wounded man.

He pulled out his phone, texted the boy in the steeple.

What's happening with the medics?

they are working, came the response, again very quickly.

Outside? Not in ambulance yet?

yes

You still can't tell anything about him?

bloody

What's he wearing?

can't see

He's alive?

don't know, sorry

The palm trees swayed in the breeze. A bulldozer, a jackhammer, both somewhere far away. He cased the workers near him on break from a jobsite, thinking maybe he could use them. They smelled strongly of paint, all of them in jumpsuits, bandanas over their heads, sunglasses, hard hats in hand, drinking refrescos. He clocked three women with children and groceries waiting for the bus, not wanting to miss their ride nor a new element of the scene. A man in a panama talked nonsensically about Christ to a young man wearing a too-large sport coat. Despite the carnage, no one was crying or wailing. No one knew the dead. But they were keyed up, eyes edging around like it could happen again, whispering as if a terrible ominous thing were coming. Like herd animals, worries chewed over like cud.

He could use this.

His phone buzzed. Another text from the kid.

they're loading him

Shit. He'd have to follow the ambulance to the hospital.

okay

If it was one of the American soldiers, Tomás needed to interrogate him—probably impossible at the hospital. And if he was a Zeta, he'd need to be silenced. Again, the hospital wasn't ideal.

Tomás moved to a better vantage on the ambulance. No lights, no sirens. Okay. He had a minute or two. A few cops with semiautos strung across their chests stood between him and the ambulance. The rest at the scene, a fútbol field or more away.

The paramedics pushed the stretcher toward the ambulance, detectives and investigators parting slowly, such was their ogling. In a minute he'd be loaded up and gone. Tomás tensed, his limbs tingling in a sudden certainty: he had to do it now. The hospital would be too hard.

He'd have to take care of it here.

He waited for an officer to go to the trunk of a squad car, away from the throng, in a spot of slight concealment behind a power-line pole not far from the cop and his car. When the cop opened the trunk and removed a shotgun, Tomás swept up behind him and in a fluid motion took the cop's shotgun with one hand and stabbed him under the ribs with the other. Little jewels of blood in the air as his knife went in and out. "This will hurt, but you will live," he said before he ran the knife across the cop's forehead. Tomás let him go, and the cop said "Gah" as he gripped his side and staggered to turn around, his face bloody, his eyes full of blood, his mouth open in an astonished rictus, pinched as though breathing were itself a tremendous labor. His lung was collapsing or collapsed or filling or filled with blood, and he was blind and mute. The cop stumbled toward the throng that remained, heedless of his predicament.

Tomás quickly put two flares in his back pocket and, one-handed, rummaged in the trunk some more, tossing small empty boxes onto the ground. He ejected the shells from the shotgun and placed them in the trunk just so. He grabbed a police radio and put it under his arm as he lit each flare. He closed the trunk on the shining casings of bullets and the red shotgun shells and leaned the shotgun against the bumper and calmly strode away.

The cop had dropped at the end of a thin spoor of his own blood, and when the shells exploded and the bullets began to pop from within the trunk, the crowd bunched and flexed as it came to mistaken terms with the noise. The trunk rocked and smoked and everyone ducked and scattered. Those who saw the bleeding cop recoiled from him and the chaos nearby as the panic grew. The policía fired in the direction of the erupting squad car, thinking the culprits were hidden behind it. The desired pandemonium.

The policía ducked and dashed and performed heroic slides into positions around the smoking squad car. A last pop brought a fusillade of bullets into the car as Tomás emerged from the ambulance, wiping his hands on his pants as though he'd finished a chore or greasy meal. He pulled the radio out from under his arm and turned it on and fiddled with it near his ear as he walked away. The policía closed in on the smoking and now silent trunk of the squad car.

A horn blasted the new quiet. An SUV rolled up to the barricade and was waved into the restricted area. Parked. Two people jumped out. Not wearing balaclavas like all the other law enforcement. One black man and a woman, both in black jackets, bulging with body armor. They kept tight together, wary and scanning, and approached the cops showing identification, working their way to a clutch of commanders.

Americans.

He texted the boy.

You see the gringos?

yes

you see the woman

yes

Does she have brown hair?

no she is blonde

So this wasn't the DEA woman. Some other gringos.

They went with a group of police to the scene of the battle, the spilled motorcycles, the charred pickups. The dead men. The man in body armor studied the ground, went where the cops pointed. The woman scanned around, and when she looked up toward Tomás, he turned and walked away.

Is she watching me?

No

Tomás saw Ernesto peeking from within the steeple.

Where is she now?

The ambulance.

Tomás got in the van. He'd have to watch these gringos, whoever they were. Tail them. It was something, it wasn't much. His phone shook on the dash where he'd set it.

did you kill the man in the ambulance

He set the phone back and could see in the side mirror the white woman shouting at the man who'd come with her, the two of them running to the SUV. The man and woman climbed in the SUV, and it pulled away.

who are these gringos

When the SUV pulled away, he started the van. They were in a hurry. Good, so was he.

He waited five seconds and pulled out. The phone vibrated in his lap. He rolled down the window and threw it hard to the pavement.

BAGRAM AFB, PARWAN PROVINCE, AFGHANISTAN

MARCH 19, 2004, 21:25

POLYGRAPHER:	Tell me about ███████.
CARVER:	The poppy warlord? He's around five-eight, two hundred pounds. Wears these yellow aviators like some kind of sheik or pedo.
POLYGRAPHER:	Shipley picked him. Why?
CARVER:	He wasn't afraid of al-Qaeda, for starters. The people in ██████ feared him, let him know what was going on. He was a serious jefe with zero charisma, but Shipley felt like he'd be the best bet.
POLYGRAPHER:	For what?
CARVER:	You know what we were doing.
POLYGRAPHER:	What did he tell you you were doing?
CARVER:	Backing the most reasonable player in all of ██████.
POLYGRAPHER:	And what did you think of that?
CARVER:	Like, ethically?
POLYGRAPHER:	Yes. And legally.
CARVER:	This is a weird question, isn't it?
POLYGRAPHER:	How's that?
CARVER:	The Agency renditions motherfuckers to black sites like Chinese takeout, and you wanna know if I was clutching my pearls over Shipley's arrangement with a big bad heroin producer?
POLYGRAPHER:	Tell me what you thought.
CARVER:	I thought about how my great-granddad ran whiskey

in Kentucky and then took that money and expertise and went into stock-car racing, even stood for mayor once.

POLYGRAPHER: I think I follow, but go on.

CARVER: I thought ▮▮▮▮▮▮ might could bring a little peace and order to ▮▮▮▮▮.

POLYGRAPHER: Okay. So how did the pursuit teams aid his operation?

CARVER: You gotta understand something. The economy up there is based on one thing: heroin. Growing it. Moving it. Protecting it. Shipley tried to warn the State Department that making farmers grow wheat wasn't gonna help win the War on Drugs.

POLYGRAPHER: Why?

CARVER: It took the bottom out of wheat prices. Even if people wanted to, no one could afford *not* to grow poppies. We weren't gonna get rid of al-Qaeda by destroying the local economy. But of course, nobody listens.

POLYGRAPHER: So what did the pursuit teams do for ▮▮▮▮▮▮▮▮▮?

CARVER: Torched his rivals' fields. Stole their pumps, shit like that. After Karzai got in power, we made sure the local police didn't fuck with him or his outfit.

POLYGRAPHER: And you employed coalition resources?

CARVER: We called in a few air strikes on the other warlords. Said they were al-Qaeda. Maybe they were. But more importantly, we made it seem like ▮▮▮▮ ▮▮▮▮ had AC-10s at his disposal. And it worked perfectly. The villagers started feeding him intel about al-Qaeda activities, which he passed on to us. Some villages in ▮▮▮▮, they just started talking to us direct. Where the enemy ratlines were. Which families were hiding weapons. Which villagers were giving aid and comfort.

POLYGRAPHER: What do you know about the incident on April 23, 2003?

CARVER:	Wait. You gotta understand something. Enemy engagements went down like 80 percent.
POLYGRAPHER:	Got it. What do you know about April 23, 2003?
CARVER:	I assume you're talking about when Special Forces intercepted that shipment? All I heard was that the runners said ▮▮▮▮▮▮▮▮ had a deal with the CIA. I dunno if it actually escalated all the way to Tenet versus Rumsfeld, but Shipley said we shouldn't expect any more intel from the Defense Department. Or help of any kind.
POLYGRAPHER:	What did he tell you about the Concern?
CARVER:	What concern?
POLYGRAPHER:	The Concern. His pet project in the Special Activities Division.
CARVER:	I never heard of any projects.
POLYGRAPHER:	He logged a lot of time in ▮▮▮▮▮ with your pursuit team in particular.
CARVER:	Yeah, nevertheless. You think I'm lying? Look at the needle.
POLYGRAPHER:	The needle isn't dispositive.
CARVER:	What does that mean?
POLYGRAPHER:	It means I'm the one needs convincing. So why don't you tell me about your time in Pakistan. About the Ground Branch's interaction with the DEA in Karachi.

CROCODILES

Harbaugh swallowed the black beans straight from the can, hardly chewing. She'd never tasted anything so salty, cold, perfect. She sopped the juice from her chin with her wrist and tapped on the bottom of the can and jammed her fingers in there to get the last beans gummed to the sides. She looked around, licking her fingers.

The house Carver had brought them to was so clean and empty that her initial impression was new construction. There was nothing in it, no furniture or decoration, the walls a basic talcy white, windows covered by faux-wood blinds. The only appealing feature was the high-end saltillo floor tile. But the place wasn't new. Nicks on the Formica counter, a chipped and stained backsplash, a cracked window. She'd thought it must be a safehouse, something the CIA kept handy. But that assumption was dodgy—why would the US government keep a house in Tampico? She had zero idea how Carver'd acquired it. Or even if he'd acquired it. They could be squatting, for all she knew.

She opened the cupboard in a renewed pang of hunger. Empty. Unless she wanted to eat the newspaper laid out on each shelf. Why did people do that? To protect the shelves? Or the dishes and canned food? She'd kill for a can of anything. Hominy, peas, tomato sauce, whatever. She yanked open an accordion set of doors to a pantry that housed only an old broom. She went through the drawers, scanned the bottom cabinets. The lukewarm fridge. Her eyes came to rest on the empty can of beans on the counter. Maybe Carver would return with another.

But she couldn't imagine taking more food from him. *Nah, I'm good*, she'd say, even though she was starving. She didn't want to seem the least bit needy. She closed the cabinets. Stood there, situating herself. It seemed important to be capable, ready for anything. She wanted him to see her that way now, after what they'd been through.

Gustavo had no such compunction. He lay splayed in the corner of the living room, passed out on the tile floor. When they arrived, she'd watched him sit against the wall, nod off, slide like a melting thing to the floor, exhausted after however many hours coked-up and adrenalized. Now he groaned in the throes of some psychic ache. He rolled over, grunting like a giant fretting fetus.

She, however, felt pretty goddamn good. Despite the bruise at the base of her neck, an astonishingly sharp pain from a scratch on her forearm, her hunger pangs (starving!), she had this . . . butterfly glee and hum in her nerves.

What the hell was this state she was in?

She started bouncing on her toes, her thighs and calves like springs. She squatted and stood and reached. Goddamn! A well-oiled and tuned-up machine—that's how she felt, like a vehicle suited for the landscape in which it found itself. Alert and at home. In this bare kitchen. In Mexico, of all places. She belonged here, in the middle of all this.

She squeezed her legs. She could run in these skinny black jeans, no problem, go for a *run* run, that's what she wanted to be doing. What it would feel like to cut through the humid morning air. How she'd perform here in the swampland outside Tampico compared to the razor cold of the Upper Peninsula or the Culver City stairs. She'd go for miles in this womby nourishing air, she'd been hardened in the Los Angeles smog, the icicle severity of Michigan, she'd go for days, and they'd see—

Jesus Christ. Just stop already. No one's watching. No one cares.

She closed the rest of the cupboards, studied her surroundings the way she would in the long minutes before a raid. The tile in here was a deep royal blue, like an ocean you could stand on. She listened to her own breathing. She heard a small plane far away overhead. Birds outside the window.

She found her mind wandering to what would come next, all the wonderful things that could be. Carver getting them on a private jet. She and Carver ushering Gustavo into a black SUV in San Antonio. The look on Dufresne's face. Beers with Cromer and the rest of Group 11. Introducing Carver to Childs. Telling the tale. How she'd been a fucking pro. How she'd done the things, and what things they were. How she'd fled the warehouse, kept ahead of mad howling stalking killers. Moman dead in his own office chair. How she'd hid there, getting the drop on the Zeta. How she'd outrun the assassins on foot at the warehouse and outmaneuvered them in the car, navigated herself and Gustavo to Carver, and how they were somehow alive yet and that because she'd kept her shit together. All the noise and sheer speed of everything going haywire—just thinking about it made her sweat again, a scared sweat—the curdled shouts, the gunfire echoing off the buildings, the scream of tires, the flash of the rocket and the muzzles, the stinging hot reek of gas afire like a punch in the nose.

And then it was over and quiet and the only thing to do was ride along, Carver driving, Gustavo in the back seat. Silence and dark. No headlights, even though it was night. She didn't ask questions, she didn't talk the whole time Carver drove them out of the city, even when he swerved, muttering "Jesus, crocodiles." Out her window the moonlit crocodiles too kept silent, thrashing away from the car in quiet muscular shadows. The night hooded all thoughts. She was too spent to even muse.

When they finally got to the house, Carver walked ahead of her as Gustavo stumbled after and then they were inside, Carver handing her the can of black beans before he left again, and it was the next day before she noticed, she'd lost hours somehow (was it afternoon now?), she had no idea how long she'd been here, she just knew she was in the time after the shocking things had happened and right before all the good things about to begin. She was *alive*. There was pride to take in that, she'd earned this moment of cuspy Christmas-morning relief, as if all that remained to do was open her presents.

Carver driving, the moonlight on his bare forearms.

They'd locked eyes as he handed her the can.

Blue eyes that practically muted him.

He'd said things she didn't catch.

The deep blue ocean of tile swelled in her vision, made her feel suddenly dizzy, almost seasick. She squatted. Caught up with herself. The blood rushing to her stomach, probably. She sat staring at the grid of grout. She tried talking herself out of hunger, out of moonlight, out of his eyes and such.

You're still deep in the woods, Hardball. Straighten up. Got a lot of ground left to cover.

On her phone, three missed calls from Childs. She typed him a quick note. **Don't worry. Coming. I'll be in touch soon.**

Across the room Gustavo twitched and squirmed. He flopped and shook his head like some kind of insect-ridden dog and then went still again. The motherfucker. Despite how good she felt, she still loathed him. He'd caused all this horrific shit, and now he was over there on the floor like a college kid trying to outsleep a hangover. A useless pile. She felt a raw, uncut dread looking at him. Not just the fat, sweaty man himself, she realized, but what he foretold: a flight back to the United States, ultimately back to Los Angeles, back to the office, the break-room microwave, her apartment microwave, her life. To Bronwyn, in some other form. Even though Gustavo was such a get that he would smooth over everything at DEA for her, her Christmas-morning feeling had turned and soured.

She knew what all the presents in all the boxes were—and she didn't want any of them.

She didn't want to go back.

She wanted this, more of *this*.

She put a hand flat against the floor, held it there against the cold hard tiles. She pressed down hard, her fingers popping out as far as they would go, shaking, her wrist and forearm trembling too, and she let herself feel this aliveness, let's call it that, she felt it in her palm, in her arm, *aliveness*, she could feel it everywhere now, in her thighs, her ass, her stomach, all over her face, along her gums, she felt it bursting through her shoulders and neck. Her whole body was smiling. She wanted motorcycles on her tail. She wanted bullets in the air, as insane as that notion was. She wanted to run. She wanted to have to run, to run or die, and then to be able to feel the panting quiet afterward.

Carver driving in the dark. She kept thinking about it.

She unzipped her flat-heel boots and took them off. She stretched her legs out. She spun her feet around and around, shoeless for the first time in two days. She brought one knee to her chest, held it there, kept the other extended. She thought about her breathing, then switched legs, exhaled, inhaled, did it all again.

After a while, she stood and dropped her arms and found the floor with her hands. Draped over her legs, she held that pose before standing and grazing the empty can on the counter next to her. Gustavo snorted. Looking at that fuckup puddled on the tile across the room, she suddenly backhanded the can to the floor. It fairly boomed when it hit the baseboards.

Gustavo bolted up so fast he smacked his head against the wall behind him. He called out something, she wasn't sure what. His eyes were open now, and one of his hands was on his FN Five-Seven where it lay on the floor. The nine was nearby, and he snatched it too.

"Morning," she said.

His eyes looked like they'd been left out in the rain. His shirt half open, only two of the bottom pearl snaps buttoned. A thick bloody scratch down his chest. His jeans had a rip in the knee, and his face was still dirty from running or falling or who knows what. She'd had a chance to wash up. He hadn't.

Finally he coughed and cleared his throat and sat up straighter and rubbed his head where he'd hit it. He shoved the Five-Seven under his gut, set the nine back on the floor, and pulled his tea bag's worth of coke from his pocket. He stuck an index finger into the plastic and lifted a bump to his nose, snorted it, and shook his head around like he'd been sprayed with a hose.

"You are a vision."

He huffed a couple more bumps from his finger before putting the baggie away again.

"Go ahead," she said. "Don't mind me."

"What, tú quieres?" He tapped his pocket, pointed at her.

"I'm hoping Carver might bring some coffee, thanks."

"Carver," he said dismissively.

"Yeah, the man who saved your ass."

"You are not smart to got trust in that man," he said, sniffing, shaking his head to clear it.

"Gotta say it's worked out so far."

"Worked for who?"

"You hear any motorcycles?"

Gustavo began shaking a foot. The heel on his boot flopped loose against the sole. He kicked down at the floor, trying to pop the bootheel back in place. "That man gonna make sure I die and probably you, tambíen. And why we not on a plane? Why we still in Tampico?"

She wished she'd listened to Carver, heard exactly what he said before he left. But those loud beautiful eyes.

"Ah, you don't know," Gustavo realized.

"Exfil is why. Carver went to set up our departure to the States." She hoped that's what he said he was doing.

Gustavo shook his head, reading her. "We're not north porque we're not going."

He shimmied out of the boot with the broken heel. He began looking at it closely, inspecting the bootheel with a kind of fretful disappointment on his face.

"Getting you to the States isn't as easy as you'd like it to be," she said.

"You always saying this to me."

"And now we're on our way. You're welcome."

"No."

"No?"

"No, this shit is not welcome. Think. *Think*. Who those men, the soldiers?"

"Operators. Delta Force. Navy SEALs."

"They not gabachos, I know that."

"And how exactly do you know?"

"Los acentos."

"Accents?"

"Sí, not gabacho, not Mexican," he said, shaking his head. "They were, I don't know what exact thing, pero ellos no eran soldados Americanos, no. Those men, they assassins, los mercenarios."

"Whatever. You couldn't hear shit in all that gunfire."

He set his boot down on the floor. "I heard them after."

"We were deaf!"

"I heard!"

"So you think this Agency spook has a squad of Polish mercs or Mossad agents on hand to save cartel turncoats? Is that your theory?"

He just looked at her, not understanding what she'd said.

"Okay," she said, "why would the CIA need foreign mercenaries to deal with a Mexican cartel? It doesn't make sense."

He snorted his nostrils clear and turned his attention to the boot, slamming the heel on the tile. The echoes banged around the house.

"Will you stop that?"

"Los Golfos have for our use paramilitares, men who was soldiers once—Los Zetas." He reached into his pocket, removed a multi-tool, and, tongue out, worked open the screwdriver. "If we got them, you think the CIA don't?"

"You actually think the CIA uses Zetas?"

"No! They got their own, not Los Zetas, but men like them."

"You gotta lay off the coke," she said. "It's giving you delusions. The CIA is saving you—"

"I didn't call no CIA!"

"What difference does it make? How can you possibly complain about being rescued?"

"Porque I called *you*, y these hijos de la chingada arrive?"

"I just didn't cover my trail, Gustavo. He found us by tracking me. And we're fucking lucky he did."

"Chale!" He slapped the wall, startling her. Over and over. Bang bang bang-bang. "No. No. *No.* You got to listen better. I called you, no? You one, you only. Pues, you come to me, yes, pero this dude Carver follow you, y también, y también, este pinche Zeta Tomás, he arrive and his Zetas, all these motherfuckers to kill us! Pero I told *only you* where I am! How there gonna be sicarios and CIA in Tampico with you? How you explain that?"

He had a point.

"Okay, okay, calm down."

"Calm down," he scoffed. "Why?"

"Maybe Moman told somebody."

"Maybe, maybe! I dunno, you dunno. But why you got trust for this American? You love him or something?" He was using the pointed tip of the knife now like a screwdriver, twisting away at the bootheel. "No es accidente this man came here," he said, pointing the knife at her. "That's why I got no trust for him, he wanna put me in a dark American hole. What you call it? The black cell?"

"Gustavo, I'm not gonna let him take you to a black site."

"You are not the boss. You say that to me, you not gonna let this or that happen, pero it mean absolutamente nada."

She didn't say anything. She couldn't.

"Me and you," he said, "we in this together. The Zetas know you know the tunnel, where it is, same as me."

"Many thanks for that."

He focused on the heel like he gave zero shits about her problems, and shook the boot around. It was loose, but better. He folded up the tool, put it back in his pocket.

"You tell the CIA man where it is?" he asked, pulling the boot back on.

"He doesn't know," she said.

"Maybe then you don't love him." He stood, tested the boot.

"He doesn't even know I know."

"Ah. Maybe you got no trust in him, same as me."

A grinding noise silenced them. They both whipped their heads in the direction of the other side of the house.

"The garage door," she said. "It's him."

A sharp screech of tires, the car pulling in. A slammed car door. Then the garage door closed. Then silence. Gustavo dug a finger into his bag of coke and did two bumps. Glared at her as though she'd summoned him and would have to answer for it. They waited, listening, keyed up. Somewhere in the house a door opened and closed.

Carver entered, set a plastic sack on the floor. He was wearing the same black T-shirt, a pistol holstered on his hip. He picked up the tension in the room.

"You two spatting, or is this just cabana fever?" he asked. No answer from either. He crouched, took a water bottle from the bag, nodded a heads-up, and tossed it to her. He did the same for Gustavo, but the man let the bottle slap the floor and skid into the corner next to him.

"Spatting then," Carver said. "Cool."

Gustavo stood up, put the coke in his pocket, removed the pistol from his front, and shoved it into the back of his jeans.

"¿El baño?"

Carver pointed. Gustavo stomped down the hall unevenly, fussing over his boot. Harbaugh guzzled down her water. So good.

"What got up his ass?" Carver asked, cracking open a bottle of water himself and leaning against the counter. His hair was mussed like he'd been driving with the top down, some sweat holding it in place.

"He thinks your operators are foreigners, that you're taking him to a black site."

"How coked up is he?"

"A few bumps since he woke."

"He *slept*?" Carver was astonished.

"It resembled sleep."

Carver polished off his water and crouched to get another, holding one up for her. She nodded and he tossed it and she snatched it out of the air. Naturals, the two of them, like a pair of jocks in a beer commercial. She set her empty by.

He was looking at her now in a vague way. An equally vague panic bloomed within her.

"What?" she asked.

He skipped whatever it was, instead saying, "There's an airstrip a few hours from here we're gonna use. I'm waiting to hear on a plane, but—"

"I have to tell you something," she said quickly. "I know where the tunnel is."

She didn't know exactly why she told him, or why now, except that she didn't want to withhold it.

He looked down, motionless. His thoughts were inscrutable. When he looked up, his blue eyes were troubled in a way that shook her.

"How?" he asked.

"He told me." She dropped her voice a half-register as the toilet flushed. "He built the thing in secret for the cartel. All those dead construction workers were killed to keep it that way."

Carver stood, looked disgustedly toward the bathroom. Water ran from the tap in there.

"He says killing them wasn't his idea. I think I believe him. Maybe. When he was the last man standing, he got spooked, and assumed he was next."

"So he bolted."

"Right."

"Why'd he tell you the location?"

"Leverage."

"What leverage?"

"He told me in front of this guy from the cartel."

"Shit." He looked pissed. "What guy?"

"One of the Zetas. But before they started chasing us. He and Gustavo talked. The Zeta tried to convince Gustavo to go back with him, that it was just a family dispute, that he'd let me go. But Gustavo told me where it was to put me in the same danger as him."

Carver shook his head as though impressed or flummoxed, she couldn't tell. He studied the lip of his water bottle.

"You're quiet," she said.

He seemed to realize he was scaring her, and his expression softened. But she couldn't be scared anymore. Maybe it was crazy, but she didn't feel fear.

"What are you thinking?" she asked.

"Just puts a new wheel on the wagon, is all."

She liked that he put it that way. Old-timey. Like these were well-worn problems.

"Should we have someone check it out?" she asked. "On the US side maybe?"

"No," he said flatly. "First thing is to get you out of Mexico. The cartel knows you know where it is, they're gonna have dirty cops looking for you. You get picked up, and . . ."

"I didn't even think of that."

"It's fine."

"No, it's not. I'm trying not to fuck up."

"Relax. You didn't. I promise."

He fetched her empty waters and put them in the sack and then grabbed the full one Gustavo didn't take and opened it and handed it to her. She waved it off. She felt full.

"You done good. Earlier, driving through all that shit. Real good. Perfect."

"Thanks."

"We should do that again," he said, taking a long draft from the water bottle so she couldn't tell what he thought or what he really meant, saying that.

She waited for him to pull the bottle away from his mouth before she said what she knew she would.

"Don't say something like that unless you mean it."

He smiled and nodded like he did mean it.

She said she wanted to get some air, but what she really needed was a minute out of Carver's presence. Little point in denying it. She was already spinning up joint task forces in her imagination. Applying to the Agency. She was not oblivious to what a dick he'd been or her own strange trajectory through American jurisprudence and law enforcement, which found her fantasizing a third move into spycraft or whatever this was . . . but she was hooked. Deep. She couldn't even imagine the woman who'd practiced law or run confidential informants or pondered a union with the likes of Bronwyn.

It was a hot afternoon that promised a sweltering evening, already heavily humid, the real heat yet to come. She stood outside in the sandy roadway, scanning the flatlands all around, the farmhouses, a windmill, the palms, the sense of nearby bodies of water. She didn't get the air she pretended she was after, so she settled for movement and wandered off the road and along a narrow path in the wispy grasses that grew in these sands, still barefoot. She was maybe fifty feet from the road when she heard a vehicle, a pristine black Chevy SUV, rolling past. It gave her the discomfiting feeling that she'd been in America all this time, in South Carolina or a Gulf hamlet, and that the blond-haired woman she could just make out in the open window from this remove—*what're you lookin' at, bitch?* popped unbidden into her mind, made her absolutely certain that the woman was someone she knew. Or would.

She'd seen an SUV like that at Moman's. Before Carver left her there alone . . .

Whatever thoughts might've come next were obliterated in the succeeding moment, when the sunlight scintillated into her eyes off a plane of water to her left, and she stopped. As her eyes readjusted, she was stunned to be mere steps from a throng of sun-basked crocodiles on a slope of drying mud. She wasn't in America anymore. In fact, "American" ceased to be a category of any meaning, as not three feet away, the nearest of the ancient and untroubled beasts rose smiling from the muck to greet her.

She'd never run so fast in her blessed life.

She only rose from the front step when Gustavo and Carver's voices hit a pitch that broke through her panting, the goose bumps subsiding. A CIA agent and cartel lieutenant were bickering in the empty house behind her. There were crocodiles everywhere. This was normal. This was fine. She actually smiled as she headed inside.

Carver squinted at the fresh light and acknowledged her but did not cease his harangue. "You put her in mortal danger with the cartel, and you think you're just gonna bounce?" he shouted.

Gustavo's hair was slicked back and his face washed, and he'd tucked in his shirt. She noticed now that he was missing one of his shirt pockets. The scratch on his chest looked like it'd been cleaned, too.

"Stop me," Gustavo said to them, his hand on his FN in his belt. The nine shoved in the back of his pants.

She didn't say anything, inhabiting a post-crocodile view on things that told her she'd already had her close call of the day. But it was curious that Carver didn't say anything either. Gustavo pressed his bootheel against the wall, leaving a black print on the white, as he took another bump and arched his back.

Carver edged his hand onto his holster, unsnapped it.

"Be calm. The only one I'm gonna shoot is me," Gustavo said.

"Not if I do it first," Carver said.

"Then do it!"

She touched Carver's arm.

"Let me," she whispered.

"Give me the water," Gustavo said.

Harbaugh picked up the bag and handed it to him.

Gustavo took out a bottle of water and drank, letting streams run down his cheeks and throat. He threw the bottle, still half full, and it smacked the floor and bounced and rolled around, water gurgling in spurts from it. Then he wrapped the black plastic bag around his fist and walked through the kitchen and out the side door. Carver made to go after him, but she stepped in front of him, her hand on his chest.

"I got it."

"I'll get the car. I'll run him over or shoot him. If we have to bring him in hooked to an IV and life support, so be it."

"Carver." Her hand was still on his chest. "He'll never listen to you. This is my area. This is what I do."

She turned her palm into a single index finger and poked him in the chest, pushed him back.

"Your area," he said, as though trying out the concept. "Okay, fine. But fucking hurry."

When she was at the door, she knew before he started saying it that he was telling her to watch out for crocodiles. But she knew all about the crocodiles. She had this.

THIS CLOSE

It was overcast, but Harbaugh had never sweated so much in her life. It poured down her back, her arms, it flicked off her fingertips as she ran. She should've brought a towel. Her barefoot gait was tentative, thrown off by the weight of the sicario's .40 in her hand. She didn't want it to jostle out of her waistband, so she sweaty-palmed the entire gun in the hope that no one would notice the barefoot woman running with a Smith & Wesson. And there were crocs, for chrissakes. But she pressed on, afraid she'd lost Gustavo.

In the distance was some refinery or plant, silver pipes and tanks against the pale sky. She ran past old farmhouses, fields of corn and palm trees. She could tell she was still near a laguna, a bay, a river, she wasn't sure, but the water was heavy in the air. Although the road was mostly dry, even dusty in places, there was standing water everywhere, sometimes huge dirty pools of it in the low bellies of the land. She startled a pair of cranes from the brush.

She didn't know which way Gustavo had gone, so she'd set off into the cul-de-sac of new builds on a pure hunch and was now worried she'd guessed wrong. In this flat land, the short trees and palms rose in a curtain, not any taller than a tractor, preventing her from spotting him even if he'd gone off road. She began to sprint. The asphalt ended, now dirt, now sand. Still no sign. She took the elevated edge of the road, where a soft duff padded her feet and fine small clouds appeared with every step. She thought about letting him escape. She thought of just keeping on running forever, she always did that.

A pair of men working on some kind of pump stopped what they were doing to watch her pass. She raised her free hand, and one of them nodded as they kept their eyes locked on her. They hadn't returned to their work even when she glanced back. A strange sight, this white woman in jacket and pants, hoofing it barefoot down the dirt road now. She noticed the gray cloud of her trail, the dust rising in the dead, hot air with the languor of a disturbed seabed.

Or moon dust.

The dream of Oscar came back to her. His boot as he leapt away from her, over the moon's horizon, the sun's flash on his visor. She wondered if the dream was the moment his spirit left the world. He'd clung to her all the way down to Mexico and then couldn't hold on any longer.

Jesus Christ, Oscar, why'd you do that?

She faced ahead and ran forward again, a little dizzy. Overheating now. The sun had peeked out and baked the air. She focused her breaths, tried not to give up even though she couldn't see Gustavo or Oscar or anyone. *You're not quitting,* she told herself, *you're doing exactly what you should. Find him. In some way this will atone for Oscar. For Dufresne. You make the boys cry but you don't let them die.*

Don't. Let. Them. Die.

Find. Him. Right. Now.

She crossed a bridge and back onto asphalt. The surface wasn't too hot to run on, but getting there. Should've put on her boots. Swamps here, lots of scrub brush and water. A marsh or floodplain.

A bright purple wall, for what purpose she didn't know. Nothing apparently. Just stuck out here and recently painted. She'd probably gone the wrong way, straight for the crocs. A bum hunch. Maybe turn around, go back and ask those guys in the yard. Gustavo didn't want to be spotted, probably stuck to dirt roads, right? Or maybe didn't care. Or he already flagged down a ride. In the bed of a pickup, doing bumps at the stop signs.

An old man on a bicycle with a battered cooler resting on the handlebars rode past her. She wondered what he had to drink in there, but she knew if she stopped, she'd quit. She wanted to quit, but instead picked up her pace. A kind of muscle memory, that. At the first inkling of surrender, she always kicked herself forward, kept on.

She topped a small rise and the brush cleared out to the west, and she could see farther ahead. Always stay on the path. That was the simplest thing, less second-guessing. Keep on.

The asphalt ended abruptly again and again gave over to sand, so much here on the shoulder that it was like running on the beach. The scrub receded, there were just palms, though not too many, skinny and squatty both—and there he was.

A lone figure to her west. Yes, fuck yes. Loping into some kind of development, boxy two-story adobes, a store with stacks of tires in front, a rusty tower of some kind. She'd have lost him if he'd been a few more minutes ahead, if she'd panicked and backtracked.

Good work, Hardball. Stay on the path.

She thought to call out, didn't, and kept running toward him.

He halted at the sound of her. Turned and looked directly at her, the plastic sack wrapped around his closed palm. About a hundred feet between them. She petered her pace down to a jog and then a walk. Didn't want to spook him. She shoved the pistol in her waistband in back.

He just stood there. Was he stopped for her? she wondered. Would he wait?

He did. She walked right up to him.

"Hey," she said, pleased she wasn't gassed, that she was so was fit and strong. "Can we try to talk this out?"

She swiped a ridiculous abundance of sweat from her head, shook it off the back of her hand. His own dripped off his nose, soaked his shirt.

"I don't care, you can talk."

"Okay. Let's get us under something. That sun's brutal."

"You can't make me go back."

They both knew that she'd come to do exactly that.

"I'm walking for the town. You come, you not come, I don't care." He looked at her bare feet as though asking her to think about that.

"Maybe there's someplace for us to stop up ahead," she said.

They walked together. Orange-pink homes, tricycles in yards, kiddie pools, concrete walls, dogs yipping behind wrought-iron gates. A horse tied to a stake next to the road, feeding on grass. A woman at a sewing machine on her porch. Beneath a shade tree an old man oiling parts of some kind on a card table. No one said a word to them. Houses became stores, became businesses. El Mini Super "Lucy." An Oxxo with a crazy castle facade, curtain wall, battlements, even a turret.

After a while they came upon a tavern, La Cantina Cosmopolita. Beach-purple exterior. A brand-new Modelo sign. Locked to a grate on the side of the building was an oil-drum barbeque pit, smoke spilling out of it. It was unattended, or she would've gone over and bought whatever there was there. She was still hungry. A man without the bottom half of his legs was scooting along the sidewalk on knee-pads. He called to her to buy his wares. She ducked her head and followed Gustavo inside.

Dark, quiet, cool. Brick walls. Two men and a bartender who grimaced up at the flood of sunlight into the place. The floor perfectly smooth, the only trouble a few pebbles of roadway stuck to her feet.

She discreetly brushed each foot over the opposite calf and minced after Gustavo.

Two men in cowboy hats, one in jeans and a western shirt, one in board shorts and tank top, mutely noted their entrance and returned to their drinks like mismatched twins.

The bartender stirred a pot on the stove, idly observing the muted morning programming. News. Harbaugh tensed. The chase, the ambush—they were on the run, after all. She and Gustavo—hell, the news just walked into the joint. It wasn't likely that anybody had seen them in the blur and violence, but still. The authorities would be asking for witnesses, someone to help explain all the dead narcos. The television was covering something else, politics of some kind.

You're just some barefoot white lady, she thought, Gustavo some vaquero, come down to the coast for a bender. An odd couple, but not exactly conspicuous. She hoped not.

They sat a corner table with Corona insignias carved into it that tilted unevenly under Gustavo's large hands. He turned his chair to face the door directly and hooked the plastic sack over the arm, heavy with bottles of water, the FN making an unmistakable expression in the plastic. She noticed the Ruta de Evacuacion drawn in green magic marker on the bricks, with an arrow pointing at the front door through which she'd just come.

The bartender came out and Gustavo ordered beer and whiskey for them both. Harbaugh almost called him back to change hers to coffee, but there seemed no point. It felt apt to remain in this weird high place her mind had arrived at. Not half bad, honestly, sitting in the new cool and waiting on a late-morning beer. How strange, though. A week ago she'd been running against the cold, and down here she was running for her life—quite a change of pace. A change of stakes.

The drinks came. They raised their glasses as if living in a normal world and downed the shots quickly. She barely felt anything, just the heat of alcohol. She put her beer against her forehead and let it set as Gustavo brooded, taking huge swigs. He burped and called for another within minutes, which she'd known he would. It felt like they'd been together for years. He looked at her in a way she wondered about. A knowing scorn between the two of them. Hers, a mild contempt typically reserved for bosses, shitty neighbors, shifty exes. But something else too—she watched him roll his jaw in a way that she now knew foretold a bump of coke, and there was a weird ease between them. With all of this. They'd become partners, of a kind. Which is why she went ahead and asked him what the hell he thought he was doing.

"Drinking." He sipped his beer, affecting weariness.

"You've just decided, fuck it, you'll take your chances alone?"

"No se." He took a drink, wiped his mouth with a backhand. "I feel maybe . . . different in everything."

"Different."

He nodded.

"Different as in you got a plan?" she asked.

No answer.

"Maybe you've decided to throw yourself on the mercy of your homeboys, your uncle?"

He arched a brow at her. She wiped more sweat off her forehead.

"Did I miss some option? 'Cause I can't think of anything else."

"I think I want to get drunk."

"Maybe do that bag of blow, too?"

"Ay, why not? And then . . ." He made a pistol of his hand and pretended to shoot himself. The same wooden face that she'd seen on Oscar. Worn, warped, self-haunted. It hurt to see it again. And then it made her mad.

"Why is it always violence with you guys? Why is that option one?"

He looked at her like she'd asked him why things drop to the ground. "Why you sometimes so stupid?" he asked.

She sipped her beer. It needed a lime. She needed to talk him out of this. He needed to see how close he was. It seemed like everything was off one notch, everything was just short. They were this close. After everything, so close. And he was ready to give up.

Gustavo breathed through his nose like a bull. In the little whistle of his nostrils, she realized that she was listening closer to everything. The emptiness of the place, the way a set-down beer bottle sounded on the bar, the silence on the tile, the bartender shuffling around in back. She yearned to hear what was outside too. What was coming for them cocked and loaded.

It wasn't just that she was so close to finishing this. She was sure that time was running out.

"You don't want to do it," she said. She didn't know if this was so, but it was important to say. If only to nudge him away from it.

"Chingate. You don't know." Gustavo rose from his chair slightly, and for a moment she thought he might leave. "Otro whiskey," he called to the bartender.

The man nodded, poured a shot, and brought it over and set it before Gustavo and gathered their empty glasses. She waited for him to leave.

"You've been threatening it for days. But you told me about the tunnel so I'd have to help you escape. You made me save you."

He grunted vaguely.

"It isn't easy to kill yourself," she added.

"And how you know?"

"Because I watched a man do it."

He searched her face to see if this was true.

"And you don't have the ingredients," she said. "You're running . . . from something in here." She tapped her temple.

"Psh. Don't be so stupid."

"Quit calling me stupid."

"Quit stupid talking."

"Come on, we've been together for a little while now. You've got a conscience. I know you do."

He cocked his head, confused, irritated.

"No se que quieres decir. *Conscious?* Estas diciendo, I'm knowing?"

"No, no. *Conscience.* As in your heart, you know, your morals . . . your feelings about what you've done. I wouldn't want to live with myself if I'd done . . ."

He was waving his hands in the air as though he could swat down her words. When she trailed off, he looked at her. Then he laughed, a big booming guffaw. The men at the bar turned to look.

"¿Qué?" he asked. "My feelings?"

"The workers you killed," she said in a low voice. "They weren't narcos, they were your men."

"They took the jobs. They understood risks. That's why the pay was very big."

"But they didn't get to spend it, did they?"

"Wives did, children did. Somebody spent the money!" He slapped the table, which wobbled under his fat palm. He leaned toward her over little ponds of spilled beer, touched his head with an index finger. "The dead are not in here." He touched his heart. "Not in here too." He drank the whiskey and set the glass on the table like a man plunking down a winning domino.

Fuck. This isn't working.

Somehow she had it all wrong. She'd gotten soft on him, spending all this time together. Grafting a morality onto him that wasn't there. Maybe they weren't close at all, maybe there was too much ground to cover. Maybe she'd never close the distance.

She stood. She needed to move to clear out her head, to clear out the moment. She took her beer to the bar, a few stools down from the day-drinkers. She clocked the man in board shorts clocking her. The bartender came over.

"Limón?" she asked, making a pinching gesture at her beer bottle.

The bartender nodded and fetched a vivid green lime from behind the bar and cut it in half and then into wedges.

Board Shorts said something then, maybe to her, but too fast for her to understand.

"Lo siento?" she said, returning his smile.

"He says your feet are naked," the bartender said. He looked at Board Shorts and then at her.

"They are," she said with a forced grin. "The tile is nice and cool."

"He says to be careful," the bartender said, even though Board Shorts had not said anything more. Maybe he'd said that at first.

Now all three men were looking at her, the one in the western shirt leaning forward to see her down the bar.

"Tell him I am careful," she said flatly. Then to him herself: "Gracias."

Board Shorts nodded. Went back to his beer. The bartender finished chopping the limes and spiffed open a new beer and put one in the bottle and set it before her.

"Oh thanks, but you didn't need to give me a new beer—"

He held up a finger and took her bottle away and touched the other toward her almost artfully with a single finger. His hair was slicked back with pomade and his eyes cinnamon colored and he recalled a hot waiter she'd seen at a wedding once, she'd loved the old-school way he did his hair, it was often little things like that that made the difference, and she was thinking of this when Board Shorts said something else. Again, a sentiment she did not catch, but definitely sent in her direction.

She turned to him and a dread washed over her at his expression— she knew this look, a kind of contempt that radiated from certain men who drank in the daytime. A derision that she now knew was there from the moment he first spoke, but which she had chosen to chalk up to her own poor Spanish.

She felt keenly vulnerable in her bare feet now. In this situation. In the glare of this horrid man's sneer. Her utter lack of jurisdiction or even a badge—which she now realized was tucked up her bag still at Moman's (dead Moman!). All this exposed in a leer.

Harbaugh was furious. And, she realized, totally unafraid. Did this man have any idea what she had been through, what killers had hounded her, what killers had failed to kill her, what she was made of and faced down, what utter—

"What did you say?" she barked at the man. "¿Qué tu decir?"

Board Shorts just muttered to his partner out the side of his mouth.

She looked at the bartender, who stood with the benign indifference of a baron or bishop.

Before she knew it, she had the .40 in her palm on the bar. The thud of its weight had alerted them all, even Gustavo behind her. She could hear him shift in his seat.

The bartender's calculation was to stand stock-still.

The other two looked alternately from the gun to her face, as though their eyes were tethered between both and could not escape.

"I asked what you said."

The bartender repeated her sentence in Spanish, or maybe said something else altogether.

The man in board shorts swallowed, nothing more.

"That's right," she said.

Back at the table time stopped or slowed to nothing. Still enveloped in her own white-hot rage—*these fucking guys think they can talk to me like some dumb bitch?*—and stewing in the quick brine of that degrading pig's common shit-talk at the bar, she could taste her indignation on her tongue . . . when all at once she realized what Gustavo's trouble was, his defining psychological iceberg: the guy was an eight-ball of pure, uncut resentment.

He didn't give a damn about anyone he'd killed or anyone he'd left alive or anyone he'd ever loved. From as far back as the moment she handed him her card, he was less a personality than a vessel of self-loathing.

That's the way in.

As she sat down and gazed upon him in this new light, she saw a man looking back at her with an almost perfect inversion of her knowing, a face in total confusion.

"Why you do that?" he asked.

" 'Cause I don't play."

"Play?"

"People can't talk to me like that."

"He said what?"

She had no idea. "I have no idea."

Sunlight flooded the room, vanished.

"They leaving," Gustavo said, alarmed.

"Makes sense."

"They will return."

"Looks like the bartender has cleared out too."

"We gotta walk now."

"Yeah," she said. "Probably. But tell me something first. Why did you leave the cartel?"

"What?"

She enunciated every word: "Why did you leave the cartel?"

"I understand the question," he said. "I said *what* porque you know why I run. They want to kill me." He stood, nodded his head toward the door. "Come on. Vamos."

"Sit down a second. How did you know your uncle was going to kill you?"

"They all got killed. I told you. All the workers."

"I know, I know. The *workers* did. But *you're* in the CDG, hell, *you're family*—"

"I said before, family don't matter no more. They—"

"You keep saying it doesn't matter, but is El Esquimal in the business of killing family? He has children, doesn't he?"

Gustavo waved a hand at her. "His children are protected. He sends them at school in Europe, at hotels in Arabia, de vacaciones—"

"Nieces and nephews. Your cousins. Has he wanted to kill anyone else in the family? Uncles? Anybody?" She'd guessed right. There was no else, she could tell by looking at him. No one prominent anyway. "But you followed orders. You built the tunnel. You even killed all those men who worked on it."

"I did not pull the trigger."

"You let it go down. You were a good lieutenant, a boss."

He sat back, his eyes searching hers for whatever she was getting at.

"Weren't you?"

"Sí. Era el mero mero," he said defiantly, crossing his arms.

"I don't know what that is."

"The best, the toughest man."

She had him.

"So if you were el mero mero," she said, staring into him, "why'd they want you dead?"

Gustavo's face darkened. He started blinking. He looked away. He shook his head.

She pressed the lime into her bottle and tipped it upside down and watched it gingerly drown upward into the beer.

"Why would your uncle want to kill someone as useful as you?"

Then she turned the bottle, slowly, right side up, and slid her thumb just so, and the carbonation spiffed out steady and neat. No mess. Her father had taught her this, shown her how to avoid spraying the pent-up beer all over the place.

"Hmm?" she asked.

"No se."

"Oh, come on. You have no idea why they're willing to sacrifice you?"

"No se," he repeated.

"What's this little bitch answer you keep giving me, 'no se'?"

He looked at her like he'd been slapped.

"Did you matter to them or not? You can answer that."

He arched back in his chair to get into his jeans pocket, and then, keeping the baggie in his lap, lifted a finger full of coke to his nose.

"Why was I to build the tunnel?" He sniffed and cleared his throat and then did another before pocketing the bag again. "They chose me, that's all."

"Sure," she said. "Or maybe they chose you because they were always going to kill you once you'd done the job for them. Maybe it was always going to end this way."

"No."

"Maybe family only ever meant something to you, not them. Not your uncle. Maybe to him you were someone capable enough for the job, someone who'd wipe out all the workers, but not trusted enough to keep it secret. Maybe they let you think you were el mero—"

He stopped her by putting his hand over hers. He dropped his head.

When he addressed her, he was holding her hand like a groom.

"Every vato knows I am el sobrinito, the nephew. They knew always. I feel them taunting me when I leave the room. But also, I don't know! Maybe I could be wrong. Because no one says nothing, no one treats me like different or nothing. I *am* family, right? They don't fuck with me. So I'm thinking then I'm just . . ."

". . . paranoid."

He looked up at her, eyes wasted and cracked. "Yes, that. Paranoid." He licked his lips and went on. "Porque I never did nothing wrong, they got no reason for this." He took his hand away, clenched his fists.

"When were you sure? Tell me what happened." She needed him to remember it. He'd go with her if he felt this again. The disrespect again. "Tell me."

"Nothing I could say was certain. Like, vatos not looking *at* you, but *through* you, like I'm a window or something like that. No one tells things happening, I have to ask for news. The talk stops when I enter the room. You know, things of this way."

"And when they put you in charge of the tunnel . . ."

Say it. Admit it out loud.

"Then I know I am deleted." He released his hands, palms up and open. His eye was on the door, then back at her. They'll have to go soon, but she almost has him. This close.

"But you knew you were in trouble long before that," she said.

"What you mean?"

"When you were arrested in the States and took my card, you knew. And you know why you kept the card and eventually reached out to me?"

His eyes flashed around in some emotional algebra, some reckoning of what he could admit to himself and to her.

He wiped his nose. His breathing slowed, his face softened.

"Ay, I know why I keep the card," he said. "Respeto. Me you treat con respeto."

"And I promise I will continue to treat you that way right to the end. You can believe that."

He sighed. He nodded.

She stood up, adjusted the gun in her waistband. It was time.

"We're gonna see your uncle go to a Supermax prison where he'll be all alone forever. We're gonna cripple the Cartel del Golfo. We're gonna show them what a mistake it was to not respect you."

She made to move, and he held up a finger. He dug into his pants and set a key on the table.

"What's this?"

"To get into the tunnel. In Piedras Negras. You take it."

He looked at the door.

"We have time for another whiskey?" he asked.

She didn't know, but she went behind the bar and fetched the bottle. The place was empty and possessed the contentment of a vacated chapel. She padded over to Gustavo. Even though all hell would break loose in a few moments, it was hard not to feel like the running was over, all troubles were past, that the end was just a couple shots of whiskey away.

LAS DOS OPCIONES

The Americans turned into the warehouse parking lot. Tomás kept going. There were many police vehicles bunched around the entrance, an ambulance too, a couple of unmarked cars with flashers. It was humid and the van's AC was no good, so he rolled down the passenger-side window to at least let the hot Gulf air blow through the van.

He waited the usual amount of time he'd wait for anyone to forget they'd seen the van or him and then made his U-turn and headed back. He pulled up at the end of a row of Pemex tankers and turned around so he could see and killed the engine. Not that there was much to see, just high concrete walls topped by razor wire and then Moman's warehouse gate. The Americans and the cops were inside, no doubt inspecting the scene. Puzzling over the beer cans on the loading dock, small bottles of whiskey, cigarette butts. And whatever else was in there. Whoever else. The dead security guard. The Zeta who'd been shot in Moman's office. Moman himself, who'd looked hardly surprised when Tomás walked in, like someone who'd suspected he'd been betting into a losing hand and was now certain of it just before the cards were turned over. Tomás immediately shot him in the face with the silenced .40. He hated when they knew it was coming like that. That resigned look of fools. At least the Glencoe kid didn't see it coming, and the Zeta he'd suffocated to death in the ambulance had been unconscious. Though maybe Tomás had wanted to look that one in the eye, maybe he was one of the two who'd nearly killed him in the warehouse, firing into the wall right near his head. He couldn't quite remember. He'd've liked to have known that.

There was no action at the gate yet, so he tore around the back of the van, seeing what the Zetas had left. More empty beer cans and a glass pipe and Gatorade bottles filled with piss and a bag of beef jerky and crumbs from chicharrones and some stinking socks. A pussy magazine and torn glassine bags and a .45 one of those dumb-asses had just left sitting here. He checked the slide and the magazine and stuffed the pistol in the back of his pants. He tore open some jerky and gnawed on it. He lifted the floorboard cover, looking for weapons. Nothing but the tire iron and jack.

He remembered the two-way radio and went and opened the passenger door to get it. He searched until he found the channel the police were using.

"—you'll have to check with Ramirez on that. Rosales made the call to the governor, but we're waiting to hear from DF. Over."

The government was involved. Interesting.

"Ah. Okay. Then I'll wait, too."

"We're all waiting."

"Yeah, no doubt. Hey. Let me ask you something. You ever buy your wife a suitcase?"

"What? Man, I don't know. She buys all her own things. What do I know what women like?"

"Yeah, yeah. But you can't say that to them. You know?"

"*You* can't. *I* say whatever I want."

"No, you're saying that *now*, but I know what happens. I've been to your house."

"Ah, you don't know what you're talking about. I'm just letting her pretend. Behind closed doors, things are different, man. Why you asking me about this anyway?"

"Well, she's been talking about vacation, but she doesn't want to if she doesn't have, you know, the proper things to display to—"

Tomás put the radio in front of his mouth and pressed the PTT button.

"Keep this channel clear, assholes."

The was a little scratch of static and then silence. He turned the volume down and climbed into the cab and set the radio on the dash. He looked around for something to read, knowing there was nothing. A mind loathed a vacuum. He wanted to know what had happened to the Twin after he'd commandeered that boat. Wondered if all the Twin's guys had died too.

He pulled out El Motown's number. He'd been feeling the urge to call, to tell him what had happened. To bitch, honestly. He didn't want to call El Rabioso yet.

He dialed.

"Lieutenant. It's Tomás," he said when El Motown answered.

"You're calling for help already? You took my best men."

"It went bad, lieutenant."

He then explained over a demonstrative silence on El Motown's end of the line. About the DEA agent he didn't expect in the warehouse. The tunnel El Capataz told her about. The chase. He stammered just a touch when he got to how the prison Zetas were led to an ambush. But also how they were trigger-happy and heedless.

"Not to insult them," he said, "but the situation did not call for such an aggressive pursuit."

"And yet you survived," El Motown said.

Accusation in the man's voice. As if this were entirely his fault. As if he could even sense that Tomás had finished off one of the Zetas himself.

"I was in the van we took from the prison," he said, evenly. "They'd insisted on motorcycles and pickups for the job. I saw no point, but no harm in it."

"Are you blaming them for dying?"

"I'm just telling you the situation got ahead of me."

"Lucky. And how will you avenge them?"

He set the phone against his chest and shook his head and looked at himself in the rearview mirror sympathetically. Almost to urge himself to get off the line. He put the phone back to his ear.

"I don't know who did it. They were ambushed in an alley. I saw laser sights. Then an explosion, an RPG I think. I heard what sounded like big guns, 416s with suppressors. MP7s too. It was military. Some kind of special forces unit. Like an FES job maybe."

"No," El Motown said, "this was not Mexican."

"Because the Zetas would know the unit."

"The Zetas would *be* the unit."

"Of course."

"Who is this DEA bitch? What's her name?"

"I don't know."

"There's a lot you don't know, Jiménez Quiñones."

Again he looked at the idiot in the mirror. *Get off the phone.*

"I didn't bother with her. El Rabioso didn't want the nephew harmed, so I had to try to convince him it was safe for him to return. For all I know, it was safe. I was going to let her go, and take him back and be done with it. It was best to play it soft. They had nowhere to run—"

"Nowhere to run? If that were true, you'd have them," El Motown said. "I'll find out who this bitch is. And what this American unit is. And they will die."

"Nobody's killed an American officer since Camarena."

"And it's a pity."

"But El Rabioso will want—"

"You think I give a shit about El Rabioso?"

"I am sorry, lieutenant." He couldn't think of anything to say to smooth the situation and save face and not make an enemy of El Motown, but he tried anyway. "I just thought you should know about your men."

He waited for a reply. He knew he couldn't hang up. Not first. He saw the black American on the loading dock and he picked up the binoculars to watch him pace the loading dock, making calls.

"You're a good soldier," El Motown said. "Too good."

"Thank you," he said, not really listening—he was trying to listen to the American's body language and what El Motown had to say both. The woman he'd been with exited the building now too. Headed to their SUV.

"It's not a compliment. Someday you'll see, Jiménez Quiñones."

Who was the black American talking to?

"The Golfos and the Zetas are not on the same side," El Motown said.

The phrase lodged in his ear, even though he already knew what El Motown was going on about: *Not on the same side.*

Of course. All these Americans were not on the same side either—the black guy was at the warehouse, looking for clues. He watched the woman get in the SUV and the black man hurry after. He didn't know why, he didn't even know who they were, what exactly they wanted, so much was yet a mystery, but he knew that following them was the right thing, his best chance.

"I understand," Tomás said, but the line was dead—El Motown had hung up. Tomás pulled the .45 from his back waist and tossed it on the seat. He had another pistol in the console. He was sure it wouldn't be long now.

He tailed the black vehicle out of town, staying well behind and as indistinct as possible. When they got out to the countryside and the dirt roads, he drifted in their dust cloud. They didn't know the way. They kept slowing at intersections, proceeding to point absent a route. He guessed they were triangulating a cell phone signal. He'd driven the same way trying to find a journalist in Monterrey whose hands he needed to break. When they slowed and turned left onto another dirt road, he kept on straight. He couldn't see where they'd gone, but he was confident he could find them.

He'd pulled over at an intersection in a sudden residential area—some outskirts hamlet or humble suburb—ready to double back and call El Rabioso to ask how much blood he should shed in capturing them. Then Gustavo and the DEA woman appeared right in front of him. Across the street, walking single file as if in a silent argument. Neither one looked over at the van or him within it. He laughed out loud, not just at his luck but the very pace of it. So easy, so fast.

After four minutes, he turned his innocuous van left and drove after them. He kept parking and waiting as they walked, making sure they didn't see him. The nephew carried a plastic sack, and even at his remove, Tomás could see the shape of a gun in it, another jammed in the back of his pants. The DEA woman was barefoot and palming a pistol, which struck him as the decision of an insane person. They were conspicuous, a walking matter of time.

They entered a tavern. Across the street he found a little copse of trees next to an old structure of brick, corrugated metal, and concrete. He parked. Took in the area. Flat land, a few buildings, a gas station, a garage, a tire shop, a convenience store, the tavern, some kind of restaurant, a taco stand. Down the way a couple of grain elevators and some kind of gin or something. Tang of ammonia in the wet air. A truck hauling a rusty turbine clattering down the road was the only bit of traffic.

Keeping his eyes on the tavern door, Tomás tried El Rabioso again. Motherfucker still hadn't called back. He kept a very close watch on the door, determined to not be caught off guard, to think of everything. He wondered why they were on the loose. Wondered who gets rescued by mercenaries and then walks barefoot with a pistol on the outskirts of Tampico, Mexico. Wondered what kind of American this DEA woman was exactly. He was as confused as a goat watching television. This was all on the other side of his ken.

He had no idea what to do. How long he had to do it. He couldn't just walk into the tavern and negotiate. Killing one and taking the other would be very difficult. He tried El Rabioso. Straight to voice mail.

He looked at his watch. Minutes crawling by. He drove around the block to make sure they weren't leaving out a back door. He parked catty-corner to watch a side entrance and the front door both. He watched the smoke from the cantina's barbeque pit trail up into the sky. He worried that the Americans he'd followed here would show up. He worried he didn't know what to worry about.

The phone rang. El Rabioso. At last.

"Bueno."

"Speak," El Rabioso said.

"We have to move fast, and I need to know what you want to do. The Zetas are dead. There was an ambush, I still don't know who. The nephew got away. But I found them. I know where they are. I can get them."

"Them? What ambush? What the fuck are you talking about?"

"Please just listen. We don't have time—"

"Don't tell me what I don't have."

"There was a woman from the DEA with him, with the nephew. You understand? And he told her."

"Told her what?"

"About the tunnel." He looked in the rearview and side mirrors, half expecting the black SUV. "They're together in a bar. I can get them, but I need to move now and I need to know how you want me to take care it."

The street was empty. El Rabioso was silent.

"So how should I handle it?" Tomás asked.

"Handle it? I want you to have already handled it. I want you to have done your job."

"I tried. I talked to him. He would've come with me, but this—"

"Shut up!"

"I am trying—"

"Man, I don't want to hear why *your* failure is *my* fault."

And like that, Tomás realized he was done with the Golfos. If El Rabioso had been sitting in front of him, Tomás would have shot him. Instead he spat out words like bullets.

"And I don't want to be blamed for how this went to shit! It is your fault, this is all your fault. I didn't give a cokehead millions of pesos to dig a hole! I didn't make him run for his life! You fucked this up! Not me!"

He'd leaned forward to holler at the man, and now he shot back in his seat, stunned at himself.

El Rabioso exhaled a cigarette, it sounded like. "You're dead," he said. "Talk to me like that? You're dead."

For some reason, El Rabioso's threat didn't impact Tomás the way he expected. An old idea had been drilled into him by El Rabioso and the ones who came before, the plaza bosses and bosses of plaza bosses, and the old idea was this: even if he survived all the things the Golfos had him do, the cartel would still have his life at the end. He'd learned the lesson. They use you until you're dead.

"Did you hear me?" El Rabioso asked. It was strange that the plaza boss was still on the phone, like he was the one who was too scared to hang up first. What an odd day this one had become. He could feel more strange reversals in store.

"You got two choices right now," Tomás said.

"Oh yeah, asshole? I got two choices? No, you got no choices."

"I can go in there and kill them," Tomás said. "That's your first choice, and it would bring justice to the man who betrayed you."

"You gotta understand something, soldier. Choices? I got all the choices," he said. "I *am* all the choices . . ."

Tomás took the phone away from his ear. The second time today he'd been harangued. He was sick of it. He looked out the window. He'd been hearing seagulls calling out somewhere, but he couldn't see them. He leaned his head out the window, looked up at the sky and the clouds stacked up there like messy bales of cotton. He twisted his head around until he saw the gulls flying in V formation. He hadn't realized they did that. Though why wouldn't they? Made sense, it was just that he'd never seen it. He watched them until the birds were just a wavering indistinguishable shape about to be lost against the clouds. Heading north. An arrow pointing north.

When he put the phone back to his ear, El Rabioso was still shouting all sorts of things at him.

"Okay, okay," Tomás said. "I'm gonna do the other choice. Do you wanna know what it is?"

"Man, it's gonna be fun to fuck you up."

"I'm not gonna be a soldier no more."

"That's right," El Rabioso said. "You're gonna be my little bitch."

"No, sir. I'm gonna make sure the nephew and the DEA get to the States. And I'm gonna make sure El Esquimal knows that you had this chance to stop them."

It felt good to say this and know there was nothing El Rabioso could do to him. Not now. It felt really good.

And then the windshield exploded.

LA BALACERA

He plunged out of the cab and onto the ground to take cover behind the Econoline's left-front end, the engine and front tires. He didn't even hear the shots, thought he'd been hit in the ear. Gone deaf. He had to move. He dove back inside the cab and reached for the .45 on the seat, but the gun wouldn't come. His arm, his hand, was slick. He had no grip. He looked at his hand like you would an empty pen. Blood everywhere. The entire right side of him bloody and wet, leaking.

He peeked into a pocket of clear glass in the windshield and saw the nephew walking from across the street, squared up, gun flashing as he advanced on the van. Fifteen meters away and closing.

Tomás tried his other hand, the left, but the gun slid onto the floor. He wiped his palm on his lap. He leaned and reached into the console for the other pistol. He put it under his right armpit and was able to hold it there and cock it. He looked at the blood all over and tried to gauge how much he'd lost. Really had no idea.

He looked around the open driver's-side door and then around the front bumper, the small nose of the van not giving him much cover. The nephew was angling, taking a semicircle path to get a better shot. The shock had worn off, and Tomás could hear the shots now. *Pop. Pop. Pop.* He scrambled backward as the headlights exploded, the front tire exhaled, and the van slumped.

He took a step sideways away from the van and fired in the man's direction, just to ward him off, slow him down. The nephew veered, the van between them again. Even now, Tomás thought they might talk. He stepped back to the cab and set the pistol on the driver's seat, picked up the .45, was able to hold on to it this time, stuffed it in his waistband and then with the other pistol fired two wild shots through the windshield at the nephew. His right arm was limp. He had to go.

Through the spiderwebbed windshield, Tomás saw the nephew running sidelong to get in front of the van. Tomás threw another wild one around the bumper and then crouched and backwalked along the side toward the rear of the van. Liquid bubbled, the radiator hissed.

The nephew came around the front of the van shaking a plastic bag off a fresh gun and fired as Tomás leapt behind the van. Bullets dimpled the rear door after penetrating the sidewall. Tomás slunk around the rear of the van to the passenger side. The vehicle pinged like some kind of busted saxophone playing quarter notes. Then quiet.

The pain focused him for a moment and he realized his right arm was a mess, he was shot through the tricep, maybe also in the heel of that same hand but that might be glass. He could only fire one gun at a time. He didn't think he'd bleed to death, but he didn't know it.

He felt the other man bump up against the other side of the vehicle. A chance to parley.

"Hey!" Tomás called out. "Let's talk. We don't have to do this."

No reply.

"You don't know what you're doing," he said. "I'm not here to kill you."

He could hear the nephew edge along the side of the van, corner, and lean against the back of it. So close they could hear one another breathing. The only sound on the deserted street.

Tomás stepped back, dropped the pistol on the ground so he could open the passenger door with his good left hand, and then removed the .45 from his pants and squared up behind the door. He aimed at the back corner of the van.

"I'm only here to talk, that's all. I'm alone."

No reply.

"You fucking shot me, man. Come out. I wanna talk."

Nothing.

And then the nephew swung around the back of the van.

Tomás let four shots go—the .45 heavy and violent in his palm—all right into the man's chest.

The nephew fell, his legs bending beneath him, his shoulder hitting the ground, and then his body flopped up and sprung over, leaving him chest-down in the dirt. Blood spread on his shirt. Like the man was a bag of wine poked full of holes. Near his head lay a boot sole.

Soft steps behind him. He turned and was immediately slapped backward and he was looking up at the sky and those cottony clouds, that's what he saw, somehow he was seeing anything at all, how did that happen, where was he.

He tried to move, but all he could manage was lifting his head. The DEA woman stood there, barefoot, maybe ten meters away with the pistol in both hands aimed at him. She was looking at him and then past him at the dead man, which is when he leveled his gun at her. As best he could.

"I just wanted to talk to the crazy fucker!"

He was speaking Spanish, and he wasn't sure hers was any good.

He could feel his focus ebbing, couldn't see her eyes, her intentions. He fired and fired. His head fell back from the effort. He expected to be shot again, but then all he heard were soft steps, receding receding receding.

Sky. He had to close his eyes against it. He'd been out for a minute, less, more, he did not know. The warm pain in his right hip. When he opened his eyes again, he lifted his left leg and twisted himself into some momentum and then used his good arm to launch himself into a roll to his stomach. He propped himself with his elbow and then the pistol to stand. He'd been shot in the hip, maybe his groin, he just knew he had to move. He couldn't walk really, but he could stand on his good strong leg and he dragged the bad one, hopping across the empty street to the tavern. When he got to the corner, he turned and held himself against the wall. He breathed, wondering what next. He made for the backside of the building, dragging his foot in the gravel. He crossed to a convenience store.

A car at one of the gas pumps. He looked inside the store. The people in there scattered when he saw them. He looked in the car, a brown mid-1980s Honda. The keys were in it. Automatic, fortunately.

He threw the pistol on the passenger seat. He started it awkwardly with his left hand, his right arm screaming.

The rumble of the engine like his father's voice on a black-eye afternoon.

The shock had burned completely off and his hip was afire and so was his arm.

He put the car in gear and pressed the gas with his left foot and drove across the road and through a wire fence. He set out east across a field.

Tomás stopped the car after going through more than a few fields and across three paved roads. He searched through the back but there was nothing except sweatpants and a half bottle of water. In the trunk a few spare tools, a gigantic monkey wrench, a bunch of plastic bags and bottles of motor oil, a child's backpack graced by a blue genie— Aladdin, he remembered seeing it when he was a child—and PVC pipe fittings and sockets, a jar of plumber's putty, and, at the bottom, a smushed and nearly-gone roll of duct tape. He could hear sirens. Distant, faint. He could hear seagulls. He could use the duct tape.

With his teeth and buck knife he tore the sweatpants and then fashioned a tourniquet with the waistband elastic. He surprised himself crying out, and sweat popped his skin.

His hip had ceased bleeding, it seemed, but he couldn't put much weight on it. The bone was shot to hell, he could feel bits of it. He hacked away at the passenger seat and pulled out pieces of cushion and held them onto his hip and side as he wrapped the last of the tape around his body. Cursing and calling out the whole time until he finally stuck a piece of car-seat vinyl between his teeth just so he could bite down and not have to listen to himself anymore. What he'd rigged ended up looking like demented padding for a player of some kind of junkyard American football.

He drank from the water, left himself a couple of swallows. As soon as he could manage sitting in the driver's seat again, he put the car in gear and crossed his left foot over to the gas pedal again and pushed down on it and drove on. He went through fields and muddy drainages and over a bridge and down easements and backroads and he had much trouble and kept finding himself with his eyes closed. Times he found himself coming to.

The Honda gave out in a ditch bottomed with old telephone poles. He pushed down on the gas and threw the gear down into low, but there was no going forward anymore.

It got dark quickly, or maybe he'd passed out, or both perhaps. He was able to pull himself out of the car and crawl up the embankment into another field. He made his way along furrows, dragging his left leg, sometimes pulling it forward with his good arm, setting it forward again and again as if he were transporting a heavy pillar in fits and starts. He could see police flashers drive past where he'd left the car, they'd missed it in the ditch. Felt like his last dregs of luck. Bottoms up.

He went on hobbling under starlight, globs of blood swinging from his arm like tree moss.

At first he thought the black mass he found before him and was heading toward was a house or barn. Realizing almost as he came to it that it was a tractor. When he got to it he sat on the plow, heaving. He could hear ship horns far out in the gulf. He sat there and imagined the lights of buoys or boats since he couldn't actually see any from this vantage. It was hard to tell how far away the water was, how far anything was.

With his good hand he felt at the plow blades. The tractor dark and towering above him.

He reached out to start climbing up into the cab. When he made his first step, his foothold went away from him. He was falling and wasn't falling and the stars were upside down and he wasn't sure where the tractor went and then he wasn't able to wonder about that or look for it.

BAGRAM AFB, PARWAN PROVINCE, AFGHANISTAN
MARCH 19, 2004, 21:33

CARVER:	We went to Karachi to figure out a way to keep ██████████'s operation stable.
POLYGRAPHER:	How?
CARVER:	He used to run his heroin through Iran. But now that Defense wasn't sharing any op intel with us, there wasn't a safe route to Iran. We had to go through Pakistan.
POLYGRAPHER:	And how did you enlist the DEA's help?

CARVER: The Karachi office had a decade of diligent surveillance on the heroin trade in Pakistan. They had informants all through the police, army, intelligence. Pakistan's gangsters wear army uniforms—the DEA couldn't touch any of them.

POLYGRAPHER: But the pursuit teams could.

CARVER: We could nab anybody. The DEA gave us a name, we'd have him strapped to a waterboard in forty-eight hours. We took a few dirty colonels off the chess board—those DEA guys couldn't get off Shipley's dick after that.

POLYGRAPHER: But how did that help move ████████'s heroin?

CARVER: It cleared the decks. Shipley helped the DEA bag a few of Abdul Kalali's rivals.

POLYGRAPHER: Which consolidated his power.

CARVER: And then we turned the spigot back on. The heroin flowed south. Fuck Iran. Fuck the Pentagon's battlespace. Pretty soon ████████ was the undisputed boss in ██████. Poppy production up, al-Qaeda production down. First time that had happened. Ever.

POLYGRAPHER: But it didn't last.

CARVER: Nope.

POLYGRAPHER: What changed?

CARVER: The DEA got informants in ████████'s operation. That really dicked everything up.

THE GRAND MAL

Y ou're sure it was him?" Carver asked her. "The one the cartel sent after Gustavo?"

"Positive," she said. "Tomás."

As far as she could tell, Carver was driving them back into the middle of Tampico. She didn't know why, she didn't know what he had planned, and she wasn't asking. She didn't even care, in a way. Gustavo was dead. She'd shot the sicario. It was a relief to have someone else at the wheel.

"Fucking hell. This guy's persistent. You said you winged him?"

"I thought I killed him. But he started shooting back," she said. "I don't know. He said he just wanted to talk to Gustavo."

Gustavo was dead. His big body bleeding in the dirt. His mouth open and still, his face like a fish that'd been slung against the gunwale and smacked dead. He'd been drunk but high and upright as they'd left the bar, sparks of paranoia and cocaine going off in his eyes as they'd stepped out into the sun. And then he'd spotted the Econoline and inexplicably walked into the intersection and began firing into it.

"He said he wanted to talk? To Gustavo?"

"After I shot him," she said. "He was down. We had guns on each other, I was trying to process everything. He shot at me. He missed. I didn't stick around for him to find his aim."

A van suddenly braked in front of them. Carver skidded their car to a stop. Men conducting some business at a sidewalk stand looked up. At her, right at her. She turned away. Carver pulled the car around, into the flow of traffic.

"Your phone," he said to her.

"What about it?"

He leaned over to open the glove box and pulled out a sack and set it on her lap. Like a change bag for a bank. It was empty. It was heavy as Kevlar.

"Turn it off and put it in there." He looked over at her. "No signals. It'll keep anyone from tracking us."

"Anyone who?"

"You got any idea how this Tomás found you? So for now, just do as I say."

She turned off her phone and opened the sack's magnetic seal and slipped her phone inside.

"You still have the gun?"

"Yeah." It was resting against her leg on the seat. She put her palm over it. "It's his."

"Whose?"

"The guy. Tomás."

"You shot him with his own gun?"

"I've had it the whole time, since the warehouse. He handed it over when he came to talk Gustavo into surrendering. As a gesture of goodwill or whatever."

He rolled his eyes at her fortune. Or something else about the gun's provenance.

"Can I have it," he said more than asked.

She handed it over. He shoved it in the door well.

"Okay, stay calm," he said as he began slowing the Bronco down.

Looking ahead, she saw brake lights and traffic cones and lights. A checkpoint of some kind. She tensed at the sight of soldiers in camo, ARs strapped around their shoulders.

Carver pulled the car over. "Stay here," he said. He had his phone out and reached in the console for his wallet. "It'll be okay." He got out of the car, held a palm up, and walked over to two soldiers who were standing on the side of the road.

He talked to the soldiers for a while, showing them documents or some such, she couldn't see what. After a while two other men came over, in uniform, not battle gear, and they walked with Carver to a kind of guard station. Another group of soldiers in black tactical gear and balaclavas were on the other side of the street, all their hidden faces turned to the car, watching. She held up a hand to them. The masked soldiers didn't respond or move and her foolishness washed over her and she looked straight ahead, her palms flat on her thighs. Carver was inside the booth for a very long time. So long that she closed her eyes and fought with herself to keep them closed so she wouldn't see anything and couldn't think about anything she saw.

Finally she heard the driver's door open and Carver sit down.

She opened her eyes when he turned the ignition.

"Is it okay?" she asked. She could smell her own flop sweat, and closed her arms tighter around her body.

"I said it would be."

"You did."

He put the car into gear and pulled forward. They passed the soldiers and then the crossbar went up and they were through, and the car was past and they were on open road again.

She didn't ask him what he'd done or how they'd gotten through. She just sat in the passenger seat, embarrassed of the wave, her tenuous grip on her own composure.

"Where are we going?"

"I have to get some things."

"Where?"

Rather than answer he just scanned the rearview.

"What's going on with the plane?" she asked.

"We're off book now, Diane."

She rested her hand on her chin, smelled the odor from her fingers. Powder.

"I've been off book since I left LA," she said. There was no explaining this much chaos to Dufresne, the DEA. Maybe she'd been off book since the beginning. Since Oscar. Before Oscar. Sacramento. Before Sacramento? Was there a beginning? She could feel him looking over at her. Maybe trying to understand how one woman could be at the center of so much trouble. She wondered if she could explain it to anyone.

"Those two just started blasting at each other," she said abruptly. "I didn't have a choice."

Carver held up his hand for her to stop.

"It's okay. I need to think."

She went silent, but soon began willing him to look over. He passed a few cars by curbing up onto the median, then swept back into traffic. The way ahead opened up a little bit. At last he looked over again.

"Gustavo was gonna go to the States," she said. "I'd talked him into it."

He sighed, nodded.

"You done good," he said.

"I don't feel good."

"Alive is pretty good." He reached over and decided to just pat her forearm. She slid his hand down into hers and squeezed them together and he held on for a minute and they both studied the road before them, the flashing brake lights, the buses, the tiny cabs. Then he took the wheel in both hands and swept up onto the median again.

———

They pushed through stop-and-start traffic for what felt like hours, small pick-ups and delivery trucks that couldn't be gotten around, and then edged through foot traffic around the plaza. He pulled into an alley, blocked it parking there, and got out heedless of traffic norms. Like he'd never see Moman's car again. Walking into the throng of people on the street, he put Tomás's gun in his belt in view of everyone and no one, and hurried her across the street and into the Hotel Sevilla.

They met a disordered line at the front desk, baggage on an unat-tended cart. Under cover of the small dickering and bickering at the counter he helped himself to bags she knew were not his own. She followed him past the elevator toward a door, nonchalantly outpacing him to open it. They entered a stairwell that smelled of the cigarette someone had just smoked there, and he peeked up the next flight of stairs at every landing. He nodded at the door to his destination floor and she held it open for him and he strode briskly toward a room, set-ting down the bags to open the door with a small device that seemed designed for opening all such doors. He held it wide for her and put the bags inside and drew the door closed as if the hallway were a nursery ward.

"See if you can find something to wear," he said, throwing the bags on the bed.

He took a canvas coat off the rack in the closet. He took Tomás's .40 from his belt and dropped it into one of the large pockets of the coat and snapped it closed.

She just looked at him.

"I'm in deep shit," she said.

She meant in particular the patrons she'd threatened at the bar. She meant that even now the police were probably in possession of a sketch of her likeness. But she kept it to herself.

"This is nothing," he said.

A knock at the door startled her, but he walked backward to an-swer it, throwing wide his arms and smiling.

"Nothing at all."

He cracked the door, and she peeked around him to see who was there. Someone very broad. A black leather jacket, a voice so deep that it sounded like a series of heavily accented growls, none of which she could fashion into words. Carver again closed the door in silence, this time turning around with a manila envelope.

"Who's the ogre?" she asked.

"A trusted colleague."

He tore open the envelope. Several credit cards. A rubber-banded roll of pesos. Passports. A set of keys. He pocketed everything in his pants or the coat on the bed according to some prearrangement. He then bent and pulled out a shoulder holster and a Beretta M9. He started to put it on. Then he stopped.

"Diane. Please." His eyes darted to the bags on the bed. "You need to change."

She'd stowed a promising sundress as well as sandals and T-shirts in a tote bag but had decided to disguise herself in a pair of baggy rolled-up jeans and a men's sweatshirt and let down her hair around a pair of huge sunglasses.

They took the stairs, exited through a service door onto the noisy street. A stack of caged birds for sale. They crossed to the plaza where men smoked cigars and had their shoes polished as they read magazines or just watched the jet-black squirrels dance in the trees. Some kind of fair or demonstration crowded around the large gazebo in the center of the plaza. It seemed like every couple she saw was holding hands. Pigeons parted in spasms and ripples as Carver strode through them. She jogged to keep up and then took his hand.

No one took notice of them the ten minutes they were walking god knows where. She had a fleeting thought of Frida and Trotsky, but didn't much muse on them as Carver spotted and rigidly strode to a red-and-white 1980s Ford Bronco angled a touch conspicuously at an intersection. Like someone had abandoned it there—which someone had—keys over the visor—which they were.

She and Carver climbed in. The Bronco smelled like it hadn't been driven for a while, it smelled like fresh grease. Her father used to refurb jalopies. She knew the smell of boosted vehicles. They smelled like hornets had nested in them, they smelled like missing pieces, of rust. This Ford, it was like that. She touched the quilted seat cover, the dusty CB radio. Carver looked at her as he turned the key. The engine roared to life. He closed his eyes and grinned as he revved the engine, and then he opened them and they motored away.

Harbaugh fell asleep against the door frame. The Ford's engine bellowed over the countryside through the open winding, waking her whenever it ricocheted back at them from village walls that dotted the little two-lane highway. The sun shone on a dark storm front moving off the Gulf and over land toward them, gray and consuming, as they sped north. Then she nodded off again in the Ford's rumble, the stir of warm wind. She was so damn tired.

Carver slowed for an overturned semi trailer sometime around sunset. The doom-colored sky to the east hung in a state of suspension, as though it kept banker's hours. In the old cab it felt like Bonnie and Clyde, and so when she asked what he meant by "off-book"— *what the hell is off-book anyway?*—she meant it in a cinematic way, a performative way. But Carver was as broody as the trouble come in off the Gulf, and he looked more at the storm beyond her than at her and just said she wasn't gonna like it.

"Not gonna like what?" she asked, sitting up.

"I'm uh . . . I'm *crosswise* of the Company now. I'm froze out. My accounts are locked. No database access. No resources." He steered around a flare in the road. "Langley's favorite way to deal with troublemakers is to cut them off and see who they run to."

"This pickup," she said, she asked. "You got a roll of pesos. You got passports."

"I got partners, I got colleagues, yeah, yeah," he said, gunning the Ford on the open road, disturbing the quietly ominous dusk. "I'm prepared for this."

"Partners?"

He nodded.

"What kind of partners?"

He looked at her.

"I'm still trying to decide how much to bring you in."

The way he withheld made her want to ask all the more. But his reticence seemed calculated to do just that. To feel her out.

"Okay. Why are you crosswise of the CIA?" she asked.

"Because they never *do* anything. They just fucking gather intel. I'm more vocal and proactive than they'd like. I'm more . . . *everything* than they'd like."

"Except specific," she said. "Except forthcoming."

"I'm just procrastinating. You're not gonna like the specifics."

"You'll cope with my disapproval, I think," she said.

"It matters to me now," he said, glancing over at her.

"What does?"

"What you think."

She looked at him like she didn't believe a word of this. This blandishment. This sudden concern for her approval. She wasn't sure she believed it.

"I've seen you in action, Diane. Seen you elude a half-dozen Zetas. You clipped a sicario, maybe he bled out, maybe he's dead, maybe that's taken care of," he said. "You're not who I thought at first sight. You're the shit."

He looked at her like someone about to breach a door, clear a room. Edging eye contact. He reached over the bench seat and dropped a leather messenger bag between them. Opened the flap and handed her a folder.

"What's this?"

"Context. In particular, a Special Activities Division report on our work in Afghanistan. My group."

She flipped through the thirty-odd pages of significantly redacted text.

"I'm supposed to read this?"

"I want you to *have* read it. Just at some point. It explains . . . me. A fuckin' miracle it even exists. But Shipley knew what he was doing. Been in Afghanistan since the eighties, fighting the Soviets, arming the mujahideen."

"Shipley?"

"My commander in Afghanistan. Somehow pulled off the bureaucratic wetwork to get that on Tenet's desk. And to Cheney and Dumbsfeld. Not that it mattered to them. But that document just proved how fundamentally game-changing our work over there was."

The light was poor and getting poorer. But she could make out certain things in the introduction. "Unconventional partnerships . . . coercive tactics that have, over time, mitigated the inherent risk of narcotics production . . . absent legal mechanisms of redress and conflict resolution, CIA Ground Branch teams have proven to be influential stewards for local syndicates . . ."

" 'Local syndicates'? Does this mean what I think it means?"

"The data is bulletproof. Everywhere SAD engaged local syndicates, not only did Taliban and al-Qaeda virtually vanish—"

"You're talking about the poppy warlords."

"So-called. The industry. Heroin manufacture and distribution. Yes."

He looked to see her reaction.

She thumbed through the report, not really reading, not really looking at him. She touched the document with her index finger. "This says you helped them."

"When you read it, you'll see we really just helped stabilize the black market, which in turn stabilized the entire region. Not just the economy—"

"And that's what you're doing down here," she said. "Isn't it?"

"Not officially."

"Unofficially then."

He didn't answer.

"Why did you want Gustavo?"

"It was a fluid situation."

"Bullshit. Tell me."

"Okay. The truth is, I was gonna to take him back to the cartel."

Her heart sank. It felt like it broke.

"What the fuck? Your partner is the cartel?"

"No, not partner. The cartel is a client."

"Jesus fucking Christ."

"The CDG isn't a flawless operation. Nepotism's an issue, obviously. And outsourcing their security to American-trained paramilitaries is a huge mistake. But the Gulf Cartel has quality product, good distribution, they negotiate well with the other cartels, they put money into infrastructure—"

"Infrastructure! All along you were just trying to protect the tunnel?"

"I didn't know about the tunnel until you told me. All I knew was the cartel boss wanted his nephew back. That we could help them solve this problem."

She held up her hand for him to stop. It was completely dark outside now. Not a scrap of light out there in the scrub for miles. Half the stars blotted by the clouds to the east. She searched her feelings and realized that the surprise in all of this was how utterly unsurprising it was.

"I knew there was something else," she said. "I thought maybe an international angle. Terrorism. Or even you wanted to kill him for what he did to those workers." She dropped the report on the seat. "But you're just working for the Golfos."

"Negative. No, I absolutely am not." He looked at her, but the dash lights were now too dim to see him by. He was silent. Maybe abject.

"What exactly is the difference between you and any Zeta? You're just another army boy turned narco."

"You have to get used to something," he said, more weary than condescending.

"I can't wait to hear what I have to get used to."

"The old ways don't work. And because of that, they cannot be justified—"

"Was there even a plane?"

He was silent and she repeated it.

"There were two planes," he admitted. "One for you. One for him."

She looked out the window at the vast nothing.

"How'd you expect that to go?" she asked.

"Not great."

"Are you taking me to the cartel right now? I'm the only one who knows where the tunnel is. Are you—?"

"No. Fuck, of course not."

"Why should I believe you? Because of your little report?"

She tossed the document over to him, it spilled open onto the seat.

The engine thundered against a stand of fences, then relative quiet. The sky bleeding black.

"Can I tell you something?" he asked.

"Totally," she said, "tell me something."

"This whole time—and I *promise* you this is true—I've been trying to keep you safe. Everything I'm doing is to really, actually, keep innocent people safe. You might not agree with how I'm doing it, but I was just thinking . . ." Carver paused, looking for the words. "I just thought maybe you're a fellow traveler. You came into this on your own. You think for yourself. You do what needs to be done."

She crossed her arms. This loitering in the foyer of the fucking point. Because she could feel a certain valence in his voice, that he was ginned up to a proposal of some kind. She knew coercion when she heard it. Fuck this. Fuck him.

But whatever was coming didn't quite make it. He was blinking rapidly and looking in the rearview. He swallowed like someone suddenly frightened at the sight of something. She turned around to see. Headlights in the far distance.

"I gotta pull over."

"Is someone following us?!"

She realized she had no reason to trust him, not one.

He let off the gas and rolled onto the rough shoulder and put the Bronco in park. She grabbed the handle, ready to bolt.

"What the hell is going on? You tell me right now."

He flipped on the hazard lights and looked at her. He'd taken the gun from her. Her phone—

"I'm about to have a seizure," he said. He turned off the engine.

"A what?"

"I have a thing . . . a condition," he said, pinching the bridge of his nose.

"A *condition*? Nope. Nope—"

She opened the door.

"Listen to me."

She had her foot on the running board. The old dome light didn't work, and they sat in the dark. The tick of the hazards was the only sound. He turned his torso to her.

"I'm going to buckle my hands into this seat belt, and I'd appreciate it if you'd pull it taut against my body. I'm gonna have a fit for about forty-five seconds or so, and when I come to, I'll have a huge fucking migraine. You're going to have to drive, Diane. You understand?"

She must've nodded. Or blinked. Something he took for assent, because he relaxed.

He pulled out many lengths of seat belt. Buckled it. He squinted enormously, his head cocked violently, and then he grinned.

"Gonna be a good one." He chuckled to himself. "Could you pull it tight?" She moved over and grabbed it, and he crossed his arms over his lap. She was few inches from his face. His eyes blinked and batted around. She thought or imagined that she could see a coming wave in them. Or rather that the water was sucking away from the shore for what was gathering and had gathered. She wondered if this was really happening. What kind of game this could be.

She cinched him in. Her hands were not steady.

"You're the only one who knows where the tunnel is. And we have to assume the Golfos know that you know. They're looking for you. We'll get you out of here."

The thought ended in a *keck*, a kind of choked gasp, and an eruption of tendons in his neck. His face went red, and she'd never seen a more anguished expression in her life. The cab was rocking when the car that had been behind them swept past, illuminating the tableau for an otherworldly moment, his hands gnarled against the seat belt. She fled the vehicle in a sudden helpless revulsion—all that muscle in agony. She couldn't sit near it. Such a long time he thrashed and spasmed in there and toward the end of it he gibbered and whimpered and she wished he'd put a belt in his mouth or a mouthpiece. Was almost angry at herself about it. Goddamn. She walked away. Where the moon rimmed the clouds, the sky was as purple as a black eye. You have to get out of here, she thought.

DAME REFUGIO

He woke up in a bed covered by blankets, daylight poking through window shutters. As his eyes adjusted, he saw he was in a small room. An old wooden icebox and a trunk covered with lace. A tall antique milk pail, streaked green by rust. None of this for daily use.

A guest room.

The blankets were dense and he was tucked in and he thought he was paralyzed until he moved his head to look around. On the nightstand next to a red faux-gaslight lamp was a glass with a straw. He couldn't reach it. Someone had kept him hydrated, though. Underneath the nightstand a bedpan. Someone had done all this. Probably cleaned him. Put him to bed. Taken care of him.

He lay there for a long while looking at the air, lines of light the shutters let in, gold bars of sunshine. It was daytime out there, an awake world, and he was alive. His strange luck.

When he shut his eyes, he continued to see those golden bars of sunshine. He wondered about them. Were they a promise. Were they a warning. Could he hold the gold light in his hands. Could he cash it in.

He couldn't sleep for the pain, for the memories of being sewn up. He tried to move, wiggling, tried to unleash himself from the bedcovers. It took time. The sharp pain in his hip shut him down whenever the blanket moved over his wound, and he couldn't even feel his right arm at all, or maybe he was feeling it so much that he couldn't locate it. The body-map in his mind was askew. But he kept slowly twisting, birthing himself. The blankets loosened and sloughed off him like a molt.

On his good side he dropped a hand to the wood floor and then put down his good foot and pulled himself up. Here he rested and sweated. He drank from the straw, leaning over a fresh agony. He looked at his arm, the bandage tight. It smelled okay, it looked okay. His hip was another matter. The bandage was loose and the stitches were ragged. He wondered what kind of doctor had fixed him. If it had been a doctor at all. He scooted himself around on the bed till he was close enough to the door to fall into it and make a noise.

He held himself on the doorknob until someone came.

When the knob turned he lost his grip and put down the right leg, the bad one, and it gave out and sent him to the floor. He couldn't see anything, his eyes wouldn't work, but he knew he wasn't dead because he could smell hardwood and varnish, and that good nice clean smell helped him go safely into black he knew wasn't death, not yet.

When he woke again it was morning. He heard the rooster.

This time he wasn't tucked in as securely and was able to rise. There was a crutch here. He drank from the straw and then stood with the crutch and got himself across the room to the door. The hallway was dark and he opened the first door he came to and stood there, unable to find a light.

One came on. A bright hallway light.

"That's not the bathroom." A woman was talking behind him. "It's down the other way. Turn around and I will help."

Tomás realized he was looking into a closet. It was full of VHS tapes, hundreds of them stacked up neatly, like a video store right there in the closet.

"Sorry," he said.

"Don't worry," she said. "Take my arm."

She was a small woman, her head barely to his shoulder, but very strong. Wiry gray hair. She held him up and guided him in shuffling half-steps to the bathroom.

"Thank you," he said when they got there. He felt like someone who'd completed a great task.

"It's not a problem," she said.

When he finished she was waiting there and helped him along, this time to the kitchen. It was slow going. They passed the living room. Furniture of wrought iron and wood. Again shutters on the windows. A TV in a wooden console, like his mother had.

In the dining room a long dark beautiful wooden table. It looked like a plank of a giant's coffin. But they weren't going to eat in the dining room.

There were more shutters on the windows in the kitchen, he'd never seen so many shutters in a house, they were open and the morning light was full and hot as it came through the windows. But the concrete was cool, as if it were still evening on the floor. He could feel it through the new white socks someone had put on his feet.

In the kitchen he sat at a round mosaic table. She put before him chicken soup with chiles and onions and hominy. A plate of radishes and cilantro.

There was a stack of almanacs on the table. He wanted desperately to flip through one but he didn't think he had the strength to read and eat at the same time. He wanted to get away. He wanted a lot of things all at once.

He ate. When he finished the soup she brought a bowl of beans and a plate of tortillas and freshly pressed white cheese. He finished all that, too.

"How long have I been here?" he asked as she washed the dishes.

"A few days. You lost a lot of blood. Didn't look like you'd make it."

"How did I not die?"

"You're lucky. We work on animals here, my husband and I. We sewed you up."

"You didn't want to take me to the hospital?"

"We thought maybe it would be worse to move you anymore. You kept screaming."

"I don't remember."

"Well, that's a good thing."

"Thank you," he said. "Your husband's at work?"

"In the field, yes. He'll be here for lunch."

"I have money for you," he said. Already wondering if his luck would extend.

She looked at him. "How do you feel?"

He was sweating. "I feel good," he said.

"We should change your bandages."

She washed and wiped her hands and came back over to him. He called out when she put her hands under his arms to help him up.

"I'm sorry," he said.

"It's all right. You're very hurt. Try again?"

He nodded, and this time he clamped his teeth down and kept them clamped all the way to the bathroom. He was ashamed to have his pants down, but she covered his privates with a cloth so he could grip the edge of the bathtub on which he sat. She made a tsking sound when she saw the wound.

"It's infected, I'm afraid."

He looked down, and the skin was bright red and inflated.

"I should go," he said, but they both knew he could not.

He didn't remember walking back to the bedroom. She gave him pills she told him to chew and brought some water.

"We've got a little portable TV," she said. "You want me to bring it in?"

"Maybe I could read."

"Sure," she said. "What do you want?"

"Anything," he said.

She came back with almanacs and magazines and more water. She told him she'd leave the door a little open and he could call if he needed anything. She didn't make any plans with him, and he suspected she wanted to consult with her husband.

"I have money for you," he said.

He'd gotten an almanac and tilted it up on his chest with his good hand, but he couldn't really make out the words. Something inside felt off. Like a magnet set next to his internal compass. He put the book down on his chest. Maybe he'd be able to do a better job later.

The almanac was still on his chest when he startled awake, again from pain. It was now night, nothing coming through the blinds. The hall light was on, and standing in the bright door were two dark shapes. He could tell they were police just by the outline and the creak of their belts. He lifted his good arm to show he was surrendering, but it was impossible for him to raise much more than a few fingers.

Maybe they'd think he was dead.

OFF BOOK

arbaugh drove as Carver shifted around on the back bench seat of the Bronco. For a long time he was quiet and she was alone with her thoughts and worries and memories, the centerline of the highway almost the only real thing as she traveled north and back in time at once. Her thoughts biased toward her father. Moments in his wake at his pantleg. The track, studying a certain gray gelding that lost him a notorious amount of money. A card game she drove him home from, all of thirteen. He was sent to the hospital a few weeks after that with broken ribs, and she realized now how often he'd been a card short, a horse-length shy, chopping cars for parts. Periods he lived in motel rooms. She wouldn't say she missed a lot of school, but she learned early on it was for suckers, her daddy in an inevitable fury over/college tuition, the outrage of having to report an income for her loans. She would become convinced that her going to college was what did him in.

Look at me now, old man. What he'd make of how afield and flung-out she'd become. On the edges, running along the rim, headed for a border. These thoughts of her father and how accustomed she'd become to different derelictions. As an attorney. With Dufresne. With

Oscar. She didn't understand women who felt shame so readily. Her father brooked not a single smithereen of it. And her mother—she kept hers in the bottom of a glass, and never let that tumbler go dry.

Carver pissed himself, but she only knew when he woke and joked about it.

"Okay," she said. "It's okay."

"Just if you look back and I don't have any pants on."

She'd learn soon that he didn't smell like anything, maybe just a little salt that would wind up on her lips, which even then felt like a kind of subterfuge.

But that was later. Right now she feared his obscurities, their every sort, shape, and bulk.

"You want me to stop?"

"Thirty-three."

"I'm sorry?"

"Inseam's about thirty-three."

"Jesus, I thought you were losing your mind again."

"And none of that bootcut bullshit. Just a good straightleg."

"I'm certain we're not anywhere near a tailor."

"Then I'll see about it in Monterrey."

"You don't have anything you can change into?"

"No."

"You usually travel so light?"

"I don't do anything usually," he said. "I better be quiet now."

"Okay."

"Talking's like hammers in my skull."

"Shush then."

He had the keys out and only his boxer briefs on when he opened a heavy noisy gate that gave onto a courtyard dense with palms and an understory of flowers. Brick paths choked with foliage, the moonlight weird to see by. They passed a cat silently slapping a floormat with its tail in front of an apartment door and went up a stairway to the second floor. The landing wrapped around the inner verdant courtyard they'd just passed through, revealing a still and untroubled fountain. Carver moved as though taking stock, as did she.

They went around the landing and she noticed that the second floor had doors on each side of the square. She reckoned eight apartments to the building in all. He let her into the place and cleared all the rooms like a bodyguard and then fixed himself something in the small kitchen. A bubbling concoction, lime-green seltzer. He disappeared into the bedroom and she pondered flight. But it felt already like an old hankering. She set her tote on the couch. She noticed where Carver had left the sack with her phone in it on the counter. She noticed the sicario's pistol on the same counter. She went to the window to notice things there, looked out over the intersection, cars parked almost to the corner. Storefronts girded with metal gates and padlocks. A paved soccer field.

She prised open the window. It stuck, but the thought occurred that she could jump through it. The street wasn't far enough to plunge to death, she noticed. She was thinking of herself as a hostage. It was like a dream in her exhaustion, and when he came out with a blanket and pillows and made a bed on the couch, she was so tired her eyes watered. She didn't argue with him about taking the bedroom.

He was awake when she got up and stumbled out of the pitch-black bedroom into the living room. He'd made up the blankets, and she sat on the couch collecting herself from the dreamless oblivion from which she'd just come. Taking in things anew. The fabric of the old couch as busy against her fingers as a head of cauliflower. The steaming cup of coffee he set on the coffee table before her black as a tar pit. There were decorative swords on the wall, several different cacti that may have been dead, a bowl of fresh fruit. Traffic outside, horns, the skirp and bleat of tires. She noticed that the sicario's gun was gone, but the sack was still in view. Her phone still inside it. Her eyes flashed away from it when Carver spoke, something about stepping out, there was fruit, some pastries, she should shower, rest again. She feigned more of the state she'd been in—a fugue—then thought better of it and asked how he was.

"Fit as a fiddle," he said.

She wanted to see if she could make him stay and talk to her. If she had even that much sway.

"What is it that you have?" she asked. "The seizures, I mean."

"I don't really know. Hit in my early twenties. Never let on to the Company. It'd be disqualifying." He could've stopped there, but he kept talking. "They're rare, and I can feel them coming on. At the FOB, I'd hit the latrine or jump in a Hummer." He shrugged. "Grandpa had fits. Older than dirt when he died, though. It's just a thing. Like a cowlick or a birthmark."

She was listening harder than she meant to. Taking this information in a kind of thirst.

"You be all right?" he asked.

"I'm fine," she snapped.

"I just meant while I'm gone a few hours. Gonna get new wheels."

She nodded.

"We'll get you to the States."

"Okay," she said.

He patted his pockets, made to leave.

"What did you mean when you called me a fellow traveler?"

He stopped. Turned around. Squared himself in front of her like this could take a minute. But all he said was, "Cops suck. And you don't."

"Well, I'm flattered all to hell."

"I'm not trying to flatter you. I thought since we both had our issues with, uh, *management*, we might occupy common ground. Philosophically." He pointed to the folder on the table. That precious report of his. "I gave you that," he said, "because I wanted you to understand the underpinnings of what I'm doing."

"The underpinnings of working for the cartels."

"I don't work for them. I underwrite black-market enterprises. Their businesses. Their operations."

"Underwrite? So you sell *insurance* to criminals?"

"In a manner of speaking."

"And this is a good thing because . . ."

He sighed. Winced a bit at the headache or the conversation or both. Maybe trying to make her feel stupid.

"I'm serious. In what universe is this okay?"

"I was trying to explain last night. The origin of all of this was the program we ran in Afghanistan—"

"I don't want to hear about Afghanistan. You were gonna take my informant back to the cartel."

"Just listen. What we learned in Afghanistan was that a small force—ten, twenty very highly skilled operators—could bring order to the heroin trade. Granted, the original mission was simply to enlist their help in stopping al-Qaeda, but we realized that stabilizing the poppy market actually led to all sorts of tangible dividends. Economic stability. Prosperity. Peace. Sure, whatever, we were helping 'criminals' secure their product. Mitigate their rivals. Evade interdiction. But when they had insurance, when they stopped worrying about that cartel shit, they started to behave like rational actors. Like regular business owners, even. Suddenly schools are going up, bridges, all that nation-building shit that State and the NGOs love congratulating themselves for. It turns out, a black market is very easy to stabilize—"

"And you're telling me that the CIA is doing that here in Mexico?"

"You fucking kidding? Of course not."

"Of course not?"

"They shuttered the program."

"Why?"

"Ultimately? The CIA doesn't want to be in the business of ending the drug war. Neither does the DEA or the FBI or the Justice Department. They want to keep it going forever."

"But *you're* doing it. Here. In Mexico."

"I took the idea to the private sector. Started an insurance business, essentially. Something goes sideways, the cartel is insured, and that means they don't need to shoot up the plaza or kill cops. We give 'em a piece of the rock, so they can do business in peace."

"We," she said, realizing what he meant. Who he meant. "That man at the hotel, those soldiers in the alley, they're not CIA or—"

"No, they're like me, most of them off-book too. Ex-military, intelligence, even a couple gangsters, guys from all over the world. Some of them moonlight in private security, different agencies. It takes a particular kind of expertise, 'selling insurance to criminals.' Figuring premiums, investigating claims—like with Gustavo. He essentially stole millions of investment dollars from the Golfos. The Concern is gonna do everything it can to avoid having to pay out a claim like that."

"The Concern?"

"Sorry, that's what we're called. It was the name of Shipley's program."

She suddenly remembered Gustavo's coked-up rant. Going off about globalistas and bankers. "El Problema," she said.

"Yeah, it got lost in translation down here. Should be more like La Empresa. The Concern—like a business. I mean, shit, we're not the *problem*, we're the solution."

"To what?"

He sighed, rubbed his eyes.

"The bloodshed, the chaos. The cartels can't call the cops when their shipments get ganked. They can't sue anyone. The only measure they have is blood. But it doesn't have to be that way. That's what we showed in Afghanistan. It's not the average Mexican's fault that America has a bottomless appetite for narcotics. Stabilizing the black market is the moral thing for us to do." He looked to see how that landed with her. "Look, if you don't see it, you don't see it. Maybe deep down, you *are* a cop. A lot of people live for the drug war—not just cops, but lawyers, judges, prisons. Millions of people making their living on the violence and chaos, none of them in cartels."

He stopped, as though he could sense he'd begun insulting her, shook his head in a way that seemed like he didn't want to make it worse. Then he tilted his head like he was getting some advice from the ceiling.

"Look," he said at last. "For someone in such deep shit at work all the time, ask yourself this: why do you stay inside a system you constantly have to game?"

He didn't ask it like he expected an answer. He stood to go.

But she had a question.

"Are you gonna take me to the Golfos?"

"What?" His shock seemed genuine. "For fucksake, no."

"I'm the only one who knows where the tunnel is," she said, searching his face for the least hint of deception. "You're telling me this . . . *Concern* is gonna cover their millions of lost investment?"

He didn't even stop shaking his head no.

"The Golfos violated the terms of the policy," he said. "They sent their own guys after Gustavo and completely jacked the whole thing. We don't do business with shitty partners. I'm not taking you anywhere but America. I know I talk shit about cops, but a dead DEA agent is unacceptable."

He wasn't looking at her, and then suddenly he was. She felt something big coming, she wasn't sure what.

"Especially if you're that agent," he said.

"Why?"

"Isn't it obvious?" he asked.

"It's not," she said.

He smiled.

"We're hiring, Diane."

—

He left.

She counted to one hundred and twenty and then bounded across the room and picked up the sack, pulled open the magnetic seal, half expecting it to be empty, but her phone was right there. She extracted it, turned it on. A few moments acquiring a signal. Messages. Bronwyn (2). Childs (7).

She dialed Childs and put the phone to her ear. She listened to it ring and looked out the window at the wired rooftops sewing the pale white sky with a thin skein of black thread. She realized just before he picked up that she didn't want him to, that she wasn't ready to talk to him, but it was too late to hang up.

"Jesus, Diane."

"Childs," she said softly.

"Where are you?"

"Monterrey."

"California?"

"Mexico. Some apartment."

"Fuck. Why? Are you okay?"

"Yeah."

"Cromer says the Mexican police are looking for you? That that American who called you was killed? Firefights, civilian casualties, what the hell is going on down there?"

She didn't know how to explain, what to explain. She just needed to get off the phone. She never should have called.

"It's okay, it's just complicated."

"Complicated? The hell does that mean? Look, you gotta get out of Mexico. The State Department's been all up in Cromer's ass, Cromer's been chewing out Dufresne, Dufresne's been taking it out on his liver, asking if you ever told me about you two's time in Sacramento. They've got the transcripts of Oscar's texts, I know that. OPR's grilled me about you. About Oscar. And now whatever you're doing in Monterrey . . ."

She absorbed this intelligence as if it were some other Diane he was talking about. She didn't feel like she was in any kind of shock, but there was something dissociative inherent in this conversation. It was like hearing a recording of the wiretap, like she was calling from an alternate timeline. So much had transpired.

"Are you listening to me?"

She hadn't been, not really. She was thinking that calling Childs felt like flipping a coin. How you'd sometimes flip tails, and realize you wanted heads all along. How calling him now was like that, was in fact an act of making up her mind. Of realizing that her mind was already made up, that she didn't want or need anything from him, from Dufresne, the team, the DEA, Los Angeles.

"Look, I'll come down—"

"No!" she barked. Then calmly, "Don't."

"Diane. This is deep shit."

In deep shit all the time. Gaming the system.

"I know I encouraged you to go, but Dufresne's right. We gotta stay in our lane—"

"I gotta go, Childs."

"It better be to an airport. Or a lawyer."

"Just . . . forget I called."

"Goddamnit, I'm your partner, Diane. Just tell me where you are, and—"

"You need to forget I called. Those transcripts aren't gonna look good, Russ," she said. "I let Oscar get close to me."

A middling silence. Him pondering what that could mean.

"I don't care—"

"It's not just Oscar," she said. "They're gonna look hard at you, Russ. Because of me. I'm sorry. And they're gonna look hard at Dufresne especially. And they're gonna find things from Sacramento. You need to listen to me on this."

"Diane."

"Really, forget I called," she said. And then she hung up, turned off the phone, and put it back in the bag.

Even what things Carver possessed here withheld. A fridge racked out with bottled water. A rusted metal medicine cabinet possessed exactly five items: an old-fashioned razor, Feather blades, a toothbrush, Colgate toothpaste, and a black comb. A bar of white soap in the shower. A diminished brick of them under the cabinet. She imagined these bars had been around the world with him. He had Fruit of the Loom T-shirts. Levi's. She already knew he wore boxer briefs. Mostly white socks. A few white dress shirts of Mexican manufacture. A pair of black loafers that looked worn exactly once. She was dying to know for what function these and the black slacks and suit coat were deployed.

She looked in the envelope he'd gotten at the hotel. At the fake passports in there. One without a picture, for a someone named Bethany Wells. She was jealous for a moment, and then her heart sang when she realized it was meant for her.

She filled the clawfoot tub and fell into a nap on a towel folded over the lip behind her. She'd brought in the tote and used the stranger's Lady Bic to shave and tried on the stranger's sundress and combed her hair with Carver's comb.

She peeled a mango with a knife and ate it with half a sweet roll and then drank cooled-to-lukewarm coffee at the window, watching nimble old men play soccer on the court outside. The day's fullness quaking the air over the court like an oven. She wondered how many miles they ran in that lot. She wondered when she would run again, and what else would happen, what events she would put in motion. How many things that mattered she would do.

He came in with a new set of keys and migraine both. He fell onto the couch with his arm over his face, so she didn't tell him that she'd used her phone. She eventually decided to never tell him by putting the bag back where it had been. A lie of omission. This would matter later, but for now she thought he wasn't the only one who could withhold now, was he? She was struggling with what she knew she wanted, with the fact that he'd noticed the dress and had maybe stifled a comment on it, and what all that noticing and reticence could mean.

She went and lay down on the bed in the bedroom and waited him out. She was tired too, but she couldn't sleep—she'd had too much or there was too much to make up or it was too hot. She turned on the large fan up in the high ceiling and watched it turn more than felt it.

He startled her with his voice in the doorway.

"What?"

"I said are you hungry?"

It had gotten on to evening. Time had some bend and flex to it.

"I could eat."

She noticed his new pants as they waited for the boy he'd called up from an apartment downstairs to bring their dinner. An entire chicken in a plastic bag. The boy left and came back with a tureen of pozole. He departed again, and returned with ribboned cabbage in a sack with vinegar and salt. A baggie of limes. The kid reappeared a final time with another bag of beers in ice, and Carver gave him a lot of money as she finished setting a table that was scored and nearly as thick as a butcher block. They ate the chicken with their hands and ate the pozole from large cups with huge spoons for the cabbage too.

He told her more about his grandfather when she asked, a runner of moonshine everyone called "Shakey" who completed his life building alcohol funny cars. Knuckles busted from wrenching up his shit. Said the seizures were a family curse going back to Ireland. Maybe, who knows? Whether so or not, the foreknowledge made his first one less an event than it would have been otherwise. A thing you could hide if you knew what it was.

They took fresh beers to the rough couch, and she told him about her father. Practicing pool left-handed so he could one day run a stupid switcheroo. Doing this practice right up to his last week alive. Never won out, but still. The man was committed to the long game.

His great enemy in life whatever was on the up-and-up. Taxes, girl-friends, umpires.

Their talk wound down. He said he'd take her to the States, they just needed to get a picture for a passport he already had for her, she could fly out of Monterrey or they could drive to the border. He realized he was just dragging her into some crazy shit. She ran her finger over the lip of her beer, trying to get the smell of him, leaning a little into his air space.

When she told him where the tunnel was, the disordered expression on his face was a fresh heaven. She climbed onto him. Feeling him beneath her, pressing herself into him, that almost did a trick on her right there, right away. She undid him and got him inside of her. She ruined her knees on that rough cauliflower couch, could feel the air on her fresh abrasions. She'd have postage-stamp scars on each for a very long time.

BAGRAM AFB, PARWAN PROVINCE, AFGHANISTAN

MARCH 19, 2004, 21:47

POLYGRAPHER: There were rumors, correct? The DEA's Karachi office had heard things about the Ground Branch and heroin trafficking.

CARVER: It came up.

POLYGRAPHER: What was Shipley's line on that?

CARVER: That it was utter bullshit.

POLYGRAPHER: So he lied to the DEA? Carver?

CARVER: Oh, is that a real question? Of course he did.

POLYGRAPHER: So what happened when DEA heard from their informants on the matter?

CARVER: I don't know that they ever did.

POLYGRAPHER: Right. Because their informants in ▮▮▮▮ were killed. But it didn't take long for the Karachi office to figure out who exposed them.

CARVER: Like you said, there were rumors.

POLYGRAPHER: It's not a rumor if it's true.

CARVER: No, everything's a rumor without proof.

POLYGRAPHER: The special agent in charge in Karachi says all his guys in ████████'s operation died or went missing after you learned their identities. He says you personally were very persistent in getting those names.

CARVER: We closed more of their cases in three months than they did in five years. We gave them actionable intelligence. Guys they wanted for years, we brought in hog-tied and ready to process. They fucking owed us. We helped them do their job, they could help us do ours.

POLYGRAPHER: Which was?

CARVER: It wasn't fighting the endless drug war, I'll tell you that much.

POLYGRAPHER: Seriously, I'd like you to tell me: what work were you doing?

CARVER: Rooting out al-Qaeda and the Taliban. Stabilizing ██████. Bringing peace and prosperity to the region.

POLYGRAPHER: You sound like a believer.

CARVER: In what?

POLYGRAPHER: The Concern.

CARVER: The Concern? Christ, I already told you. Shipley never said a word about any Special Activities Division projects.

POLYGRAPHER: Shipley wasn't supposed to deploy the pursuit teams for the kinds of things you were doing.

CARVER: You say this like I put Shipley in charge.

POLYGRAPHER: I say this like Shipley was going against orders. Did he tell you about the little report he slipped into Tenet's office?

CARVER: No.

POLYGRAPHER: The one outlining your pursuit team's work in particular? The one arguing for the deceptive misallocation of military and law enforcement assets—

CARVER: Can you take no for an answer? Look at the needle. Am I lying? Am I fucking lying? I didn't know about any program. Christ.

POLYGRAPHER: One last question: what did you personally, ethically, think about deceiving the US military? How did you feel, thwarting the work of the DEA to put millions of dollars into the pockets of a heroin operation?

CARVER: Are you asking did I sleep like a baby?

POLYGRAPHER: I'm asking, did you sleep like a baby because you were getting rich? How much did you and Shipley and the Ground Branch get?

CARVER: The only money I ever made was my government salary. Look at the needle. Did it move?

THE RUN

They kept moving about Monterrey for three days. The garden apartment was a CIA holding, and Carver said it was only a matter of time before Langley found his paperwork securing it and sent someone to look in. But they couldn't leave the city either, he said, because they were waiting on a plane.

"What plane?"

They were sitting in office chairs on an empty floor in a highrise. Monterrey notched between shark-fin mountains, city lights twinkling before them. A fingernail moon hanging like an ornament over the proceedings below.

"Not sure yet," he said and strode into an office with his beer and returned with long cushions. He did this a lot, little disappearances in the middle of conversations.

"For fucksake, dude, *explain*," she said.

"Someone someday soon will buy a plane from a Mexican in Monterrey. A small plane. A private plane," he said. "There will be a pilot who will be hired to deliver that plane."

He yanked curtains from the same interior office, fixed a pair of single beds. He nodded at his fast work. He would fall asleep at will.

He would forecast what was coming next by just starting it. Chopping an onion. Drawing a bath. It seemed tricky for him to share a plan.

"He'll leave us off the manifest?" she asked.

He nodded from the cushion, propped up on his elbows.

"Worked a case like that in LA," she said. "Only the plane was full of coke. A whole hangar of private planes. We had a warrant for one call number. Could have been anything in any of the others," she said. "No TSA screeners. Nothing."

He yawned enormously, laced his hands behind his head. His breathing slowed, whistled out his nose. He was out.

The next day, they picked up the conversation where they left off. From within an empty old cantina in the Barrio Antigua she was watching the shadows overtake the narrow old-world avenue and imagining carts, soldiers serried and marching in a small parade. Coronets. Flowers from the balconies. Clops of horseshoes.

"Those hangars are just proof that there's no borders, not really," he was saying. "Anything can get anywhere. Anyone can."

"The ports," she said. "You could DHL an army into San Pedro."

The cantina was flaky with gray grout, raw stone. She kept getting grit on her elbows where they rested on the bar.

"Exactly. Everything's a Trojan horse."

The bartender brought them two more beers, and she realized her entire life had changed. Or this was an elaborate ruse.

"What am I gonna do?" she asked.

"What do you mean?"

"In the Concern. What's my role?"

The bar looked out onto the avenue, and Carver kept checking it up and down. They'd seen a small picture of her in the newspaper. "Persona de interés." Missing DEA agent wanted for questioning. But even though her image was out there, she'd grown used to the idea of lukewarm pursuit. Even her own complacence resting in the shade of his experience with this, the tall oaks of his specific competences. She wasn't worried. She was a little buzzed. She wanted to talk next moves. She wanted him to plan with her. She wanted him to smell like something. She worried she'd never get those things, and stared at him until he was forced to quit watching for police and answer her question.

"I have yet to see a situation you cannot handle, Diane. You give off an air of belonging wherever you are. That's a rare quality. Very useful."

"Tangible things, though. What will I *do?*"

"You know the law. You know the DEA. You know things no one on our team has any idea about. And you don't quail at gunfire. And you can drive."

"*Quail?* Who even says that?"

"I do," he said, physically shifting away, just so, as though he'd brook no discussion of his words, where they came from, his past.

She thought about asking anyway, but he changed the subject.

"The tunnel, for instance," he said.

"What about it?"

"You are solely in possession of a state-of-the-art tunnel from Mexico into the United States. What should we do with it? I'm sure you have notions."

"Don't give it back to the CDG," she said immediately.

"Because?"

"Because they killed everyone who built it."

"Okay."

"Because fuck them."

"Very much fuck them."

"You can't give it to Sinaloa or the Beltran Leyva cartel, either."

"Because?"

"Same reason, different specifics," she said. "The cartels—not as constituted."

"Meaning a change in leadership?"

She nodded.

"Again, I feel like you have notions."

She did. A few lieutenants. "I might. Can you still get into TIL-LER?"

"A database we cannot access does not exist."

"I can think of a few names in the Sinaloa cartel might be worth looking into."

"See?" he asked.

"What?"

"You're already doing your job."

"What are you looking at?"

He'd bent himself out over the bar so he could see up the narrow street.

"Nine times out of ten, I'm looking for a black SUV." He pulled himself back in and situated the stool to see the street better. He appraised her there, wiping his hands of grit. "But you. For a woman on the run, you're quite at ease."

"Oh, I'm fucked," she said. "Totally painted myself into a corner."

"You don't act like it."

"What do I act like?"

"Like you're right at home."

She never felt at home. No place was ever quite right. Sacramento. District attorney's office. Los Angeles. The DEA. Always moving, always running.

She reached for her beer. When she missed and the bottle smashed on the floor, they seemed to both realize that she was kind of drunk. Maybe too at home.

Carver stood. She mirrored him, standing too. As though a sober part of her was present to chaperone the drunken part. Always ready to run. This is why she wasn't worried that anyone would spot them. On some fundamental level, she knew she could outrun anyone, anything at all.

He shuffled her out of the cantina in a hurry and then the Barrio Antigua altogether. When she asked, he said that cleaning up their glasses, the bartender had taken a long look at them, maybe trying to place them. Anyway, it was better they left the old neighborhood hideout.

He made calls and drove. She read the Spanish signage in degrees of incomprehension. She had notions of what these going concerns were, these businesses and institutions. She imagined this is what it would be like. Strangenesses such as these. Speaking broken Spanish, Portuguese, French. How she'd express herself in bent idioms. That she'd always been foreign in some way deeper than language. She watched Carver talk in swift Spanish and hang up and write down an address in the Obrera neighborhood on his palm. It was so weird. She was nowhere. She'd never before felt so at home.

In the Obrera hideout, he woke her up to show her a piece of paper he'd printed out. The new place was actually furnished, and for a minute on the canopied four-poster she was certain that this was the setting of an odd dream. Then Carver's face came into focus and her last memory was smashing a beer on the floor, the cantina grit.

She peered at the paper, squinting at the light gushing in from the windows. New memories rushing in along with it, taking shape like an emulsifying image. The night before. Smoking cigarettes and listening to records on the stereo, a slew of Mexican artists, and polishing off all the red wine in the little hours. Cigarettes, ugh, why.

Specks and motes flashed in the air between her unfocused eyes and the paper in his hand. When she managed to read "Close and Continuing Relationship Form," she got mad at her own confusion.

"What is this bullshit?"

"Gotta fill that out if you wanna keep drinking and fucking all night."

He left, and when he came back he was smiling in the doorway. A powder-blue T-shirt, a little too short, his hip bones. The doorframe was dark teak or something, but the walls were as white and radiant as pain.

"It's way too bright in here," she said.

He crawled into bed with her, where she squinted against the sun, his arrival. "If we were on-book, there'd actually be paperwork. Can you fucking believe that?"

"Hilarious." She put a hand over her face. "Shades? Curtains? Anything?"

"Sorry."

"You made me smoke."

"I had *one*. You inhaled the pack."

"Why'd you let me if—" She stopped to retrieve the phrase from the impossibly radiant white paper. "If this is a 'close and continuing relationship'?"

"Is it?"

"You're the one brought paperwork!" She buried her face in the slippery pillows. Satin sheets on this thing. A steel magnate's fuck pad, he'd said. The guy in Spain for a month.

"The paperwork is a joke," Carver said. "Early on, the thought had occurred to me that Langley deployed you to catch me out. That you're made of wiretaps and extraditions. But then you shot that guy. So yeah, I guess ours is close and continuing now."

She sighed. In principle, she loved the banter, but she wanted desperately for him to fuck off and set the sun.

"Okay."

"Do you trust me?" he asked.

"Jesus." She turned over to look at him. The sunlight was a kind of witchcraft in cauldrons of her eyewells. "Yes, I trust you."

"It's pretty life-or-death around here. And not looking to get easier. This thing I'm trying to do, it's complex. But I'm for real. I want you in."

She moaned.

"We all get hangovers, by the way."

"You make sense now," she eventually said into his clavicle.

"Why's that?"

"It's stupid, the way things are. I put kids away as a DA. Oscar shot himself . . . I hate the things I'm supposed to do, and when I do the things that need to be done, I'm not supposed to do them . . . I can't make a thought into a sentence. Do you understand me?"

"Yes."

There was no smell in his neck. Just his warmth. "Do you trust *me*?" She looked up at him.

"Yes."

"So you'll come back."

"I'm not going anywhere, Diane."

"You've got to go check out the tunnel."

"We'll—"

"Before we leave. The federales are looking for me. I have to stay here. You need to check it out before we leave. There's a key in that bag I took from the hotel. Gustavo gave it to me."

He breathed there next to her. She started to fall asleep. Dreamed she was cleaning a gun. Dreamed of crocodiles. Dreamed the moon exploded in rainbow explosions.

Woke when he stirred, again to him humming "Pancho and Lefty," *all the federales say they could've had her any day, they only let her slip away out of kindness I suppose*, and then him going on about don't leave the apartment, don't use the phone unless it's an emergency.

"Be careful," she said.

"You be careful. Don't drink so much."

"I keep questionable company."

"That's clear."

"But I picked my pony."

"I'm sorry?"

"I put all my chips in? I got nothing left."

"You got me."

"You better not say shit you don't mean."

"If anything happens, I'll get you."

"I'll get you, if you leave me high and dry."

"I'd break you out of Fort Knox."

"Don't let me get got," she growled.

"Harbaugh," he said.

"Vamoose."

She slept for what felt like days. Then the actual days elongated and spread like spilt ink. Everything to read in the apartment was in Spanish, everything on television was in Spanish, and she practically learned the language in those four days, but felt as wholly isolated and cabin-feverish as she was. She kept noticing the sack with her phone in it. As she peeled an orange, as she refilled the ice tray. She had the sack open and was turning it on before she'd really decided to do it. She immediately shut it off, before her messages downloaded, but still. It boarded the network, she saw the bars, imagined she could hear it ping the cell towers. She set it on the counter. Watched the malevolent blank screen, half expecting a ring.

He'd been gone for four enormous days. She was going stir-crazy.

She went for a run. Yes, she was wanted for questioning by the Mexican police. But she just had to. She had to move.

At this point in her life, she'd come to the conclusion that all running was either flight or pursuit. Or both. Running to the Michigan cabin, toward Bronwyn and his stew and abs and sex—she'd actually been in flight from a twitchy informant, a murder. True, she didn't know at the time that Oscar was going to murder himself, not her, but the salient thing was this: if you weren't careful, running to something or someone could deafen you to the footfalls on your heels. You had to be careful, you had to listen.

And so now, jogging the streets of Monterrey, Harbaugh kept looking behind her and around at the foot traffic, up on the landings of the second stories of lime-green and clay-red residences, into the open corner doors of markets and auto shops, feeling a tingle at the nape of her neck, like the nip of a herd dog or a laser pointer or maybe just a blink and twitch in the eyes in the back of her head. She traced the paranoid feeling of being chased back to her suicidal informant. She saw blurs of Oscar in windows, passing cars, in doorways slightly ajar.

She'd decided to do just a couple blocks to get a sweat going, but she kept on, sprinted until her heart raced, found herself panting in a park. When she jogged the way she'd come, everything in this direction looked altered and wrong, and she slowed to a walk, scanning for landmarks. That's when she heard it. Footsteps. Tires. Engines behind her. It was *so* foolish to be out. She looked around, checked that she still had the key, and started to run in the direction of the steel magnate's secret apartment.

Then she saw the black SUV slow at the intersection ahead.

A hot tingle when it lurched forward and crossed out of sight. She ran to the corner and looked, but it was gone.

When it or one just like it reappeared a few blocks behind her, she took off at a sprint, swerving around loiterers and old women, a passel of schoolchildren let out for the day and clotting the sidewalk in groups of colorful backpacks.

She heard turning tires chirp somewhere behind and to her left, and she had no idea how far away the apartment was or whether it would be safe anymore and she ducked into an archway that let onto a paved and abandoned courtyard. A pair of metal benches. Offices. What looked like a dentistry. A hair salon. Everything as quiet as scissors.

She waited on a bench for nothing in particular, nothing she could place exactly, maybe just the passage of her fear, of time, and when she stood, a woman's figure stepped out from under the archway. A man in tow. The woman small, beautiful. The man behind her, black, older than them both. Americans.

"Diane Harbaugh," the woman said.

"I'm sorry," Harbaugh said. "No."

"Yes. Please." The woman gestured at the seat.

Harbaugh did as requested. *The phone, you idiot. They tracked your phone signal—*

"My name's Samantha Carlisle. Central Intelligence Agency. That's Dennis Bowden. Also CIA."

The woman set a manila folder next to Harbaugh on the bench and then took the bench opposite, a distance almost too far for conversation, arranged, it seemed, to discourage this kind of crosstalk, though Carlisle did not raise her voice when she said they didn't do this, didn't talk to DEA agents like this.

The man, Bowden, stood against the wall of the archway, as though to prevent Harbaugh's escape. But he wasn't muscle, he had the affect of someone senior and not usually in field, not anymore. Carlisle was young and small like a dancer from Juilliard, her hair pulled back. She folded her hands on her lap.

"What's this?" Harbaugh gestured to the folder.

"Transcripts."

"Of?"

"Conversations Ian Carver and I have had. Take a look."

"You're the polygrapher."

"One of them."

Harbaugh opened the folder. Read quickly. Carver recounting his time in Afghanistan. The pursuit team. Working in redacted places for a redacted warlord. But he'd explained this, she'd heard from his lips—

"You'll note his treatment of your colleagues in Karachi," Carlisle said. "He's all too happy to use other agencies' assets—like yourself—for his own ends."

She read about the dead informants, and could feel her face flush in hot shame. Maybe for the first time. Being caught out like this, confronted, insulted, diminished. Trapped.

"What ends would those be?" Harbaugh managed to ask.

"The usual ones. Dollars. Pesos. Euros."

Carlisle made a succinct grin that disrupted her aloof beauty. A thing she'd learned young, Harbaugh guessed. A severity practiced and honed.

Harbaugh wanted to look around for a place to flee, but resisted the urge and kept her eyes fixed in the middle distance. She breathed. When she felt like she could do so with poise, she set the folder aside, tucked her hair behind her ears, and composed her hands onto her lap like the CIA woman had done.

"I'd never blame a woman for believing a man's lies," Carlisle said, leaning back and hooking her wrists over the back of the bench. "But what you *should* be embarrassed about is that you came all the way down here to meet with a cartel lieutenant only to get him killed. Along with an American businessman and about a dozen escaped convicts. Quite a spectacle."

"I didn't kill him. I almost saved him."

"You really should take this as an opportunity," Carlisle said in a therapeutic tone designed to needle and provoke, "to explore humility. Your mistakes were *profound* and *many*. No jurisdictional authority. No local backup. Was there a single protocol you followed? But now"—she bit her lip and raised an eyebrow—"look at you. Alone. Abandoned in Monterrey."

The idea that he wasn't coming back had been sitting on its haunches in the back of her mind, and now it wouldn't stop barking. *Abandoned. Of course. He got you drunk for a few days and bounced.*

"So am I under arrest?"

"You didn't do anything illegal, did you? Not that it matters. We don't arrest people. Whatever you did is Mexico's problem. The DEA's problem. Maybe State's, I dunno. Not our problem, certainly."

"Then what do you want?"

"He has a long history with narcos. When Carver dragged Quincey to Tampico, we had to put eyes on him. And then after the bloodbath down there, Langley decided to pull his clearances and left him to his own resources. He'll come crawling back, eventually." Carlisle unhooked her hands and pressed her hands to her knees to stand. "But I'm talking to you out of professional courtesy. Warning you that he's busted. And that this ends in the inevitable way for you."

"What way?"

"I don't know what he told you he's doing, but he's gone. If he contacts you, it'll be when he's out of options. He can't stay in Mexico—he's worthless to the cartels without Company assets. Though he probably has some resources salted away. Offshore accounts and such."

Harbaugh pointed at the transcript. "He says in here that he didn't take any money—"

"Jesus Christ, you *are* a dumb bitch. Let me guess—he shared Shipley's little report with you? Their fantastic project in Afghanistan? They were ordered to shut it down, but it was just too lucrative. Whatever he said is bullshit. This is a grift. We let him play in Mexico for a bit to see what would happen. And you got all mixed up in it."

The man, Bowden, stepped out of the archway. "He'll get you killed," he said.

He said it plainly, softly, and in a manner that was so sadly certain that she felt pitied. The shame flashed afresh in her chest and probably now dappled her neck. It happened almost like he'd simply pushed a button.

She clocked Carlisle looking down and over at Bowden's feet, annoyed that he'd intervened. Acting almost like she'd been scolded. Like there was a deeper disagreement about what they were after now. Or perhaps Bowden was just stepping on her toes.

"Maybe we can help you," he said. Again so soft you had to strain to hear him.

"Help me what?"

"Out," he said. "Help you get out of . . . this."

Weirdly vague. Like he didn't want to say too much.

She suddenly realized what was happening. How many times

had "Maybe I can help you" passed her lips? That glorious utterance. This man was a good spy maybe, good at running spies maybe, but he was no Midwife. No one ever says "Maybe I can help you" when they don't need something in return. They weren't here to warn her. Carver was lost—maybe she'd lost him too—but there was power in knowing this, power in knowing other things—

The tunnel.

They want the tunnel. And they don't even know to want it.

"I'm fine," Harbaugh said. "Don't worry about me."

"Don't act like you bring something to the table," Carlisle said.

"I've been called a lot of things," Harbaugh said, grinning like she had a secret. "But the only person who's ever called me a dumb bitch in my entire life," she said, dropping the transcript into a trash can, "is you."

"Then you've been underserved by everyone you've ever met," Carlisle shot back, but Bowden hissed and she quit.

There was also a third kind of running. Running to think, your feet lightly tapping the Monterrey sidewalk as you trundle onward. The thoughts pacing with your feet. And those thoughts were that there was no way that Carver had left her, because he could not. Even if he didn't care about her, or want her in his life, he couldn't just drop her.

She had leverage: the tunnel.

She bounded up the stairs to the apartment door, not realizing that the wrought-iron gate on the street was unlocked. She was thinking that he'd have to silence her if he wanted the tunnel for himself, and she just knew he wasn't as wicked as all that.

The apartment door was ajar when she pushed it open, too deep in her thoughts to notice. A very dark Mexican sat at the table with a glass of water. He looked up from his phone.

No, *her* phone.

He wore an olive T-shirt and black jacket and he opened his mouth to say something, but she spun around.

Two men advanced on the landing and she wedged herself against the doorjamb, instinctively, and like a cat enlarged herself and looked into the room for an egress as the men blocked the hall. Nothing stood out.

The man said in English to come and sit, there was nowhere to run.

THE NEW GUY

Tomás's good wrist was handcuffed to the bed. When he woke, an orderly sweeping in the hall heard the cuff clinking and went away for a police officer. The two of them conferred in the doorway as Tomás asked for water.

He wouldn't remember El Motown's arrival some thirty minutes later, though his eyes were open the whole time. His skin was a septic shade of yellow. Staphylococcus had infected his blood.

The next time he woke, he was no longer cuffed to the bed and the IV in his good arm itched. A nurse brought him ice to chew on and an ancient doctor waddled in and looked into his eyes with a penlight and declared him a miracle. His hip was expertly dressed, his shot-through hand sutured and bandaged. He hadn't eaten anything in days, and the meal was flavorless in his mouth, gummed like sawdust.

He was by this time dependent on morphine, a hankering that would harass him for the rest of his life. His fortunes had whipsawed in many strange ways. There was no mention of the cops, and the doctors said he was a special case. He had an entire room to himself. The nurses were put on orders to give him whatever he asked for, and what he asked for was more morphine and the pure black sleep that swallowed him whole.

The Twin Dawn was on his bedside table, and in wakeful times he chewed ice and read it, still not remembering El Motown's visit. He did not question the book's appearance and had an eerie familiarity with the new passages. He seemed to know the Twin's trajectory, his travels across the frozen wastes of the Northlund and the intrigues there during his time as the Wolf King's champion. He predicted the Twin would slaughter the Wolf King and join yet another order. He even knew the name, the Knights of the Wandering Jurisdiction. As the book finished with the Twin headed to the Farwest Steppes, Tomás felt like he'd written the book himself, had conjured it like a spell.

His entire convalescence took on a mystical quality. He discerned essences and auras in the nurses and interns. Time flowed laterally, the gyre of people tending to him like a musical number and dance routine. His laughter shot bolts of astonishing pain from his hip, and he aged a thousand years in its subsidence. He grew wise, he was high as hell.

And then El Motown's visit came to him like a letter he'd forgotten to read, left on a desk in his mind. He remembered the man saying he'd liked *The Twin Dawn*, and while Tomás lay in fevered sepsis, El Motown told him every last morsel of the story. He must've been in the room for hours, unspooling it. Tomás remembered too El Motown saying the police would trouble him no longer, that the Zetas had arranged things. The Zetas were his family, he would be called back to service when the time came. El Motown must've said many other things. He was there for so long that he could've told Tomás a whole library of books.

One day Tomás woke to a bulky man softly closing the door. Short hair, a cowlick like a celestial body over his right eye. Something European about him, an odor, an invisible glyph or icon. Tomás wasn't entirely sure the man was actual, even though the leather of his jacket groaned with the crossing of his arms.

"Hey fuckstick," came a nearer voice from another man. American.

Tomás looked over. A man seated on a rolling stool glided over to him.

"¿Eres auténtico?" Tomás asked.

"Am I real? You tell me."

He struck Tomás in the face with a quick punch and the next thing he knew, Tomás was off the bed and on the floor, the big man in the leather jacket holding him by his gown, the open back of which he slipped out of like a husk. The big man threw the gown aside and lifted him up by his neck and shoved him naked into a chair. Tomás was not a small person, but the big man did this without effort.

His hip and hand were screaming, but Tomás held the noise inside.

"The CDG send you here?" the other man asked.

"Fuck you," Tomás replied in English. He didn't really have the energy to fight, but the better part of him was simply made to resist. Like a locked door. The big man slapped him out of the chair.

"Asshole. Listen. Did they send you after the nephew too?"

He looked up at this man, the American, and then over at the big man.

So this is how it ends, he thought. Fuck it. Who needs secrets?

"El Rabioso me envió."

The American picked up the chair Tomás had just been knocked out of and sat in it.

"El Rabioso," the American said, shaking his head. "What a stupid piece of shit. I told him and the Eskimo both—no Zetas, none of you guys. Let us handle it. The whole point was to demonstrate that we could take care of shit like this. Nevertheless they send you assholes up here to dick it up. And even then, we *handled* the thing. It's not like *I wanted* to light up a platoon of prison Zetas in the middle of town, but we have to, we will." He looked over at the other man. "That goat rodeo's on Esquimal and Rabioso. Make sure it's reflected in the adjustment."

The other man rolled a cigarette, grunted.

Tomás sat up, his hip throbbing. Held his bandaged hand against his body. His bare ass on the cold floor. He was so confused. He'd gone from unraveling the mysteries of the universe to this painful bewilderment. He was about to ask who they were, but the confusion burned off like a fog as what the man had just said tocked into place and he realized who these men were.

"I was there," he said. "I saw you kill a dozen men in moments."

"Condolences."

"¿Mande?"

"Thoughts and prayers. You angling for a medal? What the fuck are you getting at?"

Tomás looked from the American to the other one and back to the American. "Who are you?"

"The competition," the man said.

"I do not understand."

"You're going out of business, sicario. We're the Concern."

The words went off like a red warning light. Like a hotel alarm clock buzzer. "The Concern?" He'd heard these words before.

"Get up," the American said. "You got one last job to do."

The pain rose like a sun. His hip, his hand. And a morphine hangover hovered over it all, a cloud with no shade, just another feature of his warped psychic landscape. He pitied himself for the first time since he was a child and El Frodo.

He knew he was going to die soon. He privately mourned as they drove north. He mourned that he would never read another book. He mourned in perfect silence the zip ties on his hands and feet, the scant view of sky there was to be had on his back in the back seat.

He'd been severely hurt before. He'd been burned. But this was another order of pain. It was in his spirit, fresh lenses on everything he'd ever done. He did not feel guilty or due for punishment, only a deeper resentment at the conditions of the world, that his personal honor had been so irrelevant. That he was like a faithful hammer, but a tool's integrity began and ended with its utility alone.

Hours later, he tired of these thoughts, and began to puzzle over the men in the front seat. The Concern. The European and the American and however many more were in on that ambush. *El Problema.*

El Motown had talked of them. *The problem? They are naming names like that now?*

Gustavo had ranted. *Big players, globalistas. Their networks. Security. Insurance. The Concern. Means I am expendable now.*

The American looked back on him, as though he sensed Tomás's thoughts were biased toward them. He regarded him quizzically, with a dab of disappointment.

"How the hell they'd get the drop on you?" he asked. "I mean, it *is* impressive you tracked Gustavo down, I'll give you that. How'd you manage that, by the way?"

"I followed a black truck. Gringos who showed up where my guys died."

"Those were Agency people following me. Not that you knew that. But it was smart to tail them." He snapped his fingers as a thought occurred to him. "Tight work, dude. But that just makes you getting tagged like a little dipshit all the more vexing."

When Tomás didn't say anything right away, the American jumped back in.

"It's okay, man. It happens. I mean, not to us, but then we don't really exist. I just thought you were some kind of supremo badass. Like the Golfo's numero uno."

"I quit," he said.

"You what?"

"I don't work for Los Golfos no more."

"Hear that, Goran?" the American asked the Serb, who said nothing from behind the wheel. "A Zeta who has turned on his master. Shocker. I should send you up to Langley to tell them yourself. Zetas are getting too big to be lap dogs."

"I'm not a Zeta neither."

The American turned all the way around in his seat to look down at him lying there.

"Yeah? Then why aren't you in jail? Pretty sure the Zetas made your charges go away. Which reminds me, what were you when you were straight? Army? Federal police?"

"Cuerpo."

"Ah, Cuerpo de Fuerzas Especiales! The big boys. You train with DEVGRU in San Diego?"

"Fort Bragg."

The American and the Serb traded silent looks on this. "Delta Force. Okay. Cool. You miss it? I miss it. I was just an Army Ranger before CIA, before this. There's comfort in not having to think, right? Just following orders and bitching about the orders with your guys, you know? And it's fucking nice having a mission. Something clear-cut. Take that hill. Kill these insurgents. Blow up this rathole. Know what I mean? You know what I mean."

Everything Tomás liked to read turned on the notion that a man was happiest on a clear mission cutting down enemies. He knew exactly. He knew it very much.

"I miss it," he said. It felt good to say that out loud.

"That's right you do. War is hell and all that, but the irony is it's also *fucking awesome*." Again the American had turned all the way around to look at him. "So fuck, dude, seriously. All that training? Your Delta commanders would be pissed at you getting caught out like that. What happened?"

He looked out the window at the scrub. The ribbons of clouds. Then back at the American.

"I was telling El Rabioso fuck you I quit," Tomás said. "I was distracted. And then Gustavo El Capataz come out shooting. I tried to tell him no, but he didn't listen—"

"Tell him what? That you and Rabioso were spatting?"

"Just we can talk, that's all. I wasn't taking no more orders from El Rabioso or nobody. I was out!" Tomás rolled over up onto his elbows. His hand throbbed, as though raising his voice also raised his blood pressure. Which maybe it had.

"Right," the American said, looking at him skeptically.

"I was going to help Gustavo El Capataz."

The American laughed.

"You killed the dude, dude!" he said, looking back out the windshield, shaking his head.

They drove awhile more before he turned around again.

"Be sure and don't help me, okay?"

They went all night and parked just before dawn. As the sun rose on a graveyard of cars down the mild hill below them, an auto shop appeared, surrounded by a painted sheet-metal wall near Highway 2 outside the town of Piedras Negras, just across the US border from Eagle Pass, Texas. They waited in the lee of a dead mesquite, the morning breeze shifting sand through the open windows, watching to see if anything unordinary materialized in the empty countryside. Only thin NAFTA traffic bound for the United States appeared on the highway. Tomás sweated despite his shorts, sandals, and tee in the cool air. He was maybe still sick and dying or just suffering withdrawal. His bandages itched, his head throbbed. He ate an orange the American gave him. The sugar helped.

After a time scanning the scene with binoculars, the Serb exited the vehicle, got what looked like a Savage Model 12 from the trunk, and made for even higher ground.

"Why are we here?" Tomás asked.

"You want to know everything?" the American asked.

Tomás looked out the window. There was nothing to see, nothing he could figure on his own. He nodded.

"There's a garage down yonder in all that wreckage of cars. And in that garage is a tunnel to the United States. The one Gustavo built."

Tomás looked warily at the American, wondering what was happening, about to happen, had happened.

"How do you know about it?"

"The new girl told me."

"I don't know who that is."

"Sure you do. She's about yay tall, real pretty? Likes to shoot sicarios in the dick?" He polished off a coffee they'd stopped for and crushed the cup. "Lucky for you, she doesn't have great aim."

"The DEA," Tomás said the moment he realized. Not sure what it meant. Again, realms within realms.

"Not anymore she's not." The American grinned as he pulled on a pair of aviators. "We're all kind of transitioning these days."

Tomás sat up, his mind raced. How it all seamed together. How it all came apart. Where he fit into it now. Nothing in the man's aviators but his own blasted reflection, his hair askew, scratches he didn't know where from.

The American leaned toward the driver's-side door to watch the Serbian set up his tripod position and the sniper rifle and observe the scene.

"Why are you showing me this place?"

"I gotta do *something* with you," the American said, hopping out of the car. He opened the back door, cut the zip tie from around Tomás's ankles, and helped him outside. The wind whipped up, the branches of the dead tree clacked against each other. "It's a great location. Outside of town but on a major highway, so regular traffic won't arouse suspicion. Good amount of acreage, room for expansion. From here it really looks like the kind of property we'd contract to insure."

"Insure?" Tomás asked.

"That's our gig, sicario. The Concern. Our business."

"Business? What kind of business?"

"Black-market policies are our bread and butter. We insure syndicates in Malaysia and Amsterdam. Afghanistan, of course. Pakistan. Smaller operations in the American Midwest. Australia." He was counting them on his fingers, more in his mind silently.

"I don't understand," Tomás said.

"In the straight world, you gotta have business insurance. For your trucks or your pipelines or inventory. Anything you can't afford to get fucked up in a flood or stolen? You insure it. Same thing for drugs. All that shit you need to manufacture and transport your product—trucks and tunnels and submarines and shady border patrol and dirty judges, those are assets, are they not? We insure all that stuff. Sometimes we cover *other* uninsurable activities. Illegal sports books and gambling operations, stolen-car rings, high-end burglars—you into any shit like that, we can get you a piece of the rock."

He opened a Pelican case in the trunk and started pulling out gear bags and opening them and setting them by in the trunk.

"No armaments and definitely no sex trafficking, of course. We don't fuck with slavers or stinger missiles. Here." He handed Tomás a headband with a little square camera and antenna attached. He removed a laptop and set it on the Pelican case and began typing for a moment and then gestured for Tomás to put on the headband and fiddled with it. He looked from the laptop to the camera, fiddled some more. Then showed Tomás the screen, the feed from the camera as he affixed it to his head.

"What we offer is the ability to focus on your very illegal business. Which is why we came to Mexico. Everybody here is doing shit the old way. When a cartel loses their product or a rival takes their plaza or there's federal interdiction or just plain old force majeure or inherent vice—where do they turn? You can't call the cops, you can't sue. What recourse do you have?"

Tomás realized the question was not rhetorical.

"Plata o plomo."

"Exactly," he said, snapping closed the laptop and setting it back on the roof. "And mostly plomo. Thus, surplus of assholes like you Zetas. The biggest outlay for a cartel by far is the cost of a standing army. And then you guys just engender more of the problem you were created to solve. You light up the plazas. I've seen whole wars started by trigger-happy second cousins and bored girlfriends. And—*and*—as you and I both know, war is fun. You're strapped all day, everybody starts to look like a hostile. Here."

He handed him a walkie-talkie from the trunk.

"And then your guys, they start to think maybe *they* should be the boss. This is some ancient Praetorian Guard shit. Regicide is as old as sex and just about as primally inevitable. Channel four," the American said, and he flipped on the radio. "Check," he spoke into the one in his hand, his voice issuing from his head and Tomás's device. Tomás wasn't sure what the American was saying, all these things he didn't quite parse.

"But what if there was a market mechanism to mitigate everything? And what if that mechanism freed you up from all the anxiety of being at war and instead let you focus on running your business better? What if you were covered by the Concern?"

He slammed closed the trunk, looked up the hill at the Serbian, and then assessed Tomás, chewing his cheek as he did so. Tomás was absorbing what the American had said, but it was difficult, the pain he was in.

"I suppose it goes without saying that Goran will have a bead on you. And you won't get far on foot in those flip-flops. Not with that hip. Hell, you might not make it down to the highway. You'll probably need this." He handed him a silver key, newly cut. "Find that tunnel and then get back up here."

The fence was four hundred meters away, and he felt every stone and indentation from his rocky descent down the hill. The going was less clamor-

ously painful on the flat approaching the road, but from the damp-
ness of his bandage, he surmised he'd ripped open the sutures on his
hip. It was so hard to think. He was pretty sure he would not retain
what the American had been saying about insurance, the Concern,
the cartels, business. Not that it mattered. He wouldn't live much
longer. There was a gray cast to the desert sky he was thankful for,
given what hell it would be to also bake out here. Even yet, he felt
like a wounded animal, like a lizard who'd escaped without his tail, a
creature in flight. A reptilian hope.

He stopped to look back up the hill and see the Serb and his rifle
trained on him. His pain standing there with him like another man.
A ghost, a brother, a someone who wouldn't or couldn't walk away
from him.

"Keep going," the walkie-talkie squawked.

He'd looked back only in need of something to keep his mind off
the pain. But there was no splitting it off, there was no forgetting it.
It was of a piece with him.

He put the walkie to his mouth. "Do you work for Los Golfos
then?"

"Fuck no. We *were* considering taking them on as a client."

Tomás estimated that it would take the talkative American only a
few more seconds before he'd be unable to not hold forth—

"I mean, we'd done the preliminaries, assessed their financials
externally. I thought our presentation went well enough. But the
Eskimo was hesitant. It's always the same shit, right? I mean when
we pitch to clients, they just see a kind of protection racket. Even if
they get the advantage of our services, they're still fucking gangsters,
right? You can't expect them to see the bigger picture. But a bigger
picture there certainly fucking is."

The radio went quiet. But only for a moment.

"To be fair, CDG'd be our biggest client. I get their hesitation,
and was ready to move on. But then *they* called. Said the piece-of-
shit nephew ran. And they had no idea where. I knew we could find

him, and I guaranteed it. Of course, we didn't know *why* they wanted him, not yet."

He made the empty road and crossed it. A sun-and-rubber-hammered snake shaped into an S on the road like a logo. The wind kicked up a dust devil in the lot before him. He paused at the gate.

The radio scratched.

"Just yank off one of those sheet-iron panels."

He felt for a loose one. No luck.

"Climb that shit."

He thought to say he couldn't but figured he must. He went around the side of the wall and found a mound of dirt. He cut his hands on the edge of the sheet-iron going over. He was careful of his screaming hip, but the bandage was spongy under his shorts. Full of blood. His head swam.

"How'd you find him?" he asked into the walkie-talkie.

"Shee-it. Them's trade secrets, bruh. I tell you one thing though, I never should've reported back to Eskimo where he was. Why that idiot sent another team—you and your guys—I'll never know. But it's disqualifying. Get in the shop, dude."

He was panting, had barely noticed his surroundings, though he was suddenly reminded that the American was watching the feed. Stacks of tires, rusted-out chassis, piles of interior seats, tailgates. He headed over to the building. The garage doors were chained.

He took out the key. It fit in the padlock, and he yanked out the chain.

"Like I said, we didn't want to get kinetic on your boys. But we also needed to show that we have robust recovery capabilities. That we have a shock-and-awe element, you know. That we can do wet-works, when necessary. We all have other niches, but every last one of us is an operator. Above all it is just a numbers game. Risk assessment. Knowing a killer asset when you see it. Like that tunnel down there. Hopefully. Can you listen and do shit, or is that not in your skill set? Open sesame, homeboy."

Tomás realized he meant the door and dropped the chain and heaved the thing up, clattering. A garage. Oil drums. Rags. He walked between two sets of lifts in the oil-change wells. About four feet deep for mechanics. He squatted and peered down.

"Yep, that's what I'm thinking," the American said. "There's the controls to your right."

He hopped down into the well and looked at a dirty control pad the size of a small brick attached to the length of cable. A toggle. An up and down button. He flipped the toggle. He pressed down. The lift shuddered down around him, the tracks level with the floor at his chest, and then down into the well. And then the entire floor descended.

"Bingo," came the voice on the walkie.

The floor dropped and dropped, slowly, and then a black opening rose in front of him and the entire thing shuddered to a halt. He set the control brick down.

"Go on, don't be shy."

He took a step forward and then another, and a sensor picked up his movement and on came a row of track lights as far as the eye could see, diminishing to a point on an underground horizon.

"Holy shit," the American said.

He stepped forward and touched the walls. Concrete sections, perfectly round, about twelve feet wide. A track running down the middle.

"You could drive a pickup through here," he said into the radio. For a moment he thought about breaking for it, but the tunnel was long and gave out in Texas where his chances were just about zero.

When he rode the lift back up to the top, the American was standing at the lip. The Serb was pulling down the door, the rifle slung over his shoulder.

"You're going to kill me now?" he asked.

The American sighed and looked at him. "I'll never understand how they got the drop on you," is all he said in response. "Sorry, I'm just obsessed with it."

"Now four people know this place," Tomás said, feeling blood run down his leg. "What your plans are, I don't know, but you won't let nobody keep living who knows and is not part of—what you call it?—the Concern."

"True, that," the American said, removing the camera and taking the radio from him. The Serb lit a cigarette. The American looked at him, like he was waiting for an answer, like he'd asked an important question.

Then Tomás realized what the answer was, what the American had been getting at.

"It's not important that they got me," Tomás said. "What's important is, I killed the one who wouldn't stop shooting. And I drove off the woman. My time to die was not then. And also not now."

"Is that right?"

"Simón. I think you want to hire me, cabrón."

The Serb snorted and the American glanced back at him. When he turned back to Tomás, he was smiling.

"Well, look what sprung out of the ground, Goran," the American said. "The New Guy. All fresh and bloody as the day he was born."

DO THE THINGS

She broke for the hall, had no choice but to somehow bust through the men herding her inside. She shrieked like a puma and struck the one who came reaching for her first with an exasperated look on his face as the other scanned behind them, down toward the stairs from which she'd come. She kept hitting the man coming near her, both retreating and trying not to retreat into the apartment, both fighting him off and trying not to get surprised from behind by the man at the table. Then the man coming for her had her arm and she tried to take off his ear with her bare hand and kept screaming as he forced her into the apartment. The other man right behind them, swinging closed the door.

She twisted the man's ear, but only for a moment before he punched at her—landing concussively and decisively twice. Her head snapped back and recoiled into his second punch. She fell silently to her knees. He was holding her upright by her arm and away from him like a wildcat or snake and inspecting his ear with his free hand for blood. The ear was still attached, and he shot the two other men looks of annoyance just before she grabbed his entire genitals through the loose fabric of his black track pants, sinking in with her nails and twisting and squeezing and for some reason gripping her own wrist with her freshly free hand as the man released her and tried to pull away from the torment. He made to pry her off his anguished parts, his nuts and nutsack and dick, which in her grip felt to her like they were liable to come off, as if designed for such a thing—and then blackness.

She was soaking wet and gasping for breath. All three of the men in the bathroom with her, the one from the table spraying her with the showerhead. She ascertained she was upright.

She saw a cat in the window, standing, its tail flicking and watching whatever was occurring on the other side of the window with a kind of professional curiosity. Like the animal was a student of human affairs. Her wrists were bound with duct tape and nearly yanked out of their sockets as the men dragged her back into the front room.

She was thrown into a dining chair. The man in the track pants slapped her with an open palm that spun her face and ruptured her eardrum. She knew because she'd ruptured it before as a little girl, the pain and the way things sounded were same as then.

She'd been a girl once.

The men were all yelling at her in Spanish, she was trying to appear calm in the face of their noise but taking them seriously, like she'd done with Oscar, noting her own fear within, the pain in her neck, behind her eyes, she could feel her lip was swollen and there was a throbbing over her eye socket, these assessments happening in the gale of their shouts.

What did they want?

A gong went off, a fist, her teeth felt loose.

"What do you want?" she shouted. "What? What?"

The man in the tracksuit punched her a few more times and then she sensed him being restrained and pushed back by the others. She imagined they did not want her to go unconscious again, perhaps they were afraid he'd kill her.

She couldn't help sobbing. She didn't mean to, but she hurt everywhere, even the water on her skin hurt, her head hurt, her hair hurt.

"Who killed my men?" the dark one was asking. He'd knelt and taken her face in his hand and held it up so she could see him.

"What? What men?"

"I want names. Los Golfos won't find them, but I will. I promise to kill every one of them. Look at me. I want the names. DEA, FBI, I don't care what they are. I don't care who they are."

In the course of his talking one of her eyes had swollen shut and the other had wandered off, away from the man's close dark face, his black eyes and his damp hot breath, to the window where the cat walked on the narrow ledge. Harbaugh imagined the creature hopping down to the street below, a single story, not too far for a cat. But it stopped to watch. The man was still talking to her, he waved a multi-tool in front of her face, was picking through the tools, the screwdriver.

"Sí? No?"

The scissors.

"Sí? No?"

The pliers.

"Sí? Sí."

He nodded and the men went to remove her boot, her right boot, and she kicked and toppled struggling as one of the men lay over her legs and the other removed her boot, her sock. She concentrated on the cat.

Get help, she begged at it.

When it lifted its leg to bathe itself, the dark man was in her face with the pliers.

"Nombres," he said, switching to Spanish. "Dame sus nombres."

He disappeared and the man with the track pants and red ear and scrambled testes sat on her chest wincing and angry and held down her arms. She couldn't see the man remove her toes but the one on her chest was staring into her face and saying vile things in words she didn't comprehend but which she nevertheless fully understood. He was going to take her apart like she had tried to take away his parts. Dismantle her in crude ways that would make what was happening to her now seem as painless as a haircut. Imagine that, she imagined he was saying, this pain will be a memory both remote and pleasant. Imagine that. Imagine that.

When she came to again, the cat was gone and she saw that so were the two smallest toes on her right foot. The pain was like a fire. She was upright in the chair—the jostling must've revived her—and the man was in her face again with the bloody multi-tool and he wore an expression benign and benevolent. He touched her face gently. Her blood dripped from his elbow.

"This can end fast or slow," he said.

Her face felt hot and the cold air over where her toes used to be was like an exposed ganglia, discrete fires that when she moved her foot flared and made her almost pass out again.

He opened the multi-tool. The knife.

"Names."

Carver, she thought. *You have to be here now. Yours is the only name I can give, and it won't matter, it won't be enough.*

"He'll get you killed," the CIA man had said.

"I don't know," she said.

He searched her face. Then he said things to the other men, still looking at her.

"I am going to take you somewhere," he said, folding up the tool and putting it in his jeans. "Somewhere you can scream to death."

A bag went over her head, black but not total, as she could make out through the fabric that the man had stood. The bag was the shock and it was hard to listen to herself, to hear herself thinking about what was left for her, what was possible.

There was one thing she could do, and she did not want to do it.

But the cat had put it in her mind. It would probably kill her. But she said to herself, *I do the things.*

She stood. She stifled a scream as her foot slid in the blood that still must have been issuing from the stumps of her toes, the raw openings against the wood floor. She hazarded a step and her boot slipped and she just kept her face in the direction of the light from the window. When the men laughed, she knew she had a split second to run.

She put her bound hands in front of her and knew it was only four good steps to the window over the street and two of the steps would necessarily be an untold agony, but two would be sure and painless in her boot. So many steps she'd taken, millions, and these would be the most important ones.

What she did was run. What she did was hit a pane with her fists. What she did was heave her body into the glass.

What she did was what she always did. Diane Harbaugh did the thing.

A HOLE IN THE GROUND

She remembered none of what happened in the moments after she leapt through the window. The way she pulled at the air with her bound arms and kicked her legs and twisted and tilted forward, it was all darkness to her, the whoosh of the air as she fell over and beyond the narrow sidewalk before her torso struck on the hood of a compact car and startled the driver who screamed and braked and shunted her into the street. She was already in so much pain that no more could be added. She didn't remember blacking out for a moment. A moment. A moment. She didn't remember how much she still had her adrenalized wits about her, how quickly she sat up in the roadway, legs splayed almost childlike, trying to get out of her binds and predicament. She couldn't see or remember the woman getting out of the car and upon seeing Harbaugh stepping back, covering her mouth, and then almost immediately sensing danger, looking around for what activity would deposit such a person as this onto her car and into the street. She didn't see El Motown looking out from the window or the startled pedestrians start to gather to observe her and the glass on the sidewalk.

And she didn't remember Childs running up and ripping the

hood off her head, his startlement at her swollen features, him gathering her up into the van. She didn't remember all the other DEA agents from Monterrey and San Antonio helping her into a van, some peeling off to inspect the scene and the apartment from which she'd launched herself. She didn't remember hearing shots fired or the van screeching away. She didn't remember Childs shouting "Go to a hospital!" and grabbing him by the face with now-freed hands and insisting they get out of the country. She didn't remember saying *No cops no cops no cops*. She didn't remember that she was frightened of everything. She didn't even remember the bloody triage at the DEA regional office, wrapping her fucked-up foot, someone on the radio saying they'd found her two toes, Childs saying it was lucky they'd come when they did, they were circling and zeroing in on her cell phone when she flew out the window, they were a half block away, he was pointing at the very building when she erupted from it.

The memories began when they finally got her on a chartered plane and into the air. There, finally, she felt everything hurt all at once and she remembered what those men had done to her and she remembers, still, that she couldn't stop screaming.

Four days after surgery to reattach her two toes and tend to her fractured eye socket, broken clavicle, and cracked ribs, she was released and flew home to Los Angeles for several debriefings with Cromer and the brass, the Office of Professional Responsibility, her union rep. The coffee going cold, her body cramping over so many hours in those air-conditioned spaces.

She had a story and she stuck to it. How she'd gone to Mexico to meet El Capataz, Gustavo Acuña Cárdenas. How she'd been confronted by Quincey and Carver. How she tried to get help from Dufresne. How she and Acuña Cárdenas fled north and were caught by the cartel in a small suburb north of Tampico. How he was killed and she fled to Monterrey. How she called Childs for help, how Childs tracked down her cell, how she leapt out the window.

She didn't know anything about the shootout at the warehouse or the dead Zetas in town. Of course she never brandished a gun in some little bar outside Tampico, that was absurd. Carver and Quincey stormed out of Moman's warehouse that first day, she never saw them again. Yeah, she'd read about herself in the papers. They'd blown it all up into some crazy thing. She'd only been trying to get out of Mexico.

Hers was a good story as far as it went, but there were issues with it—she couldn't explain the men who cut off her toes. And the old problems at home festered. There was Oscar, her criminal informant, the OPR's ongoing inquiry, text messages that proved an inappropriate relationship. His death still an open case in Michigan pending the DEA's investigation. There was her general reputation around the office. People heard things, about Oscar, about Dufresne. She had a reputation for messing dudes up in the head. Her nickname was the Midwife, after all.

There were months of cascading consequences. Endless follow-up interviews with the OPR about Tampico and Monterrey. A tremendous lecture from Cromer. How the Mexicans wanted to interview her, but the DEA brass couldn't permit such a precedent. How DC smoothed things over with new materiel and a promise to stick her in a cell up here.

She thought maybe she'd be able to skate, work with OPR and her union, but she was sacked for cause on a Tuesday, curbside with a box of her shit when the FBI rolled up.

Dufresne had dropped a dime on her.

It was classically trumped-up bullshit, but it happened that her jaunt to Mexico had flushed out an ongoing investigation into Dufresne's schemes. A long career of planted evidence, forged signatures, forced confessions, wholesale falsified documents, bribes and payouts, stolen evidence. She was but one accomplice stretching back years.

She was suspended by the State Bar for Brady violations and

suspect wiretap applications and indicted for the same. And of course, she was fired from her brand-new new job as a paralegal when Davis, Smiley & Wilkes found out the charges arrayed against her.

Her body had yet to fully heal. Her collarbone ached when she yawned, her ribs when she sneezed. And with her broken eye socket, she'd lost the perfect balance of her features and also certain daily permissions attending to beauty—store clerks clocked her, men ignored her, she was pitied by women on the sly. She looked shifty even to herself, couldn't imagine what a jury would make of her countenance. Her toes hadn't healed right, and after another surgery, her cane and convalescing gait situated her in another class of person so utterly that she became invisible.

She had nightmares of the Zetas, woke up in terror that someone was in the room, slept with the light on, didn't sleep at all.

She couldn't afford her Culver City apartment and moved into a studio in Glendale near the Kinko's where she then worked. Her new lawyer was a guy she barely knew from law school who reached out on the premise that he was developing a specialty defending cops, convincing judges to deny Pitchess motions to view police files. When he offhandedly said that he expected her to be sued by some of the very guilty people she'd helped Dufresne put away, for days she did not leave her bed. She let her houseplants die.

She wondered where Carver was, if he'd really abandoned her with hardly a thought. Or had something happened to him? She hadn't breathed a word to anyone about him or the tunnel or the Concern. She wondered what his game was. Nothing made sense. She knew where the tunnel was—he couldn't give it back to the Golfos if that was his plan, not without silencing her. And the longer he didn't reach out, the more likely it could be that she would tell.

She'd nearly died because of him.

"He'll get you killed," the CIA guy had said.

Every morning she entertained a wild range of anxieties and

hopes. That he would come for her. That he'd been killed. That the CIA had caught him. That her killers were en route. But the tunnel was her leverage. Or was it just a contrivance? She had no way of knowing. Why hadn't he reached out? She'd never felt so lonesome in her life.

Even good news was immediately ruined by fresh bullshit. The week she got a special insole so she might run again, she had a hearing where the prosecuting attorney reported that new information had come to light. She could be a flight risk. A redacted memorandum from the Central Intelligence Agency was submitted to the court as evidence that she'd not been fully forthcoming about her time in Tampico and Monterrey. The judge offered her the chance to speak to the document's contents, her lawyer advised silence at this time, and the judge put her under house arrest and ordered a monitor clapped onto her right ankle.

Carlisle and Bowden sat in the rear of the otherwise empty courtroom. Afterward, they were waiting outside, Bowden eating a frozen yogurt, Carlisle with her eyes closed against the sun. She knew what they wanted. She'd spent the past several months thinking that very thing.

"You don't know where he is," Harbaugh said.

"We think he's going to reach out," Carlisle said.

"Why?"

"Reasons."

Bowden tossed the yogurt cup into a trash bin and came over to her. "If you assist us, we can help with your sentencing."

"You just put me under house arrest."

"Do you love him?" Carlisle asked. "Is that it?"

She didn't love him, she wasn't in love with him. She had thought that through. She'd maybe never been in love her whole life. But she did want the Concern.

"There are things you're not telling us." Bowden handed her a card. "But you can."

———

Every night after leaving Kinko's, she ran home. Unevenly, like a jalopy. But it felt good, to bounce and use the muscles in her legs, to swing her arms. Even the pain in her knee, the burn in her lungs, those things felt good, too. As she ran, everything simplified. She treasured that.

Childs was waiting outside her apartment with a six-pack.

"Looking good," he said. Of her, of her running, maybe both.

"The hell I do," she said.

He assessed her in the same way he had ever since he'd pulled the hood off her head in Mexico, like a doctor observing her progress, silently noting what was and what wasn't permanent. She adored him for it as much as she despised being subject to it, neither of which she could put into words.

"Beer?" she said, panting. "You? Beer?"

He said his days of being a temple were over—his wife was pregnant, it was all about Baby Girl now. She let him inside and he looked around her apartment and the dead plants for a moment and then started straightening up. She coaxed him away from folding her blankets and onto the little patio that overlooked the worse apartments across the street.

"I'm surprised to see you," she said.

He'd been barred from speaking to her during the OPR investigations. When she was fired, he'd called to condole, and a few times after that.

"I'm sorry I haven't been over. Are you mad at me? You're mad at me."

"Of course I'm not mad," she said. She wasn't.

"I'm sorry anyway."

"You saved my life, Childs. I could never be mad at you."

She stood up and leaned out over the railing and scanned the street. They were like that for a minute, and then she asked how was work.

"I been checked out since we got back from Monterrey. Morale's low." He sighed. "Everyone bailing or fixing to."

"You too?"

"Got an offer from this security start-up looking for guys who know some shit. I guess I know some shit. Moving up to the Bay Area soon."

"Congratulations, Childs. That's great."

She made him pick up his abandoned beer and clink it and drink.

"You know some shit too."

She took him to mean he'd put in a good word. "That's sweet of you," she said in a way that said for him to let the matter drop.

She caught him looking at her ankle monitor. She wondered if he was thinking of a prison watchtower now, like she was. Like she did a lot of the time.

"You shower with that?"

"The worst part is I can't run at night."

He set his beer down. She knew he wouldn't drink any more.

"Can I ask you something?"

"Shoot, partner."

"Who were those guys that hurt you?"

She fingered the lip of her beer. Drank.

"Diane."

"Why do you want to know?"

"They cut off your toes!"

"Maybe I don't tell you things for your own good. Like Oscar. Like what I did for Dufresne in Sacramento."

He crossed his arms, paid out a long gorilla sigh, a growl. "I should've been down there with you."

"No, you shouldn't have. You're straight, and I'm as crooked as—"

"Fuck that, I don't care. Every time I see you now . . . I haven't been by because when I see you, I think of when I took that hood off your head."

"Just imagine mirrors. Imagine every morning."

"I can't forgive myself for what happened."

"I know, Russell." She took his hand. "But I don't blame you. You *saved* me."

He took her face in his hands. "I told you it was hard to tell which way your luck was running, but you can see now, right?" he asked, wiping away her tears. She'd been crying the moment he took her face. "It's a real bad streak you're on."

She looked away.

"Listen to me," he said and held her face until her eyes locked with his. "Dufresne is gonna do federal time in protective custody for the rest of his life."

She couldn't bear his eyes, but he waited for her to look at him.

"If there's a deal to make, make it."

That last day Carver was in Monterrey. Going on about how long it should take, what all is in the fridge, making her promise not to go outside, not to use her phone. Promises she broke, broken promises that cost her two toes. *They'll let us slip away out of kindness, I suppose, but never-thefuckingless don't go for a run and if you have to use that phone, use it on the move. In an emergency to call the States. But but but but if anything happens. And I mean this in all two thousand percent sincerity, I'll come for you. I'll break you out of Fort Knox.*

She was calling the people who hadn't picked up their orders. An English professor's reading assignments in spiral bindings. Several screenwriters. A small series of brochures for a motel in Eagle Pass.

Eagle Pass.

She thumbed through them. Stock photos. *E pluribus unum*s where text in English should be. A phone number.

She quaked. Expecting his voice, desperate to hear it again, she didn't wait to call.

"Where you calling from?" asked a not-his voice on the other end.

"Kinko's," she said, knowing it was the wrong answer.

The line went dead.

She thought about this. She dialed again.

"Where you calling from?"

"Fort Knox," she said.

A pause.

Then the voice gave an address in Silverlake. Five p.m., he said, be there two days from now.

At the end of her shift, she closed her till and left the Kinko's and walked around the block, tingling. All the things she'd been wondering were at hand. Why oh why had it taken so long. Whether this was for real. Whether the tunnel was real. Whether the call was even from him, or some kind of setup from Carlisle. Some kind of setup from him. How he'd known where she worked. Who was watching her. Whether she should just run, whether she was a loose end.

She was up all night. She called Bowden the next morning.

She met them at the Chase building in Burbank, the top floor where the FBI had taken up residence just under a dozen satellite dishes and digital antennas to monitor the Armenian mob. She'd heard of the place, but was well astonished at all the millions of dollars in state-of-the-art surveillance gear.

The conference room was already populated with Carlisle and Bowden, several other men and women, FBI or intelligence. And Dufresne, pale as a paper target next to his rumpled lawyer.

Carlisle was holding a carafe and a cup.

"Coffee?"

"What the hell is this?"

Carlisle poured herself a coffee and sat. Dufresne wouldn't meet her gaze. The coward.

"What's he doing here?"

Bowden closed a folder. "These are agents Kelly, Garland, and Yates of the FBI. You know Mr. Dufresne. That's his attorney, Mr. Riley. And over there is Ms. Hennessey on behalf of the district attorney's office. The DA couldn't make it, but she can speak for their office."

She stood in stunned silence at what was arrayed against her.

"Please sit."

"I'm out of here."

"Unlike you, we don't go off half-cocked to Mexico," Carlisle said. "We like to get all the parties together and gain consensus."

"What about *my* lawyer?"

Bowden stood, followed her out to the elevator.

"Okay, you're feeling ambushed. But this is just to set the ground rules. The FBI has been building a case against Mr. Dufresne for some time. They accelerated their investigation after your dustup in Mexico, seeing as it was connected to Mr. Dufresne's numerous illegal activities. We've assured them that that is not the case. That you were not on some mission to Tampico at your supervisor's behest. Mr. Dufresne has agreed to testify to such, and moreover that you were coerced by him, provided you help us with the sensitive matter you called about. This was my idea."

Bowden had turned around, was gesturing at the agents and lawyers watching them. When he turned back around and looked at Harbaugh with surprisingly candid and soulful eyes and beckoned her to head back in with him, she almost did.

She pressed the button for the elevator.

"We can wait for your lawyer," he said. "I thought you'd appreciate this. I mean, we could've made no gesture whatsoever."

The elevator took forever. He moved around in front of her, not blocking the doors, but almost.

"You don't deserve this," he said. "You really didn't do anything wrong. Some crafty omissions as a DA. Getting close to an informant—"

"I don't need you to tell me that I did nothing wrong."

The elevator arrived, and she climbed on. He held the door.

"What I'm saying is that you have a sympathetic audience, despite Agent Carlisle's two cents. Everyone in that room, every lawyer and agent sitting at that conference table, has bent the rules to get where they are."

"You ever wonder if maybe the system is the problem?" she asked. "And that's why we game it?"

"He really got under your lid, didn't he?"

She only just then realized that she'd been parroting Carver's words.

"*You* called me," he said, standing aside for her to come out. "Tell us what you know."

She ate her lunch and didn't go back to work, just walked into a hardware store like a regular citizen. She freed a bolt cutter from its packaging and cut the monitor off and left it and the bolt cutter on the floor and marched outside and called a cab and threw her cell phone away and rode to the address on Silverlake Boulevard.

It was a cute little house up off the street level. Stairs cut into the hill. Fresh sod, landscaping. She wondered if Carver was in there. She climbed the stairs, knocked on the door. A pair of familiar eyes looking out from behind the little gate, and then the door swung open. The sicario. Tomás.

"Oh god," she said, waiting to be shot or struck or in any way killed.

But she was not.

He stood in the doorway with a cane, looking at her curiously.

She instinctively turned and made her body a smaller target.

"You're early," he said.

"For what?" she asked warily, trying to begin to understand what exactly the fuck was going on.

"I thought we'd eat."

"Eat?"

"Pollo," he said. He looked out at the street. "And then we leave town. Come inside."

She remained where she stood, how she stood.

"Fuck that. What are you doing here?"

"This is my house. Come in, please."

"Where is it you think we are going?"

"Eagle Pass, of course."

They stood there regarding one another.

"Okay," he said, heading back inside. "Then stay there."

He returned with two plates of food. Chicken steaming and shredded. Beans, tortillas, limes, sliced peppers and radishes. He gave them to her, went inside, and returned with two bottles of beer. He nodded for her to sit and he stood next to the steps and they traded a plate for a beer and ate on the stoop. It began to seem oddly apt that they would meet again. Like all their previous encounters were missed connections of a kind, and now they could catch up.

"Carver and Goran visited me in the hospital."

"Goran?"

"The Serbian. You will meet him. And the others."

"What?"

"I'm going to bring you to Carver. That's what you want, correct?"

She wondered if she believed him or just wanted to believe him. Then she thought it didn't really matter.

"I'm with the Concern now," Tomás said.

"I see."

"Eat."

She nodded at his cane and hip. "I'm sorry about that," she said.

"A misunderstanding," he said, waving at the air. "You almost died, too. No one has ever escaped El Motown."

"El Motown?"

"The man who hurt you."

"He cut off my toes."

"I didn't know that."

"I had them reattached. I can walk, I can run," she said.

"Good."

"I want to kill him," she said, without compunction.

"You need to work on your aim," he said, grinning. "Eat, please. We must go soon."

They swapped cars in several parking garages on the way out of Los Angeles. She had only the clothes on her back. He searched and discarded her wallet. He searched her. She realized as they bore east that this was precisely the kind of thing a person might do—a person skilled in killing people—before killing someone.

As night came on and they drove toward the growing darkness, the stars over the desert, she began to think that the Concern could well be a total lie, but she also let herself believe everything she wanted to believe. What difference did it make at this point what she wanted, whether her luck was running or running out?

They drove mostly at night, sleeping the days in motels, her always waking to him with a book. Outside El Paso, she asked him what he was reading. He grinned and shook his head.

"Fantasy. Dragons and swordsmen and wizards. There is a series of novels I am loving right now. They are about a warrior called 'the Twin,' and I read them thinking about myself because my name means 'twin,' did you know that?"

She did not.

"He is a warrior. Very bloodthirsty. A very good killer. So maybe more than just that my name means 'twin' is why I read them. But also, he's looking for a place worthy of his talents. He wants to be a knight. You know, have a code, use his skills for a noble purpose."

He smiled broadly at her, his face lit up in the dash lights like a comic mask, his face so broad and joyful that she laughed. "This is also like me, no?"

It was a squat brick building on the edge of Eagle Pass, Texas. Smelling of oil and sand to collect the oil and grease. It stunk like dirty red rags and reminded her of her daddy.

Tomás took her into a back office and down an interior concrete stairwell. A breeze gave away what was behind the heavy wooden door on iron hinges.

The tunnel, twelve feet in diameter, that biased to the left and down. He gestured for her to go ahead.

"You're not coming?"

"I'm to stay here. But he's on the other side."

Tomás was holding a paperback open with his thumb, and when he was closing the door on her he rested his cane against the wall so he could keep his nose in the book until the moment he had to set it down and lock it up. It struck her as almost comical that she'd shot him, that he'd scared her so much that she did this. She wondered how long they'd be friends, how long this chapter of her life would last.

She walked down the slight and slowly descending grade. Small track lights gave off just enough light to see by. After a few laps down, the tunnel straightened. There was a lukewarm earthen breeze, and she walked along the track for miles. She wanted to run, but she decided instead to just walk. Every half mile or so, a pair of cameras pointing in each direction. She stopped and looked at one, the red light on it.

She wondered who was watching, if Carver was, and she wondered if he knew what all she'd been through, what all she'd suffer again to be here. She'd come all this way, and the end was here in a hole in the ground. She'd been running for this rabbit hole her whole life.

She walked on and on, the black terminus of the tunnel getting closer and larger. It grew warmer and for a moment seemed like an ingress to hell.

Fine, I will go to hell.

And then she heard a motor and saw a sudden column of light and a platform descending, and she could see Carver's legs. He squatted down and removed a cowboy hat from his head, and his hair was pasted to his skull like he'd come from a field or a raw labor, for all the world like a man who was building something. She saw his face then, and on it that he couldn't wait to see her and greet her, and she couldn't wait to see him and get started.

So she ran.

ACKNOWLEDGMENTS

The authors thank Dick Gregorie and Harry Giknavoian for their information on district attorney practice. They also wish to thank the Los Angeles Drug Enforcement Agency office, in particular Sarah Pullen, Vijay Rathi, Almador Martinez, and Timothy Massino for their insights into DEA protocols, culture, and interagency deconfliction practices.

The authors also wish to thank Texas State University and the faculty senate for granting Jon Marc the nontenure-line workload release in fall 2016.

Thanks to everyone in the Texas State English Department, especially Steve Wilson, Nancy Wilson, Dan Lochman, Mike Hennessy, Vicki Smith, Taylor Cortesi, Tom Grimes, and Debra Monroe.

Thanks to the Science and Entertainment Exchange.

Thanks to Susie Tilka for making it easier to go to work every day.

To Katie Kapurch—all the credit, A++.

And thanks to Ally Israelson for her support and effortless insight.

Thanks to Matt Fuller for information and background about the State Department.

Thanks to Brandon Ricks for info about the CIA and chain of command.

The authors owe a huge debt to Oscar Rodríguez, who was invaluable in helping to research this book.

Thanks to Bobby Earl Smith for the legal knowledge, and thanks to Judy Smith for marrying him.

Thanks to Dan Halpern for taking this project across the finish line.

And thanks to Nicole Aragi for being there from the beginning.

Thanks to Tomás Morín for the rights to his name (and for being such a great poet).

Lastly, the authors wish to thank each other for making this joint effort an interesting pleasure.